TEACHING
AND THE
CASE
METHOD

C. Roland Christensen

with Abby J. Hansen
and James F. Moore

Harvard Business School Boston

Instructor's Guide

Library of Congress Catalog Card No. 86-22732
ISBN 0-87584-181-3

Contents

Preface

C. Roland Christensen

Robert Walmsley University Professor

This Instructor's Guide has been developed to provide ideas, assistance, and perhaps even a bit of inspiration for colleagues at other institutions who might want to experiment with the leadership of a discussion teaching seminar. These support materials have worked well at Harvard, but other approaches to individual cases as well as the organization of the seminars are suggested and encouraged in order to meet the specific needs of your institution.

We are in debt to Dr. James F. Moore and Dr. Abby J. Hansen for developing this handbook. Special thanks go to James Moore. His willingness to experiment with the development of teaching notes which dealt with both the process of teaching the case as well as with the analysis of the specific problem proved to be a major turning point in the evolution of this effort. The results of his creativity enable us to share our experience with a wider group of colleagues. Joyce Walworth developed the case synopses found in Part V. Dyanne Holdman, with her usual efficiency, has served as administrative director of this handbook.

Part I (for liberal arts instructors) and Part II (for professional school instructors) present teaching notes and, where available, researcher's perspectives for the cases included in both seminar programs. Whether you are leading the seminar for liberal arts professors or the seminar for professional school instructors, we urge you to read the introductory notes for both seminars. In addition to specific suggestions for each seminar, these statements include general information of use to all discussion leaders. And, you might wish also to read again "Suggestions for Seminar Participants" found in Part I of Teaching and the Case Method.

Part III of this guide presents a sample mini-seminar. Such modules provide a useful follow-up format for the primary seminar programs or can be tailored to meet the needs of specialized groups. The mini-seminar involving The First Day, for example, focuses on the problems of relatively inexperienced instructors' first day in the classroom. We suggest the "Bill Curtis" and "The Introduction" cases. If you wish to extend the time frame of this module to include an instructor's first-year challenges, you might wish to add the "Suzie Simons" case.

Other possible mini-seminars might focus, for example, on issues involved in Grading and Evaluation. Complicated as the problem is in a traditional lecture setting, it is even more complex in the discussion teaching milieu where skill training is added to knowledge transference objectives. We suggest four cases: "Bob Thompson," "Pete Carmichael's Dilemma," "What Do We Do Now, Professor?" and "Charles Sexton."

Another mini-seminar might deal with a topic of high current interest, ensuring that female students and faculty members enjoy full equality of educational opportunity. For such a seminar, possibly entitled The Gender Challenge, we would suggest four cases: "Sheila Lund," "Bob Lunt," "Janice Posner," and "The Case of the Frustrated Feminist." The latter case, researched and written by Dr. Margaret Morganroth Gullette, is unusually rich and provocative. The Association of American Colleges' Project on the Status and Education of Women provides excellent support material for such a module.

Part IV contains "hand-out" sections of multi-part cases included in the two seminars. Part V includes abstracts of additional teaching cases which you may want to use at your school. Cases may be ordered from the Harvard Business School Publishing Division, Soldiers Field, Boston, Massachusetts, 02163. There is an order form at the end of this book.

A number of readings are also recommended to anyone in the role of discussion leader. Two of the articles, E. Raymond Corey's "The Use of Cases in Management Education" and Mary Jean Huntington's "The Development of a Professional Self-Image" will be of special interest to instructors working in the professional school milieu. The remaining readings will be of interest to all. We know you will find

Alvin M. White's "Teaching Mathematics as Though Students Mattered" especially meaningful. The word mathematics might well be dropped from the article's title.

We appreciate your participation in this adventure in learning about teaching.

There is little doubt that participants will find the seminar useful in subsequent classroom practice. We ourselves have learned so much from the leadership of these seminars; we hope your experience will be equally rewarding.

PART I   Liberal Arts Teaching Seminar

Liberal Arts Teaching Seminar

Introduction

Abby J. Hansen

This is a first attempt to apply the insights of several decades of thought about business and professional school teaching to another branch of learning -- the Liberal Arts. In putting these materials together, I have adopted and adapted the brain children of C. R. Christensen and his students and colleagues at the Harvard Business School. The Business School seminars have expanded to embrace representatives from the broadest possible range of disciplines, both in the Harvard community and elsewhere. As a result, a certain intellectual crosspollinization has occurred. The new cases in this section are some first fruits of this hybridization.

As a casewriter and sometime leader of teaching seminars, I have both developed teaching cases and seen them in operation. To teach these materials is to learn from them, and I -- whose educational background is in Renaissance English Literature -- have become convinced that the principles of discussion leading which Chris and his many students originally discerned from their business school experiences are equally valid for the liberal arts and indeed for any sort of teaching other than a clear-cut "transfer of knowledge" transaction, in which the instructor presents a set of plain facts for memorization.

No efforts to collect these materials would have succeeded without the generosity of colleagues and friends who collaborated with me to create these cases and supporting materials: Heather Dubrow, Larry Lynn, Elaine Tyler May, Janice McCormick, James F. Moore, and Joy Renjilian-Burgy. I am also grateful to the talented staff of the Harvard-Danforth Center for Teaching and Learning, especially John Boehrer, Margaret Morganroth Gullette, Catherine G. Krupnick, and Ellen Sarkisian, for providing me with opportunities to "road test" experimental teaching cases. Thanks also to Peter Zimmerman for inviting me to participate in a case method teaching conference at the Kennedy School of Government, where I learned a great deal watching familiar principles at work in an unfamiliar setting.

What is this module?

This module is a prototype, or blueprint, for a case-based seminar on discussion-teaching methods for liberal arts instructors. The object of such a seminar would be to help teachers at the college and graduate school levels improve their discussion-leading skills by analyzing -- and arguing about -- teaching cases. These cases, modeled on the managerial cases that form the basis for most instruction at the Harvard Business School, recount teachers' real classroom challenges and dilemmas. They should be read, analyzed, discussed, and finally absorbed by the participants in an exercise that parallels the way one processes firsthand experience.

These materials and similar documents have been used in teaching seminars populated by representatives of diverse disciplines, from medicine to musicology. Discussions that have emerged from them have aired issues ranging from the most practical (like placement of chairs, desirable size and composition of classes, advisability of serving refreshments, duration of discussions) to the most elusive philosophical conundrums embedded in the mysterious process of learning and teaching.

We hope to provoke teachers into exploring the choices open to them and recognizing the inherent subtlety of many activities we all often perform with too much facility. How should one pose questions in class? To whom? When? How can one interpret students' behavior in class and respond to it in such a way as to help them and others in the class benefit from the process? How should one move, speak, dress in the classroom? How should one listen?

What is the relation between this module and other materials in Teaching and the Case Method?

The teaching seminars for which all these cases were originally developed originated in an attempt to improve young instructors' preparation for case method teaching at the Harvard Graduate School of Business Administration. But the seminars' applicability to concerns of all discussion teachers soon created a wider demand, and representatives from a great variety of disciplines -- many of them usually classified as liberal arts -- pooled their experiences and insights with those of their professional-school colleagues so successfully that it became evident that there is a dynamic common to all discussion teaching, whatever its subject matter. All discussion leaders wish to encourage participants to apply their emotions as well as their intellects to the material, to cooperate with each other and challenge each other's positions helpfully, and to take perplexing questions home to ponder. Nonetheless, certain aspects of liberal arts teaching do seem unique. For one thing, liberal arts students tend to be younger and less experienced than those in professional schools. For another, their institutional cultures are different. Undergraduates in a Renaissance French Literature course will probably have goals, learning styles, and expectations unlike those of students in an advanced MBA course on Financial Management. Accordingly, the cases in this Liberal Arts module have been selected to highlight the challenges liberal arts instructors tend to face. But they do not exclude a few professional school cases whose basic issues seem to be universal. I invite the prospective discussion leader to browse through all the materials in this book with an eye to appreciating the intrinsic subtleties and potential of the discussion process before selecting seminar cases that appear to focus on familiar concerns.

Format

This module includes ten cases, each intended to provide the basis for a class discussion lasting about an hour and a half. I have grouped the material into four general, increasingly complex units according to each case's salient issues. But I cannot stress too heavily that these documents (descriptions of actual experiences) will squirm and wiggle when you try to pin them down. In fact, any good teaching case involves so many elements of human interaction that it could legitimately be placed under any number of rubrics in a syllabus. My message: read the cases and suggested teaching notes; modify the discussion plans to your liking; evolve your own syllabus. Your group should gather as often, or infrequently, as seems desirable. Many of the following cases could be taught in a variety of settings other than a semester-long seminar. They could, for example, provide texts for teaching workshops ranging from a single session to a weekend. Or they could combine with less-structured agendas -- perhaps topic-oriented discussions based on participants' suggestions organized in a way that suits your institution's needs. Our teaching seminars at the Harvard Business School sometimes include discussions without fixed texts. One subject we often approach in this manner is the crucial issue of how an instructor can help a group coalesce to form strong bonds of trust and helpfulness. Perhaps you might invite participants to offer the group some vexing current problems from their own experience for analysis and suggestions.

In short, this module is meant to provide a skeleton and some rudimentary musculature. It is for you, the discussion leader and organizer, to make the creature get up and walk.

The data in our cases naturally segment themselves into two or three parts for discussion purposes. The (A) case, like the first act in a drama, presents the principal characters in their setting, and leads the reader to the protagonist's first decision point. At the end of most of our (A) cases, the teacher has encountered some unforeseen difficulty -- usually in class -- and hesitates in puzzlement. It is then the seminar's task to clarify the teacher's problem, analyze its causes and consequences, make recommendations, and usually predict what might happen based on these recommendations. This is the core of the process, where the seminar participants -- guided and supported by the leader's questions and responses -- begin to <u>work</u> the material, as a sculptor works clay. This part of the discussion should be freewheeling. Participants may venture hypotheses, analyses, even fantasies based firmly on the case facts, and their colleagues should offer reactions, extrapolations, or objections to their ideas -- all in the service of collective insight.

At this point, the discussion leader should distribute the (B) case -- which describes what <u>did</u> happen, and thus engenders further discussion. We hope this latter part of the discussion will consider some potential theoretical implications of the events, viewed in the light of the group's developing insights into the dominant problem. The group can then begin to formulate some general principles based on its insights, and then proceed to refine these in further discussion. A few of our cases then continue with a (C) case -- the third segment that reveals either some long-term developments or the teacher's reflections on what he or she actually learned from the whole experience.

The discussion leader's immediate objective in our seminars is to get people to take positions and defend them. The longer-range objective is to raise as many issues -- central and peripheral -- as possible, based on the raw data that the case provides, and send participants home pondering them. In the best discussions, participants will become so interested and involved in the case that they volunteer their own relevant personal experiences for the seminar's reactions. The discussion leader's task is to create an atmosphere of trust and goodwill, monitor the proceedings, and try to prevent the discussion from deteriorating into either a superficial bull session or an arid intellectual exercise.

A good discussion will propose various courses of action as well as raise far more questions than it settles. The participants and teacher should all go home pondering. This is the broadest purpose of our teaching seminar: to stimulate people to think about the process of teaching.

Some Goals of the Seminar

Let us sing anthems of modest expectations. We offer here no step-by-step recipe for instant pedagogical perfection. This is not a "how to" manual, although we will suggest a few techniques along the way that some might label "tricks" (a term we consider too limited to capture the intrinsic seriousness and integrity of their intent).

The core of our efforts will be to stress the enormous range of choices available to teachers at every stage and on every level -- intellectual and emotional -- of their professional lives. We hope to show the rich possibilities inherent in activities that are usually taken for granted: preparation, posing questions in the classroom and reacting to students' responses, choosing students to speak, evaluating their performances, and many more.

Our focus will always be on urging teachers to consider the students -- their strengths, weaknesses, interactions in the classroom, styles of learning, and evolving grasp of the materials. This emphasis reflects our belief that only by relinquishing center stage and resisting the besetting temptation of those with advanced degrees to display their accomplishments can teachers truly harness their powers as educators. Time and again we have seen this paradox proven: when teachers focus on helping their students learn, they not only teach better but learn more themselves.

One of our basic articles of faith is the necessity of setting and maintaining an effective contract between teacher and students. Let us, therefore, attempt to live up to our own precept and state at the outset what we think this seminar can

and cannot do. As many of us agree, the classroom is a realm of largely undiscovered possibilities. Most teachers neither realize nor consciously try to control their influence on students. At the very least the seminar can address the basic issue of lack of attention to what happens in the classroom. Many factors inherent in the educational system combine to exaggerate teachers' importance in the academic microcosm -- where status, official rank, physical position in the classroom, and expertise all help dig a chasm between teacher and students. We have all encountered mistrust, distance, or downright fear in school.

It is our belief that such an emotional climate is as counterproductive as it is unpleasant. We all learn better when we feel valued; unhappy students will learn to dislike the material as much as they dislike the class if the atmosphere is acrid. These materials will suggest ways to create a pleasant, cordial climate of discussion without sacrificing discipline or seriousness. Further, we will help discussion leaders prepare to moderate discussions that help the seminar mesh its strengths to analyze the cases, extract their basic principles, and apply these as they fit the group's needs. We believe that this complex task -- and not a single-minded analysis of the material -- should be the focus of the discussion leader's preparation.

The participants' reciprocal responsibility begins with an effort to analyze the cases -- usually by considering the study questions that accompany each one. These questions attempt to guide analysis without forestalling the spontaneous emergence of the whole array of broader and deeper considerations that should evolve in discussion. As a rule, the study questions ask the reader to think and feel a little way "into" each case before drawing generalizations. First, we usually focus on actions: <u>How did such-and-such a case character behave? What other things might he or she have done?</u> Then we move to evaluation: <u>How appropriate was the character's behavior? What issues should he or she have considered?</u> The final questions usually point beyond the case into the realm of principles; they direct attention to the seminar participants' own concerns: <u>What are the implications of all this for the teacher? What are the implications for you?</u>

Of course, the discussion leader and all the participants should read and study each case before class. This is the ideal situation, but since these seminars are likely to be voluntary and conducted in the spare time (and on the goodwill) of the participants, it may occasionally happen that a participant will arrive unprepared. To spare embarrassment and prevent distracting interruptions in the flow of discussion, we recommend that participants be asked to inform the discussion leader quietly. The contract would then stipulate that the participant would not be called upon unless he or she volunteered. These materials involve neither graphs nor complex mathematical calculations. They are stories set in reasonably familiar territory. In an emergency, a participant can read them in class (while the others talk), catch the gist of comments, and fruitfully enter the discussion. Needless to say, this is less desirable than coming fully prepared, but historical example and some awareness of human foibles prompt us to warn at the outset that such occasions may arise. They should be accepted and, if possible, capitalized upon. Fresh insights might inject valuable energy into the discussion. At the very least, they should not become the occasion for embarrassment or sarcasm.

What Is a Case?

Each case is an edited version of a real and thought-provoking event which occurred in some teacher's professional experience. Accordingly, each principal case informant must sign a formal, legal release of the contents before publication. We select cases for richness as vehicles for discussion in the belief that a group of intelligent people, concentrating their minds and emotions on a common text, can teach each other and themselves lessons that bear not only on the document under consideration but also on their own personal challenges. Moreover, we believe that this goal can best be accomplished when the group's cooperative efforts are sympathetically and skillfully guided by an aware and genuinely interested discussion leader. The seminar thus presents not only materials for the discussion of teaching problems, opportunities, and challenges, but also a living model of discussion teaching and learning.

Some Critical Teaching Issues

A. Contract

One of the earliest topics we take up in our seminar -- and one to which we constantly return -- is the concept of the teaching/learning contract. Any kind of teaching requires cooperation, but discussion teaching thrives on a particularly high level of rapport, and rapport can be estab-

lished and sustained only when all participants -- "teachers" and "students" alike -- agree on just what they are trying to accomplish in one another's company. Many of the protagonists of our cases stub their toes on this very issue: having thoroughly prepared the content of their courses, teachers assume that their "good" students can and will perform whatever tasks are assigned and then attain the teacher's level of comprehension. This unexamined assumption often leads to trouble. Most students are unlikely to match the teacher's sophistication very quickly; the time true learning requires should not cause irritation. One must focus on reasonable goals. How, exactly, should the students prepare? Should they all be expected to participate heavily in class discussion? What will be their reward if they do, or punishment if they don't? (And what constitutes valuable participation?) Can they expect the teacher to reply to each of their comments and evaluate it publicly? Or should they plan to spend most of the seminar talking with their fellow students? On what criteria will they be evaluated? Will they, in turn, have a chance to evaluate their instructor? If so, what form will this evaluation assume -- written, oral, private, public?

On another level, contracts operate emotionally, almost subliminally. Students wonder whether they can expect their teachers to respect them. They wonder if their naive comments will be received as valuable contributions to the whole class's developing grasp of complex problems, or if they will be ridiculed. They wonder if they ought to expect to be teased. Must they come to class tensed to bear sarcastic repartee? Or can they expect to be babied through difficult or obscure problems and handed "answers" to memorize at the end of each session?

All these questions -- and many more that each discussion leader should anticipate asking and settling -- are strands in the knot of interactions that constitute the contract we believe exists in every teaching situation. Ignore it at your own peril, for your teaching contract will be there whether you consciously set it or not. If you ignore it, you may -- like Carol Cutler, Bea Benedict, Sue Roper, Ben Cheever, and many more of the perplexed teachers in our cases -- find yourself antagonizing students by your unintentional violations of their expectations.

To avoid such unpleasantness, it is advisable to devote some time to thinking about your honest objectives for the course and the way you would like the seminar participants to help you (and themselves) meet them. Then you should state these in class and invite responses and, if appropriate, countersuggestions.

The initial contract will evolve over time because sophisticated students do not need the same sort of help that novices do. But whatever modifications the contract may undergo, revising it is easier if the terms are understood and all concerned have long since shown a basic willingness to negotiate and cooperate.

B. The Discussion Teacher's Role

It is no accident that in this module I refer to those of you who will use these materials to lead discussions on teaching variously as "discussion leaders," "instructors," "educators," or "teachers." My linguistic uncertainty reflects an ambiguity inherent in the enterprise of teaching teachers to teach. If you decide that your course should be conducted as an assembly of peers, even though one colleague holds the reins of power for the purposes of organized discussion, the roles of teacher and student will always blur slightly. The leader of the discussion group may lag behind some of the participants in status and experience, but he or she will inevitably possess an advantage in coming to the seminar better prepared for having read all the units of the case to be discussed, browsed through the teaching notes, and spent time preparing for the discussion process. The discussion participants, on the other hand, having seen only the (A) case and study questions, will have prepared the discussion from an entirely different, far more limited point of view. This stacking of the deck enhances the leader's power (for knowledge is power, is it not?) and brings the potentially imbalanced situation closer to a normal student-teacher configuration. Nonetheless, the intelligence, sophistication, and experience of the participants will work against much of this scheme's unfairness: The discussion leader -- a teacher among teachers -- will often function less as a leader than as a colleague in the seminar. This flexibility of role provides part of the joy of this sort of teaching, for the discussion leader can often learn far more from the participants than he or she dreamed possible during the single-focused hours of lonely preparation.

The teacher in a pedagogical seminar or workshop such as this must learn to relinquish some control over the content of the discussion and stop trying to "second guess" participants' comments. This task seems deceptively straightforward, for merely stepping aside and letting the group chat will produce chaos and accelerating frustration. The discussion leader is, in the final analysis, responsible for the proceedings. But he or she must endeavor to give the group's comments shape and direction without being dictatorial or irritatingly manipulative. A good discussion is a focused improvisation on a stated theme. Leading it is no small task.

The primary way in which the discussion leader can mold the discussion is by asking questions -- not just factual questions (although these have their place in anchoring philosophical and interpretive flights to the material under discussion), but stimulating questions, questions that tickle the fancy of the participants, jostle their presuppositions, make them think and feel. All this may sound dauntingly difficult, but the art of questioning creatively is, fortunately, not as inaccessible as one might fear. There are definite mental exercises one may perform to improve one's skill as a questioner. First, think of the many types of questions there are. No two people will produce identical typologies, but most people quickly realize that there are far more kinds of questions than they had ever suspected. Questions can call for analysis, predictions, recommendations for action, extrapolations, supporting evidence for hypotheses, personal reactions and anecdotes, or assessments of the relative significance of elements in a problematical situation. They can also -- depending on how they are phrased and uttered, and on the questioner's body language -- carry powerful emotional charges. Hostile questions are delivered in sharp tones, with a tense posture -- often moving toward the respondent. They often begin with artificially precise, almost accusatory phrases. ("_Just how_ did you arrive at that conclusion? _Do you really mean_ to tell us such and such?") By contrast, supportive, friendly questions can begin with approving statements, delivered with a relaxed stance and in a calm, friendly tone of voice. ("Jim, you're an experienced teacher of history; have you ever tackled a problem like the one our case character faces?") Questions can personalize the discussion, call attention to the backgrounds and expertise of the participants, and make the proceedings inviting, warm, and friendly. Or they can calm a heated argument by calling on people to extract basic principles while they disengage themselves from overidentification with distressed case characters.

In short, questions are protean and powerful tools for leading discussion groups; and whatever else the discussion leader may attempt to do in the seminar, he or she will always perform an accepted function by posing a question: it is a teacher's most characteristic action. Getting the seminar participants to respond with questions of their own -- even to address them to each other -- is a second step in the artistry of questioning, and is one measure of the leader's success in establishing rapport and generating enthusiasm in the group.

C. Preparing to Manage the Discussion Process

The teaching notes in this module are designed to aid the discussion leader in leading a seminar. These teaching notes are unusual in that they concentrate on process rather than analysis of content. Their purpose is to help prepare the teacher for the unforeseeable actuality that will emerge during the give-and-take of discussion. If they were to attempt to forecast the interaction of unknown, spontaneous forces (the participants' personalities and discussion styles and their relationship with the text, each other, and the discussion leader), they would be absolutely doomed to fail. Their purpose, however, is not to predict, but rather to prepare -- and herein lies their uniqueness. We believe that the teacher's most significant allegiance is to the discussion process -- a sort of chemical reaction that occurs, sometimes with a flash, sometimes with a sputter, among the volatile elements of all the participants' personalities. The discussion leader is, at best, a catalyst. But simply starting a reaction and getting out of the way will not suffice to create the desired end product: a genuine educational experience. The discussion leader has to intervene again and again, but always subtly, tactfully, sensitively, helpfully, and creatively.

To aid this process, our teaching notes hope to alert discussion leaders to the enormous range of choices they possess. The choices consist not only in deciding what questions to ask, but when, and of whom. And they also include the less obvious but equally potent issue of how to react to whatever answers the participants produce. The teaching notes will attempt not only to supply a few possibilities -- mostly as examples -- but also to suggest other ways the discussion leader might approach the material and involve the group. Accordingly, they will present possible discussion scenarios and suggest spectrums of response that seminar participants might make to various kinds of questions. At best, these fantasy exercises may serve the imaginative purpose of helping teachers new to the material feel as if they had already taught these cases. At worst, they will give the illusion of true preparation when the reality of the situation is that even thirty years of case method teaching cannot prepare a discussion leader for every event that may occur when people -- thinking, feeling, dreaming, unpredictable, and ultimately unfathomable enigmas that they are -- enter the equation.

We may, for example, suggest that a particular case that deals with sexism could well be taught with a good deal of role playing, but no one on earth can tell you what exposed nerve the discussion might touch in a particular woman professor. No one can foretell what sort of ad libs your group will produce, or what strange, possibly disturbing, emotional overtones any strongly expressed opinions may create for some participants. To invoke a metaphor that comes up over and over again in our seminars, the discussion leader may find that he or she has "unleashed the tiger." The question then will be what to do with the beast: shoot it, ride it, run from it, or let it romp (or rampage)? No teaching note can fully prepare you for that decision. But it is our intention that these suggestions at least alert you to a reasonable proportion of the possibilities inherent in the material and the situation.

The most basic purpose of discussion teaching is to get students to teach themselves. To borrow from Henry David Thoreau in Walden, "Give a man a fish and you've given him a meal, but teach a man to fish, and you've fed him for life." The sort of teaching we are considering applies to materials that require each person to exercise intuition, understanding, empathy, and judgment, as well as intellect. We propose to teach people to fish, and with no pretense to clairvoyant foreknowledge of exactly what they will catch.

The flat truth is that no one can bestow insight, retention, or proficiency. In a way, it is impossible to "teach" anybody anything. You can only demonstrate, clarify, give pointers, and provide moral support while the students work toward their own learning. But you can't learn for them. Still, the teacher has a responsibility: to provide coherent educational materials that give a fair chance of success in mastering an unfamiliar skill, and guidance and encouragement while students struggle.

To summarize: In a sense, all these teaching notes are shots in the dark. Treat them with due skepticism, because real life can usually be counted on to surprise you. The exigencies of the unexpected will probably trample whatever private script -- ours or yours -- you have envisioned. This unpredictability is a major strength of case method teaching. It both minimizes boredom and helps trigger the sort of creative energy that can make discussions memorable, because spontaneity is an exciting, powerful stimulus to original thought.

Rejoice, therefore, in the unexpected. The best way to prepare for it is to remember that it lurks "out there" in discussion method teaching and can explode at any moment, possibly trailing clouds of insight in its wake. If our teaching notes merely resolve your anxieties about dealing with new material and a new methodology, they will have served a purpose. Sample them; then make up your own lesson plans. Our basic intended goal is to urge you to stress classroom process in your preparation.

D. A Walk Through a Teaching Note, Section by Section

Each of these notes begins by introducing the case as a document upon which to structure a discussion. We note any unusual features of the material that might skew the discussion process in some particular fashion. Then we try to identify the predominant mood of the case. When discussion teaching works well, the participants' emotions come into play as well as their intellects, and the mood inherent in the case itself can profoundly affect the way the group will react. We therefore offer a few words about the potential emotional valences in each case. Then we go on to point out any sensitivities -- potentially painful issues like racism, sexism, problems of handicapped students -- as further signposts for the discussion leader who is mentally drawing a map of the terrain. We then present what we call the "blocks of analysis," which are possible topics that might emerge in the discussion. Like real blocks, these can be stacked in numerous ways, but a sense of their size and weight may help the discussion leader stay oriented when the group starts juggling with them. Our suggested blocks merely reflect one way to carve a case into manageable chunks; we recognize the existence of innumerable alternative systems. Choose your own. But we do strongly recommend that you develop some sense of pattern. It is easier to gauge which topics have been overlooked and which pumped

dry when one has a sheet of paper in view that notes some salient rubrics and briefly lists substantiating details from the case itself.

The real nerve center of each teaching note is the second major section -- "Preparing for the Discussion" -- which includes detailed suggestions on managing the class process as it occurs. The choice of the first speaker is crucial, for the impression created in the first five or so minutes sets a tone for the rest of the class hour. If it is a negative tone, the discussion leader will have to work hard to overcome the poor start. Do you want to ask a black participant to open a case discussion that involves an incident of alleged classroom racism? Do you want a woman to begin the discussion of a case that describes a sexist insult? Do you want an inexperienced teacher to open a case involving a young teaching assistant's blunder? What do you seek in an opening speaker -- a clone for the case character, or someone with a very different perspective? How you, the discussion leader, answer these questions will have great impact on your choice of an opening speaker. And his or her performance will, in turn, help determine the tone, pace, attitudes, and emotional overtones of the rest of the class meeting. Finally, each note ends with a section called "The Discussion Questions," in which you will find a long projection that simulates a possible discussion scenario. Unlike real scenarios, these may bear little resemblance to what will actually occur in class. They are not meant to be scripts; the participants in your group will probably never see them. Their purpose is to strengthen and limber up your ability to direct the real discussion.

E. How to Use These Teaching Notes

Those who happen to be familiar with the traditional teaching notes that accompany management cases may find the notes in this module a trifle peculiar. Instead of "reading" the cases -- giving the "inside dope" -- they stress imaginative projections of how a discussion based on each case might shape up. They are, in other words, not analyses, but fantasies. Those who thirst after analyses of content should turn to the "Researcher's Perspective," in which I, who wrote most of these cases and have road-tested several, offer my own insights -- not as definitive interpretations, but rather as personal, perhaps quirky, but frank opinions about the "meaning" of each case. These are possibly closer to conventional teaching notes than the pieces that this module labels Teaching Notes.

This difference from established procedure reflects a basic philosophical credo, namely that the teacher is best served by spending time planning how he or she will orchestrate the conjunction of the material at hand with the diverse minds and personalities if those who have gathered together to study it. Merely analyzing the cases -- even if one's analysis is airtight -- may actually obstruct one's teaching in cases like these; opinion and point of view can be significant and distinctions subtle. Participants' reactions and recommendations can vary widely with perfect justice, because there are genuine enigmas involved in human interactions like teaching. What matters is the process, and that should be the focus of the discussion leader's efforts.

The very first time I spoke with Professor Christensen about discussion teaching, he mentioned his belief that "the assumption that content alone runs a class is the first line on the tombstone." That statement has stayed with me, like a time-release capsule, as I have observed classes, taken a few myself, and led discussions. First, of course, the image of the epitaph lends the idea a certain vividness. Second, I have become more and more persuaded that the observation is simply correct. In fact, I have come to marvel at how few teachers realize that classroom process -- whatever it is that occurs among the participants, instructor, and materials at hand -- is the key to success or failure in discussion teaching. The essence of the insight is a choice. One can emphasize either content, things, people, or process. Of course, neither alternative excludes the other, but there are only so many hours in anyone's day for preparation. Will you spend them going over and over the class assignment, to make sure your command of its intricacies is nearly perfect? Or will you devote the time to trying on the students' mental shoes and imagining, or remembering, how it feels to be a beginner -- perhaps an untalented or ill-prepared beginner -- tackling new and confusing material?

I have spoken with many teachers who report frustration and impatience with their students' slowness, ineptitude, or apparent lack of preparation. Some of their complaining is, no doubt, justified. But much of it should be ascribed to an error they, the teachers, have slowly come to make: they have forgotten the enormous edge their years of postgraduate training and privileged familiarity with the material (often provided by teachers' notes, instructors' manuals, and the like) give them vis-à-vis their students, who often approach the assignment with five others hanging over their heads and a softball game in progress just outside the library window.

Choosing to emphasize process does not obviate the necessity to maintain a good grasp of the primary material under study, but it does require that the discussion leader consecrate substantial chunks of time and mental and emotional energy and devote them to empathizing with the particular group of people whom choice or chance has thrown into the class. Who are they? What are their backgrounds, their personal styles, discernible peculiarities, strengths, weaknesses? What sort of social groups seem to be forming in the class? Who appears to be dominating the proceedings? Who seems shy? Are there any worrisome misfits, any stars? In other words, what do you, the teacher, know, guess, feel, or suspect about this group that will help you figure out how to lead it "into" this material most effectively, encourage active participation, and prevent trouble?

There may be readers who find this content/process distinction obvious. But in my experience, most teachers beyond the secondary school level tend to ignore it almost entirely. Why? Because most college, university, and professional school teachers chose their professions out of a deep love of their subject. Even those who find teaching intriguing and want to help their students learn have often found their own deepest personal satisfaction as scholars or practitioners. This means that even if they would like to teach well, their instincts and training emphasize their own performance rather than the elusive art of coaching others.

In academics, one is often hired to teach, but simultaneously expected to perform time-consuming administrative tasks and produce serious research. In many institutions, teaching gets lost in the shuffle. Even in places where teaching is a genuinely significant consideration in promotion decisions, there is rarely any support built into the system to help professors improve their skills. As a result, many college and university professors have been too busy to take the time to sit back and ruminate about the teaching process per se. They have, therefore, tended to recapitulate their own experience as students -- selecting readings much like those they studied, producing syllabi modeled on those they followed, writing quizzes and exams like the ones they took. Most important, they have approached classroom interaction more or less as most of their professors did: as a sophisticated form of monologue. Most academics are familiar with the infamous "fake Socratic method" in which a teacher asks the class questions that are really only lightly disguised requests for cues to trigger the next few paragraphs of his or her discourse. In discussion teaching, this can engender resistance in the students, because they sense that the focus of attention should be on them and their developing competence. A true discussion teacher succeeds by helping students improve their performance, and the classroom dialogue is the means by which he or she attempts to effect this beneficial change.

F. Some Practical Hints

1. Names. The quicker that people get acquainted, the quicker the group will jell. To this end, it is helpful for the discussion leader to learn and use participants' names and encourage the group to do likewise. To speed this process, it helps to display people's names accessibly. If the participants are seated at desks or around a table, fold-over cards placed in front of them will be legible from several vantage points. (Have their names written on both the front and back of these cards so that participants seated at awkward angles may read them.)

From the discussion leader's point of view a fallback is also useful, particularly in the early meetings or during one-shot workshops. As the group introduces itself, sketch a seating plan and keep it visible. Then for your own benefit and the group's, try as gracefully as possible to use people's names when inviting or responding to their contributions. This device is both a good mnemonic and a way to convey a pleasant cordiality.

2. Eye contact. Most people are either "right-eyed" or "left-eyed," just as they are right- or left-handed. The practical consequences of this normal asymmetry is that one unconsciously tends to pay less attention to either the right or left side of a room. In a discussion class, this means that one section of the room is likely to feel ignored. Consciously ascertaining which way you instinctively turn, and then compensating for this natural tendency, will help you avoid frustrating a whole segment of the group.

One extremely successful teacher I know begins each new course or workshop by consciously making brief eye con-

tact with each member during her opening remarks. To accomplish this task smoothly, she mentally divides the class into pie wedges and turns her attention first to the the faces in the outer left wedge and then to those in the outer right, proceeding, as she speaks, to fill in all the wedges. This approach has become so habitual that it has lost its original, slightly mechanical feel and has become second nature to her.

3. Body language. An all-embracing term that achieved wide popularity in the 1970s, "body language" includes all manner of expressive gestures, twitches, blinks, grunts, murmurs -- in short, anything that conveys a message without words. Much body language is unconscious: we flinch (signifying fear) when a foreign object comes flying at us; we grunt softly ("hmmph!") when surprised. Similarly, we tend to sit up straight when we are interested, and slump when our thoughts stray from our conversational partner's droning to private fantasies that we find far more engrossing. The discussion leader will do well to pay attention to some of these physical signals and -- without becoming paralyzed with self-consciousness or endeavoring to adopt a set of uncomfortable mannerisms -- begin to use body language positively. There are many ways to encourage a speaker without yelling "Right!" during his or her remarks. Sitting forward on one's seat, straightening one's spine in a posture of attention, smiling slightly, or inclining one's ear to the speaker's words can all convey interest and attention.

Body language can also help "cue" another discussion participant into readiness to pick up the conversational ball. Inclining one's ear to one participant while making eye contact with another and nodding slightly can accomplish this task and help the discussion proceed seamlessly, with as few intrusive stage directions from the discussion leader as possible.

4. Hand gestures. One can convey expansiveness by extending the hands, palms open; signal attention by raising a hand; or urge speed in wrapping up a statement by moving the fingers rapidly (as if saying "more, more, come on"). Needless to say, one should use only hand gestures that feel natural, but practicing them can expand the repertoire. Although a discussion leader is neither an orchestral conductor nor a baseball umpire, a little staginess, judiciously applied, can go a long way in teaching as long as it does not deteriorate into a bid for attention.

In a large classroom, the discussion

leader can sit, stand, pace, walk toward the participants, or back away. Remember that to a seated participant, the standing discussion leader looms large. Moving toward a speaker can express interest, but it can also be threatening. Backing away by contrast, can give a symbolic gift of freedom, if one's face shows involvement in the particular participant's comment.

All of the discussion leader's motions derive exaggerated impact from the centrality and status of the position itself. Even in a classroom where the discussion participants outrank the leader, the leader has higher status because he or she "calls the shots." Directing a discussion confers a sort of automatic (but not permanent) promotion. One's gestures thus carry more than customary weight and should be modified according to the impression one hopes to convey. If seriousness and a sincere intention to work energetically seem desirable, one's physical presence, clothing, stance, gestures, and choice of words should reflect this choice. Dressing sloppily conveys quite a different message, as do slouching, murmuring, and tentative gestures.

5. *Speed*. In a discussion leader, excessive speed of speech or physical movement is likely to irritate the group or cause nervousness. Excessive softness, or a very high pitch, will probably imply lack of confidence. If your natural tendency is to speak too fast, consciously try to slow down when leading a discussion group. If you tend to mumble, speak as clearly as you can. If the room permits, walking around can help break the potential monotony of talk if one proceeds at a relaxed pace, but it will seem like edgy pacing (or worse, prancing) if you move too fast.

6. *Voice level*. It is advisable to raise one's voice slightly when leading a discussion. Without shouting, try to remember that you are addressing a number of people. If you tend to bow your head in normal conversation, raise it when leading discussions. If you mumble or keep a hand in front of your mouth (many people do, unconsciously), fight these tendencies when teaching.

7. *Apparel*. As our protagonist in "The Day the Heat Went On" discovered to her dismay, wardrobe matters. The issue may seem petty at first, but the exaggerated visibility of the discussion leader's position makes his or her visual impression ("image") unusually significant. There are no magic formulas, but observing the culture of your institution should help set a tone for your attire. Women certainly need to consider the matter of dress with different criteria than those which determine men's choices. Freud's observation "anatomy is destiny" comes to mind when one compares the implications of a woman teacher's publicly removing her suit jacket with a male colleague's doing the very same thing. However intrinsically innocuous the gesture -- a simple matter of freeing the upper body for more natural gestures -- the fact remains that our case character Ellen Collins elicited a wolf whistle when she shrugged off her blazer in an overheated classroom. The safest advice in this matter is probably to adopt the general style of the institution in which you are teaching (tweedy? tailored? casual? uniform?) but for the purposes of leadership, take it "one step up." In other words, if most people wear suits, wear a particularly crisp one. In leading a discussion populated mainly by professors in sweaters with elbow patches, however, the female discussion leader would look threatening in a black suit. If participants wear sweaters, try a simple jacket. For women, a reasonable piece of advice might be: neither emphasize nor contradict your gender with clothing. Simply put, the objective for women is to appear professional but not severe or "mannish." Whatever else you do, make sure that your clothing is comfortable because, as we have noted, good teachers move while teaching.

8. *Mirroring*. This is a catch-all term I use to designate a ubiquitous phenomenon: unconscious imitation. Human beings are mimics -- never more so than in classrooms. If the teacher is nervous, the discussion group will pick this up and get edgy, too. By the same token, confidence is contagious; so are good humor and energy. By modeling, the teacher can exert surprising control over the style with which the class will operate. To encourage casualness, for example, act casual. But beware: like the instructor in "The Offended Colonel," you will risk unwelcome resistance from some member of the group who takes exception to your breezy manners and relaxed stance.

Mirroring can operate subtly, but there is scarcely a human encounter from which the phenomenon is absent. Nonetheless, I do not mean to suggest that you can remake a discussion group in your own image simply by modeling values or a particular intellectual approach. The teacher in "I Felt as if My World Had Just Collapsed!" made this error: she thought that declaring and embodying her passionate ethical convictions would automatically inculcate a similar set of beliefs in her students. She learned that classroom modeling has limitations, but many teachers have yet to appreciate the dynamic at all. Mirroring can aid or obstruct the classroom process. The message here is: try to be aware that your mood, approach, and attitudes will probably be both more apparent and more contagious than you might normally expect. Still, they will not completely dominate the class simply because you are its leader.

The Seminar Outline

I.   Early Class Sessions: Setting the Instructor-Student Learning Contract; Gaining Students' Respect; Adapting to a New Environment; Cultivating Rapport

      Cases: "The Offended Colonel"
               "The Day the Heat Went On"
               "One Teacher's Nightmare"

II.   Leading the Class: Direction versus Control; Classroom Dialogue; Maintenance and Revisions of Contract; Retaining Authority

      Cases: "A Night School Episode"
               "Assistant Professor Graham and Ms. Macomber"
               "The Dethroned Section Leader"

III. Responsibilities of Leadership: Protecting Students

      Cases: "Henry Jasper"
               "The Handicapped Heckler"

IV.   Operations: Day-to-Day Classroom Management; Implications of Teacher's Actions; Importance of Detail; Moral Issues

      Cases: "The French Lesson"
               "I Felt as if My World Had Just Collapsed!"

Note on the Seminar Outline

In the final analysis, this outline has no more validity than any other the seminar leader might construct. Ideally, after teaching these materials and (we hope) generating enthusiasm in the participants, you may wish to write your own teaching cases. This would fulfill the deepest purpose of these materials and the case method of study in general -- bringing the stuff of life, still fresh, into the classroom.

Before, during, and after every case method teaching seminar, the discussion leader should invite participants to develop and share their own cases. That is how many of ours came to exist.

I have organized this teaching seminar into four general units: Early Class Sessions, Direction versus Control, Responsibilities of Leadership, and Day-to-Day Classroom Management. These roughly parallel the way a group develops over the course of a semester, but the issues with which a teacher must deal can vary widely from this pattern: problems common to the beginning of most classes can crop up at the end, and vice versa. Nonetheless, in the interest of bringing order from chaos, let us consider these rubrics and explore some of the reasons I have organized the cases in this particular order.

I.   Early class sessions. This start-up unit includes cases particularly likely to raise issues germane to meeting new people and beginning to help them form a learning group. Any teacher has to establish authority without appearing lax, on the one hand, or stuffy and dictatorial on the other. He or she must set a workable contract swiftly, or it will set itself. What do you want to accomplish with this group? What do they want to do? The teacher must also begin to create an environment conducive to the sort of discussions that can actually help expand and deepen participants' appreciation of teaching even though they may have been teaching for years, possibly with diminishing enjoyment and effectiveness (burnout is common in the profession). The challenges to the teachers in these early cases center on issues of contract setting, establishing rapport, proving the teacher's authority without pomposity, and finding a niche in a new (and in one case potentially hostile) environment.

II.   Direction versus control. The critical skills here are posing questions and really listening to answers. Classroom dialogue is the crux of discussion teaching. The teacher who attempts to control the proceedings too tightly falls into the classic trap of trying to play ventriloquist. This almost invariably produces bilateral frustration. The students fail to perform the dummy's role satisfactorily, and the teacher strikes them as a martinet with no imagination. Directing the proceedings is quite another matter; it requires more subtlety, greater attunement to the participants' thoughts and feelings, and a shift in focus away from the teacher to the students. It also requires listening.

The most powerful techniques in directing a discussion are questioning and responding -- and we use these terms far more broadly than most people might assume. Questions go beyond the mere eliciting of information. They possess an inescapable emotional component, which discussion teachers ignore at their peril. Assistant Professor Graham's classroom behavior highlights this truth. Think, for example, of the different overtones of "How did you arrive at that calculation, Janice?" and "Just how did you arrive at that calculation, Ms. Macomber?" There are almost endless types of questions -- hostile questions, questions that conceal commands, encouraging questions, patronizing questions, questions that stimulate the fantasy, questions that stifle speculation, questions that accord respect to the participants, and questions (often sarcastically phrased) that belittle and discourage. A discussion leader can use any of them.

The cases in this section also invite discussion of ways to evaluate and maintain whatever teaching-learning contract the initial class meetings have established. All relationships between human beings change over time. The initial equilibrium between the discussion leader and the class -- be it formal, friendly, arm's length, dependent, chilly, whatever -- will eventually alter. The chances are that by the third or fourth session, the seminar will have begun to "feel" different to all concerned. This can upset some teachers, who begin by establishing authority and then dread its erosion as the seminar wears on. What attitude should they take to their classes' developing independence? And what should they do?

III. Responsibilities of leadership. All teachers should be protectors by virtue of their de facto authority. But the true nature of protection -- whom to protect, how, when, and how to recognize genuine weakness -- is by no means obvious. This unit deals with problem students, and helps focus teacher's attention on various ways to spot them, appreciate their impact upon the rest of the class, and begin to think creatively and usefully about ways to offer real assistance.

IV. Day-to-day classroom management. This section takes up issues that schools of management classify under "Operations." How does one move, speak, question, respond, give assignments, behave in the classroom? What are the overtones of all these actions and words? How can teachers begin to appraise and manage these often unconscious procedures?

This is the section in which we consider details. We end with it because it is the most subtle. It should demand the greatest sophistication from the group's abilities to perceive and analyze intricacies in classroom interaction. We also end with it because it highlights implications that we consider absolutely crucial to teaching. The teachers in this group of cases unwittingly preside over situations that seem to damage students, yet neither teacher in this section should by the furthest stretch of the imagination be accused of malice. On the contrary, both are experienced, successful instructors whose philosophies of teaching include humanitarian goals. Why, then, do they encounter precisely the sort of problems they would most like to avoid? The implications of their classroom behavior may be seen to summarize most of the issues the seminar has considered from the beginning: contract, direction versus control, responsibilities of leadership, and the minutiae of what one actually does and says in the classroom, occasionally with surprising effects. We end intentionally on this note of complexity in the hope of raising more questions -- more personal questions for each teacher -- than we answer.

It is our intention to underscore the infinite richness of the classroom dynamic -- not to create a generation of self-conscious instructors, but simply to demonstrate the potential in discussion teaching and suggest that the enterprise can be improved by thoughtful contemplation of its complexities and refreshed and renewed by the constant effort to step outside oneself, imaginatively, and try to feel how the members of the group perceive the things one does and says. For teaching is, above all, an act of communication, and communication requires far more than simple self-expression. In discussion teaching, it is not enough to pinpoint what one really knows about the material and express it clearly. One has to figure out how to lead particular groups of disparate individuals through different points of view about the materials and then let each of them make a separate judgment. This is a far more difficult enterprise than most teachers suspect. But it is also an extremely effective and satisfying way of teaching.

Note on Group Process

Basic to the task of leading a case-based seminar on discussion teaching is the need to encourage the members of the seminar to form a cohesive group that can function synergistically. Ideally, with

the leader's help, the individual participants should come to pool their experiences
and insights in an increasingly productive
way. The following suggestions (and I am
heavily indebted to the contributions of my
colleague James F. Moore) are intended to
help liberal arts instructors set goals for
this component of their mission as seminar
leaders.

Involve all members in discussion. A
primary objective for the first seminar
meeting is to get all section members involved in the discussion. This sets a norm
of participation and allows the discussion
leader to begin to learn about the individuals and the chemistry of the group. In
addition, the leader should try to model
good listening skills for three reasons: to
encourage participants to listen to each
other, to hear what the group actually has
to say, and for the inherent benefits of the
exercise itself. Good listening may well be
the most underrated skill any teacher or
discussion leader can possess. The leader's
second task would be to use his or her
responses, both verbal and nonverbal, to
show appreciation for the diversity and
richness of experience that the participants
bring to the seminar.

Encourage respect among participants.
In the second session, it might be desirable to refine these behavioral norms by
moving from simply encouraging participation to encouraging seminar members to
respect and take active note of each other
during the discussion (in other words, to
begin to form cordial relationships within
the group). One way to do this is to
encourage the use of participants' names.
For example, when a seminar member refers
to a colleague with a pronoun -- "as she
said . . ." -- one might intervene briefly
with "Yes, what Jane said. . . ." It is also
advisable to use one's authority as instructor to insist, when necessary, upon courtesy. In addition, one might begin at this
point to look for ways to involve students
who are hanging back, even if this means
ignoring more aggressive participants in
order to create opportunities for quieter
members to join the discussion.

Praise the process. Early sessions
provide a setting in which to begin to
"praise the process," by which we mean
highlighting the cooperative nature of the
proceedings rather than the excellence of
any particular comment. Whenever an
especially good interchange or whole section
meeting occurs, the discussion leader
should bring this to the attention of the
group. This rewards and reinforces cooperation and team play and dampens the

urge to compete. In addition, it begins to
make the participants aware that a group
process is under way, and that this phenomenon has value.

Stress diagnosis over action. Also in
the first few sessions of the seminar, the
discussion leader might do well to emphasize
diagnosis over action plans or explorations
of larger theoretical issues; this should get
the participants to look deeper into the case
material itself as well as improve cohesion
before launching into potentially divisive
issues like plans for action or personal
philosophies of teaching.

Take notice of the learning process.
In the first several meetings -- let us say
three or four -- the discussion leader's
evolving sense of who the seminar members
are, their individual strengths, and ways in
which these can mesh, is in flux. The
discussion leader should, therefore, periodically take a personal survey of the process, silently asking, "What do I notice
going on in this seminar? What learning do
I perceive taking place? What makes me
think this is so?" One way to approach
some answers to these questions is to come
a bit early to discussion meetings and stay
a few minutes afterward in order to be
available for informal conversations with
participants. These moments often offer
the instructor significant glimpses into their
worlds and clues to their reactions to each
other, the group as a whole, and the
learning process.

Set Goals for Group's Development

In summary, during the early sessions, one might consciously pursue certain
process goals for the seminar that focus on
the group's development. During later
sessions, when the group has established
norms that support self-directed, productive conversations, the discussion leader
can shift focus to individuals and their
development, trying to create classroom
experiences that may challenge particular
people. In earlier sessions, we tend to
concentrate on getting wide participation
and creating a climate of respectful,
accurate listening. We usually try particularly hard to encourage participants to
focus the discussion on a carefully detailed
examination of each case text. But in
"Assistant Professor Graham and Ms.
Macomber," which we suggest for the fifth
session, the content of the seminar shifts
from the teacher-student learning contract
to the instructor's pattern of question
and response, which requires a corresponding shift in the style of case analysis.
Instead of looking for general patterns of

interactions, participants should now try to see how those patterns are expressed in specifics.

Encourage consideration of other options. In looking at particular questions and responses, the leader can encourage participants to consider what other options the instructor might have chosen. This moves emphasis from diagnosis to action, and simultaneously increases potential risks. Making recommendations for action is an inherently dangerous activity, since participants must commit themselves, at least temporarily, to their own recommendations. This can be a drawback. But at the same time, discussions of action can create excitement and involvement, partly perhaps because of the risks, and also because participants must put themselves into the characters' roles and feel the urgency of the case situation.

Both risk and involvement are further increased in the "Graham and Macomber" case by asking participants to evaluate, on the basis of segment (A), how Janet Macomber experiences Charles Graham's intervention, or to predict the long-term effect of the intervention before reading the (C) segment. Predictions, like recommendations for action, force participants to put their judgments on the line. There is an element of challenge in this, and an opportunity for immediate feedback when the next segment of the case reveals what <u>did</u> happen. But, again, the risk is also real. The discussion leader has the responsibility for creating a climate in which participants feel basically safe. In particular, the leader must be ready to protect participants who make unpopular recommendations or wildly incorrect predictions, or who espouse positions that further discussion shows to be unwise.

Inherently contradictory cases like "Graham and Macomber" often produce some widely divergent opinions in the group. Some participants side with Charles (whom subsequent discussion usually casts in rather a bad light), posit value in "toughening students up," and assume that the other students in Charles's class realized that Janet had "cracked the case." Such a defense of Charles usually stimulates intense disagreement, which can be valuable to the seminar because it is inherently exciting and because it underlines the message that "reading" a case or a real situation is often a difficult matter in which reasonable, intelligent people of goodwill can take opposed positions. Additionally, a measure of passionate disagreement can increase involvement in the discussion and

lead to richer, more intense exploration of the case situation and its basic issues. But when participants advance unpopular opinions, the instructor will have to be careful to extend support to the dissidents and highlight the value of their opinions for the discussion process as a whole.

Create "safe" climate to increase participation. There are many ways an instructor can minimize the negative emotional consequences of "being wrong" or taking unpopular stands. In general, it will help to frame disagreements in the section as clashes of ideas rather than of people. One useful technique is to make sure that any idea is expressed and developed by several participants, rather than just one. Most ideas will find some support or elicit further development somewhere in the seminar, if only for the sake of argument.

An instructor can also make the climate safer by stressing the inherently dialectical nature of case discussion. A good seminar session benefits from contemplation of the material from a variety of perspectives. In hindsight, some of the ideas may seem more useful than others, but each idea expressed along the way helps advance the process. Even "wrong" ideas can help highlight positions that approach "truth" more closely, if only by intensifying their luster.

The goal of all our discussions is to help participants see that it is not necessarily easy to comprehend teaching situations swiftly, and that the effect of a teacher's actions can be quite different from what one might initially expect. Making action recommendations is a tentative, chancy business that needs to be grounded in analysis (and then, one hopes, blessed by luck).

Emphasize teamwork; encourage mutual respect. The central consideration for the discussion leader -- whatever the stage of progress of the group process -- should always be to emphasize teamwork: as a group of professionals we are cooperating to explore questions about teaching. This image of the seminar should help reduce competition and defensiveness and create an atmosphere in which participants can reveal their deepest concerns and most precious insights. To aid this process, the seminar leader should model respect and openness throughout, and insist that respect be shown by others. The phrasing of specific questions can abet this task: for example, "Can you please help us understand the situation confronting Case Character X?" is quite different in tone and impact from "What is your personal opinion of Character X?" One can also encourage a supportive position with the phrasing of a question. "As a friend and colleague of Professor Graham, what would you tell him to look for in this situation?" might signal helpfulness and focused analysis rather than censure -- ideals both for the group's approach to cases and for each participant's approach to the others in the seminar.

Participants should be able to expect their remarks to be heard and respected, as well as critically examined. Once the group coheres around these values (which typically takes at least a month), the seminar leader can permit more autonomy in the process, and turn his or her attention to the individuals in the group. This is a turning point both for the participants and the group leader. The discussion leader may wish to take this opportunity -- the increased self-sufficiency of the group -- to sharpen his or her skills as a listener and make sure that seminar members are taking the time to hear each other.

Two other important shifts might begin to take place at this pivotal point in the seminar's progress. First, the leader might wish to work to increase the emotional involvement of the participants in the discussion process. Role playing is a classic technique for achieving this end. Second, cases that involve emotionally charged issues like racism ("I Felt as if My World Had Just Collapsed!" which we suggest to end the seminar), handicapped students ("The Handicapped Heckler"), and potentially disturbed or extremely shy students ("Henry Jasper") can be used when the group has coalesced and learned mutual trust, and the discussion leader, too, has gained confidence.

The Focus Shifts as Seminar Progresses

From diagnosis to action. In earlier meetings, we often spend a good part of the seminar hour on diagnosis, understanding the situation. In the middle period of the term, we tend to shift to about 50% diagnosis, 50% action. As the term progresses, toward the end of the seminar, we further shift that balance to include discussions of generalizations. Ultimately, one hopes by encouraging participants to articulate the wider issues that link all of the cases that they will begin to apply some of their own and others' insights to their own teaching. We now ask, for example, "What questions does this case raise for you in regard to your own teaching? What do you consider the central issue this case raises?"

Has anyone here ever experienced a situation like the one facing Character X? How did that situation affect you? Given that you actually had a similar experience, what was it like for you to read the X case?" We try to save at least the final few minutes of the latter sessions for discussions stimulated by these sorts of questions.

From group to individual. Last in our process planning, we as instructors try to pay individuals more attention within the firm context of a strong, cooperative group. By the end of the seminar -- say the last three or four cases in the syllabus -- the group usually has become reasonably self-maintaining and the seminar usually has come to "feel" like a different group from the assembly of disparate individuals who first came to the early meetings. The group may even have seemed to assume a collective personality -- jokey, for example, or quiet and empathetic, or tough-minded, or whatever. Regardless of the group's particular chemistry, if the seminar leader has succeeded in creating a climate of cooperation and support, he or she may now focus attention on the needs of individuals. For example, if a participant has remained reluctant to speak, the leader may develop strategies to encourage him or her to participate, perhaps by emphasizing experiences similar to ones the participant has very probably had. Or if a member is very good at analysis but less adept at action planning, the leader may start pressing that participant to speak about actions. In this way, a "rounding out" process begins to come into play, and participants can develop in areas where they seem to have deficiencies.

Summarize Value of Seminar and Group's Progress

The last session should probably include not only a case discussion but also a summary and overview by the seminar leader. This summary should emphasize the values of the seminar itself and dwell on the group's progress as well as the insights -- into particular cases and into the whole complex endeavor of teaching -- that this seminar has produced.

A Practical Note -- Organizing the Seminar

How does one set up and run a case-based teaching seminar, especially in an institution where the enterprise and method are unfamiliar? Our experience suggests several preliminary considerations.

First, where shall the group meet? A pleasant, informal room (perhaps a library), where movable chairs can be pulled into a circle, provides both a relaxed atmosphere and opportunities for good eye contact during discussions. Second, how large should the group be? This will, of course, depend upon the institution's faculty, facilities, and the participants' availability; but from the point of view of the discussion process, we have found that somewhere between ten and twenty-five participants can constitute a constructive discussion group in a small room. If -- as in many professional schools -- a large amphitheater-style classroom should be available, the group could greatly expand (even a hundred is a manageable number in such a setting).

Finally, locating potential participants and publicizing the seminar's modus operandi (with regular, assigned readings and faithful attendance extremely important) present steps in the process of applying these materials. Certainly, one may post announcements that herald a practically oriented, case-based discussion seminar on improving one's discussionteaching skills. But is it not risky merely to tack up some posters and see who turns up? We suggest actively requesting department heads and others with direct responsibility for evaluating the effectiveness of teaching in their areas to publicize the seminar and suggest possible participants. Word of mouth is usually the best advertisement, and in order to permit the word to circulate effectively, one should clarify what this seminar is: a series of case-based discussions aimed at teachers at all stages of their careers.

What does the seminar offer? Approximately a semester's worth of weekly meetings with colleagues who care about teaching. The participants can expect to work with others who wish to sharpen their discussion-leading skills, gain perspective on their own strengths and weaknesses, and satisfy their (perhaps latent) curiosity about what their colleagues think and do about some of the difficulties that dog the mysterious process called teaching. Part of the pleasure of the seminar resides in a sort of communion, born of trust, that can flower among the participants once they have allowed themselves to exchange competition for cooperation.

What is the uniqueness of this process? If the seminar meshes, its members will help each other and themselves by focusing their mental and emotional energy on empathetic analysis of "cases": sugges-

tive descriptions of episodes that really happened to teachers. Each case offers an open-ended range of problems that can stimulate exploration on two levels: the specific and the general.

The discussion leader will function less as a teacher than as a moderator. This means that he or she will both prepare the cases and give thought to the subtleties of the classroom process and the best ways to help the seminar group pool its skills, energies, and insights to create an experience richer and more useful than any one participant might expect to have in solitude.

Each case has its origin in a pedagogical technique developed in the Harvard Graduate School of Business Administration to reach management. Accordingly, one may detect a certain tendency to consider teaching managerially. This is by no means to say that we view teaching as a species of assembly-line processes, quantifiable in terms of profit or loss. On the contrary, we take the central concept of process management as broadly and creatively as possible -- more as an art than a science. The elusive task of translating the teacher's preparation and good intentions and the students' potential into growth for all concerned is what shapes our endeavor. We try to work with what actually occurs in the classroom -- questions are asked, answered, and referred for further discussion; insights are volunteered, challenged, and refined; summaries are offered and sometimes transcended; human beings interact. This constitutes a process for which the discussion leader (or teacher) is accountable by virtue of his or her role. Managing this complex process is the central focus of our efforts, and the seminar itself often becomes the central focus of the seminar's discussions because the participants' own normal task is to lead discussions; and they are only temporarily "playing student" during the seminar. In any teaching situation, participants and leader alike manage not only the materials but themselves in relation to all the others present in an ever-changing dynamic. Our materials attempt to honor these complexities without (to paraphrase William Wordsworth) "murdering to dissect." Our emphasis on process as a living entity may well be the drawing card that attracts participants to the seminar, for our practically-oriented focus upon process is, at this writing, a reasonably rare and, we think, powerful pedagogical approach. Experience suggests that a seminar such as the one we present really can make a difference.

The Offended Colonel

Teaching Note

Special Features

The salient event in this case involves a teacher's difficulty with a cultural issue: linguistic propriety. Ben Cheever, a visiting professor of economics and management, leading a model case method discussion at a military policy institute, tries simultaneously to enliven a lackluster discussion and prevent a "premature conclusion" by greeting a participant's comment with a familiar, but still off-color, expletive ("Bullshit!" to be precise). This so offends a colonel in the group that he later demands a public apology from Ben, not only on his own behalf but also to the "ladies present." This element in the colonel's protest is jarring because there is actually only one woman in the group, and he could not possibly have seen her reaction to Ben's language.

Mood

This case makes a good icebreaker because it is short and lively. Participants often find Ben's exclamation amusing and quote it repeatedly. (The discussion leader who finds this language disquieting or inappropriate to a teaching seminar should decide in advance how to handle this probable aspect of the discussion.)

Suggested Uses

Despite its suitability as a lead-off, "The Offended Colonel" has enough intrinsic complexity to repay deeper analysis than may be possible in an introductory session. One might choose to reserve this case for a point in a discussion group's evolution when participants have developed enough sophistication to discern and draw on the implications behind case details.

In teaching this case, most of your class time should be assigned to the (A) segment. Recommendations for action and comparison of these with what Ben actually did are less valuable here than thorough and insightful considerations of the subtle implications inherent in the situation itself.

This researcher, accordingly, would schedule two-thirds or more of the discussion time for the (A) case and the rest for the (B) case.

Conflicts, Sensitivities

The central event of this case is potentially offensive (it certainly offended the colonel) because it involves a breach of etiquette (although a minor one) by a respected professor in a formal setting. The discussion leader will have to use discretion in assigning this material. Are some of the people in this particular group so straitlaced that the material -- and the implications that will probably be explored in discussion -- might so offend them that they will withdraw from participation and possibly disrupt the group? Discussing this case might trigger a replay of its problems in the teaching seminar itself. This would <u>not</u> necessarily be a bad thing. Many participants will agree that Ben Cheever won his confrontation with the colonel. Nonetheless, the discussion leader should be aware of these possibilities.

Second, the final paragraph of the (B) case mentions that several members of Ben's discussion group accompany their apology to him with the information that the colonel was a "born-again Christian." The discussion leader should also prepare to handle vehement reactions (pro or con) to this detail.

Teaching Objectives

A fundamental issue behind this case is the establishment of rapport -- an essential ingredient for discussion teaching. Ben Cheever unwittingly offends a member of a discussion group. When challenged about his language, Ben is intransigent. He refuses either to apologize or change his style. Doing either, he implies, would be hypocritical. This, in the researcher's opinion, is an overstatement born of conflict. No teacher as experienced and canny as Ben appears to be is likely to be blind to the fact that there are many styles of

This teaching note has been prepared by Dr. Abby J. Hansen as an aid to instructors in classroom use of the case series "The Offended Colonel" (A) 9–383–061 and (B) 9–383–062.

communication, and teachers -- more than most people -- have several of these styles at their command. Teachers do not speak or move the same way in casual conversation as in teaching -- particularly when they appear before large groups in auditorium-like settings. There is far too obvious an analogy to stage performance implicit in these occasions -- and the teacher, like Ben, who self-consciously plays devil's advocate to stimulate a more interesting discussion cannot be blind to the dramatic overtones of what he is doing. Ben's choice of dress, style, and diction seems highly conscious. The issue is whether it was wise. As often happens in a teaching seminar, the discussion leader may be scrutinized for his or her handling of the same problem: establishing rapport. How can one strike the right note with this particular group to produce trust, friendliness, and openness in order to have genuine discussion? Sensitivity to the participants' professional position, experience, personal styles, and motives for joining the seminar -- combined with an awareness that the discussion leader has options in approaching these people -- might spare the leader some of Ben Cheever's discomfort.

The central issue here is how to use the options of behavior, language, dress, and classroom setup to help establish the right atmosphere for useful discussion. No discussion leader can afford to sacrifice all of the creative tension that goes with the formality of the teaching situation. Nor should the leader abdicate his or her responsibility to keep order and give direction to the proceedings. But teaching seminars are often conducted by and for one's peers, if not superiors. One dreads seeming pompous in their presence. Casualness is an attractive antidote to this danger, but extreme laxity can lead to chaos. The problem is, and always will be, how to find the happy medium. This case should produce a discussion in which the multiplicity of possible teaching styles becomes apparent. There is no single way to teach. Ideally, a teacher should behave differently (within reason) with every new group of students.

The "Blocks" of Analysis

The researcher has discerned several general rubrics into which discussion of this case might fall:

1. Methodology. Ben Cheever comes to the Commanding Officers' Senior Executive Institute as an apostle for an alien methodology: the case method. There he

meets military officers whose educational experience, both as students and teachers, has probably included only lectures, with a few supplementary small-group discussions. The question arises: How well can one introduce an unfamiliar educational approach like the case method, which requires time for a group to learn to work creatively for full effectiveness, in two days' time?

2. Culture clash. The obvious civilian/military disparity deserves attention. In the military world, rank and hierarchy prevail. Academics, by contrast (certainly at the senior levels where Ben Cheever operates), generally regard themselves as a loose confederation of peers. In their research, and often in their teaching, professors tend to think of themselves as extremely independent. Ben is trying to encourage military personnel to set aside their professional constraints temporarily for the sake of his educational demonstration. The enterprise involves obvious difficulties.

3. Expectations. Ben seems to have limited enthusiasm for the whole workshop. What, then, can one expect of his audience? Many of them have come under orders, and this workshop is going to take two days of their normally free time. We see obstacles to full, enthusiastic participation on both sides.

4. Environment. The room seems to be a conventional auditorium where participants can see Ben, but not each other. This setup is appropriate for lectures, not discussions.

5. Characters. Ben Cheever seems competent, experienced, and perhaps a bit jaded by his twenty years of teaching. The military personnel seem self-protective. Their reluctance to jump into case method discussion in the presence of fellow officers (whose interconnecting webs of obligation this case does not detail) is understandable. The colonel comes across as a "crank," alienated from his colleagues. It is noteworthy that only one other participant leaves the room with him. In the (B) case, some participants actually apologize to Ben for the colonel's hostility. In this section, one would hope to encourage participants to pay attention to the case's descriptions. How, exactly, do people dress, speak, move? The colonel, for example, is in uniform, as are several others in the group. The rest wear rather conservative civilian clothing. Ben seems to be more casually dressed than most of the participants. What signals are being sent?

6.   Communication. Dress, stance, tone of speech, actual words -- all comprise a complex phenomenon called communication. The colonel implies much by his stance (rising to speak when others have stayed seated), dress (having chosen to come in uniform), and tone. He speaks with obvious hostility, using a rhetorical question -- "Don't you think you ought to apologize?" -- as if he were speaking to a naughty child. This is condescending. The sum total is an impression of self-righteousness. One would not expect such a man to be a beloved member of this group. Language is the all-important crux of this case. No discussion of "The Offended Colonel" would be complete without some attention paid to the professor's expletive. Was he wrong? Did he unwittingly break the conventions of leading a case method discussion? What is the effect of vulgarity in an otherwise fairly formal situation? How does such a break in tone affect the participants? What do we see happening in this case? Although people possess varying degrees of sensitivity to subtleties of language, virtually all of us both notice and adapt to linguistic conventions in the groups with which we come in contact. It doesn't take most college freshmen long to call the "American Civilization" course "Am. Civ.," or refer to the local soda shop, whatever its real name, as "The Spot." These familiar abbreviations and nicknames set members of a group off from nonmembers. To use them is to belong. The same phenomenon operates within any group. What is Ben communicating to this particular group of people by being the first to introduce mild vulgarity into their discussion?

7.   Challenge to authority. Ben reacts rather defensively to the colonel's demand for an apology. What is Ben defending? And does his defense succeed? How seriously should any case discussion leader treat such an unexpected personal criticism? What is at stake for Ben? If he does apologize, is he damaging his credibility, losing respect?

8.   Rapport. Ben, like any other case method teacher, has to establish some sort of rapport with the group. In fact, unlike other teachers, the case method teacher also has to try to encourage the group to establish its own rapport. The trust should not be extended merely from student to teacher, but also from student to student. It would seem fundamental to this enterprise that the discussion leader size up the particular group, sense its specific quirks and sore spots, and endeavor -- at least in the early phases of their associ-

ation -- to be, if not ingratiating, at least not irritating.

Unlike lecturing, where simple competence and cogency (combined with a little showmanship) may carry the day, case method teaching is greatly enhanced by amicability. It helps if the participants _like_ the teacher, and vice versa.

9.   Characters' attitudes. This is a sensitive, elusive, and important topic that warrants exploration. Ben "sensed from the outset" that he would have trouble "getting the workshop moving in the right direction." When the discussion started, it shaped up as "particularly lackluster." What is the relationship between the discussion leader's expectations and the group's performance? What could Ben have done, first of all, to prevent the group from becoming "wary, tentative, and unsure of how to proceed," and second (given that the group was hesitant and relatively uncooperative), what could he have done to improve the situation?

10.   Symbolism. Under this rubric, the researcher would include style of dress, physical movement and stance, and tone of voice. What should one make of Ben's apparently deliberate choice of casual clothing, a "breezy, informal approach" to the discussion, and a humorous style? What was he trying to accomplish? Did his tactic backfire? If so, why? What should he have done differently?

Preparing for the Discussion

Exhibit 1 lists suggested Study Questions, to be handed out to participants for use when preparing the case before class. Exhibit 2 contains a summary of the Discussion Questions, to be used by the seminar leader in preparing for class and in guiding the case discussion when necessary.

If participants have considered the study questions in Exhibit 1, they should have paid some attention to the unpromising details of Ben's situation. He seems unenthusiastic about the whole enterprise, having come to "get his ticket punched." And he is an alien. Despite his extensive military experience, he comes to this workshop as an apostle from the civilian world of academics. He dresses far more casually than most of the participants, and the commanding officer of the institute has given him a daunting buildup. It is challenging, to say the least, to be introduced as "the best." Furthermore, he is introducing and demonstrating a new methodology to people who are not only unfamiliar with the case method, but also largely uncommitted to teaching as a profession. Last, Ben is taking up time that these people normally devote to leisure.

Under these circumstances, it is not surprising that Ben found the ensuing discussion lackluster. His choice of a moderately shocking slang word to enliven the proceedings seems to have accomplished his purpose: it caused enough of a rupture to shake people and loosen them up a bit. Like most unexpected uses of mild profanity in rather formal situations, it got a laugh. But what was going on under the surface? Were others in the group beside the colonel upset that this expert from the world of scholarship chose not to behave professorially? Perhaps the slang is a symptom of Ben's real frustration, and the colonel's reaction a sort of lightning rod for other people's (milder but real) dissatisfaction.

Opening Speaker; Backstop

This case involves an "alien" (a civilian academic demonstrating case method teaching at a military institute) and a "crank" (a born-again Christian with a particular aversion to profanity and obscenity, however familiar or mild, apparently) who tries to speak for the group's moral standards. If the teaching seminar includes participants who might conceivably fall into either category, diplomacy would suggest that one avoid singling them out to speak for either of the principal characters. (On the other hand, if the group is obviously good-natured and uses labels with reliable affection and acceptance, it would seem reasonable to take advantage of the existing group dynamics and ask the obvious people for their comments.)

The arrogance of the colonel's unsolicited protest on behalf of the "ladies present" does not usually escape the attention of women in the seminar. It might be advisable, thus, to ask a woman to open the discussion of the colonel's remarks, but by all means, men should also be encouraged to provide interpretations. The sheer lack of observation involved in referring to a single woman in the plural highlights the peculiarity of the colonel's protest. He seems far more out of step with the group than does Ben.

If there are any current or former military officers in the group, the discussion leader will have to decide whether or not to stress the unique setting of this case by choosing someone with military experience to begin the discussion. Certainly the cultural clash inherent in the material could be highlighted by having a military officer appraise the situation from the audience's point of view and describe how Ben Cheever's teaching style might have struck the staff of the institute. One way to downplay the military setting without completely ignoring it would be to ask someone with military experience to "backstop" the opening comments.

The Discussion Questions

To get the seminar started, the following questions (Exhibit 2) can be addressed after the (A) case has been read:

1. **[To the opening speaker]: Please outline the situation for us. Let's review the what, when, where, and who, to get our discussion started.**

This question ought to focus attention on the groundwork for any discussion. Neglect for the specifics can only produce vagueness. In this case, there are many significant details to consider. As part of the what, one should note that Ben is attempting to introduce case method discussion in two days of demonstrations and discussions. How feasible is this? Discussion teaching requires the evolution of group trust and cooperation. What can one expect from the very first case discussion of a concentrated workshop? The when might bring up an explanation for the rather understandable lack of enthusiasm on the part of the participants (many of them there because their superiors volunteered them). These people have not come out of curiosity, and certainly not out of dedication to teaching. The where points to the environment, both metaphorically, as an organizational system, and also in purely physical terms. The room seems unsuitable for discussion teaching because it is apparently an auditorium, set up for lectures rather than conversations. Auditoriums focus undue attention on the discussion leader and guarantee that the participants will suffer difficulty in seeing and hearing each other. Culturally, the where also involves the web of command and obedience that constitutes a military organization. Surely this setting must condition the expectations and social behavior of its personnel.

Other details to consider include the fact that it is Friday morning (normally free time for the staff), Ben's unacknowledged status as an outsider (visiting Washington, D.C., from a home base in New England),

and the impact of the commanding general's "warm and humorous speech" that mentions Ben's military experience and the fact that Ben had once been his boss. The general's parting comment -- according to Ben's report -- that "he considered case method teaching something they ought to know a bit about and that we [Ben and his university's faculty] were the best" must have had an effect on the audience. What was it?

Some participants will add these factors up and assess Ben's situation as perilous: the general's introduction has placed him on a pedestal -- rather an exposed perch for a discussion leader with a potentially hostile group to lead -- and, in this case, simply an exacerbation to Ben's status as an outsider. Others may see the general's buildup as beneficial to Ben; these people will find Ben's subsequent difficulties with the group as surprising as Ben did. The discussion leader's task will be to explore both points of view and try to get participants who naturally gravitate to one or the other attitude to see each other's lines of reasoning. One would hope that this opening section of the discussion would produce enough varying reference to specific details to provide material for a substantive discussion. The case is both brief and rich enough in circumstantial facts to allow the discussion leader to encourage frequent specific references to the case.

2.   [To the backstop]: Would you please help us begin to evaluate Ben Cheever's actual "offense?" What do you think provoked the colonel to protest?

The backstop's personality will condition his or her response to Ben's remark. Some will find it harmless; some, annoying; some, juvenile; some, perhaps, offensive. Whatever one thinks, however, Ben's exclamation is the dramatic core of this case. It usually causes amusement, and members of the seminar often quote it repeatedly. If the discussion leader wishes to prevent this (based on an appraisal of the group, or on his or her own sensitivities), it would be advisable to preface the initial question with a friendly, good-humored request: "Please, spare us Ben's predicament; you don't have to quote him here!" Most members of our seminars consider Ben's language run-of-the-mill, but recommend using such expressions cautiously. This case shows how they can damage rapport. If discussion were to remain on the stylistic level of Ben's remark, the result would probably lack intellectual content: the

vocabulary of profanity is quite limited. Another possible reason for preventing overzealous repetition of Ben's exclamation is the potential for insulting seminar members who share the colonel's sensitivity, if not his whole outlook. They could be extremely useful to the discussion. The articulate presentation of a conservative point of view -- without the colonel's self-righteousness -- would be a great contribution to the elucidation of this case. After all, the colonel had a point: why shouldn't a visiting professor leading a model case method discussion observe the normal proprieties of classroom conduct? Vulgarisms, however common in everyday experience, are still substandard as public speech. When a professor uses this sort of language, a conservative member of the group may well feel offended and suspect him either of contempt or unusual insensitivity. Ben could have spoken differently. (Most of us do not use the same vocabulary when we, let's say, wrestle with recalcitrant income tax forms in private as when we address convocations of our colleagues.)

Profanity has its uses. It makes an effective emotional safety valve by substituting name-calling for physical attack. But why should Ben Cheever bring this language into the classroom? Perhaps the colonel is not too far from the mark in sensing a touch of contempt, however inadvertently expressed.

Another question that the backstop might raise is the extent of Ben's responsibility to the whole group. Even granting that most of the officers found his exclamation unremarkable, did Ben have the right to risk insulting even one of their members? This line of reasoning points out why it might be advisable for the discussion leader to plan in advance how he or she will handle Ben's actual exclamation.

3.   What about the colonel's actual demand? Could we take a look at his words and begin to think about some of the implications behind them?

The matter of precisely what provoked the colonel to protest involves an adjustment of focus. Rather than concentrate exclusively on Ben's exclamation, the discussion should widen at this point. The backstop may not provide this broadened perspective. If not, the leader should ask questions that direct the group's attention back to the case for circumstantial details. The timing of the colonel's objection, for example, seems significant. He waited through the whole discussion. Then, when Ben opened the question period and called on him, he stood up (unlike the other members who had all remained seated) and delivered an extremely hostile rhetorical question. His wording -- "Do you always use profanity when you teach? Or is it that you just feel you have to talk down to us servicemen?" -- is not a question. It's an accusation.

Furthermore, some seminar participants may detect in it a certain contempt for Ben. The colonel's tone is schoolmarmish. His words have the same ring as, "Young man, don't you think you ought to take that chewing gum out of your mouth and sit up straight?" Questions like this are thinly veiled commands.

The second part of the colonel's protest includes the reference to "ladies present," which usually provokes women in the teaching seminar to accuse him of arrogance. It is also possible to defend the colonel and define his intent as chivalrous. If these two viewpoints emerge, confrontation may be avoided by keeping this section of the discussion as analytical as possible. Prompt the group to deal with the colonel's words, not so much in terms of their emotional responses to them but as evidence for interpretation. (In practice, this case does not tend to produce acrimony in the seminar, but the discussion leader should be alert to possible flashpoints, and this is one.) A way to divert attention from the male/female issue here is to ask if anyone else in the group Ben was leading might have been offended by Ben's exclamation. Was only the colonel just a crank, or might he have had a silent constituency? (Whoever made the comment that provoked Ben to respond with "Bullshit!" had reason to feel insulted.) It is relatively rare in case method teaching for the leader to jump in so directly. One usually tries to get participants to expose each other's fallacies. In a sense, Ben violated the conventions with his comments.

Some questions the discussion leader might use to probe for thorough discussion of this section of the colonel's remarks would include asking the seminar to think about the layout of the classroom. Could the colonel have known if the woman was offended? Do we have any indication that she expressed dismay by some remark, a gasp, a shift in posture? (No.) What are the implications, then, of his speaking up for her? Further probing in this area might go beyond the specific incident to some theorizing about the whole enterprise of case method teaching. Success requires participants to speak as openly, sincerely, and alertly as possible because open discus-

sion is the primary tool in this educational method. To hold back or disguise one's reactions is to cheat oneself and, in a sense, deform the whole process. Given this responsibility to be honest, which falls on every participant, the colonel's decision to speak for another participant (with neither permission nor encouragement from her) is a violation of the basic contract. He doesn't know what she is thinking and therefore cannot present her viewpoint. Furthermore, the implication of his statement is that she is incapable of speaking for herself. This implies contempt.

4. **What should Ben do? What are his risks and potential gains in this situation?**

If the foregoing discussion has exposed a broad range of the subtleties that can be drawn from this case, this question should elicit a similar variety of suggestions. Upon first reading, one might think Ben had two simple choices: apologize or not. To apologize would be to admit a breach of etiquette. To refuse would be to stand his ground and defend his right to self-expression in the face of protest by a stuffed shirt.

Some participants will doubtless counsel apology, and there are many reasonable arguments for this course of action. A dignified admission of error can enhance a leader's authority. Not every capitulation is a defeat. On the other hand, others may suggest that -- since only the colonel protested, and, in fact, Ben's remark brought a laugh and picked up the tempo of discussion -- the colonel should be treated as the wet blanket he is. Another possible response to this question is to look for compromises. Ben could make a personal apology for having -- even unintentionally -- offended a discussion participant. Then in the next breath, he might suggest that he is, however, glad to see that no one else seemed offended.

Experienced teachers may point out that most instructors facing sizable groups (and, therefore, occupying the spotlight) instinctively see all challenges as threats. Ben might be expected to react self-protectively.

What is at stake? Possibly his credibility as leader, the group's respect for him, and the whole workshop. In a sense, like every teacher, he may have felt -- in that split second that he had to consider how to react to a direct, unexpected criticism of his competence -- that his fundamental right to be standing before this group had been attacked: an overreaction, perhaps, but not an unimaginable one. Others may downplay this whole aspect of confrontation. The colonel is a crank. Military personnel hear (and use) language far saltier than Ben's remark every day of their lives. Ben should shrug this off and get on with the task at hand. A canny participant may note that the colonel's remarks have a great deal to do with the matter at hand. Ben is leading the last segment of the discussion which is an analysis of the case discussion these people have just held.

In the course of their discussion, Ben used a deliberate technique -- a modified form of role playing, with a distinct change in verbal tone -- to jostle the group out of a rut. This was a pedagogical tactic, and its success or failure could provide material for this section of the workshop.

It often happens that hindsight reveals a shining opportunity in the most seemingly devastating threats. Ben could, perhaps, have turned the colonel's peevish complaint to pedagogical advantage by saying something like, "Wonderful question, Colonel! Could we discuss this? What do you other participants think of the technique I used there? What was its purpose? What kind of tactic was it? Did it succeed?"

But few teachers think that quickly on their feet. The purpose of this section of the discussion is to gain insight into how Ben might have felt when faced with the colonel's unexpected, hostile question, how the colonel might have felt as he delivered his challenge, and what some of his reasons might have been.

It will be valuable to discuss the overtones of the several responses available to Ben, if only because they illuminate some of the complexities inherent in teaching by discussion. The particular response the group recommends for Ben is less important than an open-minded consideration of the many possibilities.

*   *   *

After the (B) case has been read:

1.   **What do you think of the way Ben responded to the colonel's challenge?**

Proponents of apology will doubtless express their disappointment or annoyance with Ben. They may, perhaps, begin to like him less in the character of intransi-

gent leader than they did as beleaguered colleague. Certainly, Ben reacted defensively. Both his critics and defenders will probably notice the self-protective tone in his description of the way he felt and what he said. Ben scanned the classroom first -- a good, sensitive move. After all, he had just been accused of inappropriate behavior in the name of the whole group. Trying to gauge people's reactions from their expressions would be the obvious corroborative gesture.

The faces in the room did not look angry, and Ben chose to stand his ground, rejecting a sarcastic, teasing retort he could have made. He seems to have decided that, rather than strike at the colonel, he would simply explain himself.

The discussion leader would do well at this point either to quote Ben's words or ask participants to do so. "Look!" Ben says, "It would be hypocritical of me to say 'I'm sorry.' So I won't. This is the way I talk. I'm just being myself, and that's that." There is much here to analyze. From this point on, the discussion should keep referring to Ben's words.

The same attention to tone that is recommended in analyzing the colonel's remarks ought to be paid to Ben's reply. What is the impact of that introductory "Look!"? It usually prefaces an argument. Perhaps it says something like, "You fool! I'm going to point out something that's obvious to me even if you haven't noticed it." (Would you believe someone who asserted his or her good spirits by saying, "Look, I'm not angry!"?) Having the dialogue read aloud will greatly help analysis here. Some discussion participants will focus attention on the word hypocritical -- a label Ben (specifically) rejects. Apparently he values honesty above diplomacy. The discussion leader might probe this point. What is honesty in teaching? How much of one's true self is it appropriate to reveal? Where is the boundary between leadership and manipulation, courtesy and hypocrisy? (These issues should come up again and again in this discussion.)

After Ben's reply to the colonel has been examined, consider the colonel's reaction. Again, the discussion leader should direct attention to the details. The colonel "stiffened" before his exit line: "If that's the case, well, I don't feel I care to stay." What does this stiffness convey? (Some will note the extremely personal tone -- the colonel repeats the word "I" twice, and refers to his emotions: he doesn't "feel" that he "cares" to stay.)

But in truth, even as he stiffens, the colonel has given ground. Instead of defending public morals, he is now leaving because <u>he</u> feels uncomfortable.

Ben has reacted with instinctive (and understandable) defensiveness. Interestingly enough, his slight shifting of ground -- from arguing about the word he used to defending his whole personal style -- has made the colonel shift accordingly. The confrontation has narrowed to a private test of wills, and the colonel backs down -- not by ceding a point, but physically, by leaving the arena. The colonel probably considers his exit a moral statement, a gesture of protest. But he also seems to be something of a spoilsport. The fact that only one other officer follows him suggests that they are "odd men out" in this group.

2. **Briefly contemplating the following reply -- "Hey fellow, are you really serious? I learned this language from a Marine!" -- how might it have worked?**

The effect of this reply is quite sarcastic. It would be antagonistic to call the colonel "fellow," and unpleasantly ironic to ask if he is really serious (he is). There may be several points of view on this: participants who, like Ben, express themselves with frequent punctuations of profanity (and there are many, many such people in all walks of life, from the manual trades to academe!) may find this reply basically good-humored. Others might find it provocative, even unfair. The colonel seems to have had little sympathy from the group. Playing on this apparent alienation by teasing him might have seemed almost cruel and thus lost Ben some of the sympathy that the group had probably felt at seeing him attacked for a remark that, in fact, only brought a laugh.

3. **What effect do you think the colonel's exit had?**

There is likely to be little disagreement on this point. The colonel and his colleague have isolated themselves. Moreover, they have cut off the dialogue by removing themselves from the arena of discussion. They are the ones who refuse to exchange viewpoints. It seems fairly obvious that this permits Ben not only to retain his leadership, but also to gain enhanced esteem for having survived a confrontation that threatened his authority. He and the colonel were eyeball to eyeball, and the colonel not only blinked, but ran away.

The discussion continued after the colonel's exit. The discussion leader might ask participants what they make of the fact that people came up to speak to Ben after the session. Most experienced discussion teachers consider it a good sign if participants seek to prolong the momentum of the class. Certainly, seeking the discussion leader out is no signal of rejection. Among those who approached Ben was the only woman in the room who came to assure him that she had not been offended. This fact provides an opportunity for the seminar to consider why she remained silent when the colonel took it upon himself to speak for her. Ben mentions having looked directly at her to read her reaction, but she seems to have wished to remain silent in public. The point of this question would not be to guess the woman's real reason for not rescuing Ben, but rather to emphasize the undesirability of putting discussion participants on the spot. Whatever her reasons for silence, Ben, as discussion leader, behaved responsibly in respecting her right to keep quiet.

As it turned out, instead of Ben apologizing, he ended up receiving informal apology from some of the participants. The tables were completely turned.

4. **Do you agree with Ben's assessment of his handling of the situation?**

Here, the discussion leader might cite Ben's own words, that on the whole "he'd handled this situation appropriately." What does "appropriately" mean? What were his goals? What was at stake? Did winning this confrontation constitute success? Are there <u>other</u> ways in which we might define "appropriateness?"

5. **What larger issues does this case pose for you?**

The purpose of this last section should be to pose open-ended questions on a higher theoretical level than much of the preceding discussion. Some salient issues that most people will extract from the case are rapport, respect, and challenges to authority. But the most telling one -- at least for this researcher -- is the elusive, fascinating human problem of communication. The nuances of the various interchanges in this case are extremely complex, and it is likely that no two seminar groups will assess them the same way. Diction (choice of words), tone of voice, and physical posture in communication all carry enormous impact; teachers who ignore them do so at their own peril.

In teaching this case, you will want to encourage participants to consider what messages they wish to convey by such details as dress and diction. Leaving aside the questions of <u>appropriateness</u>, was Ben wise in seeming <u>more</u> casual and slangier than the discussion group he was leading through a case method demonstration? What is the difference between projecting calmness and a feeling of ease and unintentionally conveying disrespect? At the very least, all teachers should be aware of the complexity of communication.

Exhibit 1

The Offended Colonel (A)

Study Questions

1. How would you have appraised Ben Cheever's chances for success at the opening of this teaching demonstration? On what details do you base this appraisal?

2. What do you think of Ben's use of slang to prevent the group from reaching a "premature conclusion?"

3. Why did the colonel's demand for an apology catch Ben by surprise?

4. What issues does the colonel's challenge raise for you?

5. How would you have advised Ben to respond to the colonel's demand?

Exhibit 2

The Offended Colonel (A) and (B)

Discussion Questions

After the (A) case has been read:

1. [To the opening speaker]: Please outline the situation for us. Let's review the what, when, where, and who, to get our discussion started.

2. [To the backstop]: Would you please help us begin to evaluate Ben Cheever's actual "offense"? What do you think provoked the colonel to protest?

3. What about the colonel's actual demand? Could we take a look at his words and begin to think about some of the implications behind them?

4. What should Ben do? What are his risks and potential gains in this situation?

*   *   *

After the (B) case has been read:

1. What do you think of the way Ben responded to the colonel's challenge?

2. Briefly contemplating the following reply -- "Hey, fellow, are you really serious? I learned this language from a Marine!" -- how might it have worked?

3. What effect do you think the colonel's exit had?

4. Do you agree with Ben's assessment of his handling of this situation?

5. What larger issues does this case pose for you?

The Offended Colonel

Researcher's Perspective

Ben Cheever faces several obstacles to a successful demonstration of the case method. He is a civilian, albeit one with a military background and a personal friendship with the commanding general. Furthermore, the pedagogical method he is trying to demonstrate differs radically from most military procedures. In a group of "85% colonels, lieutenant colonels, and some majors," Ben is facing a large number of people who are more used to giving orders than reaching a free consensus of ideas with peers. Furthermore, Ben and his colleagues, despite their military experiences, have come to this institute as civilians. They are academics, representatives of a distant professional school of management. In this character they have traveled from their university to the military institute for two days. Perhaps Ben's expectations for the very first case method discussion under these circumstances are overly optimistic. Unfortunately for him, he seems to have drawn the short straw: it is his task to follow the commanding general's fulsome praise with an impressive demonstration of case method teaching. The task of creating the initial rapport with this stiff and basically unpromising audience has fallen to Ben, and the issue of the scope of method teaching is well worth considering. But Ben has agreed to participate, and he has many problems to overcome.

The classroom in which Ben finds himself seems to be of the familiar auditorium design. He stands facing an audience of seated participants in a configuration likely to remind most of them of all their years of conventional schooling, beginning with first grade. In such settings the discussion leader -- regardless of age or experience -- wears an invisible sign saying "adult," while the participants wear corresponding signs that read "children." Especially when some of the participants are older than the discussion leader, these roles can chafe and produce resentment. In this case, it is possible that the "offend-ed colonel" expressed a hostility that others in the class also felt. Unlike the others, however, he attached his hostility specifically to Ben's rather commonplace, mildly scatological exclamation.

Whatever the source of the colonel's irritation, Ben might have taken his objection more seriously -- not as a signal to eliminate profanity, necessarily, but as a tip that he had made some fundamental errors in establishing rapport with this group. Rapport is perhaps the most essential ingredient to success in case method teaching. A lecturer can succeed through superior control of the material, but a discussion leader's material is, in a sense, the participant's. It is the leader's complex task to elicit pieces of analysis from the class, and then, with fine tact, structure the emerging discussion without overtly controlling the proceedings. The case method teacher does not quiz students. It is not his province to ascertain whether they can solve quadratic equations. Rather he is a guide who leads the whole group -- himself included -- on a voyage of discovery through a complicated problem grounded in the messy circumstances of real life. Most students need some time to realize this.

There are no pat answers in case discussion because cases are true events -- disguised, but presented with as much complexity as the actual problems possessed when they perplexed the original case characters. Discussion participants must learn to take public risks in the name of exploration. Newcomers to the case method usually begin by assuming that their status depends on producing unassailable correct answers. Ben has to combat this assumption in inimical surroundings. His real challenge -- if his discussion is to demonstrate the case method at its best (as the commanding general promised) -- is to produce enough enthusiasm and trust in this group to permit its members to advance hypotheses and constructively disagree with

This commentary on "The Offended Colonel" was written by Dr. Abby J. Hansen, research associate, for the Developing Discussion Leadership Skills and the Teaching by the Case Method seminars. Its objective is to help instructors in the development of their own teaching plans for this case.

each other. He must enable them to give and take criticism in a spirit of cooperation.

A military organization, hierarchical by nature, provides unpromising soil for the swift cultivation of such free-wheeling equality. Furthermore, the members of this group exhibit their fair share of the common human tendency to reduce tension by avoiding open conflict. They shy away from disagreeing with each other. Ben describes the result of this as a "lackluster" discussion in which the participants are "wary," "tentative," and "unsure." He also pinpoints several other obstacles to success. The lack of committed teachers is one. His own lack of commitment to the institute is another. But possibly the worst is the scheduling of the workshop. Ben is trying to start the workshop on Friday morning -- a time the faculty usually has free. Ben is inadvertently competing with the participants' daydreams of what they'd rather be doing than sitting in a classroom looking at him.

Ben knows he has to create rapport by getting these people to relax, but his tactic -- adopting casual dress and language -- backfires and produces open resentment from the colonel. Perhaps the image that Ben presented with his sporty clothes, slangy speech, and jokes disturbed a significant proportion of his audience. Certainly their style of dress -- conservative civilian clothes and some uniforms -- communicates a measure of stiffness.

Ben's demeanor indicates just the opposite, yet he comes to these people stamped with the prestigious label "professor" and certified by their commanding general. He may be sending crossed signals to an audience that would prefer to cede him formal authority. Similarly, his title implies intellectual accomplishment, but his choice of vocabulary and use of humor to warm up the group may also have baffled many of their expectations. "I expected a professor," some might have been thinking, "but this guy is telling jokes." Ben might have done better to dress conservatively -- suit and tie -- and signal relaxation by shedding his tie. Similarly, he might have spoken somewhat formally at first, and then relaxed, introduced some humor, and ventured into a few slangy expressions when he could sense the group relaxing along with him.

Ben seems to dislike hypocrisy. Challenged by the colonel, he replies: "This is the way I talk. This is me, and that's it." He isn't the sort of man to apologize for form's sake, but nonetheless he is willing to do some playacting. He plays devil's advocate when he drops that coarse, familiar exclamation that so infuriates the colonel. But it seems significant that Ben's remark comes in response to a comment with which he actively disagrees. Given his morning of frustration with this group, isn't it possible that his reaction was heartfelt, spontaneous, and very much in his own voice? At any rate, its slangy tone produced a laugh from the group in general. In the classroom, profanity and vulgarity, used unexpectedly and with good humor, usually do provoke laughter -- possibly because they break decorum. They are mildly shocking, and if they carry no threat, their very inappropriateness will seem funny. Ruptures in the normal scheme of things usually do amuse: think of people's first reaction when somebody trips and sprawls on the sidewalk. But this sort of laughter carries a nervous edge, and a case method teacher will have to manage this nervousness.

The colonel is in uniform. Perhaps this shows a particular desire for formality in him. Perhaps he wishes to stay hidden behind his institutional identity. He seems to have felt some personal threat or challenge behind Ben's breach of decorum. One wonders: Could Ben have noticed this colonel and read some warning in his reactions throughout the discussion? Was the colonel showing a mounting anger? Could Ben somehow have headed off his interruption and avoided being insulted?

The outburst itself is instructive to examine. It attempts to call attention to Ben's differentness -- making the group "us servicemen" and Ben the alien interloper. But, since Ben's language did not, in fact, deeply insult most of the members of the group, the colonel's challenge boomeranged and ended by isolating the colonel and one follower. It is they, not Ben, who leave the room. The colonel has abrogated an implicit contract of free discussion by simply assuming the right to speak for the whole group. It is he who has insulted them.

More specifically, he has insulted the only woman in the room. Alluding incorrectly to "ladies" when there was just one female -- and further alluding to her assumed outrage at Ben's language when in fact the colonel, sitting a few rows behind her, had no way of gauging her reaction -- the colonel has implied that this poor female couldn't possibly be expected to speak for herself. This presents a complication of the challenge to Ben: what is his responsibility to this woman? Should he ask her to comment for herself? Should he apologize to her? Should he ask the colonel to apologize for daring to speak for her without consultation? Or should he resist the temptation to get out of the heat and avoid putting the woman into the spotlight?

In the heat of the moment -- surprised, annoyed, and generally frustrated by a less than stellar discussion -- Ben seems to have reacted only to the colonel's challenge to his authority. He treats the colonel's demands like a showdown, and he wins the confrontation. But perhaps Ben has lost an opportunity to examine the tactics by which he attempted to set a contract with this group of strangers.

Many of the thorniest issues in this case cluster around the elusive matter of the desirable social tone to set in the classroom. Certainly, different groups will elicit different styles of discourse. What's appropriate for a military institute will probably not be appropriate for a group of Gestalt psychotherapists. But the question of the proper sort of language to use remains somewhat universal. Profanity and vulgarity are current coin in many subcultures -- the armed services and many university graduate departments, for example -- but the classroom (particularly when a formal teaching demonstration is taking place) should be the setting for intellectual communication of the highest order. The content of many of our slang expressions is at best embarrassing and at worst downright sickening or sadistic. These associations are unavoidable on some level of consciousness, no matter how familiar the terms or how dead the metaphors. To use scatological or obscene or racially insulting language is to arouse emotional overtones in the participants' minds -- overtones that lead in directions that can have nothing to do with the intellectual work of the class. Not that emotion is inimical to learning -- on the contrary. But the emotion of the classroom should be focused on the issues under discussion. Locker room language instantly makes women feel conspicuous because women's bodies are the focus of so much of its lexicon. The same is true of all racial slurs and stereotypical slang remarks. These tend to focus unwelcome attention upon any members of the group under discussion who happen to be participants. Even if these people take the remarks in stride with good humor, they have nonetheless been singled out for distracting attention. Furthermore, most obscenities greatly impoverish one's range of verbal nuance. It takes a brilliant speaker, a trained and talented actor, to use obscenity with elegance in the service of real communication. And surely communication is the most basic goal of classroom dialogue.

In teaching this case, the discussion leader might wish to enter a plea for diplomacy. It isn't necessarily a virtue to insist on one's right to speak the same way all the time. It is the teacher's duty to gauge the audience and adapt accordingly. After all, no one speaks the same way all the time. There are many kinds of discourse -- baby talk, pillow talk, locker-room banter, social chitchat, prayer, howls of anger. Classroom language should be adjusted to the occasion and should always be in the interest of establishing the best sort of rapport with the group that one has agreed to lead through the voyage of discovery that is case method discussion at its finest.

The Day the Heat Went On

Teaching Note

Special Features

"The Day the Heat Went On" could be considered, more than most cases in our syllabus, a "woman's case." The protagonist, Ellen Collins, finds herself heckled in a particularly gender-specific way: when she removes her blazer while teaching in an intolerably stuffy classroom, a loud wolf whistle rings out. This mild impertinence assumes serious overtones only in context. Ellen is one of the very few female instructors at a large, well-known school of business and public management, and she happens to be the only female teacher assigned to this particular group of students for their first-year master's degree program. Furthermore, as we learn in the (B) case, Ellen considers the female students in the class "demoralized," and the prevailing institutional culture unsettling, alien, and basically hostile to women. Since a wolf whistle conveys an intrinsically condescending appreciation for a woman's figure, the "me Tarzan, you Jane" overtones of this interruption to Ellen's finance class could scarcely have escaped the students. Symbolically, the wolf whistle shifts Ellen's identity from "discussion leader" or "finance expert" to "woman on display," and turns a simple action -- removing one's jacket on a hot day -- into a striptease. The challenge she faces is, thus, more complex and charged with risk (loss of dignity, diminished effectiveness as a leader, personal embarrassment) than might at first appear. It is the discussion leader's task to make sure the seminar considers the implications.

To deemphasize the gender issue, the discussion leader can try to emphasize the "everyman" aspect of this case and treat Ellen Collins as a member of a minority group in the mainstream culture of a large, urban school of management. The wolf whistle may be considered representative of a form of public heckling, and the challenge to Ellen's authority typical of the sort of hazing many new instructors endure from spirited, rather immature, students. Certainly this approach to the case will bear fruit. But the specifics do call for some attention to the problems of young women professors in business and professional schools in general.

Mood

This is a peppy case. The trigger incident is a wolf whistle, and the case informant lively and resilient.

Suggested Uses

"The Day the Heat Went On" deals with events in the last part of the academic year, but the teacher is relatively new to this group of students, due to peculiarities in the academic schedule of her institution. She is, moreover, this group's only female teacher, having inherited the students after they have worked exclusively with male teachers for the better part of the year. Part of her challenge is to establish a working relationship despite this group's habituation to dealing only with men in authority. It is, thus, a "contract" case; the wolf whistle jeopardizes the contract that Ellen would like to establish. The section of the course in which contract issues cluster would seem the natural home for this case, but it could also be positioned in that part of a syllabus that deals with day-to-day classroom procedure (or Operations, as it is termed). How does any teacher respond to an unexpected bit of disrespect in the classroom? Unanticipated impertinences can pop up at any time.

Conflicts, Sensitivities

The discussion leader should beware of polarizing the group on the issue of sexism. The obvious way to defuse this potentially sensitive material is to stress the broader aspects of the case: the underlying challenge to authority that Ellen experiences in her way could have assumed a different form when directed at a male teacher.

This teaching note has been prepared by Dr. Abby J. Hansen, research associate, as an aid to instructors in the classroom use of the case series "The Day the Heat Went On" (A) 9-384-098 and (B) 9-384-099.

Teaching Objectives

Paradoxically, part of the rationale for using "The Day the Heat Went On" directly contradicts the advice of the previous section of this note. This case <u>does</u> have sexist overtones. One salutary effect on discussion might be to allow men in the group to empathize with Ellen Collins's anger at being singled out for unwelcome sexual appreciation. On another level, of course, it should provide a means to air the grievances felt by members of any minority group in a culture with palpable elements of prejudice, condescension, or hostility.

The "Blocks" of Analysis

1. The teacher. Ellen is young, attractive, soft-voiced, competent to handle her teaching role, and ambitious. She is also sensitive to nuances in her classroom, and extremely aware of the symbolic content of students' and teachers' gestures. She understands the unfolding classroom dynamic quite well. This is both an advantage and a handicap, for she not only recognizes a challenge when it occurs, she also knows how much rides on her response.

2. The institution. Fleming Graduate School of Business and Public Management in Toronto seems to be a large school of excellent reputation where advancement as an instructor is extremely desirable. Certainly, Ellen conducts herself as if she would like to be tenured there. The students seem lively, and the curriculum is extremely demanding. Women are a minority at Fleming, but their numbers are significant; there may be just enough of them to constitute an irritating presence.

3. Subject. Ellen Collins is teaching finance -- a serious, difficult, and high-status subject in the school of management. She is, in a sense, poaching in a traditionally male preserve, for women in this sort of professional school have traditionally taught the "softer" subjects, like industrial psychology, or business English.

4. The students. The Fleming method is to segment its first-year MBA students into groups of eighty to a hundred students who take all of their courses together. The "Learning Groups" (LGs) meet daily from 8:30 a.m. to 2:30 p.m., and we gather that they spend much of their free time socializing together. This system would tend to encourage strong social identification in the student groups, while positioning the instructors on the outside. Add to this the fact that Ellen is the only female teacher of LG VI, and we can see her vulnerability vis-à-vis the students.

5. The "trigger" event. The wolf whistle can be considered a trivial impertinence, a naive but sincere compliment, or an insult. Whatever point of view emerges most strongly in the discussion, it is advisable to try to elicit the others. In all likelihood the student who whistled meant no harm, but his naivete does not remove the insulting implications of the whistle, especially when addressed to a thoughtful woman teacher who has given time to considering the symbolic overtones of precisely this sort of cultural convention. (All of the above interpretations of the whistle may be valid for different members of the class.)

6. Basic issues. Among the principles that structure this case, the researcher has discerned these: challenge to authority, self-management under stress, response to a potential insult, the instructor's authority (and its tenuousness), and contract.

Preparing for the Discussion

<u>Exhibit 1</u> lists suggested Study Questions to be handed out to participants for use when preparing the case before class. <u>Exhibit 2</u> contains a summary of the Discussion Questions to be used by the seminar leader in preparing for class and in guiding the case discussion when necessary.

Opening Speaker; Backstop

In this case, choosing a man to open is advisable because the material <u>is</u> so heavily slanted in the direction of women -- preferably a man who could put himself in Ellen Collins's position. As he responds, listen very carefully for reactions that might suggest differences between the way men and women treat challenges to their authority. For the backstop, a good choice would be a woman, to both balance the opening speaker's recommendations and to signal that despite the presence of sexism as a live issue in this discussion, your group will approach the issues from all sides.

B. The Discussion Questions

The following questions (<u>Exhibit 2</u>) can be addressed after the (A) case has been read:

1. [To the opening speaker]: If you

were Ellen Collins, what would you do when you heard that wolf whistle?

A male speaker might suggest some vigorous rejoinder to the whistle. One extreme would be to demand to know the identity of the whistler and then ask him to leave. Another would be to turn in the direction of the whistle and briskly say something like "You're out of line, buddy. And this is the last time this sort of thing is going to happen in my class!" Another suggestion for a response is a sarcastic joke: "Well, I guess _your_ social life has been uneventful lately!" On the other hand, the first speaker might try to put himself in character, noting that Ellen describes herself as quiet-voiced, not given to large, dominating gestures in the classroom, and generally conciliatory rather than combative. Speaking from Ellen's point of view, one might feel more inclined to stonewall the event, continue the class with minimal fuss, and maintain one's "cool." But she _is_ angry.

Another alternative might be to seize the opportunity to make a speech, either on classroom manners (stressing the unacceptability of heckling, catcalls, and whistles in a professional school) or on sexism at Fleming. All of these courses of action should find both their adherents and their detractors. There will probably be a range of responses in the group that includes people who have thought long and hard about the problems of women in society, some who may be bored and discouraged with these issues, and people who have not yet considered these matters in great depth.

As with all cases, the discussion leader should be concerned at first with expansiveness -- opening up the discussion to as many points of view as possible. In this instance, the choice is to begin with "action," not necessarily because this case is more operations-oriented than theoretical, but because examining Ellen's options and their consequences will lead naturally to considerations of her position in the closed society of Fleming Graduate School of Administration and Public Management.

2. [To the backstop]: Could you help us appraise Ellen's position? What do you consider to be the critical elements in her situation at Fleming?

At this point, discussion will have to focus on the inescapable gender issue. Ellen is a highly qualified tenure-track assistant professor of finance at a major institution. She is thirty, married, of medium height, with collar-length hair and a soft voice. She does not practice a "tough" style of teaching (as some of her respected male colleagues do), and she is acutely aware that her teaching wardrobe is important. In other words, she is self-conscious, and the focus of this self-consciousness is the fact that she is female -- different from the dominant mold of Fleming teachers, who are male. She looks different, sounds different, adopts a different attitude toward students, and has to keep different criteria in mind when she selects her clothing. The "backstop" can hardly fail to mention at least a few of these considerations. Other considerations to expect would include the prestigious, success-oriented school, with its annual graduating class of five hundred master's degree candidates -- the great majority of them being men. Another factor is the Fleming method in which the large Learning Groups form strong, sometimes complex, social bonds. Class participation counts heavily in Fleming's grades, so students must learn to assert themselves in discussions with their groups. Teachers who "float" from classroom to classroom to meet the LGs for their classes are almost automatically "odd man out," as the LGs form cohesive social units and gain group identities as the year progresses. This incident occurs in April -- seven months after the beginning of the LGs' first year. Seven months are a long time for eighty to a hundred students to spend in each other's company, taught -- as the case tells us -- exclusively by male instructors. A significant ingredient in Ellen's situation is her conspicuousness as LG VI's only woman teacher.

Alert participants will also notice Ellen's reference to Charlie Brennan, LG VI's tyrannical instructor in industrial psychology. Charlie is a "tough" teacher who, according to Ellen, had "wiped the floor" (symbolically) with all the women students in the class by calling them together for a special meeting in which he treated them with insulting condescension. Unfortunately for Ellen, she teaches the LG immediately after Charlie's class. No wonder she finds the group tense and the women "demoralized."

Certainly germane to Ellen's predicament is the mood in which she usually finds the class: it is flirtatious. The nervous humor that Charlie inspires in his tense students characteristically assumes sexual overtones, and Ellen has to cope with these. Her method for dealing with the moderate suggestiveness of LG VI's jokes had been to permit the group to let off a little steam. Ellen chose to "shrug off" the unwelcome implications in their jokes. Her only reaction to the sexual overtones in some of their humor was to "hope that the jokes would not escalate."

All of these factors, plus the observation that "no one found Charlie Brennan's condescending attitude toward his female students particularly unusual," define the situation in which Ellen finds herself at Fleming with LG VI. These, plus her inexperience (this is her first year at Fleming as a tenure-track instructor), make things difficult for her.

Attention should also be paid to Ellen's description of the general Fleming culture: the "high-level of obscenity in the LGs' humor," and the "assumption . . . that women students couldn't possibly say anything worth hearing." The three "extraordinarily bright women" in Ellen's class, she notes, "seemed to be having as hard a time" as "the less gifted, more intimidated ones." For the bright, assertive women, the problem was social ostracism. Their very intelligence seemed only to have provided their fellow students with a sarcastic label for them, and their best comments in class often inspired bored chuckles. To Ellen, the basic, inescapable fact was that "women -- all women -- have a very tough time at Fleming." We assume she includes herself in this group.

A discussion participant might draw attention to some of Ellen's central decisions in creating a teaching image: what to wear, and how to move in the classroom. As Ellen herself makes us aware, these are not trivial considerations. Ellen draws the parameters sharply: "Look too frilly, and you come across as an airhead; but if you look too severe, you're a schoolmarm." She also mentions the institutional custom (for men) of beginning class by removing their jackets and rolling up their shirt-sleeves. Given the sexual tension in the air in LG VI's meetings, Ellen felt that following this custom would be completely inappropriate for a woman. She uses the "striptease" analogy to explain why.

Another element in her immediate situation at the end of the (A) case is the unpredictability of the Fleming heating system -- quite a familiar problem in most schools. On the first warm day of the year in Canada, the heat went up, not down, and the "temperature must have gotten up near 90°." Ellen and the students were all struggling to continue a serious discussion despite increasing physical discomfort and growing mental fuzziness. Everyone must have suffered at least some loss of mental acuity.

All of these factors bear directly on Ellen's situation.

3. **Although a male teacher would have been far less likely to inspire a wolf whistle, do you find some elements in Ellen's predicament that might apply to teachers of both sexes?**

Speakers will probably isolate a few common elements of threat from Ellen's specific challenge: first, she has been unceremoniously interrupted during a class. This violation of conventions would irritate and distract most teachers. Second, she has been symbolically booted from her role as "teacher" or "possessor of superior information and insight" down to a lower level: female creature. This instantaneous loss of status could happen to a man if he felt that an ad hominem attack (a prank, insult, or disrespectful personal joke) had occurred in class. If the wolf whistle is taken as just another form of heckling, the challenge to Ellen is not so much sexual as grounded in her right to stand before LG VI at Fleming and act as their leader.

4. **What do you think the whistle implied?**

Responses to this will vary according to how sympathetic the speaker feels toward the whistler. One may take a lenient attitude and call the whistle a good-natured joke, or even treat it as a sincere, if inappropriate, compliment to Ellen's looks. A hard-line feminist would take it as an insult, a symbolic reduction of Ellen to an inferior, available, "sex object" -- all the more infuriating because it comes from a member of a group that is, in the nature of the situation, inferior to her. After all, who is the teacher here? Who should set the rules of classroom behavior?

At this point, it would be useful to make sure that attention has been paid to the way Ellen reports reacting to the whistle. She says "anger crashed" over her for a split second. And the verbal content of her anger was this: "What nerve! How childish! What an insult!" We note that Ellen makes no mention of having felt flattered by the whistle.

5. **What should Ellen have done?**

At this point it might be interesting to circle back to the territory we opened with the first question and note whether participants have altered their initial positions. What responses might Ellen have made?

They range from tough to lenient, hot to cool. She could have turned on the whistler and demanded that he apologize. Or she could have interrupted the class for a lecture on appropriate manners for MBA students. Or she could have delivered a feminist tirade delineating the unwelcome implications of a wolf whistle. Or she could have made some sort of joke, possibly including sexual overtones of her own, to show that she was not flustered. Or she could have ignored the whistle and continued the class, but made silent plans to deal with the underlying issues at some future date.

As is customary with cliff-hanger questions that precede distribution of the (B) case, the discussion leader should allow the seminar participants time to discuss the pros and cons of a wide range of responses before giving them the (B) case, which contains the description of how Ellen Collins actually did respond to the wolf whistle.

* * *

After the (B) case has been read:

1. **Ellen considered several options. Would you have included any others?**

She considered turning to the women in the class for help and support -- after all, she had been insulted as a woman, and her position as role model for the female students might have dictated recognizing a certain solidarity with them. What might have been the result of this course of action? We know that the women in LG VI were not a distinct social unit -- the bright ones had been ostracized by their female as well as male colleagues. We also know that the dominant impression they made on Ellen was one of demoralization. Ellen's decision not to address them in her need was probably correct: they might not have come to her defense. An appeal to them could have seemed like further evidence that women couldn't survive unscarred at Fleming. If a woman teacher crumbles under attack, what can one expect of her students?

2. **What do you think of the response she actually made?**

Ellen decided to keep cool, physically turn away from the whistle (symbolically reject its very existence, momentarily close off the whole area of the room from her realm of attention), and deliberately continue the class. She called upon a male student -- one she knew to be competent --

and tossed him a "direct and simple question" relating to something she had just put on the board. In other words, she acted competently, professionally, and perhaps just a touch condescendingly (a "simple" question could be interpreted that way). Most important: she kept control of the situation. Then she did something that is advisable for all teachers in moments of stress: she used the time while he answered to "collect her thoughts." In other words, she bought time, and she would have calmed down enough by the end of the student's contribution to concentrate on leading the rest of the discussion coherently. Not surprisingly, Ellen mentions, "the class went on with no further jarring incidents."

Most participants will endorse her actions, but there may be some "hardliners" (either feminists or those simply given to bolstering teachers' authority in the face of challenge) who criticize her leniency. These people will maintain that she failed in her responsibility as a teacher when she purposely ignored the impertinence and meted out absolutely no punishment or reprimand (no negative reinforcement for unacceptable behavior). The class could profitably consider this question: What is the best treatment for childishness that verges on insult in class? If a teacher reacts with quiet, cool maturity, may one rely on the heckler's innate sense of propriety and decency to reassert itself and teach the appropriate lesson? May the teacher assume that the student's classmates will gather around him (or her) afterward and lavishly express scorn for such foolishness? In other words, can the lesson about decorum be taught indirectly? Or does it fall squarely on the teacher's shoulders to address the issue in public? What, in short, is the most effective method of teaching the necessary lesson here?

3. **What effect would a pointed -- perhaps sarcastic -- joke have had?**

Many will assert that a joke, particularly a sexually charged joke, would have been disastrous because it would have symbolically lowered Ellen to the heckler's childish level. Some participants may, however, espouse this sort of rejoinder as palpable proof that the teacher is neither shocked not rattled. But jokes are always dangerous: they frequently evoke embarrassed, rather than appreciative, laughter. A joke in this context would probably have had such an effect. Humor's many implicit complexities provide an inexhaustible topic -- one that certainly could surface in this direction. What is the effect when the victim of an insult makes the joke? Are there any humorous ways Ellen could have deflected the condescension of the wolf whistle and turned the situation to the whistler's disadvantage? Would she have lost dignity by engaging in this sort of repartee?

4. **Can we compare the impact of "muddling through" (as Ellen managed to do) with an angry retort and a lecture on classroom manners?**

This topic should have been broached at least indirectly during consideration of the various options Ellen could have taken to respond to the wolf whistle. Many teachers find themselves in a state of hyperacute concentration when they encounter an unexpected challenge or symbolic insult in the classroom. It is surprising how often they report instantaneously considering a wide variety of responses, almost as if a screen were rapidly flashing these alternatives before their eyes. Generally speaking, those who choose the least unsettling response -- making <u>no</u> direct rebuttal to an insult, and playing for time while their tempers cool -- reap the benefits of their instinctive reluctance to create a scene. They generally receive a reward: increased cooperation from the class.

5. **What do you think of Ellen's statement, "Women live under microscopes at places like Fleming"? Is this true of other groups as well as other places? What are some consequences of this situation?**

This question ought to open the discussion to the consideration of other minorities. The thrust of thought here should be to call attention to their conspicuousness and self-consciousness, and the inescapable tension that these cause. All "aliens" suffer awkwardness of some sort in a mainstream culture -- particularly one like Fleming where the potential stakes of "belonging" are high. Women and other visibly different and underrepresented groups are, presumably, taking their MBA degrees at Fleming because they, like the males of the dominant, traditional business culture, want influential and remunerative positions in the corporate world. But they realize that the folkways of this culture do not come naturally to them, and the culture does not welcome them unequivocally. They have not been bred to its unstated norms, and they know perfectly well that many of its folkways define them as inferior. Note the scorn with which LG VI greeted classroom contributions by women -- <u>even</u> the extraordinarily bright ones -- because, as

Ellen observed, women were traditionally ostracized in this culture. The brilliance of a few women made no appreciable dents in this prejudice.

What are the consequences of life in a goldfish bowl? Participants will probably mention Charlie Brennan's irritating influence (notice how he calls attention to the trappings of women's clothing and accessories and thereby heightens their self-consciousness).

The women in the group seem to have reacted, by and large, by losing self-confidence. What does this mean -- that they internalized the culture's lack of confidence in them? That they truly doubted their own capacity to contribute and excel? That they labored under extra pressures in an already tense atmosphere and therefore performed all the more poorly? The same generalizations may be ventured about other "standout" groups.

6. **What steps might you advise the administration to take to improve the institutional culture for women?**

This is patently a "take-home" question. It is unlikely that the discussion group will produce a coherent, effective blueprint for social progress in graduate schools of administration and management in the ten or fifteen minutes or less left at the end of a case discusssion. Is it sufficient to bring women (or other minorities) without preparation into a culture that is not only alien but demonstrably (if sometimes subtly) hostile? If not, what sort of preparation? (Support groups, teacher-student conferences, special advising, introductory orientation programs, counseling?) Is it the institution's responsibility to help prepare these people? Or is it the students' sole problem to survive the unfavorable odds against them and come through their years at Fleming all the tougher? Will the situation improve on its own, without administrative interference, as the numbers of Fleming MBA women in the corporate world increase and improve their status? Should efforts be made to recruit Fleming's women graduates as visitors, counselors, contacts, and unofficial advisers to women students? What might be some potential negative results of creating special support services for women?

This last discussion question, in essence, asks the seminar group to solve a besetting problem of all academic institutions whose dominant culture for many years had been male-oriented. But the issue is indisputably important. Talented, competent, and basically self-confident people like Ellen Collins are now populating these previously closed societies in increasing numbers. The problems these women face -- and the problems they pose to the institution -- deserve the most serious and immediate considerations if valuable skills and talents are not to be wasted.

Exhibit 1

The Day the Heat Went On

Study Questions

1. From Ellen Collins's point of view, what is at stake at the end of the (A) case?

2. What immediate course of action would you advise for her?

3. What dynamic do you perceive working in these events? What are some underlying principles? Is this uniquely a "woman's issue?"

Exhibit 2

The Day the Heat Went On

Discussion Questions

After the (A) case has been read:

1. [To the opening speaker]: If you were Ellen Collins, what would you do when you heard that wolf whistle?

2. [To the backstop]: Could you help us appraise Ellen's position? What do you consider to be the critical elements in her situation at Fleming?

3. Although a male teacher would have been far less likely to inspire a wolf whistle, do you find some elements in Ellen's predicament that might apply to teachers of both sexes?

4. What do you think the whistle implied?

5. What should Ellen have done?

*   *   *

After the (B) case has been read:

1. Ellen reports having considered several options. Would you have included others?

2. What do you think of the response she actually made?

3. What effect would a pointed -- perhaps sarcastic -- joke have had?

4. Can we compare the impact of "muddling through" (as Ellen managed to do) with the alternative that some teachers choose: an angry retort and a lecture on classroom manners?

5. What do you think of Ellen's statement, "Women live under microscopes at places like Fleming"? Is this true of other groups? Other places? What are some consequences of this situation?

6. What steps might you advise the administration to take to improve the institutional culture for women?

The Day the Heat Went On

Researcher's Perspective

This may be regarded either as a "woman's issue" case or simply as a case in self-management in the face of a moderately insulting form of heckling. Ellen Collins faces several obstacles besides her gender: she is young enough to lack the automatic aura of authority that age bestows on teachers; she "inherits" her class extremely late in the semester; and she is different from LG VI's other teachers because besides being female, she is soft-voiced and somewhat more formal in style (she always wears a jacket when teaching). Although in this case the disruption takes the form of a wolf whistle when the teacher sheds her blazer for the first time in the classroom, it might have been some other form of needling -- a catcall or other rude noise, perhaps -- addressed at a man. Nonetheless, Ellen herself emphasizes the fact that Fleming presents special problems to women -- students and faculty members alike. It is not only a male-dominated institution, it has a mission to prepare students for a generally male-dominated field: public administration. It is thus no surprise that the women in the group Ellen is teaching strike her as demoralized. They are reticent in discussions; they avoid making themselves conspicuous; they are silently offended by many of their male colleagues' jokes; and they join in ostracizing the three women in the class who don't happen to conform to the norm -- the "outstanding, outspoken" ones.

The general institutional culture seems to sanction the rough-tough style of teaching that Charlie Brennan is espousing (he's considered an "old pro"). Surely his condescending speech to the women of LG VI implies that he thinks little of their ability to grasp the simplest social rules of the professional world into which they aspire to assimilate themselves, and we do not hear of his giving any analogous speeches to the men in LG VI. The final piece of evidence we have for the difficulties women encounter at Fleming (and institutions like it) is the sort of pranks that are considered traditional there. These, we gather, often take on a sexual cast, show poor taste, and present women in a purely physical role. But they are traditional, accepted (by male and female students), and, apparently, destined to continue. For a woman to protest against this sort of humor would mark her as a spoilsport and further isolate her from the dominant culture. This presents a dilemma for both Ellen Collins and her women students: adaptation to the prevailing mode implies accepting it, but accepting it can also imply a tacit certification of one's own inferiority. There's a Catch 22 for women in schools of administration and similar institutions. Ellen must respond to the symbolic insult of the wolf whistle both as a new instructor and as a female leader of a 75% male group. She cannot escape the issue of gender.

But she can underplay it, and this is what she does. Ellen's tactic is to rise above the challenge. She realizes instinctively that revealing her instantaneous fury would be the worst thing she could do. Thus Ellen masks her reaction, focuses attention far from the whistle's point of origin, and continues the class as briskly as possible. She does not relinquish control; she makes the next call, and resists the temptation to choose a woman speaker (which could have inflated this fairly minor irritation into a threatening male-female confrontation). Ellen's calmness achieves a multiple purpose: she keeps the reins in hand, continues the discussion and -- most important -- gains time to compose herself and let her anger cool.

Ellen faces a sex-specific version of a common challenge to any young instructor in the second semester at a high-pressure professional school like Fleming: establishing and maintaining authority over a group of students not much younger than oneself who have formed a strong internal social

This commentary on "The Day the Heat Went On" was written by Dr. Abby J. Hansen, research associate, for the Developing Discussion Leadership Skills and the Teaching by the Case Method seminars. Its objective is to help instructors in the development of their own teaching plans for this case.

organization while enduring intense academic and social pressure since early September. She handles it successfully by simply continuing to do her job: lead the discussion. April is a crucial month in academics: not close enough to the end of term to signal the imminence of release, but still far enough along for students to feel both fatigued and yet fairly experienced and powerful within the system. An unseasonably warm day at this time of year in a cold climate like Toronto's tends to kindle spring fever, and Ellen seems to have run into a sample of just this sort of thing. It could have been much worse.

Like many young instructors beginning their academic careers, Ellen may also have felt somewhat uncomfortable in her new role of leadership. Permitting one student to flirt (in the interest of relieving the group's tension after a class with Charlie Brennan) might have telegraphed a camaraderie Ellen did not really intend. Ambivalence about having suddenly joined the power structure (holding not only the reins of discussion but the power of the grade over people who are not so very different in age from oneself and possibly even more professionally experienced) is endemic among younger instructors. Ellen, thus, has her own feelings to manage as well as the potential disrespect of her class. The wolf whistle clearly went too far in the direction of reducing the distance between teacher and students. It was tasteless and insulting in implication, if not in intention. It may have been a useful signal to Ellen that the time had come to tighten the reins a bit.

Had Ellen retorted with an impromptu reprimand, she would have risked infantilizing the group and thereby encouraging the same sort of resentment a naughty child feels at being chastised. Further, all the members of LG VI would have felt embarrassed, and some of them might have felt that Ellen, being female, had acted "schoolmarmishly."

Aside from being LG VI's only woman teacher, Ellen has other problems. Her late entry into the academic lives of LG VI is another great stumbling block. The segmentation of the Fleming student body into LGs creates social units that act in a self-protective manner -- that is, they band together against instructors. They fear that teachers may try to "wipe the floor" with them -- and the Charlie Brennans do so, proving their fears were right. Thus they attempt to support each other and forestall instructors' possible abuse. Sometimes such self-protectiveness escalates into hostility; when an instructor is friendly, it can turn the student body's reaction into either a peculiar sort of group adoration or into contempt (if the teacher shows technical incompetence). When a teacher is genuinely helpful, concerned, competent, fair, and good-humored, a good rapport -- and good teaching evaluation -- will likely result. We may see Ellen profiting from such a situation here. Teaching directly after Charlie Brennan may be a real blessing for her. If he is the heavy in this case, she is its heroine. Ellen gets the superior teaching evaluations from the LG VI -- possibly because she is sensitive enough to make the effort to see her students' needs. By serenely ignoring the tasteless wolf whistle, she also shows LG VI evidence of her maturity. She demonstrated self-confidence and a general worthiness to lead them. Grace under pressure is an admirable quality in any leader.

But, issues like grace and leadership aside, the sexual element in this case should not be ignored. Ellen presents Fleming as an institution with antifemale prejudice embedded in its structure, and she furthermore offers this incident as but a minor example of the sort of harrassment that women instructors often encounter here. Despite her apparent efforts to steer a middle course and keep a low profile -- avoiding the stereotype of the overdressed siren or severe "radical feminist" -- Ellen runs into a mild but identifiable form of sexual harassment. She seems very willing to make adjustments to adapt to a male-dominated culture, but she cannot escape symbolic hostility directed specifically at her gender. The "woman's issue" aspect of this case can be played down, but it won't disappear, and it involves far broader concerns than the fairly simple choice of whether or not to wear a jacket while teaching.

One Teacher's Nightmare

Teaching Note

To start the discussion after the (A) case has been read, one might begin most dramatically with the point of decision: "What do you think Jeff ought to do?" There probably will be a range of responses: "He ought to change the grade and save his skin." "He ought to nail the bastard and report him and his brother to whatever academic disciplinary body exists for students." "He ought to consult the department chairman and the dean to discover what precedents exist in cases like this." "He ought to quit and go home to New York!" "He should start attending football games; he might learn to like them." Each answer -- like the myriad other possible responses -- could be used in one of two ways: the discussion leader could either probe for further elaborations on the same theme, or take another tack -- call for other responses until a rather full range of possible responses for Jeff lay "on the table" for the group's further consideration. The group could then take up each path of reaction and its implications and discuss these for several minutes apiece.

Each reaction to Jeff's range of opportunities brings with it a special set of implications and assumptions. "Jeff should change the grade" implies that (1) it is Jeff who is out of step, (2) Southwestern is a football school, (3) Constitutional History is not the be-all and end-all of life, (4) Jeff should learn to live in his new environment and play by the new rules. This is the course of adaptability.

"Jeff should stand firm and flunk the kid." This reaction implies an inflexible attitude: (1) the teacher has set policy, (2) most students have observed the teacher's wishes, (3) the maverick must suffer for his nonconformity, (4) it is Jeff's right to set whatever standards he thinks appropriate and his duty to maintain those standards, once set.

"He ought to get advice" implies a more sensible course of action. Paramount in this case is Jeff's newness and discomfort in an unfamiliar cultural climate. He seems to be trying to operate in a vacuum, all alone with his office telephone. Cultural adaptation requires contact with the natives, and this Jeff appears to avoid. He would probably be well advised to seek advice from experienced colleagues -- not, of course, abnegating the final responsibility of making his own decision and sifting through the advice, judging the worth of each person's suggestions according to his own lights. Jeff acts precipitously. He agonizes, squirms, ponders, relents, and reaches for the fatal pen to change Bob Crane's grade. All of this takes very little time. This writer's opinion is that Jeff acted hastily and in the absence of potentially useful advice; but the issue of how he might have sought advice is worth exploring. How much time should he have invested in seeking advice? What sort of informant or advisor should he have sought?

The possible suggestion that Jeff "quit and go home" could be used, humorously, to set one pole of possibility. Jeff is an alien, but need he remain so? What are the real differences between his devotion to scholarship and Southwestern's apparent devotion to moderate scholarship and passionate athletic participation?

The other extreme -- in contrast to the stiff-necked cultural rejection of Southwestern's values -- is complete capitulation. Could Jeff become a rah-rah, pennant-waving football fan, redesigning his courses for the convenience of the quarterbacks? The class will probably consider such overstated vision of adaptability with the derision it deserves. But positing the two scenarios of rejection versus acceptance of an unfamiliar cultural milieu and set of values might serve as a useful way to set the parameters of the discussion.

More fruitful -- particularly as a means to help the discussion participants

---

This teaching note was prepared as an aid to instructors in the classroom use of the case series "One Teacher's Nightmare" (A) 9-384-063 and (B) 9-384-064.

plan their own early days in new courses -- will be a discussion of Study Question 1:

1. **How do you think this situation came to exist?**

Here, the discussion leader might probe for an imaginative reconstruction of the way Jeff Freeman probably went about planning his course (alone, with his own notebooks open and glancing at the primary material, readings, and academic calendar). How else could he have done it -- particularly given that there were norms already in operation and he was teaching in tandem with a staff of experienced instructors? Did Jeff bring this upon himself? In a way, yes. By failing to warn Bob Crane that he, Jeff, was not like the other easygoing teachers in the course, Jeff allowed Bob to live in a fool's paradise, confident that he could slide through the course with no effort and get a passing grade. Jeff should have set an explicit contract, allowed the students time to react to his proposals, and considered their counterproposals, if any, with real open-mindedness. Teaching a class is a two-way street.

2. **Should Jeff change Bob's grade?**

The question of whether Jeff ought to change the grade is less simple than it might appear. One is tempted, at first, to say, "Absolutely not!" Extortion like Matt's belligerent threats and subsequent wheedling is repugnant; it incites one to resist merely by its impudence. There will very likely be a fairly outspoken faction in any discussion group who will argue for Jeff's need to stand firm. And they will have logic on their side. Jeff had the right to set his own standards. The other students managed to meet them. Why should Bob Crane receive a special dispensation because he's a jock with a loudmouthed big brother? But there may be another faction in the class who take a different point of view: Jeff did not give adequate warning to Bob. Bob had no way of knowing, when he signed up for this section of the course, that this particular new instructor intended to break with the famous tradition of giving easy B's. Jeff had no one's approval for his unusually tough standards, and the option of giving Bob "No Credit" does, in fact, describe the situation with great accuracy. Bob did virtually no work; he is getting no credit for it. His penalty will be the necessity of making up the course -- next time, presumably, by expending some more effort on his studies.

3. **How do you think Jeff might have done things differently?**

There are many things he could have done. He could have spent more time consulting the other instructors in the course about the ways in which they taught. Did they really let students get by without doing any work, or did they, perhaps, have ways to make the material more accessible, simpler to digest, more fun to work with? What sort of work did they consider acceptable? (He might have asked for samples of written work, with the grades they had received.) He might have met with some of his colleagues and tried to set group standards -- perhaps a bit higher than the traditional ones, but less rigorous than his own -- (compromised, in other words). Most important of all, he should have (1) warned his students that he had particularly stringent standards, (2) hoped they agreed with him that they would get more out of the course by following his guidelines for performance, and (3) wanted to hear their reactions and suggestions before setting final policy.

4. **What larger issues does this case raise for you?**

Here is the group's opportunity to present personal material. This writer has encountered quite a few professors who have found themselves in situations reminiscent of Jeff Freeman's. Students do try to extort higher grades from professors -- sometimes by belligerence, sometimes by veiled threats of bizarre behavior, depression, even elliptical allusions to suicide. How should the teacher react in these intensely uncomfortable situations? Whose well-being is paramount -- the teacher's or the student's? Whose is the opportunity to grow, to learn? And what are the lessons implicit in these confrontations? The besetting problem of adjusting to an unfamiliar cultural milieu is another one that can profitably be discussed under this rubric. Academics tend to move a lot. It is not unusual for a career to start in California, continue in Texas, move on to Connecticut, and resume again somewhere in the deep South. What sort of resilience does this demand from the academic? How can he or she make these various moves with minimal psychological damage to all concerned? Again, the personal experiences of the participants will vary widely. If the proper atmosphere of trust and honesty has been established thus far in the discussion group, many useful, sympathetic, and heartening anecdotes may emerge -- or many cautionary tales of errors committed, which will perhaps warn the listeners and help them avoid similar mistakes.

Final Note: Some role playing might be useful in discussing this case. Asking a discussion participant to imagine the students' reactions to Jeff Freeman might open up some of the subtleties involved in this seemingly simple cultural confrontation. Most teachers will, most likely, instinctively side with Jeff. In fact, there is much to be learned by making some imaginative leaps and examining his situation through others' eyes. (For any teacher, the mental exercise of trying to think how the student might receive his or her teaching is always profitable!)

*   *   *

After the (B) case has been read:

1. **What is your appraisal of Jeff Free-man's action?**

There can only be two possible responses. One can either approve or disapprove of Jeff's capitulation. As we have seen, the discussion to this point will probably have succeeded in exposing subtleties not immediately apparent upon a quick first reading of the (A) case. One might feel initial moral outrage at Jeff for caving in under pressure from a couple of pea-brained louts. One might, despite this outrage, feel sympathy for his fear of reprisal if he should not change the grade: nobody wants to be fired or, perhaps, beaten up. But cowardice isn't attractive, and the (B) case shows that Jeff felt queasy, uncomfortable, and sour. Clearly, he felt disappointment with himself for giving in.

But another point of view would be to approve of his action and chalk it up to his learning. Certainly, he could have seen this coming; he could, perhaps, even have prevented the actual confrontation by getting Bob Crane out of his section or warning him earlier in the term that he was heading for a D. But Jeff wasn't clairvoyant. Few of us are. By granting Bob the opportunity to stay on the team and in the fraternity, he was, perhaps, giving charity where it was not particularly well deserved, but the "No Credit" option has an undeniably logical appropriateness to this situation. Bob Crane will not emerge completely unscathed; he will have to take another course. And Jeff will have to give some careful consideration to what went wrong this time. One hopes he will consult some colleagues, accumulate further data on the institutional norms, and try to present his own expectations more clearly and honestly at the beginning of the next course he teaches.

One Teacher's Nightmare

Researcher's Perspective

I read this as a case about both teaching and ethics. The pedagogical issues of grading and its larger effect on the student's life are present, but the primary impact of this episode is on the teacher, Jeff Freeman, whom I see as a victim of a clear, crude extortion. Jeff's problem is how to react to implied threats made by a football player and his big brother. Violence seems to lurk close to the surface in these brothers' words and actions, and Jeff is, therefore, put into a double bind: he is being asked to flout his principles, revise his honest judgment of a student, and cave in under pressure. His reaction -- anger and fear -- seems understandable.

Jeff is a newcomer to the football culture that seems to prevail at Southwestern. Scholarly and, one gathers, not an ex-fraternity member himself, he appears to find the world of football and frats alien, threatening, and intrinsically repugnant. Yet he is being asked (commanded, rather) to place the values of this unfamiliar and unpalatable world above his own. How has Jeff gotten himself into this fix?

One source of the trouble seems to be his initial decision to depart from the norms of the course. Constitutional History had the reputation of being easy, and Jeff found his fellow teachers fitting this mold. He chose -- possibly as a means of defining himself against the new culture -- to depart from the mold, and the result was this miserable confrontation. Should he have chosen to steer a different course? Should he have gathered more information from his fellow teachers before setting his section's standards? Should he, perhaps, have tried to make his unusually rigorous approach clearer at the outset and given dissenting students (like Bob Crane) a chance to get out of his clutches? One wonders whether Jeff taught similar courses with equal stringency during his graduate student days at Columbia. Defensiveness -- bridling at a new and uncongenial environment -- seems to color his actions. And he pays for his defensiveness in an extremely unpleasant way, with a situation that involves genuine offensiveness: the belligerence of the brothers Crane.

Jeff Freeman's situation seems emblematic of the cultural clashes that occur more and more frequently in these years of the infamous "tight job market" in the liberal arts. Academics who have done their graduate work and perhaps a few years of full-time college teaching in institutions famous for scholarship and research are, these days, often finding themselves taking new jobs at acknowledged "football schools" in geographical areas these young professors would, under other circumstances, probably prefer to leave unexplored. Adaptability is the order of the day.

What lessons might a teacher in circumstances similar to Jeff's derive from empathetically watching Jeff squirm under pressure from the jock contingent at Southwestern? Perhaps one might devote some time and careful analysis to the prevailing cultural norms before setting one's own standards in a new environment. Perhaps one might speak with experienced faculty members whose work one considers respectable and ask them, quite frankly, what they think is fair to expect from their students. Perhaps one might take some class time in the earliest sessions to "walk students through the course" and make one's expectations clear, giving students a chance to present their expectations, in turn, and then -- perhaps over the course of the semester -- taking occasional moments to see how teacher and students perceive the "learning contract" to be working. Too many learning contracts are set by simple fiat or, worse, never set at all -- just simply assumed by the teacher and (often differently, even antagonistically) assumed by the students. This appears to be the situation in Jeff

This commentary on "One Teacher's Nightmare" was prepared by Dr. Abby J. Hansen. Its objective is to help instructors in the development of their own teaching plans for this case.

Freeman's section of the Constitutional History course, and we see here how explosive the results can prove.

Let's take up the question of what Jeff actually did: he gave in to the pressure. Was this the appropriate action? I think -- in the purest of all possible worlds -- not. His stated reasons for changing Bob's grade appear to be pure rationalizations, spurious in the highest degree. Bob got his "No Credit" simply because he and his brother put the muscle on the new teacher. Their aggressive belligerence must have created painful fantasies for Jeff: visions of meeting half the football team in a back alley some dark evening, visions of a rich, alumni, Big-Daddy type demanding his immediate firing, visions of his reputation as a "spoilsport," "uptight Easterner," "tyrant", or just "bad fit" -- blazing like a brushfire through the department and the whole university. One can see how much (besides a few nights' sleep) Jeff has to lose in this situation. The power he holds over his students -- power to set their curriculum in the course, power to evaluate them and give them grades -- is more than overbalanced by their power over him.

Most damaging to Jeff, I think, is his apparent lack of help and support among his colleagues. Perhaps out of strangeness or shyness, he seems to feel he has to tackle this problem completely alone. I would have recommended that he take more time -- both to plan his course and his approach to the material and students in this new situation, and to react to the Crane brothers' intimidating behavior. He would probably have found help and sympathy from his colleagues and the dean. Jeff needs help. He needs to know what precedents exist for situations like his. He needs a sympathetic ear to listen to him and a feeling that he is not alone.

The principal lessons I would draw -- for myself -- from studying this case would be the advisability of scouting new terrain thoroughly before attempting to build my personal, private log cabin in the wilderness. I might find somebody else's time-tested blueprints far more useful than my own hastily considered plans. If an Eskimo professor comes to teach at the University of Southern California, he would be well advised to build a beach bungalow, not an igloo.

A Night School Episode

Teaching Note

This note will concentrate heavily on the discussion process, loosely following the suggested study questions for the (A) case and the discussion questions for the (B) case. The instructor may wish to forgo the study questions and simply distribute the minicase in class for "instant" discussion. The brevity and relative simplicity of minicases tend to generate discussions in which the rehearsal of case content plays a very minor role and the management of the discussion process itself becomes the primary challenge. The advantage of this primacy of process is that the discussion leader has an excellent opportunity to get to know the group and begin to encourage teamwork. Minicases may inspire some off-the-cuff, even ill-considered, remarks, but the loss of premeditation is balanced by a gain in momentum, which the discussion leader can use to steer the group fairly quickly beyond the rather accessible primary materials to a discussion of basic teaching issues.

The discussion leader should try to guide the group to cover the basic areas of analysis by relating various participants' points to those of their colleagues. The whole discussion will begin to approach completion when the basic questions -- What _is_ this situation? How did it come to be? What should one do about it? -- have been explored and the class has begun to take a look at general issues. Success in teaching any case resides in the richness of the discussion. The instructor should always bear in mind that the primary task is to stimulate the group to consider the material from a variety of perspectives. The atmosphere should be friendly and courteous enough to permit participants to disagree with each other's points in a spirit of cooperation. Most important, the teacher should strive to listen to the participants and get them to listen to each other. Although a discussion leader need not assume the opacity of a classical Freudian psychoanalyst, a certain reticence about one's private opinions is often useful to help create an encouraging climate for discussion. The role of leader confers status in itself: many participants, perhaps unconsciously, defer to the instructor and hesitate to espouse contradictory opinions. Instead of agreeing or disagreeing with a comment, the discussion leader can adopt one of several genial but noncommittal modes of response. One mode is simply to repeat or rephrase a participant's contribution, inviting further comment. Another is to avoid words altogether. Body language -- an encouraging nod or smile or a positive hand gesture -- can convey the message that the comment is welcome and worthwhile.

Preparation

One effective method of preparation for teaching a case includes (1) careful reading of the case to extract its basic issues, (2) thought about teaching goals, and (3) some effort of imagination to project oneself forward to the discussion and anticipate the sorts of comments participants are likely to make. The third element is especially good preparation for teaching minicases, where, as we have noted, the discussion process is apt to be lively, spontaneous, and tied less to the case facts than to their implications.

One of the first questions the discussion leader should ponder during preparation is: Whom should I ask to open the case by offering the first comment for subsequent discussion? In this particular minicase the protagonist, Sylvia Nevins, is a female facing challenges on a matter connected, however tenuously, with her gender. Should you invite a woman to open this minicase? What would the implications be -- for the particular group you are leading -- if you were to do so? Would these implications change if you were to select a woman from an age group very different from that of the protagonist? By the same token, what might it imply if you were to ask a man to open this discussion? Might it be desirable to pick a man and a woman and ask them to form an impromptu

This teaching note was prepared as an aid to instructors in classroom use of the series "A Night School Episode" (A) 9-384-085 and (B) 9-384-086.

team of two -- one to open and the other to "backstop" (i.e., provide the group with clues to areas the initial speaker may have overlooked)? The discussion leaders' decision on these matters will have considerable impact on the first few minutes of the discussion.

The "Blocks" of Analysis

This writer has found it helpful to break case analyses into "blocks" -- general topics that the material seems to suggest. In this instance, several arise. For example:

1. Leadership. Sylvia Nevins is a young woman leading a coeducational group including men and women old enough to be her parents, and the course includes material that some of these students might find embarrassing. Issues that arise from these circumstances might include (a) leadership in general, (b) special challenges for a woman leading a coeducational group, and (c) special challenges for a young instructor with much older students.

2. Preparation. Sylvia is caught unaware by her student's criticism, partly because she has not anticipated how widely his point of view might diverge from her own. Her personal convictions are so strong they have made it difficult for her to put herself in her participants' shoes. Sylvia is comfortable thinking about issues like abortion, divorce, and contraception, for example, but before this incident, it has not really occurred to her that these are highly explosive topics for many people. Accordingly, Sylvia's preparation to teach these materials ignored the crucial exercise of planning to deal with potential prejudices among her students. What place has Sylvia's personal conviction in her classroom? How could she have made herself more sensitive to the different convictions of her students?

3. Insecurity. Challenged by one student's objection to her terminology, Sylvia feels threatened. Her reaction is to become defensive, because she perceives her authority to be in jeopardy. The whole issues surrounding the teacher's right to lead the group and the group's right -- or likelihood -- to challenge that authority are almost inescapable in any teaching situation. To what extent do such issues manifest themselves in this minicase?

4. Contract. Sylvia describes herself as having invited the students to present their honest reactions in class, even to interrupt her lectures. Why, then, is she so upset when a student takes her up on this offer and presents an honest, negative reaction to her teaching? What are the implications for all teachers and their contracts -- stated or implicit -- with their students?

These are some "blocks" that occur to this writer. Other instructors will, doubtless, create their own systems, but the technique of writing these out on a single sheet and keeping that sheet in view during the class can give the discussion leader a sense of the structure of the proceedings and a quick reference point to show what areas of the case may have been insufficiently explored or, perhaps, entirely untapped.

Study Questions

For students' use when reading the (A) case:

1. **What has triggered this particular episode?**

Two extremes of the range of possible response to this question might take the forms of a defense or condemnation of Sylvia. One participant might reply, "Sylvia triggered the episode herself. She asked for honest criticism and then broke a cultural taboo: many older people -- men, especially -- feel uncomfortable hearing a younger woman talk about matters related to sex. This embarrassment was Sylvia's own fault." The opposite pole might be represented by an opinion like: "Sylvia could not have anticipated this challenge because her previous experience with the course material gave no inkling of possible trouble of this sort. The class included adults; she was an adult; the course description must have made the material clear. The man who took exception to her terminology was way out of line."

With these two opposed analytical positions stated, the discussion leader is in an ideal position to ask the other participants to help explore the reasoning and assumptions behind each position. Several "blocks" will doubtless be broached in the ensuing discussion. Sylvia was caught unprepared by the discussion process; how might the members of <u>this</u> group (the one discussing the minicase) have advised her the day before her class so as to prevent this incident? How serious was the man's challenge to her authority? What motivated him to object? To what extent <u>did</u> Sylvia create this situation herself? What really is at stake in this incident -- for Sylvia, for the man who objected, and for the class as a whole? The discussion can move among several blocks as the students toss out variations on their analyses of the causes of Sylvia's embarrassment. Is this a case of hypersensitivity? If so, whose? Is this a case of cultural disparity? If so, what should Sylvia have done to take this into account? Is Sylvia really being challenged? If so, why, and what should she do about it?

2.   What should Sylvia do, immediately, in class, to respond?

The group's answers to this question will, of course, be colored by the general trends of the earlier discussion of causes. One's ideas about what Sylvia should do will depend on one's views of her and her students. Some might say, "She should thank the man for his honesty, but state clearly that her terminology was perfectly appropriate for the material and that she intends to continue to use frank expressions. If the man feels uncomfortable under these circumstances, he may withdraw from the class." Others might say, "She should apologize and change her style of presenting the material to this particular group. This man was brought up in a far more conservative era than Sylvia. He might even be old enough to be her grandfather. She has probably offended him quite deeply. Surely there are ways to discuss issues of family life without trampling an older gentlemen's refined sensibilities." These two opposed points of view should both be explored. What does Sylvia owe this man? What does he owe her? The usual considerations of risk and reward should be broached. What does she lose or gain by apologizing? What does she lose or gain by standing firm? What does she lose or gain by reprimanding the man for prissiness? What are the consequences of each course for the group as a whole? Some of the blocks covered in this section of the discussion will include leadership, insecurity, and contract. (The reader may have noticed by this time that almost all of the blocks pertain in some fashion to every point of discussion; that is why it is a good idea to note them on a sheet of paper and let the discussion float naturally among them. There is no need to overstructure a discussion or try to direct a group methodically through the various topics of analysis in the order that happens to have occurred to the discussion leader. The various points of entry into a discussion can be connected naturally in a free discussion with no great loss either of coherence or content, so long as the discussion leader remains alert.)

Sylvia's response to the man's challenge will do much to condition the group's future response to her. After all, she is the one in the spotlight; that is the teacher's natural habitat. Her response can either antagonize the man, create a confrontation between him and her, or somehow broaden his challenge to involve the group as a whole in some educationally fruitful line of inquiry. It might be useful to try to have the class explore some of the consequences of each course. What are the risks/rewards of confrontation? How might Sylvia profitably include other members of the group -- or should she? (What might she lose by widening the confrontation?) What is the "worst case" scenario? Where might Sylvia most effectively seek support in this group? How can she best turn this moment to advantage? In what sense does this challenge present her with an opportunity for teaching -- or for learning?

3.   What are some "gut issues" in this situation?

Certainly Sylvia's gender and relative youth present two "gut issues" that might lead to consideration of several others. Power -- the tenuous reciprocity of rights and responsibilities in a classroom -- is always, in this writer's estimation, an issue that lurks beneath the surface of almost any interchange. In this case, Sylvia has several obstacles to surmount: the material is intrinsically sensitive, and its potential for offending some segment of the student population has to do with issues of sex. Sylvia is a woman leading a group that includes men; this itself is another situation in which the issue of sex plays an unavoidable role. Finally, Sylvia's age presents another potential handicap. It is difficult for a younger person to assume unchallenged leadership of a group that includes older people. The group might very profitably explore shades of opinion on these topics and begin to evolve some strategies for dealing with them.

A popular way to end the discussion of an (A) case is to ask participants for predictions. With Sylvia's options all "on the table," and the risks and potential rewards of each having been explored, participants might like to speculate about which option they think she actually did take.

Discussion Questions

For use after the (B) case has been read:

1.   Sylvia seems to have regretted her

first response almost immediately. What is your appraisal of the first thing she did to "minimize the personal aspect" of the confrontation?

As usual, there may be a range of responses to this question. Some participants may think that Sylvia's first response was perfectly natural and exactly what they might have done in her place. Others might say (especially since the case shows this response backfiring) that Sylvia's urge to appeal to the rest of the class was disastrous from the outset, as it simply offered them a chance to align themselves against her as a group, thus maximizing the "personal aspect" of the confrontation by placing Sylvia, alone, on the spot. Other participants might remark that Sylvia's instinct included a strongly negative aspect: instead of seeking to remedy the situation she perceived as deleterious to her leadership, she exacerbated it by inquiring after further bad reactions to her teaching. She might have done better to ask a positive question: "Who agrees that this terminology is appropriate to our course material?" or "Who would like to reply to Mr. A's objection?"

As it turned out, when Sylvia asked who else had been offended, she got a sexually polarized response, thus turning the initial challenge into a potential male-female confrontation. This seems to fulfill Sylvia's own "worst case" scenario. Why? It might, at this point, be valuable to have the class spend some time discussing what a woman teacher has to lose when the class becomes polarized in this fashion on an issue involving sex. It might also be useful to ask the class to turn its attention to ways in which women teachers might avoid such confrontations, or respond to them if they should happen to occur despite their best efforts.

2. **What is your opinion of her second response?**

Sylvia's second response was to turn from the class to the material. Her purpose was, presumably, as before, to lessen the tension she perceived in the room by diffusing the source of anxiety. Her method was to inject a personal opinion, placing herself, as it were, on a par with the student who had objected. Sylvia tells the whole class that she, personally, finds the Victorian ideology offensive. This is a political statement, on an emotional level. It is, possibly, an irritant to some members of the class, and certainly -- if they should wish to take it up as such -- an invitation to further argument. Some students may

praise Sylvia for her honesty -- for having dropped the professorial mask for a moment to participate in her own class as a person rather than a symbol. Others may fault her for this very behavior: it wasn't her place, just then, to descend to the student's level and inject personal opinion into the class material. She should have shored up her right to lead the group by maintaining the discussion on an intellectual level. As a tactic for "minimizing the personal aspect" of a challenge, inserting a personal opinion into the class discussion is surely very peculiar.

But Sylvia's expression of dislike for the Victorian ideology seems to have mollified the man. Some explanations of the reason for this might include (a) her injection of personal emotion into the discussion, thus creating a sort of camaraderie between herself and the man; (b) simple lapse of time without any painful pauses in the flow of talk, and (c) Sylvia's continuation of control in this potentially dodgy situation: no matter what was said, she did not relinquish the right to redirect the flow of discussion, nor did she (apparently) appear rattled or upset by the (to her) unpredictable course of that particular class.

3. **What do you think of Sylvia's long-term handling of this incident?**

This question takes up Sylvia's unexpected and certainly unplanned "private" chat with the man, whom she happened to notice sitting alone during a class break in the very next session of the course. Sylvia "gathered her courage" to go over to the man. The discussion might spend some time in probing what his feelings might have been at that moment, as well. This might even be an opportunity for some role playing: what is the man thinking as he sits alone? (Why is he alone, not chatting with other students?) What is Sylvia thinking? What might other class members be thinking if they happen to be watching this little drama? In any case, Sylvia reports that, having had time to consider some implications of the man's challenge to her in the light of her own policies, she forced herself to thank him for his "honest, forthright comments." The man's surprise and his comments might tell us something about him: perhaps his own school days, decades ago, led him to expect retribution (rather than thanks) from a challenged teacher. (It is useful to remember that in the role of student, all of us, whatever our calendar age, regress at least a little.) Sylvia describes her "urge to placate" (a social urge) dominating her "instinct to tell him how annoyed" she really had been (a human, but less adaptive, instinct in this situation).

Sylvia herself ended by being glad that she had "trusted the urge to make peace" (the social urge). One of the least comfortable facts of teaching is the frequent necessity of the instructor to favor the socially adaptive response over the one that the ego might prefer. In terms of the class dynamic, Sylvia succeeded in several ways. She signaled acceptance to a potential isolate; she behaved graciously in sight and hearing of other members of the class, thus offering them the assurance that they too might expect gracious treatment from her; and she created peace where further confrontation might have erupted. Sylvia's payoff was that "the man became a more cheerful, friendly, and active member of the class." Surely this had a good effect on the whole group; cheerful, friendly, and active participants usually help create a good class atmosphere for the other participants.

Sylvia gives her own overall assessment of the incident, and this writer happens to agree with her. Perhaps some class participants may not. There may be hard-liners who say that Sylvia should have thrown the dissident out. Others may fault her for having taken two tries to arrive at the successful formula for reacting to the man. Some of the lessons to be derived from reviewing this incident surely cluster around the always paradoxical means by which discussion teachers best maintain their authority. They wield power through empathy, openness, and accessibility to legitimate challenge. In Sylvia's case, the best ultimate response to challenge was to welcome and absorb it in a spirit of cooperation. Sylvia's initial contract statements did ultimately condition her dealings with the student, and her own long-term evaluation of these contract terms was positive.

4.   **What basic issues does this case pose for you?**

To this writer, the blocks of analysis contain the basic issues. Leadership, gender, insecurity, preparation, contract, the reciprocal rights and responsibilities of the teacher, the individual student, and the class as a whole comprise a loosely related system of issues that may be interrelated in as many ways as the class chooses. This section of the class discussion is both the most important and the most difficult to second-guess. In this section, the participants' personal experiences may with greatest appropriateness be described,

analyzed, and compared with those of their colleagues. As I have mentioned, a schematic chart of topics, (or blocks), may prove useful at this point in helping the discussion leader maintain coherence in the discussion and suggest new directions for the group to consider.

Exhibit 1

A Night School Episode

Study Questions

To be used with the (A) case:

1.   What has triggered this particular episode?

2.   What should Sylvia do, immediately, in class, to respond?

3.   What are some of the "gut issues" in this situation?

Exhibit 2

A Night School Episode

Discussion Questions

After the (A) case has been read:

1.   What do you think caused this incident?

2.   If you were Sylvia Nevin's friend, sitting in that classroom, what would you hope to see her do to respond to the student's criticism?

*   *   *

After the (B) case has been read:

1.   Sylvia seems to have regretted her first response almost immediately. What is your appraisal of the first thing she did to "minimize the personal aspect" of the confrontation?

2.   What is your opinion of her second response? How do you account for its effect?

3.   What do you think of Sylvia's long-term handling of this incident?

4.   What basic issues does this minicase pose for you?

A Night School Episode

Researcher's Perspective

[Note: This brief essay will address itself to the study questions for the (A) case and the discussion questions for the (B) case.]

The (A) Case

The researcher's unique perspective -- a privileged view that includes knowing not only the episode but also its protagonist and aftermath in the context of the principles and assumptions of the seminar -- leads this writer to the opinion that Sylvia would have served both herself and her students best by paying greater attention to her own explicit learning contract in the first place. The (A) case mentions that Sylvia began the course by inviting students to contribute their own "family histories," behave spontaneously, and even interrupt her lectures if their inner voices so prompted. These instructions must have given a clear signal to the students: "This is your class, not mine. Even when I'm 'performing,' you should feel free to up-stage me." Like most teachers, however, Sylvia seems to have cherished a few private, probably unconscious, reservations to her own policy of free speech. Few teachers really welcome interruptions, especially if they contain (or seem to contain) a kernel of challenge to the teacher's authority. This case shows Sylvia facing one direct consequence of her own open invitation to the students. Fortunately, although she falters, she also manages to show a certain graciousness. She does, ultimately, ratify her own contract.

Part of the problem seems rooted in Sylvia's unfamiliarity with this group of students. She has taught this material before, but to a considerably different audience: undergraduate liberal arts students nearly a continent away. Her students in the night school in New York must be culturally quite different from the late adolescents she teaches at Farwestern. The particular student who unsettles Sylvia with a public criticism of her teaching is a generation or two older than her typical students. In fact, he is probably old enough to be Sylvia's father, and this is likely to account for some of his discomfort. One can well imagine a man in his sixties (seventies?) blushing to hear a young woman making public references to matters that his background has conditioned him to consider supremely private. A great cultural divide separates Sylvia from this particular student. But she has failed to anticipate problems arising from this disparity. This minicase shows Sylvia learning something about judging her audiences.

Given the explicit contract Sylvia has set with her students -- openness in the classroom -- her best response to the man's objection would have been the one most consistent with her own policies: she should have thanked him for his frank contribution and turned the remark into the basis for further class discussion. How might she have done this? By tossing the ball right back to the class with some abstract, analytical questions to cool any rising blushes (including hers). Abstractions are always useful to defuse potentially tense situations. She might have asked some young student (likely to hold opinions like her own) to present the class with an assessment of the cultural content of the term offensive, both for Victorians (the subject of the class discussion) and contemporary college students. The man who objected had taken a step in the direction of confrontation, saying "I find such and such offensive." Sylvia had reacted to this, and immediately felt personally defensive. She might have taken up the challenge with a calculated risk (assuming she had been able to think fast enough to plan a few analytical "fallback" questions), asked the man to analyze his own objection, and then offered the analysis to the class for discussion.

This writer thinks Sylvia overreacted. The man's challenge was there, but mild.

This commentary on "A Night School Episode" was prepared by Dr. Abby J. Hansen. Its objective is to help instructors in the development of their own teaching plans for this case.

He did not demand an apology; he merely expressed a personal opinion. She reacted a bit touchily, but this is understandable in a young woman in an unfamiliar setting teaching a group of people whose backgrounds are rather foreign to her. All women in coeducational institutions face the challenge, explicit or covert, of establishing and maintaining their authority in the classroom. When challenged by a male -- especially an older male -- they may well overreact a bit. Perhaps, knowing this, they should be doubly vigilant against overreacting.

Sylvia hasn't as much to lose as she fears. She seems to have been leading the class satisfactorily up to this point, and she has, apparently, conducted her lecture impeccably -- surrounding the "offensive term" with bibliography on the chalkboard that should make it clear that the term is not her own coinage, but one of established scholarly currency. What she can gain, in this researcher's opinion, is enhanced authority. Any challenge, if well and gracefully met, bolsters a teacher's position as a leader. Furthermore, the man may well be speaking for a significant segment of the class in voicing his discomfort with the term. The material of the course does, in fact, contain issues that raise many people's temperatures: womanhood, manliness, contraception, abortion, child labor, and so on. If Sylvia has taught the course previously without encountering contentiousness among the students, she has been unusually lucky. These issues are all potential grenades. Wise preparation for teaching such a course might well include some speculation on emotional outbursts that may occur, and what course the teacher might take to contain them or turn them to use.

What can the students lose? If she falters badly, they can lose respect for her and also the opportunity to explore some of the unexamined prejudices many of them have brought to the course. What can they gain? If Sylvia skillfully turns the man's objection into an opportunity for class discussion, they may gain insight into themselves -- individually, and as a group.

Some of the larger issues that this writer sees implied by this minicase are the dynamics of power in the classroom, the advisability of a teacher's psychological preparation for possible challenges, the necessity of abiding by one's own contract, and the inevitability of finding cracks and seams in the social structure of any extremely heterogeneous discussion group. It seems fair to say that women teachers, especially younger women teachers, might do well to prepare themselves for meeting challenges gracefully. Such challenges will probably occur, and serenity in meeting them will make its mark.

The "gut issue" is sex -- in this case expressed indirectly through the Victorian ideology. But without poaching in the psychiatrists' preserve one may guess that a young woman discussing matters of sexuality with a coeducational group of various ages has enmeshed herself in symbolic conflicts on several levels. First, she is a woman leading men (many men find this uncomfortable; some, intolerable). Second, she is a young woman (daughter figure) speaking about sexual matters, however dryly, to older men. Symbolically, and very subtly, she may even be treading near some sort of cultural incest taboo. All these unconscious issues and resonances "float around" in any situation where women and men work together. It is this writer's opinion that, having recognized these resonances, one should give them a silent nod and simply attend to the business at hand courteously but without hypersensitivity or undue self-consciousness.

The (B) Case

Sylvia's first response backfired to produce exactly what she least wanted: controversy between the men and women in the class. Why should this be particularly undesirable? In this writer's estimation, the reason lies in many women professionals' fear of stereotypical situations. If a woman presides over a discussion that degenerates into a battle between the sexes, this means she has failed to guide the class to a truly intellectual consideration of the unique problem at hand. Worse, an observer might infer that the women in her class are "sticking together" to oppose the men out of camaraderie, not conviction, and that the situation is the same with the men. Not an ideal academic environment! Sylvia's question to the class -- asking who else felt offended by her terminology -- was fairly certain to spread bad feelings around the room. She would have done far better to shift the grounds of discussion from emotion (feeling offended) to abstraction -- analyzing the intellectual content of the man's objection or looking more closely at the other scholars' uses of the objectionable term.

Sylvia's second response seems to have been just as unfortunate as her first. Instead of intellectualizing the situation, she herself reacts on the emotional level.

She finds Victorian stereotypes personally offensive. Fine. But <u>why</u>? The appropriate discussion topic isn't who feels offended by what: education will be better served by analysis of these feelings and their cultural assumptions.

Lest we be too hard on Sylvia, let us remember that she found the man's challenge upsetting. Much of what she did in the classroom was instinctive. Caught off-guard, she tried to protect her dignity. Finding the best method took her a bit of time, but she did ultimately solve her problem. Her most successful gesture toward the man was to approach him during a class break and force herself to thank him for his honest comment. This was the best teaching tactic and the most consistent with her own stated policy. Her graciousness gratified the man, reassured him, showed him Sylvia's generous side, and ultimately integrated him better into the group. This researcher agrees with Sylvia's considered analysis of her own reactions, by and large. The man who objected to her terminology was, in fact, following Sylvia's contract better than she was. When he voiced an honest reaction, as the class had been invited to do, he had a right to expect Sylvia to welcome his contribution. In a free discussion, all opinions -- if courteously expressed -- are admissible and worthy of analytical consideration by the whole group, teacher included.

Assistant Professor Graham and Ms. Macomber

Teaching Note

"Assistant Professor Graham and Ms. Macomber" deals with a classroom interchange between Charles Graham, an instructor in his second year of case teaching, and Janet Macomber, a first-year, first-semester MBA candidate. The incident described involves Ms. Macomber's presentation of her analysis of a case problem, Professor Graham's response, and the reactions of Janet and the other students to the exchange.

"Graham and Macomber" is an extremely popular case. Though it was developed for the professional school seminar, it has been used widely in other settings ranging from liberal arts to medicine. We believe that at least part of its appeal stems from the universal importance of a skillful question-and-response style. This seminar is based on the premise that the essential artistry in case discussion leadership rests on the use of questions and the selection of responses to students' comments. The present case, which describes a dramatic cross-examination of a student, raises participants' awareness of (1) the power of questions in shaping students' classroom experience, (2) the different sorts of questions one can use, and (3) the likely effects of particular types of questioning. "Graham and Macomber" describes a situation in which the professor is unaware of the impact of his questions. As a result, his intervention does not help his students learn, and it actually damages one person's self-esteem and willingness to participate in class discussions.

In one of our syllabuses, this case usually follows the "Bill Curtis," "Henry Jasper," and "Ernie Budding" cases, all of which focus on the issue of establishing and maintaining a constructive learning contract. "Ernie Budding," which often directly precedes "Graham and Macomber," includes a short description of classroom interaction; discussion of that case often turns to how the concrete, moment-to-moment interaction between instructor and students shapes classroom learning. This detailed examination of instructor-student interaction is then developed further in discussion of "Graham and Macomber."

"Graham and Macomber" is presented in three brief segments. Generally seminar participants are asked to read and consider the (A) case before the class discussion. The (B) and (C) cases are handed out in class.

The (A) and (B) cases deal with the interchange between Professor Graham and Ms. Macomber -- first from his point of view, then from hers. The (C) case presents the thoughts of Professor Graham as he reviews his records on student participation some three weeks later, puzzled by Janet Macomber's marked drop in performance since the early class sessions.

Case Summary

The Institutional Context

This case takes place in an MBA course at "New Dominion," a pseudonym for a large, highly selective business school with a case-based curriculum.[1] At New Dominion, the first-year class of MBAs is divided into approximately 10 sections, each containing 80 students. Each section is assigned an amphitheater-shaped classroom, in which the students assemble daily at 8:30 a.m. for the first of three classes; each class lasts 80 minutes. The instructors move from one section's classroom to another's during the day.

---

1. For further information on New Dominion's real-world counterpart, see Abby Hansen's "Background Information on a Graduate School of Business Administration," HBS Case No. 9-382-153.

This teaching note was prepared by Dr. James F. Moore in collaboration with Professor C. Roland Christensen as an aid to instructors in the classroom use of the case series "Assistant Professor Graham and Ms. Macomber" (A) 9-379-020, (B) 9-379-021, (C) 9-379-022.

Section members work together throughout the day during the entire first year. Personal interaction between students is very high, and intense social dynamics of one sort or another can develop within a section. At the beginning of the year -- the time of "Graham and Macomber" -- students are often highly concerned about the image and reputation they are establishing within the section.

The Course

Quantitative Analysis and Operations Management (QAOM) is a technically oriented course in which students learn quantitative methods of analyzing problems in the design and organization of manufacturing processes.

The Instructor

Charles Graham is an assistant professor in his second year at New Dominion. He is described as having "a sincere commitment to the case discussion teaching methods and philosophy." No information is given in the case about his background, age, or appearance.

The Section

The section consists of 80 first-year MBA students. Since the course has barely begun, it can be assumed that section members do not yet fully understand what is expected of them in classes, nor have they yet gotten to know the strengths, weaknesses, and personalities of their peers.

Janet Macomber is an atypical student in several respects: she is younger than most students (the median age of New Dominion's MBA candidates is 27); she is female in a largely male-dominated school and content area; and she has strong quantitative skills developed at California Institute of Technology.

The (B) case, which focuses on Janet's experience of the incident, introduces a second student -- Peter Anderson, "an already popular figure who usually sat with a group of cohorts in the middle of the right-hand bank of seats."

The Teacher-Student Relationship

In contrast to the cases discussed earlier in our seminar, "Graham and Macomber" focuses on the teacher-student relationship as it exists in a relatively short span of time -- i.e., during a 10-minute classroom incident.

During the previous 70 minutes of the class, students have been discussing a management problem presented in the case. Charles's thoughts are described as he listens to the final few minutes. In his judgment the discussion does not reveal an adequate analysis of the case. He concludes that the discussion has "gone nowhere" and that "he would have to exercise the basic dictatorial prerogative of any instructor; he would have to tell them how wrong they were." "One more comment," he thought, "and then they are in for it." These statements suggest his impatience and irritation with the discussion, and his readiness to treat the students as wayward subjects in need of correction.

The (A) text gives very little information about the students' orientation toward the course and/or toward Charles. It is probably safe to assume that they are still "feeling out" the school, the course, the instructor, and their peers. Thus it is a time of uncertainty about one's role, one's competence, and the rules of the game. Students are trying to read signals from peers and instructors in order to determine unspoken rules of conduct.

The Incident

The (A) case describes the incident from Charles Graham's standpoint, detailing the crucial interaction between instructor and student. The text includes quotations from both participants, and observations that Charles could have made.

The focal incident of "Graham and Macomber" is an exchange between Charles Graham and Janet Macomber -- a student who, in the closing minutes of the session, finally offers the kind of analysis of the case problem that Charles had been expecting. Through a series of pointed questions, he forces her to describe the steps through which she proceeded to "crack the case," but studiously refrains from indicating his agreement. When she has finished, his only comment is an ambiguous "Well, well!"

The (B) case describes the same incident from Janet Macomber's point of view. She experiences her recitation as a terrible ordeal. Without any feedback from the instructor, she wonders whether she has gone off on completely the wrong track. After class ends, the other students cluster around her desk and tease her. Clearly, they do not realize that her point was correct, nor that Professor Graham was impressed by her insight. Peter Anderson, the popular figure in the class, ridicules her loudly and christens her analysis "The Macomber Memorial Matrix." Janet feels crushed and resolves not to expose herself to further ridicule by sticking her neck out in discussions.

The (C) case takes place three weeks later, as Professor Graham reviews the participation records of the students. He is puzzled by Janet's performance, which has slipped markedly. She no longer volunteers comments in class, she often seems unprepared, and she shifts seats so often that he is not sure whether she is attending all sessions of the class. She often looks sleepy or bored. He wonders why her behavior has changed and what, if anything, he should do about it.

A Note on Study and Discussion Questions

Typically at least two sets of questions are prepared for use with each case. The first set (Exhibit 1) consists of study questions, and can be handed out for participants' use when preparing the case before class. The discussion questions (Exhibit 2) are used by the instructor of the seminar in preparing for class and in guiding the case discussion when appropriate.

The discussion questions constitute a question-based teaching plan which gives the instructor a general direction to pursue, but is not so restrictive as to prevent the students from developing their own alternative interpretations of the case. In this way, participants are encouraged to structure their own approaches to understanding the case situation. Through careful use of question and response techniques, the discussion leader can then manage the ensuing discussion to develop the participant initiatives that emerge. That is, by using selective calling, "bridging" between comments, the insertion of summaries at key moments, and direct questioning of participants, it's possible to move the discussion in potentially profitable directions.

Such an approach to managing class discussions is in sharp contrast to that apparently used by Professor Graham. Charles appears to have spent the class period waiting for students to discover "the" answer. Very likely he has overlooked valuable student-initiated alternative views of the case. The case text suggests that for most of the class session he has followed a fairly passive style of question and response, rather than using questions to raise issues or to shape the evolving

discussion. Then in the final moments he switches his style dramatically and pounces on the student who makes the long-sought discovery -- pulling out from her the line of argument he seeks.

The discussion questions listed in Exhibit 2 reflect an open outline such as might be used in discussing "Graham and Macomber." A set of "discussion probes" are also provided, which can be used to lead participants more directly to some of the features that in our judgment are central to understanding the case. The "Analysis" section provides detailed notes for all the discussion questions (but not for the study questions).

One final comment: instructors may find it interesting to compare the question-based teaching plans for several seminar cases. For example, because the "Graham and Macomber" case is used to examine the crucial role played by questioning, the discussion plan emphasizes the use of prepared questions to direct the seminar's explorations. By contrast, the "Bill Jones" case is used to emphasize the importance and complexity of instructor responses to student comments. Accordingly, the discussion plan relies relatively heavily upon instructor response to the students' initiatives, and uses only a few prepared questions. Ordinarily the correspondence between teaching plan and case content is not so neat. Nevertheless, it should be valuable to skim through several of these teaching notes and to exchange views with other instructors in order to get a feel for the range of question-based plans that can be used.

A Suggested Process Plan for the Case

Our overall goal is to help participants see how the instructor's questions and responses shape the experience of students in the classroom. We hope to raise awareness of the effect of such factors as the selection and timing of questions, and especially the manner in which a question is phrased.

We use "Graham and Macomber" as a prediction case. Participants in the seminar are asked to read the (A) case, reflect on what Charles does in the interchange and how he sees it, and then predict how Janet and the other students might experience it. The (B) case allows participants to check their judgments against an account of what actually happened. In discussion we encourage an exploration of why this result occurred, and what it suggests about the nature of students and sections, and about the effect of an instructor's style of questioning.

We feel it is important that the section spend a good deal of time examining in detail the interchange between Charles and Janet. If an opportunity for this discussion arises while the (A) case is being considered, we may prolong that discussion and spend relatively less time on the (B) case. In some sessions, however, the (A) case is discussed without going into detail about the interchange. We are then likely to move ahead to the (B) case and seek a later opening to direct the section's attention back to Charles's interrogation. In such situations most of the seminar time is spent in the (B) discussion. We generally spend about 65 minutes on the (A) and (B) cases -- including reading time for (B) -- and 25 minutes or less on (C), which raises the issue of how instructors can learn to read the impact of their actions and interchanges with students in the classroom.

In working with the (A) case, we focus on Charles's definition of his situation, and on what he did, and why he may have done it. Participants are encouraged to scrutinize the elements of his interactional style, for we feel that such details are often crucial to a teacher's success. We also underscore the link between a teacher's instructional philosophy and his or her operating style in the classroom.

We then move to a discussion of the probable effect of Charles's actions on Janet Macomber and on other members of the section, using clues provided in the (A) text. Often the discussion becomes quite spirited at this point, with some participants condemning Charles's approach out of hand, while others argue that his approach may be constructive, even if abrasive.

The (B) case can be a real eye-opener for the latter group. We encourage a careful exploration of the new data on the immediate results of Charles's actions. Participants typically concentrate on both Janet's experience and the section group dynamics revealed by Peter's comments about the "Macomber Memorial Matrix." As the seminar discussion develops, we call attention to the (A) case's detailed account of Charles's questioning and response, asking what elements in his comments contributed most to the final effect. We find that doubling back in this way to reconsider the (A) material helps participants appreciate the significance of details

and the critical role played by an instructor's style of questioning and response.

The (C) case raises the broader question of how an instructor can understand the students' experience of his or her actions. We acknowledge the difficulties involved in accurately reading the effect of one's questions and responses, and typically conclude the session with a discussion of how instructors can overcome these problems. Because we use this case to stimulate a detailed consideration of questioning and responding, there is often little class time to discuss the (C) case. In such instances we hand it out to be read at home. In the long run, little appears to be lost by this approach, because the issues we wish to emphasize most are raised by the (A) and (B) cases. We find that participants are stimulated by the (C) case even without an in-class discussion, and often return to the issues it raises in subsequent class sessions.

Notes for Discussion Questions

These notes parallel the suggested discussion questions presented in Exhibit 2. They indicate the pedagogical intent and use of each question and provide an "answer." These analytical responses are provided primarily to alert the instructor to key issues in the case as he or she prepares for a discussion. We do not regard these responses as the definitive solutions to the questions raised by the case. "Graham and Macomber," like other cases, can be profitably analyzed from a variety of viewpoints. We hope each new discussion of the case will provide fresh insights of value to both participants and instructor, for this has been our experience as discussion leaders.

The first five questions are related to the (A) case. They assume that participants have read only that case and have considered the study questions.

1. **How do you think this situation appears to Professor Charles Graham? How does he see the situation facing him, here in the second week of classes, in the discussion session described in the case? What might he see as the problem? What might he focus on as the two or three key features of the situation?**

We open with this broad question because we want to encourage participants to present their own analyses of the case without being unduly influenced by our directives. However, there are several issues that we feel should be raised early in the discussion. If they do not arise spontaneously, we use special probes to elicit them, as indicated below.

> a) **As a teacher of this section, what does Charles see as the critical challenge facing him?**

Usage Note

This probe focuses attention on the problem as Charles himself defines it. Since the problem, as he defines it, is one that participants have probably encountered in their own teaching, this approach helps them develop some empathy for him.

Analysis

Charles appears to believe the problem is related to the content of the course. As he puts it, the class has "entirely missed the point of the case." Time is running out, and it seems improbable that any student will make the discovery that would "crack the case."

Further, Charles is concerned about setting a bad precedent early in the first term. He seems to believe that if he does not confront the class with the deficiencies of their analyses, he will be tacitly encouraging mediocrity. As he states it, "I could not conscientiously allow 80 apprentice managers to leave class thinking that the last hour passed for an adequate case analysis."

The assumptions that underlie Charles's understanding of his situation are worth examining. First, he appears to assume that there is a single answer that solves the case, and that once discovered it will provide a key for understanding the situation and making sensible recommendations for action. And he apparently sees case discussions as a time for collective thrashing about in search of this answer, followed by an examination of its implications for action.

In our judgment, Charles's view places undue emphasis on discovering keys to the case. While certain critical recognitions are often important to a case discussion, they are seldom sufficient in themselves to permit either an adequate analysis or adequate action recommendations. Much of the learning that goes on in a case discussion revolves around the complex task of determining how to build on critical insights in order to act effectively.

Moreover, Charles apparently has not designed a sequence of questions that could lead students to the insights he believes are crucial. He seems to feel students must discover them on their own. Particularly in the first days of a new course, students cannot be expected to know how to carry out an effective analysis, and they must be guided in some manner. Several approaches are possible. One is to use specific, highly directed questions to lead students to key points. (Our seminar discussions of "Ernie Budding" reveal the limitations of this approach.) Alternatively, an instructor can use a carefully designed set of questions of varying degrees of openness. Open and exploratory questions can be used to direct the students into profitable areas of consideration, while leaving them free to develop their own approaches to analysis. More closed questions can be used to ease students toward a critical insight when their own search has gone astray.

In the first weeks of a course like QAOM, which draws on specialized quantitative methods of analysis, students may well fail to discover the key points of a case independently. Unfortunately, Charles has apparently developed no way to point students toward a critical solution. He sees no alternative to the unpleasant task of making a speech to the class in the closing minutes of the session -- to give them the "answer."

> b) **What is Charles's concept of the section leader's role?**

Usage Note

This question directs participants' attention to Charles's operating philosophy of case method teaching.

Analysis

Charles sees a case discussion as a search for an answer that solves a case. This answer appears to be <u>his</u> answer and not necessarily that of the class. An alternative view would see the case discussion as a disciplined process of exchanging and testing ideas.

Charles seems to feel the instructor's role is to judge the adequacy of the class performance. He is to inform the section when it has gotten the answer and indicate whether their search process was adequate. Charles does not seem to feel it is appropriate for him to guide or even actively facilitate the search.

Further, he seems to assume that the class has failed if it does not come up with his answer. He does not acknowledge that the instructor has some responsibility to help the students attain overall learning goals. Irritated by their "failure," he feels an impulse to chastise the section. Thus "One more comment," he thought; "then they are in for it."

2. How well, in your judgment, did Charles handle the questioning and response with Janet Macomber?

This question provides the first of several natural opportunities to encourage the section to examine in detail the elements of Charles's interaction with Janet. We now shift the discussion into the critical area of the skilled use of questions and responses. We hope to sharpen participants' awareness of the various ways an instructor can intervene in a discussion, and the different effects created by different kinds of question-and-response techniques. Finally, we hope that participants will begin to develop their own "contingency theories" to guide them in the use of questions and responses.

The following probes can be used to direct the discussion further when necessary.

a) What was Charles's approach?

Usage Note

By asking participants to consider Charles's "approach" -- that is, to interpret his behavior as a set of intentional, strategic actions -- this question provides a framework within which his use of questions and responses can be examined. A careful dissection of his comments is vital to sensitize participants to the impact of their own comments as instructors. The seminar leader may wish to use a chalkboard to record (and thus reinforce) the observations.

Analysis

A crucial feature of Charles's approach is his sudden, unannounced shift from a laissez-faire posture to a highly controlling, dictatorial style of managing the discussion. This transition is made somewhat ambiguously, for his first comment to Janet ("And just what is your analysis?") is a broad question of the type often used at the beginning of a case discussion. Such a question suggests that students should lay out their thoughts in their own way, show-

ing their initiative and creativity in organizing a useful approach to the case problems. But Charles follows up this opening with a series of questions that tightly control the dialogue and thus force Janet to present her analysis in a manner that he chooses.

The ensuing interchange resembles a courtroom cross-examination. Like an advocate moving in on a hostile witness, Charles asks, "And what exactly did you have?" "And what did you find from this matrix?" "And what did you conclude based on this observation?" He uses short, logically linked questions that walk his subject through an argument he himself lays out. This style of questioning strips Janet of her initiative and autonomy, and makes her merely a supporting actor in his presentation. Further, Charles uses what might be termed "hook words" -- beginning sentences with "and" and lacing his queries with "exactly" and "just." These words evoke the image of a prosecutor moving in for the kill, and implicitly place Janet in the position of a guilty defendant.

In the middle of his cross-examination, Charles asks a personal question, "And how long did that take you?" which prompts snickers from the side of the room, and leaves Janet nonplussed. In our opinion this question is problematic on two levels. First, it can be construed to imply that her approach involved a foolish investment of time -- thus discouraging student explorations that require substantial effort. Second, by focusing on Janet's process of working, rather than her results, Charles's question shows a lack of respect for her ability to work independently. He has treated her as a subordinate whose efforts must be closely supervised, rather than one capable of autonomy.

It is also significant that Charles does not indicate his displeasure with the previous performance of the section or his satisfaction with Janet's work. At several points in Janet's comments, he chooses not to show his approval. The first is when she clarifies the company's problem (i.e., how to move work-in-process through the plant) and observes that the class's recommendations miss the point. The second is when she points out the significance of multiplying the two exhibits together, thus cracking the case. And finally, Charles in his summary avoids any signal that would clarify either the significance of Janet's comments or his reason for taking time -- at this late point in the period -- to allow her to lay out a new analysis.

Charles's careful avoidance of praise raises an important question: When (and how) should a discussion leader use praise? If excessive, praise can establish a teacher-student contract built around "pleasing the teacher" rather than openly exploring the issues of the case. Yet praise can be useful in motivating students and providing feedback about the value of their work. In general, we tend to use praise sparingly, and to address it either to the section as a whole or to specific comments that are helpful to the class's work. We avoid praising individuals, which can encourage "teacher's pet" behavior.

Finally, by commenting "Let me understand" -- rather than "Let us understand" -- Charles signals that the dialogue is being conducted primarily for his benefit (and perhaps for Janet's). He misses an opportunity to suggest that the other students have something to gain from her comments.

b)   Why do you think he chose that approach?

Usage Note

This question helps participants see that Charles's intervention style was not simply the result of a random error, but reflected his conscious appraisal of the situation. He thought he knew what he was doing. Our hope is that when participants recognize that Charles's mistakes were deliberately chosen and not merely careless, they will become more alert to the possibility of similar errors in their own practices.

This question may also help participants maintain empathy for Graham. In the fast-paced, complex, and ambiguous environment of a case method discussion, it is perhaps not so surprising that Charles errs in reading and responding to a student comment.

Analysis

The case text tells us that Charles wanted the class to understand the import of Janet's analysis, but gives little indication of the thought process that led him to the intervention style he chose. However, we can speculate that he was concerned primarily with getting her complex analysis out fast (only a few minutes remained in the class period) and thus wanted to speed up and prestructure her remarks so they would be as clear and as concise as possible. He may have thought that a crisp, rapid-fire cross-examination would accomplish this most effectively.

Just before the exchange with Janet, Charles was gearing up to exercise the instructor's "basic dictatorial prerogative." He seems extremely frustrated at the direction the discussion has taken. His reaction seems to be to abandon his earlier noninterventionistic style in favor of dicta-torial control -- perhaps for its own sake. Many instructors must wrestle with the urge to exercise excessive control over discussion. Often this desire stems from simple impatience, and a desire that students discover as many key insights as possible. Instructors sometimes forget the long years it took them to master the field, and hope to bring their students "up to speed" unrealistically quickly. The desire to overcontrol a discussion can also reflect insecurity about one's grasp of the material being discussed, and/or one's ability to manage a more free-flowing exchange. Our experience suggests that case teaching requires a firm grounding in the field of study, joined with a cultivated taste for ambiguity and serendipity in the discussion process.

Some members of our seminar have commented that Charles's tone is angry, ironic, and attacking. Psychologically oriented participants have suggested that this tone may be a reflection of his frustration at the preceding discussion, directed toward Janet as a consequence of his suppressing his amazement at her correct "answer." Although this interpretation is largely based on conjecture, it raises important questions about instructor self-management. Case data indicate that Charles feels it is the students' responsibility to get the answer, and that praising them for success amounts to pampering them. Thus he shows no reaction to Janet's remarks. Unfortunately, his suppression of amazement seems to have left him still stewing in his anger toward the rest of the class. The case text reports that "he only wanted the class -- each and every one of the other seventy-nine -- to realize the import of Janet Macomber's words." Charles seems to believe that the anger he expresses through the tedious interchange with Janet will be felt by the section as a criticism of their earlier work. Unfortunately, the students appear to assume that his irritation is with Janet, and not with them.

c)   What was the impact of his approach on Janet? What signals was Janet sending that might have helped him anticipate and monitor his impact?

Usage Note

This crucial question shifts attention from Charles's intervention to its impact on Janet. Participants now are asked to identify the clues or signals that might have enabled Charles to anticipate the effect of his questioning.

This question asks participants to assess Charles's impact without having any more data than he did -- no easy task. It is useful to press participants to commit themselves as to what they think is the likely impact of Charles's comments. The (B) case will then allow them to test their speculations against Janet's actual experience. This exercise lets participants assess their abilities to read the signals, and tends to build involvement in the discussion.

Analysis

In our opinion, Graham's approach was intimidating and left Janet feeling vulnerable to ridicule from her new classmates and confused about the value of her contribution. She had signaled her timidity and difficulty in asserting her viewpoint by sitting in the back of the room, by speaking in a quiet voice, and by pausing and restarting apologetically when interrupted by the shout of "Louder, please!" from across the room. Nevertheless, Graham responds initially with the sarcastic and domineering "And just what is your analysis, Ms. Macomber?"

Other students probably interpret his challenging, guilty-until-proven-innocent courtroom style as a sign of contempt for her contribution. For the same reason, they snicker when he asks how long it took her to do the calculations. Charles's responses give Janet no sense of the value of her contribution. Thus she feels she has been ridiculed by the instructor and branded as a "number cruncher" at best, and perhaps also as an overachiever.

d)   What background information would help him choose a more effective approach to Janet as an individual?

Usage Note

The appropriate use of background information is one aspect of the broader issue of understanding and managing the dynamics of a section of students.

Analysis

Charles knows that Janet is younger than many others in the section, that she has little work experience, and that her academic background is technical and quantitatively oriented. This information might alert him to the possibility that she would feel intimidated by the rough-and-tumble case discussions in which many participants draw on their personal backgrounds in business and industry to inform their comments.

Other students apparently do not share Janet's quantitative orientation. Until they become more sophisticated, they may have difficulty with concepts that come relatively easily to Janet. Thus the instructor may need to explicate Janet's comments -- for example, by labeling the ideas as valuable and asking other members to develop the ideas, and/or asking her to explain her responses for the benefit of the section.

3.   At the end of the interchange, Charles says, "Well, well!" What do you think of this response? What will be the effect of this response? How else might he have responded?

Usage Note

This question raises the broader issue of how to use feedback to enhance individual and section learning. When should instructors refrain from assessing the value of a contribution? When should they give feedback on the process of discussion? When should they comment judgmentally on the content of student contributions?

Analysis

Charles's response to Janet is intentionally vague, giving no information as to the value of her comments. As a result, both Janet and the section are left confused as to how to evaluate her insights -- insights which call into question the entire previous discussion.

Understandably partial to their own ideas, the other students are likely to dismiss Janet's comment as irrelevant, particularly in view of the evident lack of respect shown by Charles's adversarial questioning. Thus his failure to support (or reject) her challenge to the section discussion probably leaves her feeling vulnerable in her relationship with the other section members.

Instead of guarding his neutrality,

Charles could have acknowledged the importance of Janet's insights and expressed gratitude for her willingness to risk bucking the tide of the discussion. Such a response would give the class and Janet clear feedback -- reducing their confusion, giving them a sense of direction in their work, and accomplishing Charles's original goal of letting them realize the inadequacy of the earlier discussion. In addition, it would encourage other students in the future to risk bringing up analyses that run counter to the consensus of the group. The multiplying of viewpoints which is so important to case method teaching depends on the willingness of group members to take such risks.

4.   **What is your evaluation of his summary? Was it appropriate to this class session?**

Usage Note

This question directs attention to another important instructional tool -- the end-of-class summary -- and it encourages participants to consider how summaries can be used (and misused) in influencing the learning of students.

Analysis

Charles's summary simply relates the case to the course plan, and he carefully avoids "passing judgment on Janet's analysis or on the preceding case discussion." Thus it compounds the problem of inadequate feedback.

Summaries are among the most potent teaching tools available to a case discussion leader. They provide valuable opportunities to reinforce important points, and to comment on the section's developing ability to function as a forum for the exploration and testing of ideas. To the extent that Charles's section had missed the point of the case under discussion (and we are not sure his views on this point are reliable), he could have helped them by suggesting some directions for further exploration of the case material. In our own practice we sometimes feel that a section has missed considering an important aspect of a case problem. In such situations we often conclude our summary with a short provocative question that signals the importance of this dimension and reinforces the class's sense of the complexity and richness of the issues raised by the case. Charles could have concluded the session by calling attention to the critical problem faced by the company and the potential value of the quantitative data contained in the case text.

5.   **Should Charles have dropped by the group around Janet's desk?**

Usage Note

This question raises awareness of another tool available to the case discussion leader: the informal, after-class chat with students. Many discussion leaders cultivate such opportunities to speak with students, since these encounters may provide clues to otherwise hidden section dynamics and may allow the instructor to reinforce student learning and give less formal feedback on student participation.

Analysis

In our judgment Charles would have been wise to drop by Janet's desk in order to get a feel for what was going on. He realizes that something important is happening, but apparently assumes that the students are congratulating her and/or seeking to learn from her approach. Had he stopped by her desk he could have checked out his assumptions rather quickly, and then made whatever intervention seemed appropriate.

*   *   *

At this point in the discussion, we suggest that the (B) case be handed out, read quickly by the participants, and discussed, using the following approach:

6.   **What is the situation from Janet Macomber's point of view?**

Usage Note

With the data of the (B) case, it is possible to compare Janet Macomber's experience of the incident with 1) Charles's own experience and 2) what he assumes her experience to be. This question -- which is often nearly superfluous, given the powerful expression of Janet's point of view in (B) -- opens up discussion about her experience and underlines the broader question of how instructors can know what their students are experiencing.

Analysis

Janet seems to be a conscientious student who finds herself in the difficult position of holding views very different from those of the rest of the section. In the closing minutes of class, she marshals "all the courage she could muster" and presents her analysis. She points out that "the class's recommendations simply do not answer the company's problem. . . ."

In bringing forward an analysis contrary to the consensus, she takes several risks. First, she effectively takes on the entire class -- by contradicting their work. Second, if she is right, she risks being stereotyped as a teacher's pet. Third, by presenting a highly quantitative analysis, she risks being stereotyped as a "number-cruncher." Fourth, if her analysis is wrong, she risks making a fool of herself in front of the class.

Charles's adversarial cross-examination adds to what she calls her "ordeal." When it is over she feels "like a defendant released from hostile cross-examination." Charles puts her under pressure, effectively ridicules her in front of the class, and then gives her no feedback. ("The ordeal was over but the verdict was still out.")

She does get feedback from her peers, ranging from "good-natured teasing to open incredulity" at the highly mathematical approach she had taken. One of the most popular members of the section caps off the session by saying, "We are going to call your achievement The Macomber Memorial Matrix!" Thus she feels she has made a fool of herself and added little to the case discussion. In the absence of any signal from Charles, neither she nor the other students have any information to contradict this verdict.

7. What was Peter Anderson signaling?

Usage Note

This question directs attention to another element of section dynamics: peer relationships and peer pressure. A student is always managing two sets of relationships, and two sets of self-images -- one with instructors, the other with peers. Both are of vital importance to the student. Clearly an important part of Janet's experience is the indirect result of Charles's comments as they influence the section's view of her and the section's relationship to her.

Analysis

Peter Anderson appears to us to be summing up the sentiment of the group, and in effect announcing one of two possible verdicts: 1) that Janet has made a fool of herself by presenting an analysis that seemed to the rest of the students to be ridiculously off target, or 2) that she has

shown up the section and thus become a "rate breaker" violating section norms.

In our experience, students who attain early popularity often do so because they have a highly developed ability to read the attitudes and values of the group, and to act as a standard bearer for it. Thus it is likely that Peter is signaling and in some ways crystalizing the sentiment of the group through his comment about "The Macomber Memorial Matrix."

8.   What might Janet have done afterward? Why didn't she speak to Charles?

Usage Note

Teaching is a two-way interaction, and students as well as instructor have choices and responsibilities. This question directs attention to the ways students can influence their relationship with the instructor, and the ways instructors can make it harder or easier for students to approach them directly.

Analysis

Both Janet and Charles would be better off if she had spoken to him after class. At a minimum, she could have gotten Charles's assessment of her contribution. This would have relieved her confusion and, while not altering her relationship with other students, could have encouraged her to continue participating actively in the class. Ideally, she might have been able to tell Charles about her feelings during and after the interrogation, and/or the reactions of her classmates. A sensitive, supportive response from Charles would have done much to help her regain confidence and self-esteem. In addition, Janet's comments could perhaps have helped Charles improve his teaching style and even take specific corrective action in the section.

Unfortunately, it seems unlikely that someone in Janet's situation would choose to speak with Charles. To do so would be emotionally, and perhaps academically, risky for the student -- particularly in the first weeks of a new and highly competitive graduate program. To take such a risk usually requires that the student feel some trust for the instructor. But Charles has apparently not taken any of the steps by which instructors can make themselves more approachable (e.g., remaining in the classroom to encourage chats after the discussion session, establishing periodic routine conferences with individual students or student groups). Moreover, the last risk

Janet took with Charles -- speaking in class and contradicting the consensus on a case analysis -- was rewarded with abusive cross-examination. She has no reason to assume that a meeting with him would be handled any differently.

9.   **What was it, precisely, about Charles's comments that created the devastating impact?**

Usage Note

If participants have not already discussed the details of Charles's question-and-response style, this question provides an opportunity to direct attention to that crucial issue. Since participants now have developed an understanding of Charles's impact upon Janet Macomber, the discussion can focus on Charles's techniques as such rather than their effects. We find it is crucial in guiding discussion of this question to push the seminar to examine Charles's use of questions and response in word-for-word detail.

Analysis

Several aspects of Charles's approach are particularly important: the sudden, unexplained shift from a noninterventionistic approach to a highly controlling one; his adversarial stance toward Janet, including the use of short, logically linked questions and provocative "hook words"; the personalization of the interrogation by asking about her process of working out her analysis; and the studied avoidance of a clear signal to Janet or the class about the value of their contributions. A more detailed sample analysis of Charles's approach to Janet is presented in the notes to Question 2, Part a.

10.   **More generally, how does an instructor encourage student risk taking?**

Usage Note

This question asks the seminar members to generalize about the case, focusing on risk taking and the ways in which a safe climate for participation can be created in class. The key idea here is that the instructor who wants to get students to take risks in discussion must also assume the responsibility of protecting students who have taken a venturesome position.

Analysis

There are a variety of ways in which an instructor can create a climate that encourages students to explore ideas, challenge the status quo and conventional wisdom, and take initiative in creating new approaches to the problems presented in the cases. From the opening of classes, the instructor can seek to establish a learning contract in which intelligent student risk taking is valued and protected by the instructor.

Such a contract is shaped by both the instructor's words and his or her behavior. For example, the discussion leader's opening comments can describe the section as a place for discovery and experimentation with ideas, and not simply a place for defense and attack. It is useful to emphasize the importance of multiplying perspectives, and of examining conflicting ideas in a reasoned, respectful discourse.

By their behavior, and by what they demand from the students, instructors can establish mutual respect as a basic operating rule of their classes. Such respect helps to ensure that students will not be ridiculed for their contributions -- and that indeed students will feel valued when they participate in discussions.

The instructor should try to recognize when a student has taken a particularly risky stand, and to respond in a supportive way. It is often helpful for the instructor to take a respectful but not patronizing stance toward a comment that seems to be made with much difficulty. Peer support can be built by asking other students who agree to build upon the contribution. Finally, we try always to keep in mind that student comments really are the stuff from which discussion classes are built. We will sometimes thank a student, on behalf of the section, for making a particularly risky -- but often also valuable -- contribution to our learning.

Though like Charles, we may all occasionally undercut a student who is trying to make a contribution, it is important to stay alert to such unintended slights. We try to talk with the student, apologize if appropriate, and work to support the student -- both as an individual and as a member of the section -- in the future.

*   *   *

At this time the (C) case can be handed out, read, and discussed. We suggest the following discussion questions:

11.   **What is Charles's diagnosis at the end**

of the fifth week?   How is he likely to handle this situation?

Usage Note

The (C) case shifts the focus from the encounter itself to its longer-term effects. This question asks seminar participants to examine Charles's ability to diagnose the problem at this point, when he has had an opportunity to read signals sent over a period of several section meetings.

Analysis

In the first weeks of the term Janet came to class obviously well prepared, and participated eagerly in discussions. Charles notes that her comments "had been intelligent, succinct and to the point . . . and that on one occasion [the time of the incident] . . . Janet had performed an analytic tour de force, smashing the case wide open." Now Janet is silent, no longer participates voluntarily, arrives late, and changes her seat position every day.

Charles thinks Janet "seemed sleepy -- or bored," and "quite evidently had been barely following the discussion." He has "a strong presupposition" that she is unprepared.

As Charles reflects on the situation, he does not question his reading of Janet but rather his handling of what seems to him a clear-cut problem. He notes he has refrained from calling on her so as not to embarrass her. He chastises himself mildly, noting "such benevolence ought not to continue."

Though the text does not indicate what he is likely to do, his comments suggest that he feels a need to take corrective, and perhaps somewhat punitive, action. It seems likely that he will make it a point to call on Janet in class, perhaps with a sense of applying discipline, and challenging her to prove her preparation for discussion. If so, it is likely she will be further intimidated by him.

Alternatively, he may decide to speak with her in his office. The two of them might then finally be able to communicate their respective experiences of the incident, and to reopen communications. If so, there is a possibility of reestablishing mutual respect, trust, and thus a workable learning contract.

12. **What else might someone in Charles's shoes do in this situation?   What would be an effective way to handle this situation?**

Usage Note

Asking participants to put themselves in Charles's place tends to increase involvement and helps them realize the variety of options open to someone in this situation. It also helps them develop their ability to respond creatively and inventively to challenging teaching situations.

Analysis

Participants are likely to come up with many valuable suggestions. The common theme will probably be the need to open communication between instructor and student, whether by calling Janet in for a conversation or by talking with her less formally after or before class.

The point of such a conversation must be to ask her what the problem is, from her point of view. Charles persists in assuming he knows her experience of the class and his interventions. He does not. Instructors need to find ways of checking what students' experiences actually are. Often the simplest approach is to ask the student directly but tactfully, and with respect for the difficulty he or she may experience in responding.

13. **Faced with the situation as he sees it, what questions might he have asked himself?**

Usage Note

This question invites participants to consider how instructors can challenge their own complacency and recognize that their perceptions of reality may not be entirely accurate.

Analysis

Clearly, Charles should have asked himself, "Why is Janet acting this way? What is her experience of the section?" More generally, we find it important to keep asking these questions about our own students -- and to note particularly the little details that seem surprising and perplexing. Such details (like the shift in Janet's participation) are often clues to realities of which we have been unaware.

In some ways a more important question is, "Why do we, as instructors, so often take for granted the accuracy of our 'reading' of teaching situations? How might we teach ourselves to question our interpretations more often?" We have found that the simple pressures of time, and the absence of ready opportunities to talk candidly with students about their learning, inevitably create a tendency to take quick readings and rely too heavily on them. There seems to be no easy solution to this problem. In many situations, the most helpful approach may be to arrange frequent, informal meetings with small groups of students and deliberately cultivate their willingness to give us their candid views.

14.   Charles believes his class is going well. Do you agree? Why or why not?

Usage Note

This question raises a broad issue to which we return again and again in the seminar: How do you know when your class is going well?

Analysis

The case text gives very little data on the progress of the entire section. Nevertheless, we doubt that the class is going as well as Charles may believe. First, we wonder about his concept of an ideal class session. He characterizes the session in which the incident with Janet occurred as "everything a case discussion should not be: floundering, disjointed, indecisive, and entirely irrelevant to the company's problems." But sometimes floundering is an indication of real work being done. We, as instructors, may want things to flow logically -- but for students, "floundering" can be a groping exploration of difficult questions and issues that is immensely valuable. Students often feel such discussions are very productive and useful.

Second, just as Charles imagines he can understand Janet without difficulty and without testing his attributions, we suspect he may believe he can read the section's progress with the same ease. As he reflects on their accomplishments, there is little evidence of self-critical questioning of his assessment. He thinks to himself, "Individually and collectively, the class had come a long way in five weeks." Charles grins: he supposes, if surveyed, "the class would say the same thing of him." But would they? There is no evidence that he has carried out such a survey -- formally or informally.

15.   What broader questions does the case raise for you?

Usage Note

This question asks participants to generalize from the case, making connec-

tions to general themes and questions that will recur throughout the seminar and probably in their own teaching practice.

Analysis

"Graham and Macomber" raises a number of important questions for teachers. Some are general: How does an instructor respond to discussions that don't go as he or she planned? What constitutes a productive discussion session anyway? How does an instructor learn to read a section and understand the experience of the members, the group dynamics between members, and the learning process that is taking place? How can an instructor anticipate, monitor, and afterward test out the effects of his or her questions and responses? How can an instructor renew a constructive working relationship with a student who has become intimidated and resistant to his or her interventions?

Other questions revolve more concretely around the use of questions and responses: When and how is it helpful to praise or criticize the classroom contribution of an individual student? When and how do you critique the classroom work of an entire section? Do you offer your critique immediately after the contribution, at the end of the day's session, or perhaps during your opening remarks in the next session? How can you praise an individual student's contribution without setting up peer counterpressure?

One suggestion that emerges from our own practice is to "praise the process of the section" in the first weeks of the term. That is, we try to give the section members a sense of how the section as a whole is performing as a discussion forum. In this way we avoid singling out -- and potentially isolating -- individuals while at the same time helping the section become self-aware, self-reflecting, and self-correcting in its own discussion process.

One final observation that has intrigued us: while we as instructors focus our attention on our individual questions and responses, the students use these same questions as a basis for making much broader inferences about us. Particularly early in the term, students are trying to discern our style of class leadership, our manner of discipline or praise, and who we are as persons. Thus interventions that we may regard as relatively disconnected are interpreted by students as indications of overall personal style and "policies" and thus establish expectations that become part of the student-teacher learning contract.

Suggestions for Building the Seminar Group

During this discussion, which occurs early in the term, we concentrate our attention on the evolving process of the seminar. At this point, we are still trying to get a better sense of who the seminar members are, what their individual strengths are, and how these can be played together (almost like the various instruments of an orchestra) to create dynamic, searching discussions. And we are alert to the group dynamics of the section, watching for any situations that might lead to a "Janet Macomber" effect. After all, we are not immune to the processes described in this case, and we hope to take preventive action by seriously asking, "What is going on in the seminar? What learning is taking place? How do I know this is so?"

One way to gain some answers to these questions is to come a bit early to the seminar meetings and stay a few minutes afterward, making oneself available for informal conversations with participants. At these moments the instructor is often offered significant glimpses into the worlds of the participants, and the reactions of both individuals and the group to the learning process of the seminar.

In addition, we consciously pursue certain process goals for the seminar. These are modified from year to year and seminar to seminar, but we have found the basic perspective enduringly helpful. During the first four to six sessions, we focus on the group and its development. During later sessions, when the group has established norms that support self-directed, productive discussion, we turn our attention to individuals and their development. We try to attend to those in-class experiences that would "stretch" or challenge particular participants, and work to help create such opportunities for them.

"Graham and Macomber" is typically used for our fourth or fifth class session, when we are still working on the development of the group. In earlier sessions we have concentrated on getting wide participation, and on creating a climate of accurate and respectful listening. We have also encouraged participants to focus the discussion on a carefully detailed examination of the case text.

In "Graham and Macomber" the content of the seminar shifts from the teacher-student learning contract to the instructor's question-and-response style. A corresponding shift in case analysis is needed; instead of looking only for general patterns

of interactions, participants should now try to discover how general patterns are expressed in specific interventions.

Further, in looking at specific questions and responses, we want to encourage participants to consider the other options the instructor might have chosen. Thus emphasis shifts from diagnosis to action recommendations. Making recommendations is inherently risky, since participants must commit themselves to their suggestions. At the same time, discussion of action often creates more excitement and involvement in the seminar, perhaps because participants put themselves into the roles of the case protagonist and begin to feel the urgency of the case situation.

Risk and involvement are also increased by asking participants to predict, on the basis of the (A) case, how Janet experiences Charles's intervention (or to predict the longer-term effect of the intervention, before reading the (C) case). Predictions, like action recommendations, force participants to put their own judgments on the line. Participants are typically excited by the element of challenge, and the opportunity for immediate feedback (in reading the remainder of the case sequence).

It is important that the case discussion leader create a climate in which participants feel safe to take risks. In particular, the instructor must be ready to step in to protect participants who take an unpopular approach, or make a wildly incorrect prediction, or commit themselves to an action recommendation that subsequent discussion reveals to be unwise.

Early in the discussion of "Graham and Macomber," some participants commonly argue that Charles's approach is a good one. Like Charles, they may sense a need to "toughen up" students, and they assume that other students immediately recognize that Janet's answer cracks the case. Such a defense of Charles often stimulates intense discussion and can be profoundly valuable to the seminar. It brings home the message that reading one's section is a difficult matter, and that reasonable, intelligent, caring people often make different interpretations of the same data. This fact is of course central to the case content itself. Additionally, a measure of passionate disagreement raises involvement in the discussion, and leads to a richer, more intensive exploration of the case situation and the issues it raises.

The defense of Charles is often a

minority opinion, however. Like Janet Macomber, these dissidents deserve to have the instructor support the value of their contribution to the discussion.

There are many ways an instructor can minimize the negative emotional consequences of being "wrong" or taking an unpopular stand in a case discussion. In general, to avoid creating competition between members of the section, the instructor can frame the discussion as an examination of -- and perhaps competition between -- ideas. One useful technique is to make sure that any idea is expressed and developed by several persons, rather than just one. Most ideas expressed will find some support elsewhere in the section. Encouraging the expression of that support will tend to associate the idea with a group rather than an individual.

An instructor can also make a climate safer by stressing the dialectical nature of the discussion process: A good discussion requires consideration of central issues from a variety of perspectives. In hindsight some of the ideas may seem to have been more useful than others, but in fact each of the ideas expressed along the way helped the seminar to understand the case situation more deeply. A clear example is the devil's-advocate position, which can make a very valuable contribution to discussion.

Exhibit 1

Assistant Professor Graham and Ms. Macomber (A)

Study Questions

1. What is your diagnosis of the situation confronting Professor Charles Graham as of the end of class?

2. Should Professor Graham stop by the group gathered around Janet at the end of class?

Exhibit 2

Assistant Professor Graham and Ms. Macomber

Open-Focused Discussion Questions

The first five questions are directed to the (A) case.

1. How do you think this situation appears to Professor Charles Graham? How do you think he sees the situation facing him, here in the second week of classes, in the discussion session described in the case? What might he see as the problem? What might he focus on as the two or three key features of the situation?

    a) As a teacher of this section, what does Charles see as the critical challenge facing him?

    b) What is Charles's concept of the section leader's role?

2. How well, in your judgment, did Charles handle the questioning and response with Janet Macomber?

    a) What was Charles's approach?

    b) Why do you think he chose that approach?

    c) What was the impact of Charles's approach on Janet? What signals was Janet sending that might have helped him anticipate and monitor his impact was making?

    d) What background information might have helped him choose a more effective approach to Janet as an individual?

3. At the end of the interchange, Charles says, "Well, well!" What do you think of this response? What may be the effect of this response? How else might he have responded?

4. What is your evaluation of his summary? Was it appropriate to this class session?

5. Should he have dropped by the group around Janet's desk?

*   *   *

At this point in the discussion, the (B) case is handed out to be read quickly by the participants and discussed, using the following approach:

6. What is the situation from Janet Macomber's point of view?

7. What was Peter Anderson signaling?

8. What might Janet have done afterward? Why didn't she speak to Charles?

9. What was it, precisely, about Charles's comments that created the devastating impact?

10. More generally, how does an instructor encourage student risk taking?

*   *   *

At this time the (C) case can be handed out, read, and discussed, using the following discussion questions:

11. What is Professor Graham's diagnosis at the end of the fifth week? How is he likely to handle this situation?

12. What else might someone in Charles's shoes do in this situation? What would be an effective way to handle this situation?

13. Faced with the situation as he sees it, what questions might he have asked himself?

14. Charles believes his class is going well. Do you agree? Why or why not?

15. What broader questions does the case raise for you?

The Case of the Dethroned Section Leader

Teaching Note

Special Features

This case portrays a young instructor (twenty-six, still a graduate student) in a college Shakespeare course who faces a small classroom revolt against her leadership. The struggle that lurks beneath the surface of much classroom interaction appears with unusual clarity in this case, but many other perennial problems of teaching are also embedded in its events. For example, Bea Benedict operates without a workable teaching contract: she fails to listen carefully and respond constructively to her students; she tries to control the class rather than direct or guide discussion; and she reacts hastily and self-defensively to Jack Kesselman's "attack." Finally, the question of evaluation -- Who has the right to criticize whom? -- is also important in this case. In short, most of the issues our teaching seminars probe can be extracted for preliminary consideration from this brief history of Bea Benedict's adventures with her Shakespeare section.

Mood

A contentious case, "The Case of the Dethroned Section Leader" portrays a public confrontation and its attendant embarrassments. The material incorporates a good deal of classroom dialogue, and can stimulate spirited role playing. (Almost every teacher can identify with the protagonist's dislike of the fractious student.)

Suggested Uses

This case has special appeal as an opener for a seminar or workshop because it provides glimpses of many teaching issues we normally consider during the whole course of a semester. These include: 1) setting and maintaining a teaching contract, 2) creating a free, open climate for discussion, 3) the critical skills of posing questions and responding to students' contributions, 4) classroom management -- especially self-management, 5) the important difference between directing and controlling the discussion process, and 6) evaluation. Let us go through these briefly.

1) Student-teacher contract. In this case we see Bea Benedict leading her students according to an unstated, probably unconscious unilateral contract -- the kind many teachers set without much thought about reciprocal rights and responsibilities, unaware that they have latitude in designing a syllabus, making up assignments, and selecting a format for opening the discussion sessions. Bea seems unaware of the breadth of her options in determining what the section will do and how it will do it -- much less of the students' options.

2) Classroom climate. The climate Bea creates with her dominating style and rigid assignments seems chilly. It could hardly be expected to promote the kind of spirited, engaged discussion that Bea herself probably wanted.

3) Question and response. Bea's style of speech, which is quoted in the case, betrays the classic tendency of the inexperienced teacher to overwhelm the students (at the risk of arousing hostility and boredom). Bea's verbal responses seem hasty and ill-considered, and they show no attempt to engage the students with each other. Her reply to Jack Kesselman's complaint, for example, seems almost self-destructive (Did she <u>really</u> have to preside over her own impeachment?).

4) Classroom- and self-management. Faced with a revolt, Bea veers between schoolmarmish authoritarianism and self-defensive whining -- neither of which seems likely to engender respect and cooperation in the students.

5) Direction versus control. Directing a section resembles moderating a panel discussion. The discussion leader gives the

This teaching note has been prepared by Dr. Abby J. Hansen as an aid to instructors in the classroom use of the case series "The Case of the Dethroned Section Leader" (A) 9-382-177 and (B) 9-382-178.

students' comments shape by rephrasing them, poses questions that suggest directions in which the analysis might profitably move, and offers new ideas for the students to consider. Direction is not dictatorial. Control, on the other hand, connotes rigidity. The teacher who tries to control a discussion risks turning the students into parrots. Bea transmits confusing messages in this area. She looks casual: she wears slacks; she sips coffee during the discussion; she meets the students on their home ground, within earshot of a frisbee game. But she also stands while they sit, uses a rather conservative style of opening, and gives such long introductions to her questions that she practically answers them herself.

6) Evaluation. Although most colleges and universities routinely ask students to evaluate their teachers, the balance of power in this respect is still tipped toward the teacher, who has the customary role of providing feedback, not only in class (by praising or criticizing students' contributions as they are offered) but also in the concrete form of grades. Jack Kesselman breaks this convention publicly; this accounts for much of Bea Benedict's feeling of having been attacked.

The purpose of this rehash of Bea's foibles is not to excoriate her. On the contrary; Bea's errors are due mainly to her inexperience and lack of guidance. (Her senior professor seems to have offered no advice about teaching.) Given that Bea wishes to improve her effectiveness as a teacher -- that she really wants to help her students learn -- she must shift her focus from herself and how she handles the material to her students and how she can nudge, guide, charm (but not push or drag) them to a more sophisticated grasp of Shakespeare, according to their lights. Like all discussion teachers, Bea must create some stimulating, open-ended questions and think carefully about how to phrase them in order to get her students to talk more than she does in class. These are far more difficult tasks than simply showing off one's erudition, but they are necessary for success.

It should be apparent by now that "The Case of the Dethroned Section Leader" is a fertile case. Although relatively brief, it contains the seeds of quite a variety of important teaching issues.

One of the most salient of these is contract -- the agreement that sets the form the teacher-student relationship will take. This is a common concern in the early stages of all courses, and the maintenance of the relationship continues to be important, for it will change over time. This case shows a radical disruption in contract; many other teaching situations change, but with less drama. Whenever the issue of contract is à propos, this case is relevant. One very basic question it raises -- how to exercise power in the classroom -- is always of interest, for students' attitudes toward their classwork and teachers often approach rebellion or belligerence.

Still, a young woman teaching Shakespeare in a liberal arts college is the focus of this particular case. Some seminar participants in very different disciplines or at more advanced stages of their careers may feel little fellowship with Bea Benedict. The discussion leader should try to steer these people past the specifics to general considerations of classroom dynamics as swiftly as possible.

Conflicts, Sensitivities

The most potentially sensitive point in this case is the inescapable fact that Bea Benedict is female, and Jack Kesselman -- who questions her leadership -- is male. In discussion, some participants have interpreted his protest as simple sexism, and the discussion leader should be prepared for this. One way to prevent the seminar discussion from focusing only on this observation would be to give this point of view some "air time," but then ask participants to brainstorm a bit. (What if a male teacher had behaved precisely as Bea did? Would Jack have reacted differently? What elements in Bea's style might have triggered his protest?) Calling attention to the rigid way she seems to conduct class -- contrasted with the casualness of the setting and her attire -- should help broaden the focus. Bea's confusing signals have nothing to do with her gender.

Teaching Objectives

This case offers a fine opportunity to explore such important topics as how one helps students grapple with primary materials without cramming one's own interpretations down their throats. What are genuinely stimulating questions? The crucial pair of skills -- question and response -- may also be approached through this case: Bea Benedict makes some blunders in both areas, and Jack Kesselman, in his blunt way, points them out. This case gives seminar participants a chance to think about whether they have committed similar errors, and, if so, how to avoid them in the future.

The "Blocks" of Analysis

As always, every comment in the discussion may be associated with some major category of interpretation that relates to the past, present, future, or theoretical aspects of the events. The "past" includes what Bea and the students did before the decision point in the (A) case. The "present" includes the clearest possible assessment one can make of her situation at the end of (A). (Was Bea really attacked? Had she been insulted? Did she have to step down as leader?) The "future" category includes prediction and prescription. The situation has to change for better or worse. How should it change? What should Bea do? The theoretical issues include the basic principles that operate in this set of events. In this case, power, question and response, and contract should certainly come under discussion.

Study Questions 2 and 3 (see Exhibit 1) refer to Bea's constraints, as opposed to factors she could control. Each of these could constitute a "block."

1. Constraints. Bea has to teach, as part of her graduate fellowship. She does not run the whole course, and she finds Professor Glendower's lectures "superficial." This leads her to supplement his material in her sections. (She also has to do her own graduate work while teaching. This double focus usually produces stress.)

2. Choices. She chooses to dress casually and wear her long hair loose. She chooses to teach after dinner in a residence hall in a formal conference room and bring her coffee mug. She chooses to assign oral reports and set the rules for their delivery. She chooses to read and excerpt criticism for her students but discourages them from reading it themselves. She also chooses to begin the section by writing key terms and dates on the blackboard, suggesting that these should organize the evening's discussion.

3. Power. This issue is deeply embedded in these proceedings. Who has the right to direct the class? Who has the right to say who shall speak, to whom, and when? Who has the right to evaluate? How? All these issues surface when Jack criticizes Bea in class.

4. Character. Consider Bea Benedict's personality and background. Still a student playing the role of teacher, she does not seem comfortable exercising power over other -- albeit younger -- students. Also, she is competitive and -- one gathers from her reasons for attending graduate school -- primarily interested in studying literature, rather than in teaching students. And Jack comes across as a rebel, or at least in a rebellious phase.

5. Environment. This includes the physical setup, the course, psychological atmosphere, time of day -- any factors that surround and condition the classroom dynamic.

6. Classroom dialogue. There are infinite numbers of ways to pose questions and infinite numbers of ways to respond to students' answers and suggestions. Tone of voice, physical gesture and posture, and choice of language have subtle but enormously powerful effects.

7. Methodology. One basic challenge of discussion teaching is that the teacher learns the material and wants to help the students learn it too. But this cannot be accomplished by a simple transfer of knowledge from brain to brain. Most teachers choose the profession because they have been successful and happy as students. But effective teaching requires the exercise of different skills. Some teachers never learn this, and their students suffer (causing them, in turn, the frustration of feeling less outstanding as teachers than they have been as students).

Preparing for the Discussion

Exhibit 1 lists suggested Study Questions, to be handed out to participants for use when preparing the case before class. Exhibit 2 contains a summary of the Discussion Questions, to be used by the seminar leader in preparing for class and in guiding the case discussion when necessary.

Opening Speaker, Backstop

This case features a woman teacher and a male antagonist. The discussion leader's choice of opening speaker and backstop will depend upon the immediate goal for the opening mood of the discussion. Do you want to begin with an emotional "high" and generate some involvement at the risk of detachment? This will leave cool analysis for a later point in the discussion. If so, pick an assertive woman to speak for Bea Benedict's point of view and an equally assertive man (possibly even a contentious one, if you have such a participant on tap) to speak for Jack Kesselman.

On the other hand, asking a man to speak for Bea and a woman to speak for Jack could have the opposite effect: it would signal empathy as the opening mood. In fact, there is no reason the discussion leader should not state this choice of opening mood quite openly, saying, for example, "Poor Bea! Mary, as a woman teacher yourself, perhaps you can help us sympathize with her." "Sam, would you play devil's advocate and step into Jack Kesselman's shoes for a moment to provide us with some reactions he might have been having to Bea's teaching style?" Choosing opening speakers from disciplines quite divergent from Bea's would be a way to signal that identification with Bea's predicament need not be rooted in a similar background. (All our teaching cases are meant to raise issues that puzzle most teachers at some point in their careers.)

The Discussion Questions

I would suggest running a discussion of this case with primary attention to general concerns that emerge from the whole range of events in <u>Exhibit 2</u>. I have supplied an equal number of questions on (A) and (B). but the operational issues seem less crucial than the more general, basic questions we have noted.

After the (A) case has been read, the following questions may be introduced:

1. [To the opening speaker]: **What's going on here? What do you make of Bea's remark that she "felt attacked?"**

There may be divergence of opinion on this point, depending on how people feel about authority. Jack behaved in a manner that some might find insulting simply because it is insubordinate: He "slouched," looked away from Bea, and then blatantly ignored her instructions to report. Instead of analyzing the assigned passage from <u>Richard II</u>, which Bea had just exhaustively introduced, he launched into a criticism of her teaching style and included the bombshell-statement that instead of listening to her introduction he had timed it and, furthermore, found her presentation "pretty boring." It was at this point that Bea felt attacked.

Most teachers would probably feel the same. But what, in particular, insulted her is worth considering: Was it Jack's criticism of her lecture style? Or was it his rejection of her right to tell him what to do in class? It may be worth probing a bit to expose this. What is damaged besides Bea's ego?

One may also assume that preparing the minilecture must have cost Bea both time and effort: she had grounds for feeling both insulted and unappreciated. Most teachers will empathize with her defensiveness. But there may be differences of opinion over how she should have responded to Jack. Hardliners will probably say she should have tossed the upstart out of the classroom. Others, taking a more lenient stance, might defend Jack's right to protest. After all, his education (and those of his fellow students) is at stake here -- not Bea Benedict's right to show off. Some may excuse Bea's handling of his criticism. She actually gave him permission to defy her because she was caught off guard, felt hurt, and, possibly, felt guilty and embarrassed at having taken up so much class time with her minilecture. Still, her reaction was ill-considered and her querulous rhetorical question ("Don't you think I've got anything to teach you?") was unfortunate.

The opening speaker will probably side with either Bea or Jack, and the discussion leader should find an opportunity to elicit support for whichever point of view the opening speaker has not espoused. This could be done with a pointed ("<u>Why</u> do you say such and such?") question or some role playing. To expand the focus this early in the discussion would signal a certain welcome amplitude. This case will support a variety of interpretations. (It is this researcher's feeling that a reasonable degree of ambiguity in a case produces the most useful discussions.) The leader should try to keep shifting ground and probing for shades of opinion and different ways to view the events and characters and their implications. The advantage of case analysis over real life is that one can view and review case events. They "stay put" better than episodes in one's own experience, and permit one to profit from many vantage points.

2. [To the backstop]: **How might things have looked to Jack?**

Some participants have suggested Jack's protest was just a cover for lack of preparation. He simply hadn't done his homework. Another point of view is that he was actually telling the truth. He had both read and thought about the assigned passage. (Bea's assignments seem to be brief and compact; he <u>could</u> have done his assignment right before class.) But Jack is described as a performer and "political activist," familiar with the rhetoric of formal, public protest. Had he, quite sincerely, felt that he and his fellow students were being ill-served by an egotistical discussion leader's attempts to exhibit her erudition at their expense, public protest would have suggested itself as an appropriate means to improve the situation. This might have been a matter of conscience for Jack.

Bea describes him as "something of an operator" -- a manipulator of the system. Perhaps he did affect the rhetoric of ethical protest to camouflage his own laziness. But we must remember that we have only Bea's descriptions in this case, and she admits that her feelings for Jack after this episode coalesced into solid dislike.

3.   How about the others in the class?

Bea gives us other descriptions: Elke Gunnarson is a sporty, socially conventional sort of person, it seems. Her boyfriend, Cliff, appears to be a male version of Elke. They might be expected to occupy the middle ground of a political struggle. One certainly would not anticipate their marching to the cry of "Revolution!" from Jack. The other student Bea recalled in any detail was Skip Townsend, a Californian who, unlike Elke and Cliff, might either promote a rebellion or, at least, be amused by any sort of anarchism that might crop up in a formal situation. Anyone who writes "beachcomber" under "Professional Plans" on a student information card shows both a sense of humor and a tendency not to take authority too seriously.

There is, thus, a balance of personalities in this little group: two conservatives, two radicals. The others seem to have impressed Bea so little that -- at a distance of a few years -- she was unable to furnish any information on which to evaluate them.

One can imagine the class reacting along a political spectrum, with the conservatives groaning inwardly at Jack's familiar line, and the radicals thinking something like "Right on!"

But primary attention should be paid to the disruption that Jack's ploy (whatever its intent) created in the normal operation of the section. If one believes that the business of a Shakespeare section is Shakespeare, Jack was destructively diverting attention from the task at hand -- an offense much more serious than any "boring" lectures from Bea. If, on the other hand, one believes that education cannot be pigeonholed by subject, and that there are many things to learn in a classroom and many ways to learn them, Jack

may be furnishing a more educational episode than the students could have experienced if the class had proceeded more normally.

Some seminar participants may offer their own recollections of the time at which this case occurred. The early 1970s are still vivid in the minds of many academics. They were a time of protest, frequent political demonstrations -- some fairly good-humored, some literally deadly -- and widespread, highly publicized civil disobedience. As a student, Bea must have taken this atmosphere for granted and felt comfortable working within it. One gathers, from her extremely controlled and orderly structuring of the class, that she was probably not a radical herself. Certainly, she was no anarchist. But the popularity of public protests in her milieu may have, at the very least, created some guilt for her regarding autocracy in the classroom. Perhaps the students looked at her -- long hair, running shoes, and blue jeans -- and saw a potential comrade. As we have noted before, Bea's appearance could have misled them: she behaved like a teacher, but looked like a student. All of these factors may have combined to unsettle the students in her Shakespeare section.

4.   How did Bea get into this fix?

At this point, the discussion leader's task will be to try to direct attention to those factors in Bea's environment that we have mentioned in the "blocks" under Constraints and Choices. There were some aspects of her environment that she simply had to accept: her students, the class size, primary texts, Glendower's lectures. On balance, though, it seems that she also had quite a broad area of choice. Did she unwittingly stack the deck against herself? The discussion leader might point out some items to consider. ("What about the room in which she was teaching?" "Could she have changed it? To what?" "What about the meeting time?" "Do you encourage students to eat and drink in your discussion classes?" "How about those frisbee players right outside their window?" "What do you think about her opening gambit -- putting terms on the board?")

The object is not to pillory Bea for gross foolishness in setting up this section, but rather to show the extremely significant effect of such small choices as whether or not to "condition" a discussion with key terms (or let them emerge in progress), whether to permit or encourage eating and drinking, whether or not to run a discussion around a conference table, whether or not to try to discuss Shakespeare in competition with frisbee players' shouts. There are many other aspects to this question: one way Bea "got into this fix" was by accepting a fellowship at Fairchild University that entailed teaching. Is she ready to teach? Is she interested in teaching? Has she given enough consideration to how her students learn? After the discussion has dwelt on some of these extremely basic considerations, one should move into the "action" area (which, as I have noted, I find essentially less important in this case than in many others, even though the threat of deposition makes it dramatic).

5. What should she do?

One hopes for brief, trenchant suggestions here. Bea hasn't got too many options: like anyone handed an ultimatum, she can take it or leave it. What she should do, thus, boils down to a choice of whether to accept the ultimatum or not -- complicated by a not-so-simple (because partially unconscious) choice of style. Much will be implied by the manner in which she responds. She could react personally, saying, "You have really insulted me, Jack; your manners are atrocious!" She could cling to her official role and lecture him: "This is inappropriate behavior, Jack. I think we should go on with our discussion as planned. Please either present your report or leave and allow us to continue." Or, she could capitulate gracefully, and with some retention of authority -- say, by taking a vote herself, standing at the board in the "teacher's place." She could also capitulate ungraciously, by stalking out. An unpleasant refusal to give in might have sounded something like, "Okay, Jack. You want to run things? Let's see you come up here and give a coherent and interesting fifteen-minute minilecture on Richard II!"

Participants almost invariably enjoy role playing and supplying dialogue for the "prediction" sections of discussions, and this case can provide material for lively contributions. It might be advisable for the discussion leader to end this section of the seminar meeting on an upbeat, high-energy note, with suggestions for Bea and guesses about the outcome of this dramatic confrontation.

*   *   *

After the (B) case has been read:

1. What is your appraisal of how Bea responded to Jack's challenge?

Varieties of response to this question will probably align themselves along the same axes as response to the first question on the (A) case. How one feels about Bea's permissive response will correlate with one's feelings about a teacher's proper role. Bea acted instinctively -- as one usually does in teaching, where crises develop too fast for much planning. She combined a democratic acceptance of the students' right to vote (some participants may scream at her pusillanimity) with a tacit refusal to relinquish her intrinsic right to lead. She "stood at the board" and gave a deceptively tough-sounding order: "Hands up, those who want to have no leader." In fact, she leapt to a self-destructive conclusion. There were many middle courses between her previous controlling style and her leaderlessness, but she ignored them. Ironically, she may be seen to have engineered her own downfall. Some participants may detect in her action an essential ambivalence about power: Bea Benedict invites her own deposition in terms of crisp command! The discussion leader should solicit reactions, and try to respond to them by directing participants' attention to the precise details of the (B) case. Bea Benedict stood at the board and viewed the vote against her. Jack and Skip -- the radical and anarchist (in gross oversimplification) -- raised their hands. That left the two conservatives and the rest of the students, whom Bea couldn't even remember without her gradebook. We'll never know why Elke and Cliff chose to vote with Jack and Skip; perhaps they also found Bea boring. Perhaps they were environmentally attuned to protest. Perhaps they found the novelty intriguing. Perhaps they were influenced by Jack's forceful personality. But they did raise their hands, so (again, some seminar members might scream "pusillanimity") Elke and Cliff joined the majority. The dynamic here is worth discussing. We have a very small section with a clear conflict and three general groups -- left, right, and middle. What happens in this situation is probably a microcosm of many far larger events. A squeaky wheel makes noise, attracts attention, rattles authority, and manages -- by energy, or novelty, or perhaps even intrinsic rightness -- to effect a revolution.

At any rate, the group's vote against Bea was unanimous. From the point of view of her self-respect as leader of this group, this is the nadir of the situation. She has just been unconditionally rejected. The discussion leader should try to direct attention to the <u>manner</u> in which Bea accepts this defeat. She describes a clear sequence of actions in terms that reveal a certain bitterness. She "surveyed the democratic assembly that had just ousted" her (feeling just like a deposed political leader, apparently), "put the chalk back on the ledge" (relinquished the scepter), and "sat down" (symbolically stepped down from power to join the group on its level -- no lower. She could have left the room.

"What is the impact of Bea's watching the vote?" might be a useful question to ask. "What do you think you might have felt as you watched her put down that piece of chalk and take a seat?"

An important question here is "What do you think the impact of her 'abdication speech' might have been?" Bea reports saying three words: "Okay, Section -- discuss!" She's still giving orders. At this point, all we know is that Bea has allowed herself (even helped, some might say) to be voted out of authority. Her previous contract -- to lead the group in discussion of Professor Glendower's Shakespeare lectures -- is completely void. But no contract has taken its place. In a sense, Bea has no right to her parting shot. No one has said <u>what</u> the class is going to do now. The new direction must emerge from the section itself. It can't come from Bea.

If the seminar has polarized around reactions to Jack Kesselman and what he stands for in this case, reaction about what <u>did</u> happen next will also be vehement. Jack "began to talk about the passage" (people who think he was totally unprepared may be surprised at this), but he spoke "mainly in terms of personal likes and dislikes" (another hint that, maybe, he <u>hadn't</u> prepared after all). Was he reading it for the first time right there? Was that why he gave only superficial reactions?

But there is a serious issue embedded in the rest of Bea's report of the sort of comments Jack was making. He spoke of his personal reactions to a literary character, without historical context, and without reference to published scholarship. He spoke naively but, we gather, honestly. Bea, the graduate student, would have done it differently. "What's wrong with Jack's 'report?'" one might ask. Participants should spend some time on the issue of the teaching potential of naive comments as a teaching tool. Is there value in simple "gut reaction" commentary like Jack's? Many teachers (privately, at least) think not. The discussion leader should ask

participants to try to suggest ways to use naive remarks to get the students in the class to examine the primary data. In literature, one would ask what descriptions, kinds of diction, images, bits of dialogue (or whatever) might be making Jack feel he "doesn't like <u>Richard II</u> very much." Jack's reaction seems genuine; it could lead to extremely important observations -- observations that the rest of the class could furnish, building from Jack's simple contribution.

Bea's task is to use her sophisticated appreciation of the material to focus the students' attention on details to which they are (perhaps unconsciously) reacting. All teachers of introductory courses should bear in mind that they were once as innocent and ignorant of their special subjects as <u>their</u> students are now. This seems obvious; but in practice, most teachers -- particularly the more experienced ones -- often forget this truism. Contempt for one's average students (be it unconscious, veiled, or even denied) is widespread and debilitating in the teaching profession.

2.   **What about the aftermath of her abdication? What factors do you see at work here?**

This section of the discussion provides the leader with an opportunity to strike theoretical bedrock. What happened was "the other students didn't seem terribly interested in Jack's personal reactions." Why? Are we looking at some clue to the essence of an interesting, involving discussion -- a hint at the difference between one person's purely private reaction to a subject (be it literature, art, music, history, or politics -- anything with human content) and a <u>useful</u> classroom approach from which many students can profit? How can someone like Bea present students with the fruits of years of advanced study without stifling their emotional involvement?

The problem with Jack's reactions to <u>Richard II</u> as <u>material for educational discussion</u> is that they are too personal to sustain the other students' interest for long -- we all know that sinking feeling when a fellow student's report or class commentary threatens to drag on and on, leaving us with fixed expressions, pretending to pay attention. This is the signal of a class in limbo. No good teacher will allow such a situation to persist for long. The reason that undiluted personal testimony fails is that emotion is ultimately not truly communicable. It is very difficult to share another's pain, pleasure, or boredom; but we <u>can</u> communicate ideas. It is the teacher's task to balance emotion with thought. For effective learning, you can't have one without the other. Students' unpracticed and unconsidered attempts to lead class discussions almost always err by excluding one element. But pure emotional effusion will alienate the other students just as certainly as dry intellectualism (unless it is full of true genius) will end by boring them.

The question for us is "Can Jack's personal reactions constitute a useful report? If so, how?" The answers will lie in attention to problems of pacing, artful questions, referring one student's insight to another student for criticism (rather than responding oneself, as the teacher), and the judicious introduction of critical and historical material. All this is the "meat and potatoes" of discussion teaching.

Bea goes on to describe the whole aftermath. After a "desultory and unfocused" attempt at discussion, the hour ended. Bea "said nothing" during this period. But afterward Cliff and Elke stayed to talk to her. Both were "very embarrassed." Why? At their treachery, because they both voted to oust her? At Jack's impoliteness? At the damage to Bea's self-esteem?

A good question to ask the section at this point is "What do you think of Cliff and Elke's perception that Jack has become their new section leader?" Many participants will agree: There seems to be two strong personalities in this case -- Bea and Jack -- whose revolt could be boiled down to a good, old-fashioned personality conflict.

The discussion leader should focus attention on several remarks Bea makes in the (B) case. She mentions that she confided her anger at Jack to Elke and Cliff, but combined this with her opinion that she "had been fairly and squarely voted out of authority." The issue of authority seems to surface over and over in this case. What do your seminar participants make of it? What authority did Bea have at the beginning of the case that she relinquished? Of what authority did the vote deprive her? Was she forced to take that vote? What else might she have done? What did she lose (or gain) by the vote?

Bea also makes a revealing remark about her approach to discussing the section's behavior with Elke and Cliff. She calls herself (with the advantage of hindsight) "unprofessional." Is she? What is professionalism in a situation like this?

Has she acted unprofessionally in other ways? What ways? When? How?

It might be useful to point out that Elke proposed to call a new vote at the very next meeting, and Bea rejected the suggestion. Is Bea being manipulative? If so, why? What is her ultimate aim? (What would yours be in her situation?)

The (B) case describes (in compressed, summary form) events that took weeks to develop. Bea mentions that the seminar limped along with no one actually leading it. In the realm of symbolism, someone in the seminar is likely to point out that Bea sat "in the seat farthest from the chalkboard" and "no one sat in the teacher's seat." What is the significance of these details of position? (The discussion leader might call attention to them if they do not emerge by themselves from participants' comments.) The manipulation of classroom space is always significant.

It may also be noted that the second vote, unlike the first, was held in Bea's absence. Having haunted her section for two weeks (one wonders about the effect of her silent presence in that room), Bea seems to have retreated a bit. At least she let her students vote a second time away from her gaze, without taking the opportunity to make mental notes of her partisans and enemies.

The section of the discussion dealing with the "factors at work" during the aftermath is likely to touch on a number of points without exhausting any. There is, in fact, a great deal suggested in these encapsulized events. Bea remained in the room, but refused to participate as a student. It is likely that her presence had a dampening effect on the students' discussions. Did she help create the disorganized confusion she criticizes?

Once Bea was voted back, she found the students relieved to have her back. One might ask whether they were relieved to have her leading them again, or simply relieved to end the embarrassing arrangement whereby she watched their "formless," self-conscious discussions. (One cannot imagine an assertive person like Bea sitting expressionless during a discussion of which she basically disapproves!)

It is probably not surprising that Bea felt that the semester went "quite satisfactorily" after the students voted her back into power. The discussion leader might probe for some reasons for this. Was Bea simply pleased to feel vindicated, ratified, and appreciated? Wouldn't anyone enjoy a vote of confidence? Or did the situation really improve, once Bea had learned, from personal embarrassment, how brittle a teacher's authority can be? Did Bea endeavor to involve her students more? Write fewer directives on the board? Spend less time disguising lectures as questions and try to ask more genuinely stimulating questions?

3.   **What were the critical turning points of Bea's situation?**

The crucial turning points in this case begin with Jack's initial refusal to present a report, and his unsolicited public criticism of Bea (in the (A) case). How might Bea have reacted, instead of allowing him to provoke her into taking the all-or-nothing vote that ousted her from power? (This may already have been covered in the discussion of the (A) case, but one could summarize remarks from that portion of the discussion.) The second "turning point" was Bea's private discussion with Elke and Cliff -- two social leaders in communication with the rest of the students. Elke, a student-government type, is probably as competent as Bea to take the situation in hand, and she seems to have pegged Jack Kesselman as a heckler anxious to overturn the applecart partly for the thrill of it and partly to flex his muscles. She probably could have done Bea's "dirty work" quite efficiently. Should Bea have allowed Elke to take a vote at the very next class meeting? Should she have tried to get more information about the other students from Elke and Cliff? If so, what kind? What is appropriate information, and what isn't?

The next turning point is, of course, the vote that restored Bea to power. The class should take up the question of <u>contract</u> here. How should Bea run the section now? What should she have learned from Jack's insurrection? What elements of her teaching style should she modify? In essence, what was she doing wrong at first?

4.   **How does power operate in discussion teaching?**

This is one of the most basic, far-reaching, and important questions -- not only in this case, but in the whole seminar. The class will certainly not exhaust it in the space of ten or so minutes of discussion. The discussion leader should ask the class to consider both the (A) and (B) cases. What specific details in the (A) case tell us how Bea exercised power? (Power, for discussion purposes, may be

simply defined as the ability to make other people do what you say.) What factors in Bea's situation gave her this ability? The issue of evaluation is pertinent here. Seminar participants will probably mention that she had the absolute power to grade her students. She had the power to make class assignments, to tell the students when to present oral reports, and, presumably, written papers. She had some power to decide where the class will meet, and she could say whether the students would bring food and drink to class, who would speak, when they would speak, to whom they would speak, when and what they would or would not read. (They were required to read certain passages of the play for their reports; they were discouraged from reading criticism.) Such details will probably emerge fairly easily in class.

The more difficult aspects to plumb will be the students' power. What could they do to Bea? In this case, Jack Kesselman affords us a particularly blatant example: he criticizes openly, grabbing the power of evaluation out of her hands. All students evaluate teachers, both inwardly and in informal gripe sessions with their friends, but it is very rare for students to break the conventions and criticize teachers in class. A student can also refuse, tacitly or overtly, to be taught. If this happens, the teacher's function has, in effect, been nullified. The teacher-student relationship is reciprocal. It requires trust and acceptance on both sides. The teacher must trust the student to be making an effort to learn; the student must trust the teacher to be guiding his or her developing perceptions in useful directions. Either side can break this relationship -- a point many teachers forget. The teacher-student relationship always has contractual elements, and all contracts require cooperation.

The symbols of power -- position in the classroom, right to write on the board -- are also prominent in this case. So is the issue of dress (costume, if you will): What is Bea signaling by dressing like a student and bringing her coffee mug to class? Does she seem to be aware of the symbolic overtones of her choices? The seminar should discuss these issues -- not to praise or criticize Bea, but rather to make each other more alert to the many subtle details of the teaching situation that the teacher can control. Unconsidered choices may send unintentional messages.

Other issues of power in the classroom have to do with information: Why did Bea read criticism, but suggest that her students should not? Why did Bea write historical and critical catchwords on the board, rather than give research assignments to her students and ask them to write on the board? Why did Bea ask such long-winded questions? How much time should a teacher spend talking? Who should ask the questions? Who should talk to whom? (There is no student-to-student dialogue in Bea's class before the "revolution"; afterward, it exists with no moderator.)

All these are meant to be provocative questions -- certainly not answerable in ten or fifteen minutes' worth of discussion time at the end of the seminar. But they are central, and should be returned to again and again.

Exhibit 1

The Case of the Dethroned Section Leader

Study Questions

1. Bea Benedict "felt attacked" by Jack Kesselman's protest. How would you describe and evaluate her situation at the end of the (A) case? (Think not only of her point of view, but also of Jack's and that of the rest of the class.)

2. Under what constraints was Bea working?

3. What elements in her situation could she control?

4. Evaluate her choices in setting up the teaching situation.

5. What would you advise Bea to do at the end of the (A) case? Why? What is at stake, and what can she gain?

Exhibit 2

The Case of the Dethroned Section Leader

Discussion Questions

After the (A) case has been read:

1. What's going on here? What do you make of Bea's remark that she "felt attacked"?

2. How might things have looked to Jack?

3. How about the others in the class?

4. How did Bea get into this fix?

5. What should she do?

*   *   *

After the (B) case has been read:

1. What is your appraisal of how Bea responded to Jack's challenge?

2. What about the aftermath of her abdication? What factors do you see at work here?

3. What were the critical turning points of Bea's situation?

4. How does power operate in discussion teaching?

The Case of the Dethroned Section Leader

Researcher's Perspective

In the view of the case researcher, the Bea Benedict case depicts a power struggle that she herself engendered. By her own (unexamined) attitude toward the students, Bea almost guaranteed some sort of resistance. The particular time of this case (1973) happened to be propitious to open rebellion, but her behavior would have triggered truculence in the section under any circumstances. This commentary will suggest some points in the case that lend themselves to this view.

The Instructor

Note Bea's background: She is an honors graduate of the same institution in which she is now teaching. Unmarried, and back at her own former school, Bea is probably feeling herself something of a *revenant*. Not quite a faculty member, but no longer her own former undergraduate self, she hasn't yet adopted a completely new adult identity. She lives with students, dresses like a student, and -- at least part time -- *is* a student. Furthermore, Bea's statement of her purpose for being back at Fairchild University ("I felt ready for a good, nourishing drink of great literature") doesn't mention teaching at all. We can only infer that teaching is secondary to studying among her reasons for having returned. It seems reasonable that we should examine Bea's teaching style for evidence of competitiveness: outtalking the students, refusing to relinquish authority to them, reluctance to grant them class time to find their own tentative analyses of the material. Bea is so impressed with her own increasingly sophisticated appreciation of Shakespeare's plays that she tends to force her interpretations on her students, hoping thereby to accomplish their instant elevation to her own state of comprehension while simultaneously impressing them with her brilliance and preparation. Inexperienced teachers frequently fall into this trap, partly from a desire to demonstrate their legitimacy as leaders, partly from the habits of long years of competition with peers in the classroom, and partly from simply not having directed their attention to what they actually want to accomplish in the classroom -- namely, helping their students learn how to come to grips with the material.

The Setting

Bea has chosen a difficult teaching situation. Not only is she on the students' territory, she is teaching at a particularly relaxed time -- right after dinner, and in an atmosphere full of distractions (e.g., within earshot of the frisbee games). If she wished to teach a Falstaff House section, she might have taken some time and trouble to find a more secluded room in which she would not have had to sit facing her students around an excessively large conference table. One of the "common rooms" (similar to a living room) with arm chairs, sofas, and coffee tables) would have lent itself to creating an informal discussion circle. Bea also might have tried to have the section meet <u>before</u> dinner, as most students tend to <u>think</u> of the evening as a social time, or at least a time when <u>they</u> may use the hours as they please, not as a section leader dictates.

The Course

Teaching a discussion section of a large lecture course involves specific constraints. The discussion leader must work within a framework not of his or her own design. Bea felt it necessary to work against the grain -- presenting supplementary material in a way implicitly disparaging to Professor Glendower's course organization and presentation. Her approach may have raised some resentment from undergraduates who liked Glendower (a popular raconteur) and found Bea's fact-laden, intense graduate-studentlike style pedantic.

The Students

Here Bea shows her greatest weakness. She has analyzed literature, not people. She describes the students rather

This commentary on the "Case of the Dethroned Section Leader" was prepared by Dr. Abby J. Hansen. Its objective is to help instructors in the development of their teaching plans for this case.

baldly, giving little information about their personalities and styles of learning. This implies that she gave little, if any, attention to the primary problem of discussion teaching: finding how to present the material to this particular group. The discussion teacher should take the opportunity to find out as much personal information about each student as possible, within the bounds of propriety. Bea's student-information cards were a step in the right direction, but she seems to have failed to read students' attitudes from their behavior. She ought to have spotted Jack as a potential threat to her authority, if maintaining authority was one of her primary concerns (as it seems to have been). Bea's descriptions of the four students she remembered show Jack to be rebellious, Skip to be a potential accomplice to him, and Elke and Cliff to be conventional middle-of-the-roaders, capable of allying themselves either with authority or rebellion.

Bea's Style

The distinguishing characteristic here is dominance. Note the way Bea asks Jack her initial question: she all but answers it herself, launching into a capsule analysis of her own, and even interrupting herself to underline a previous lesson to the class (her reference to the importance of middle acts of Shakespeare's five-act structure).

Bea's desire to control everything in the classroom is further shown by her habit of standing at the board to write catch-words that she hopes will organize the hour. No discussion so programmed is truly free. One gets no sense that Bea intended the students to have any real control over the content or direction of their own discussion. Her classes seem to have been lectures in disguise.

Given Bea's apparent need to control the class, direct its discussions almost as if she were writing scripts, and thereby demonstrate her intellect and authority in the classroom, it is not surprising that she perceived Jack's (admittedly impolitely phrased) resistance to her teaching style as an "attack." She takes it quite personally (reflecting on how much she dislikes him) because her teaching style has placed enormous emphasis on power. Her ego must have been bruised indeed by Jack's statement that she had been "boring" as a teacher.

The Lesson of the Rebellion

Possibly the most salient lesson is that a discussion teacher should carefully attune his or her approach to the constituency in question. Students should have a say in how they are going to be taught. Bea might have actually devoted some class time to questions of format, asked the students to generate some recommendations for topics they'd like to discuss, and offered some critical readings for them to present to each other in the form of reports or discussion questions.

Bea's experience shows a pendulum swing from too much structure in the classroom to none at all. Neither is optimal for students' learning, but, as the (B) case implies, no structure is probably the less desirable alternative of the two. The best alternative, however, is a middle path. Bea had the fruits of superior skills and several years' worth of study to offer her students. She simply failed to learn from the group how she might make her offerings both palatable and accessible to their inexperience.

It is not surprising that, instead of a truly leaderless section, Bea's group simply exchanged their assigned teacher for an informal leader: Jack. Jack had a somewhat exhibitionistic element to his personality: he was a performer and, at this point in his life, manipulator of authority in the system in which he found himself. The classroom struggle between him and Bea included an element of pure competition. She liked the limelight, and so did he. Given that Bea possessed the natural advantage of superior preparation and expertise, it is not surprising that after a period of floundering the students voted Bea back into authority. Jack didn't devote any more time than Bea had to finding out what his fellow students wanted from the discussion process. The lesson of rebellion is, all too often, that one tyrant simply replaces another.

Apparently Bea did modify her style to allow for more freedom for the students. One gathers this from Bea's remark that Skip later in the semester actually took her up on her invitation to interrupt her when she slipped into lecturing instead of leading a discussion. This shows that Bea learned by her experience.

Underlying Issues

Authority. Simply by virtue of position, any teacher enters a class with authority. By standing to teach seated students, or otherwise taking stances that reinforce the idea of superiority over the group, the teacher is simply gilding the lily and acting defensively. Defensiveness, in turn, tends to engender a certain edginess in students that can turn to sullenness or even open rebellion, as in this case. When this happens, issues of power in the classroom come to the fore and the teacher can only lose face, either by forcing the issue and remaining, uncomfortably, in control, or -- like Bea -- being (albeit temporarily) dethroned.

Operationally, the teacher should guard against (1) cutting off students' comments, (2) answering his or her own questions in lengthy introductions before students have a chance to speak, and (3) signaling (by boardwork or otherwise) a rigid agenda for a supposedly free discussion. Informal meetings with students early in the semester might provide the teacher with clues to the group's social organization and help the teacher identify, for example, the group's natural leaders, "troublemakers," and middle-of-the roaders. Finally, the teacher would profit by bearing in mind, quite explicitly, that the best technique for leading a discussion is asking provocative, open-ended questions that will trigger the students' creative responses to the material. The object of the exercise is getting students to learn. Simply demonstrating one's own intense interest in, and mastery of, a subject will not accomplish this end.

Role change. Bea demonstrates the confusion of role that is a common trait of inexperienced teachers, particularly those who have not yet (or only recently) completed their own studies. She behaves too much like a student in the classroom, answering her own questions, competing with her students, and depriving them of a chance to participate fully. This failure to appreciate her true role -- that of teacher, not fellow-student -- shortchanges her students, who look to her to help them learn Shakespeare, rather than flaunt her own knowledge. Many of Jack's criticisms of Bea underscore these failures of hers.

Contract. Bea seems to have given no thought to the expectations that her competitive behavior, studentlike dress (jeans, track shoes, very casual hair style), and the setting (directly beside the students' recreational area) imply, namely, that the members of the section will treat her like a fellow student. In a sense, she has brought herself from a position of potential authority down to their level by behaving like one of them. Thus, her attempts to exert power over the students have confused and annoyed them. To unbend further from her position of equality would mean lowering herself to a status inferior to theirs, and this is what does happen when Jack "dethrones" her. A new contract is forged, under the terms of which Bea may not even participate in the section she has been hired to lead. She should have given some attention to the sort of behavior she wanted to elicit from her students, and then worked out strategies to help gain her ends.

Henry Jasper

Teaching Note

This case describes the predicament of a graduate student facing her first teaching experience -- focusing attention on the critical issue of the teacher-student "learning contract." This working agreement comprises both formal, explicit elements and informal elements that are partly or completely implicit. For example, it includes the spoken and unspoken academic rules of the institution; the formal procedures set up by the instructor for student preparation, participation, and evaluation; the informal norms that guide behavior of instructor and students; and students' expectations as to the educational results of the course.

The learning contract evolves over the course of the semester and is negotiated both overtly and covertly between instructor and students. The contract profoundly shapes the learning that occurs.

In our alternative seminar outline, "Henry Jasper" is usually preceded by "Bill Curtis" and followed by "Ernie Budding." These cases all address questions about learning contracts. The "Bill Curtis" case deals with the problem of establishing instantaneous rapport and a quick working relationship with a section of students. In contrast, "Henry Jasper" explores how a learning contract becomes set over the course of a semester. In particular, it highlights the degree to which such contracts are negotiated and established outside the awareness of the participants. And it points up some dangers for the instructor who remains unconscious of the contract he or she is setting with the students. In the "Ernie Budding" case, we take a closer look at the kinds of contracts an instructor can make with a section, examining a situation in which an instructor consciously chooses to change the contract as his goals for the section change.

Other important themes that emerge from "Henry Jasper" are (1) the problems that may occur when a learning contract is inadvertently violated by the instructor, (2) the problems of moving from being a student to being a teacher, and (3) some ways in which the instructor can begin to read the often subtle signals given by a section and by individual students about their hopes and fears, their strengths and weaknesses.

Case Summary

The case summary in longer cases such as "Henry Jasper" provides a focused outline of key constraints or dimensions of the situation described in the case. Few supporting details from the case text are listed. The seminar leader needs to examine the case text and note supporting evidence; discussion of the case will provide an opportunity for participants to identify many of these details and to note their significance.

The Institutional Context

The "Henry Jasper" case takes place in an undergraduate statistics course at Northern University, a selective Ivy League university with 1,200 undergraduates and 3,000 graduate students. Northern does not feature case method teaching.

The Course

Most of the students in this statistics course are not quantitatively oriented, and are taking the course only to fulfill the requirements of their majors. It has large lectures three times per week (during which many students read the college paper or sleep!) and weekly section meetings in which problem sets are worked. Because these problem sets provide direct preparation for the examination questions, students attend section meetings regularly.

The Instructor

A young woman barely older than her students, Carol Cutler is inexperienced as a

This teaching note was prepared by Dr. James F. Moore in collaboration with Professor C. Roland Christensen as an aid to instructors in the classroom use of the case series "Henry Jasper" (A) 9–378–036 and (B) 9–378–037.

teacher and not very familiar with the quantitative material in the course. She is finding both the process and substantive content of the course difficult to manage. She has taken the teaching position primarily because it is a requirement of her financial aid package.

The Section

The section consists of 24 sophomore students, including 20 women mostly majoring in human ecology. There are 4 men in the class. One of them, Henry Jasper, stands out from the beginning because of his atypically neat and unstylish dress, his isolation from the other students, and his anxiety about the course, as expressed in weekly visits to Carol Cutler during her office hours. Unlike others in the section, Henry is majoring in industrial relations.

The Teacher-Student Relationship

Carol Cutler aims for an emotionally supportive style of teaching. She believes that most of the students are suffering from various degrees of math anxiety, and that the way to help them is to be "as cheerful and supportive as possible."

Carol does not challenge her students intellectually during the section meetings. When she does a demonstration problem, she asks for a volunteer to work the example, and if none is forthcoming she herself does the calculation on the board.

Carol provides many hours of individual conference time each week, and devotes a great deal of her time during section meetings to individual coaching.

The Incident

The focal incident of this case occurs in the middle of the term. Carol Cutler begins a section meeting by summarizing the major points covered by Professor Wilbar that week in lecture, and then presents what she perceives as a simple problem. As usual, she asks, "Can anyone get us started on solving this?" No one volunteers. "Well, Henry," she says, "why don't you give it a try?"

Henry Jasper at first just stares at her, and then replies "in a loud, agitated, violent way" (as she described it):

Look, I'm sick of you women teachers always picking on me. I'm not going to take it any more. You women are always trying to castrate me. That's just it, you're trying to

castrate me and it's been that way since I was in elementary school. Well, you're not going to get away with it now. Professor Wilbar is going to hear what you're trying to do to me. I'm not going to let you women try to castrate me any more. You'll be sorry!

Henry then remains standing by Carol's desk. She looks at him, then at the class, then back to him, frantically wondering, "What's going on? What do I do?"

Study and Discussion Questions

Two sets of questions are usually prepared for use with each case. These questions focus participants' thinking, and are used as guides for discussion. Study questions can be handed out with the case, for use in preparing for class. Discussion questions are used by the instructor in preparing for the class and for guiding the case discussion when appropriate.

The instructor must decide how focused or directive the discussion questions should be. In teaching "Henry Jasper," for example, the instructor can try to focus the attention of participants on the learning contract issue by using a set of questions that raise this issue and ensure that it is explored. One could give an advance reading assignment about learning contracts, and begin the discussion by asking, "What sort of contract has Carol made with her section?"

Alternatively, the instructor can take a less directive approach. We usually like to use a somewhat more open approach, for at least two reasons. First, we want to find out what sorts of interests participants have, and what sorts of analyses the section as a whole tends to support. This is particularly important near the beginning of the seminar semester, when working with a new group. A good way to uncover the character of the section is to allow it enough freedom to demonstrate its preferences. Second, open-ended discussions give the participants a better sense of discovery. Participants (and the instructor!) tend to find these sorts of discussions much more exciting and engaging. Instructors still shape these discussions by encouraging the development of certain participant responses, while letting others drop.

Study and discussion questions for "Henry Jasper" are shown in Exhibits 1, 2 and 3. Of the two sets of discussion questions, one set is intentionally broad and open (for beginning the class), and one set is more focused, to be used (if it seems appropriate) for zeroing in on the topic of learning contracts.

For each of the two sets of discussion questions, we provide detailed teaching notes. For the broader introductory questions, the teaching notes indicate some of the predictable responses participants may make, and give discussion process suggestions for the instructor. For the topic-focused questions, the notes contain a sample analysis of the case. The major theme of this analysis is that a learning contract violation on the part of Carol Cutler is central to Henry Jasper's outburst.

A Suggested Process Plan for the Case

An Overall Plan

Using the open-focused discussion questions in Exhibit 2, our typical overall plan involves directing the discussion toward diagnosis, holding the action recommendations until the end (or omitting them entirely). The point of emphasizing diagnosis is to deepen participants' ability to appreciate and make sense of the infinite complexity of teaching situations. In addition, we wish to build the cohesiveness of the seminar group before promoting the sorts of electric clashes that often emerge in discussions that emphasize action recommendations over diagnosis.

We typically start the diagnostic discussion by asking, "What are one or two key factors that contributed to the present problem?" This question gives the participants great latitude in choosing issues to bring into the discussion, while encouraging each one to identify the items he or she believes to be most salient.

As more and more factors are introduced into the discussion, it is useful to turn the section's attention to the temporal dimension of the case by asking, "When did Carol's trouble begin?" This question helps the participants to begin putting the various factors into a sequential order and to see how some factors build on the others to amplify the problems. In addition, participants begin to appreciate how early Carol Cutler, and others in a similar spot, could begin to get help and/or make preparations that would minimize later difficulties.

As the discussion continues, the participants get a sense of the sequential

development of the problem. Then we begin to ask them to generalize from Carol's experience and examine the wider issues raised by the case. This shift can be encouraged by asking, "What questions does this case raise for you about teaching, and about your own teaching experience?" This sort of questioning helps participants to identify and think about themes that were first introduced in the "Bill Curtis" case, and will be central to the entire seminar. These themes include the need to establish a good learning contract between instructor and students, and the importance of preparation for teaching, instructor self-management, and knowing when and how to get help. Raising these wider issues also helps participants realize that Carol's problems are not unique, and enables them to relate the case discussion to their own teaching experience.

An Emphasis on Diagnosis

Thus we encourage an overall movement in the discussion from diagnosis to a consideration of time and sequentiality in the diagnosis and finally to the general issues raised by the case. Only at the close of the period do we ask participants to suggest what Carol Cutler might do.

Richard Beckhard, a noted management consultant, claims that 90% of organizational problems stem from managers' tendency to rush to action without first making an adequate diagnosis of their situations. While Beckhard's claim is probably intentionally overstated, we find it very important in the early sessions of the seminar to encourage the participants to spend a great deal of time on diagnosis. On first reading a new case, inexperienced participants often feel it is simple and transparent. Only upon rereading, and through rich discussion of alternative diagnoses, do they begin to respect the complexity of the human reality expressed in apparently simple cases. Participants are often amazed to discover the limits of their own styles and biases in understanding situations.

As part of our emphasis on diagnosis, we push students to attend to the details of the early cases. They are asked to back up their diagnoses with quotations and details from the case. When students differ on matters of interpretation, we refer the section to the case to look for clues as to what is going on. This practice sets a norm for future sessions, ensuring that discussion will be based on a close reading and rereading of the text. It also teaches students to examine again and again what seems commonplace, until they find new and deeper meaning in it. The book selection on "Louis Agassiz as a Teacher" is particularly relevant here: the great naturalist forced a new student to spend several days examining a single embalmed fish. Each day the student made new discoveries, noticing patterns that had been invisible to him during previous sessions.

The second section of the "Henry Jasper" case consists of Carol Cutler's reflections, years later, on the factors she believes contributed to the problems in her teaching and particularly with Henry Jasper. We never learn how she responded to Henry Jasper's outburst, or how their relationship developed after the incident. But we are given her rather thorough diagnosis of the situation. Thus the nature of the (B) case underscores our emphasis -- at this phase of the seminar -- on diagnosis rather than action recommendations.

Responding to Action Recommendations

During the discussion of the case, we are usually willing to entertain suggestions about action, but we try to reserve these for the last few minutes of the session. And even when accepting these suggestions, we handle them in a fashion that supports the emphasis on diagnosis. We generally accept whatever suggestions are offered, pushing the participants to make explicit the assumptions behind their suggestions, and the probable consequences (including risks) of the possible actions. We do not stimulate discussion of particular options, however, nor do we try to build toward a class consensus for action, or even a clear set of alternatives.

In later class sessions we will sometimes handle action suggestions quite differently, exaggerating differences in suggestions, pushing participants to imagine themselves in action roles, and pointing up conflicting approaches. This approach will build emotional involvement and encourage participants to plan actions and commit themselves to their chosen courses. But at this early point in the seminar, we are more interested in helping participants develop the understanding needed to choose and support a committed stance, rather than in actually making those choices.

Special Features of the Case Text

In this two-part case series, the (B) case is essentially a reflection by Carol Cutler on the events in the (A) case. It is her response, at a much later date, to the discussion question "What one or two critical factors contributed to Carol's problems?"

Handing out the (B) case early will tend to scoop the discussion. That is, participants may give too much credence to Carol's insights and not develop their own. In no sense do we, as instructors, believe that Carol's analysis is the "correct" one. It is valid and well argued, but not definitive.

Thus we tend to hold the (B) case until very late in the hour, or hand it out as a take-home piece. If it is used in class, we might ask, "How does Carol Cutler see this situation?" "Do you agree?" "Why do you think she places her emphasis where she does?"

A second important feature of the case text is that it includes interviews with almost everyone who is centrally involved except Henry Jasper. It should be emphasized, if the participants do not pick this up on their own, that we see Henry Jasper only through Carol Cutler's eyes. Thus the information we have about him is not only limited but may be distorted by being filtered through Carol Cutler's perceptions and memory.

Notes for the Open-Focused Discussion Questions

These notes parallel the suggested discussion questions presented in Exhibit 2. The notes for Question 1 are particularly extensive, because the question is broad and the resulting discussion sets the stage for the rest of the session.

1.   **What do you see as the one or two critical factors contributing to Carol Cutler's current problem?**

Usage Note

This broad question tends to elicit three general types of responses: (1) decisions and actions taken by Carol Cutler that have negative consequences; and/or decisions and actions taken by others (e.g., Henry Jasper's outburst, Barry Gerber's interruption of Carol's student conference); (2) summary statements referring at a low level of generality to such actions and consequences, such as "She is not prepared to teach the content," "She doesn't understand how to teach these students," "She is not able to read the section and/or individual students accurately enough to respond to their needs and strengths"; and (3) comments at a high level of generality about teaching issues raised by the case. For example: "She does not understand the contract she is making with the students," or "Sexism is really the root of much of her problems," or "One always has to expect that there will be difficult personalities in one's classes" -- such comments attempt to identify the root problems underlying key difficulties described in the case.

We allow the discussion to bubble for a while, as more and more features of the case are brought into the discussion and tentatively linked to previous points. We regard all three levels of response as useful to the discussion at this time, but we find it important to note (for ourselves) what sorts of comments are coming up. In general we will try to work back and forth between the three levels of analysis. For example, if a student brings up the contract issue (a comment at a very high level of generality), we may ask, "What specifics in the case support this interpretation?" or, "What actions that Carol has taken have contributed to this trouble with the contract?" On the other hand, when a series of participant comments have focused on actions and decisions that contributed to her difficulties, we might ask, "What sort of difficulty are these things leading her into?" and/or, "What is the crux of her present predicament?" Thus we work to integrate across levels of analysis.

Cases incorporate a richness of detail that mirrors real-world situations. Accordingly, their interpretation involves complex considerations, and cases can often be profitably considered from a variety of angles. Each approach is likely to show that the case is "about" different fundamental issues.

During discussions, we attend to what themes or analyses are emerging, and point out connections between comments when we can. Thus, we build bridges between apparently related ideas, highlighting shared themes.

In addition, part of the task of the instructor is to ensure that certain issues are emphasized in any particular case discussion. Only in this way can one create a coherent course of instruction centered on a systematic consideration of issues. While remaining open to participant initiatives, the discussion leader must see to it that certain preselected issues are covered adequately. In practice this requires guiding the section's approach to each case. Throughout the seminar on case method teaching, we examine ways in which such "controlled spontaneity" can be achieved.

In a discussion of "Henry Jasper," Question 1 invites participants to take a variety of approaches in diagnosing Carol's situation. We suggest that the instructor manage the ensuing discussion to emphasize several key themes, as discussed later. In addition, some students will probably be attracted to certain angles of attack that can create difficulties at this point in the course. We suggest that the instructor manage the discussion to deemphasize those themes.

Analysis

One central theme concerns the instructor-student learning contract. In particular, participants may conclude that Carol Cutler established an ineffective learning contract with her section and/or Henry Jasper. Further, they may feel that she invited trouble by subsequently violating her contract.

Students may also raise the issue of instructor preparation for teaching. They may conclude that Carol Cutler's problems stem primarily from her lack of adequate preparation for either the substantive content or the process aspects of her teaching role. Participants may describe their own understanding of adequate preparation, and point out how Carol Cutler's falls short.

A third theme is instructor self-management. In particular, Carol Cutler's attitude toward her students -- assuming that they labored under high math anxiety and required reassurance -- may have blinded her to their real needs and strengths. Participants may note that Carol's assumptions about the students seem more appropriate to her situation than to theirs, and may be the result of projection on her part. This raises the issue of how instructors can become aware of and manage their anxieties, and, more generally, how they can stay aware of and manage their attitudes toward the students.

Participants may mention the instructor's need to read cues given by students and the section as a whole -- to discover who they are, what they are experiencing during the discussions, and what their attitudes and intentions are toward the instructor and the learning process in the class.

In "Bill Curtis," a relatively fast reading must be made of the Miller Scholar and the class. In "Henry Jasper," Carol Cutler has much more time to observe and interact with Henry and the rest of the section members, and the questions raised by Henry's behavior are much more involved than simply determining (as in "Bill Curtis") the momentary motives of a student. Carol must assess Henry's potential to master the course material and to handle the social demands of speaking in class; she must also judge whether he has emotional or psychological problems severe enough that she should seek help in dealing with him.

How can such judgments be skillfully made? Participants may want to discuss what data are available to instructors seeking insight into a section and individual students. They may also want to explore what sorts of inferences are necessary and appropriate to teaching (e.g., psycho-diagnosis may not be appropriate, but it may be important to monitor how capable a student is of meeting the demands of the course). In addition, they may want to discuss how the instructor can use outside-of-class sources to supplement observations and to check hypotheses (e.g., one can sometimes discreetly speak to a member of the class to gain further information; one can speak directly to the student or students in question, and so forth).

The case also raises issues about how to get assistance when teaching. Both Bill Curtis and Carol Cutler might have gotten more help, both while preparing for teaching and during their actual teaching time. Instructors need to learn when and how to ask for help -- from other colleagues, their superiors, and the students themselves -- and how to manage the process of being helped.

Though we tend to play down this issue, the case can lead to some consideration of how to handle a surprising outburst in class. Participants sometimes will point out that issues of control, including self-management and self-control, are indeed central in responding to surprises. How the instructor follows up on the incident can be as important or even more important than how he or she responds immediately. Follow-up is particularly important as a way of reestablishing rapport and a learning contract with the section.

Two discussion themes inherent in the case data are difficult to handle productively at this stage in the life of the seminar. Some guidance from the instructor will probably be needed to prevent the discussion from dwelling on these themes to the detriment of other issues raised by the case.

The first such issue is the psycho-diagnosis of Henry Jasper. As discussed further later on, the case does not include enough data to support a valid psychodiagnosis. Still, a focus on this theme is encouraged by the title of the case ("Henry Jasper," not "Carol Cutler") and by the content of Henry's outburst.

To minimize discussion of this theme, we generally just discourage comments along this line as they come up. For example, when students begin to speculate on Henry's psychological problems, the instructor can warn against "putting him on the couch." We can divert attention from the psychological analysis by emphasizing Carol Cutler's problems (also the problems that arise well before the incident) and by amplifying comments about the situational factors that might have been responsible for Henry Jasper's outburst.

An alternative way to manage discussion of this theme is to encourage participants to begin with a consideration of Henry Jasper and his alleged psychological and social problems. In this way the section gets it out of its system; at the same time, the instructor can help participants recognize the limits of the data. He or she can, for example, ask humorously if there is enough evidence here to commit Henry Jasper, or to make a treatment plan. After this theme has been thoroughly examined, the instructor can encourage the participants to switch to a situational approach by asking, "What else might be going on here?" "What are Carol Cutler's contributions to this situation?" From this point the discussion can be handled as outlined above.

A second problematic theme is that of sexism and gender-based conflict. The case is organized around Carol's problems with men in her teaching life, as reported by Carol. All of the problems mentioned involve men -- the incident with the jocks, Barry Gerber's interruption of her student conference, and the situation with Henry Jasper. Carol's own analysis, in the (B) case, suggests that a central problem was sexism and gender-based conflict which created difficulties in communication control of male students. Thus this case could be used to examine the influence of sexual stereotyping and gender-based conflict in teaching. This is a very important theme, particularly as the number of female university faculty members increases. We encourage discussion of this theme later in the semester.

In the present case, however, we deemphasize this issue for several reasons. First and foremost, it is a powerful and attractive theme, once it becomes established in a discussion. As such it can easily distract from the issues of contracting and preparation which we believe need to be covered early in the seminar. We have built later units on the assumption that this matter will have been explored early.

Second, the theme of sexism and gender-based conflict can be very difficult and divisive, especially this early in the life of the seminar. Opinions run strong, and the group can quickly break apart into hostile camps. In a few years, these issues may be easier to discuss. But at this point in our society's history -- 1986 -- they are difficult.

Our approach to this problem is to try to get the discussion centered on the matter of contracts before the question of sexism is raised. Then when the issue is introduced, it can be seen as one of a variety of problems that can interfere with the establishment of a productive learning contract. One way to encourage the early development of the contract theme is to pick lead-off discussants who are likely to be more sensitive to the contract issues and less to the gender-based issues. In practice this means that we tend to open this particular case discussion by calling on two men. In addition, using our license as instructors, we amplify comments and build bridges between comments in a way that encourages a central focus on the issue of establishing learning contracts.

2. **When did the problem begin? What decisions or actions did Carol take before the day of the blowup that may have contributed to Henry Jasper's outburst?**

Usage Note

This question introduces a temporal dimension into the discussion. Participants should be encouraged to develop a sequential list of Carol's key decisions and actions and then to note how (1) some mistakes kept building on others, thus compounding her predicament, and (2) early on she missed opportunities to prepare for her role and to get assistance and support.

To help participants develop a list, the instructor can ask someone in the section to array Carol's mistakes in a time sequence.

Or alternatively, as her decisions and actions are mentioned, the instructor can record them on a chalkboard, listing them in approximate time sequence. Either approach gives participants a list to work from.

Once the list is developed, the instructor can ask participants, "How did Carol's later problems build on earlier decisions and actions?" To shift the focus to missed opportunities, one can ask, "What might she have done, early on, in order to reduce her later difficulties?"

Analysis

Carol's early mistakes include spending the summer in Europe and arriving at Northern just before classes, when she might have been better off visiting Northern and perhaps getting moved in and acclimated during the summer months. She also did not contact Professor Wilbar in advance, either to get a copy of the course text and other materials, or to tell him about her own background deficiencies and attempt to work out a plan for preparation and/or support during the term.

In addition, she did not think through (and discuss with others more experienced) the process of teaching the course. She might have reflected upon at least (1) the general pedagogical plan underlying the course design, (2) the range of abilities of the students -- and how to check out students' abilities individually and respond to each one's different needs, (3) her own attitude toward the course content and toward the students, and how this might influence the teaching-learning relationship, and (4) ways to get ongoing feedback and support for her teaching during the term -- for example, by having another teaching assistant sit in on her section and tell her what sort of implicit contract she seemed to be establishing with students.

3. **Why didn't Carol Cutler see these circumstances developing? Why did she have such a difficult time in her first semester?**

Usage Note

These questions (which we tend to use together and/or interchangeably) shift attention from Carol's decisions and actions (and their consequences) to her overall situation. This shift in focus can make seminar participants more sympathetic to Carol. At the same time it helps them see how they themselves might get into a similar situation, or might even have been in one.

Analysis

Participants tend to note that Carol is having difficulty making the transition to being a graduate student, particularly since she must also shift from a student to an instructor role. They also note that Carol is not prepared; she does not understand the requirements of her new task (in fact, she probably does not realize the extent to which she is not prepared); and she has not developed adequate means of ongoing support and feedback.

4. **What is your appraisal of Henry Jasper's outburst? a) What do we know about Henry (details, clues, etc.)? Of what significance could these observations have been to Carol Cutler? b) Why did Henry Jasper feel wronged? Why the intensity of his attack?**

Usage Note

This question introduces the complexities of reading a section and/or individual students. In general, the instructor needs to press participants to identify the inferences they are making about Henry Jasper, and to support them with material from the case text. In addition, participants can be asked how much confidence they have in their inferences -- based on their limited knowledge. And building on this point, the instructor can ask participants how they might get more information about Henry Jasper -- and thus check their inferences -- if they were in Carol Cutler's shoes.

Analysis

Carol has missed opportunities to read Henry Jasper. She could have noticed that he is probably a loner, perhaps with limited social skills, and that he is apparently seeking to establish a special contract with her through such actions as sitting especially near her desk and meeting regularly with her during office hours. Further, he is particularly anxious about his performance in the course (probably in part because he has been informed by the registrar that he must pass the course to get his degree, and perhaps in part because of other factors unknown to Carol), and seeks continual reassurance from his teacher.

If these observations had been read as danger signals, Carol might have (1) examined more carefully than usual her contract

with Henry, (2) tried to renegotiate it, while being careful not to violate it inadvertently, and/or (3) sought the help of Professor Wilbar and/or some other university resource person (perhaps a student counselor) to evaluate the situation with Henry and to explore further action.

It is also important to note that we _cannot_ reliably read about Henry Jasper. The case text does not include enough information to permit a psychological diagnosis of Henry, nor do most participants in the seminar have training that would enable them to make such a diagnosis even if more data were available. Thus they can be led to realize that an instructor in Carol's position need not (and probably should not) try to psychodiagnose his or her students.

On the other hand, instructors do need to be able to diagnose the contracts they are making with the student, and to recognize when difficulties in establishing a learning contract indicate that outside assistance might be helpful. Such difficulties may indicate that the instructor could benefit from feedback and suggestions on contracting, or that the student could benefit from counseling or other assistance.

5. **What questions does this incident pose for you as a discussion instructor?**

Usage Note

This question lifts the discussion to a higher level of generality, and lets participants examine themes and issues raised by the case. A supplementary question we often ask is "Have any of you ever had a similar experience? Would you be willing to tell us about it?" This question can also be asked in a way that focuses on the more general issues in the case -- for example, "Have any of you recently made the transition from graduate student to instructor? What was it like for you?" In either case the instructor needs to (1) listen and support the participant in sharing this bit of personal history -- especially as this sort of sharing can be risky for participants early in the seminar, and (2) help identify issues that are common to both the participant's and Carol Cutler's situations. One can ask, "How is this [the participant's] situation similar to that experienced by Carol Cutler?" "Is there a common issue or even common set of dilemmas raised by these two situations?"

At this point the instructor may decide to highlight and develop the learning contract theme -- perhaps even using the discussion questions presented in Exhibit 3.

But the case also raises many other important educational issues, and it is not necessary to focus narrowly on the contract issue. It can be of great value for the participants just to begin identifying broad teaching/learning issues and relating them to their own experience.

6.   What can Carol do now?   In the class? After the class?

Usage Note

We try to defer suggestions for action until the last few minutes of the session. Often there is not enough time left to discuss action recommendations -- and from our perspective, which emphasizes diagnosis in this case, that is not a problem.

When participants present action suggestions, we handle them in a fashion that supports the emphasis on diagnosis. We recommend accepting whatever suggestions are offered, pushing the participants to make explicit the assumptions behind their suggestions, and the probable consequences (including risks) of the actions. As noted earlier, however, we do not encourage discussion of particular recommendations, nor do we try to get the section to come to a consensus on a course of action.

Analysis

In considering action recommendations, a number of factors need to be taken into account. One must somehow (1) get Henry to sit down, (2) take charge of the section, (3) develop a continuing learning contract with the section during the rest of the hour -- and the semester, and (4) choose how to deal with Henry.

A *Special Note on the Use of the (B) Case*

The (B) case is often handed out at this time. Usually, it is not discussed, but is given to participants at the close of the period, with this comment: "You might find it interesting to think further about this case. This (B) case includes Carol Cutler's thoughts, written a number of years after the events we have been discussing."

As we have noted, the (B) case centers on diagnosis, and raises both the contract issue and the sexism issue. Participants often find it interesting to compare their thoughts on the case with those of Carol Cutler. However, as instructors we make clear that Carol Cutler's analysis is not in any sense the "official" or

last word on the matter. Handing the (B) segment out after the seminar discussion helps ensure that participants will keep Carol's remarks in perspective.

Notes for Topic-Focused Questions

In the following pages we present a sample analysis of the case, based on the premise that Henry Jasper's outburst, while resulting from a confluence of several factors, is primarily a response to Carol's violation of her learning contract with him. These notes parallel the discussion questions presented in <u>Exhibit 3</u>. The questions are all used to focus discussion closely on the contract issue, and thus we have not included separate usage notes here.

1.   What was Carol Cutler's contract with her section?

A contract has been established between Carol Cutler and her students. Some of the expectations that constitute this contract are formal and explicit -- for example: the testing and grading procedures, the assigned hours of the section meetings, and the problem sets to be solved at each meeting. Many of the expectations encompassed in the learning contract, however, are informal and implicit. The most important of these have to do with the ratio of support to challenge that Carol provides, and the nature of her support.

The case text indicates that Carol gives students a great deal of substantive and emotional support, and a modest amount of academic and intellectual challenge. For example, when presenting the section with sample problems to solve, Carol asks, "Can anyone suggest any way to solve this problem?" And she reports that "if no one raises his hand, I go ahead and work it out myself, explaining while I do it." When students consistently have difficulty with the problem sets, she attaches a note to their papers suggesting they "stop by my office and we'll try to clear this up once and for all."

Much section time is spent clearing up the mistakes of the students rather than breaking new ground. As Carol writes, "Often the individual discussions in the lab are as much about the mistakes of the prior week as they are about the problems of the current week." Thus in her actions she takes over much of the responsibility for correcting students' mistakes and helping them keep up the pace of learning. Another instructor might use section time primarily to clarify new material and challenge the students to master it.

Carol believes the students need a great deal of emotional support, especially in the form of gentle encouragement. She writes that in the section, "I try to be enthusiastic and supportive because I know so many are overly anxious about the math." She schedules six hours of student conference time each week (a relatively large amount) and some students come every week. Some of these weekly visitors are top students seeking to fine-tune their work. But many others appear to come for emotional support -- or at least that is how Carol Cutler perceives them and appears to respond to them. She writes, "I think that they're frightened by the very idea of a Stat course and in some ways have a mental block against it. . . ."

An important constant in Carol's behavior is that she does not put students on the spot publicly. She does not ask students to solve problems for the class as a whole unless they volunteer. And she writes that during the individual working time of the section, "I wander around the lab so that people can stop me and show me their problems if they need help." Thus students need not even raise their hands or otherwise acknowledge publicly that they require help; if they just wait, she will come to them.

2.   Did Carol Cutler have a special contract with Henry Jasper? If so, what was it?

A special contract has evolved between Carol and Henry Jasper. In many ways, it is an amplified version of the contract she established with the other students. Carol not only provides Henry with substantive help in working out the difficult problems; she checks his homework so closely that she finds and corrects simple arithmetic errors.

He meets with her weekly and though she does her best to be reassuring, as the semester goes on he still says he feels insecure about his ability to master the material. And she continues to be as reassuring as possible, stopping only just short of guaranteeing him a passing grade.

We find no evidence that Carol Cutler regularly calls on Henry or asks him to speak in front of the class. On the contrary, we are told that Henry sits very near her desk, and when he has questions during the study period he can simply turn to her and ask them. Thus he need not even raise his hand or wait for her to come by his desk in order to get help.

3.   What do we know about Carol Cutler's actions on the day of the outburst? How might her actions have contributed to the outburst?

On the day of the outburst Carol starts the class in her usual way, by asking if anyone can "get us started on solving" a sample problem. No one volunteers. At this point she departs from her usual practice of working the problem for the class, and instead calls on Henry Jasper, saying, "Well, Henry, why don't you give it a try?"

This action violates Carol's contract with the class. By "cold calling" a student when no one has volunteered, she has moved from a supportive to a challenging style of teaching, and she has put a student publicly on the spot. One would expect such a shift to be unnerving for class members, and to put anyone called upon under a great deal of unanticipated pressure.

By calling on Henry, Carol also has violated her implicit contract with him, which includes more emotional support and a special sensitivity to his needs. Thus he can be expected to feel a sense of personal betrayal as Carol asks him to do something he probably perceives as beyond his abilities and beyond what has been demanded in the past of other members of the section.

Especially since Henry seems to have little rapport with the other members of the section, it seems clear that he will be placed under overwhelming stress. In fact, he not only defies the challenge but angrily expresses his sense of betrayal. While his language is strong and includes accusations of castration, generalization to other females, and a threat to go to Professor Wilbar, it is perhaps understandable when seen as a desperately angry outburst, and not the considered reflections of a more peaceful moment.

4.   Are personality factors, or situational factors, central to Carol's predicament?

At first reading, this case appears to be mainly about dealing with a student with emotional problems -- and in particular how to deal with this student when he, apparently without warning or cause, blows up in class. Such an interpretation is encouraged by the dramatic design of the case; it also follows naturally from the way in which most untrained observers attribute causality in social situations. That is, most people tend to attribute individuals' actions to features of their personalities and to under-rate situational influences.[1] Thus we might expect case readers to overlook the situational factors initially.

Perhaps because we have developed our approach at a school that has a long history of emphasizing the analysis of situations, we believe that the psychological interpretation of this event is not the most useful one. While there are definite indications in the case material that Henry Jasper is not a typical student -- and we believe a skilled instructor should be able to read and respond to these signals -- we do not believe so-called personality variables adequately explain what happened. And we do believe there is ample evidence in the case of situational factors, under the control of Carol Cutler, that could provoke such an outburst.

First of all, closer examination of the case material reveals very little data on which to base a psychological analysis of Henry Jasper. We have no direct comments from Henry on his experience of the section and/or the outburst; we know nothing of his personal history; nor do we know about his behavior out of class. We do know that he does not dress and act like a typical Northern student, and does not mix well with the others in the section. And it is clear that he is frightened about his ability to master the course, and comes to Carol Cutler unusually often for assistance and reassurance.

But all of this is well within the range of normal behavior. Colleges are full of shy, somewhat unstylish students. And many students are frightened of math courses. Further, Carol is extremely reassuring, and encourages Henry to come back to her by responding consistently and without confrontation to his requests for support. Henry is merely a sophomore, and it is quite possible that he is simply not aware that his behavior is atypical. And he is given no signals from Carol Cutler that would tell him differently.

In teaching this case to seminars including psychiatrists and clinical psychologists, we have noted that such professionals are particularly reluctant to jump to a diagnosis of Henry based on the data given. In general, they tend to see Henry Jasper as a young man, probably not socially adept, who has been caught in an embarrassing and humiliating spot and is reacting angrily in a way that is normal and understandable under the circumstances.

Second, the case text provides considerable evidence that Henry Jasper's outburst is a broadly predictable response to a situation that Carol Cutler has in part created, and could perhaps have avoided or ameliorated.

We prefer to focus the analysis of the case on the nature of Carol Cutler's learning contract with her section members, and especially with Henry Jasper. The text includes a great deal of information about Carol Cutler and her way of understanding and working with the section members. We have direct statements of her perceptions of the overall teaching situation that semester, her ongoing interaction with Henry Jasper, and her experience of the flare-up. Her preparation for teaching the section is also described, as well as her attempts to gain assistance both before and during the semester. We also have Barry Gerber's observations of her general appearance and personal presence, and her interactions in conferences with students in her section.

On the basis of the information given in the text, we believe that the outburst can be explained largely in terms of situational factors within the control of the instructor -- that is, Henry's outburst is a direct result of Carol's violation of her learning contract with the section, and especially with him. This explanation also makes it possible to identify a variety of factors that may have led up to the problem with the learning contract, and to suggest ways in which instructors can avoid similar problems.

Suggestions for Building the Seminar Group

This case is generally used in the second or third meeting of the seminar, and thus our section-building aims are different from those of the first meeting. Then our primary goal was to get all section members involved in the discussion, setting a norm of participation and allowing us to learn as much as possible about the individuals and the chemistry of the group. In addition, we modeled good listening skills in order to encourage participants to pay attention to their listening practice, to sharpen up our own ability to listen, and simply to hear what the group had to say. We used our responses to encourage participation and to convey an appreciation of the diversity

1. Walter Mischel, "Continuity and Change in Personality." *American Psychologist,* 24 (1969):1012–1018.

and richness of experience that our participants brought to the seminar through their comments.

In the second session we try to refine the behavioral norms guiding discussion. We want to move from simply encouraging participation to encouraging students to respect and take note of each other in the discussion process. We work toward this goal in several ways. For one thing, we encourage the use of participants' names. When a student refers to another by using a pronoun (e.g., "What she said . . ."), we may make a correction by responding with the participant's name (e.g., "Yes, what Jane said . . .").

We also use our authority as instructors to insist upon courtesy, when necessary. In addition, we begin at this point to look for ways to involve students who are hanging back; this may mean ignoring the more aggressive participants in order to create space for quieter members to join in.

In addition, we begin what we call "praising the process" of the section. That is, rather than praising (or condemning) individual contributions, we focus attention on the evolving learning dynamic in the entire section. When a particularly good interchange or whole section meeting occurs, we bring that to the attention of the group. This rewards and reinforces discussion-building behavior on the part of the participants, and counters excessive competition between individuals. In addition, it begins to build the participants' ability to monitor and evaluate learning section dynamics -- which of course is our overall objective for the seminar.

Finally, we continue to emphasize diagnosis in order to get the students to look deeper into the case material, as well as to build group cohesiveness, before launching into discussion of action -- which can be more divisive.

Exhibit 1

Henry Jasper

Study Questions

1.   How did Carol Cutler end up in this situation? What is going on here?

2.   What are the most important factors that contributed to her predicament? When did her problem begin?

3.   What can we learn from this case about the problems confronting a new instructor? Any instructor?

4.   What can Carol Cutler do now? What would be your goals for her right now? How might she achieve them?

Exhibit 2

Henry Jasper

Open-Focused Discussion Questions

1.   Can you help our seminar group understand Carol Cutler's situation? What do you see as the one or two critical factors contributing to her current problem?

Or, (somewhat more provocatively): How did Carol Cutler get into such a mess? (She obviously had the best of intentions; she worked hard; and she tried to improve her work and be helpful to the students.)

2.   When did the problem begin? What decisions or actions did Carol take before the day of the blowup that may have contributed to Henry Jasper's outburst?

Or, (more provocatively): What was her first mistake?

3.   We suggest that one or both of the following questions be used:

a)   Why didn't Carol Cutler see these circumstances developing?

b)   Why did she have such a difficult time in her first semester?

4.   What is your appraisal of Henry Jasper's outburst?

a)   What do we know about Henry (details, clues, and so on)? Of what significance could these observations have been to Carol Cutler?

b)   Why did Henry Jasper feel wronged? Why the intensity of his attack?

5.   What questions does this incident pose for you as a discussion instructor?

6. What can Carol do now? In the class? After the class?

Exhibit 3

Henry Jasper

Topic-Focused Discussion Questions

1. What was Carol Cutler's contract with her section?

2. Did Carol Cutler have a special contract with Henry Jasper? If so, what was it?

3. What do we know about Carol Cutler's actions on the day of the outburst?

How might her actions have contributed to the outburst?

4. Are personality factors, or situational factors, central to Carol's predicament? (By focusing on Carol's action, we create an analysis of the case that emphasizes the situation or context around Henry as the chief cause of this outburst. If we focus instead on Henry Jasper and ignore the context, we tend to create an analysis that emphasizes his personality -- and possible psychological problems -- as the chief cause of his outburst. Which sort of analysis do you tend to favor? What are the limitations of each? Is there a way to bring both types of analyses to bear on this problem? What would this suggest for teaching practice?)

The Handicapped Heckler

Teaching Note

Special Features

"The Handicapped Heckler" presents arresting details that should engage participants' emotions and create a lively, committed discussion. The central student character, Frank Edgerton, is a paraplegic. His instructor, Paula Wilson, labors under manifest stress -- a crumbling marriage, too little time to prepare the course, an unfamiliar environment. And, finally, the administrator to whom Paula turns for advice is blind. All of these elements are unique to this situation, but their specificity should not obscure the universals that power this case. The teacher pities Frank, but she is reluctant to rebuke him for his unacceptable behavior, not only because she does not want to hurt him, but also because she wishes to avoid the unpleasantness of a confrontation -- a familiar human urge that often creates more problems than it prevents. Frank is dramatically disabled, but bitterness, cynicism, and the need to attract attention by disruption sometimes appear in students with no visible handicaps (disabilities can be psychological, too). Finally, although the advisor in the Office for Disabled Students is blind, her suggestion to confront Frank and try to control his rudeness would have been valid no matter who had given it.

In short, despite the unusual elements of this case, it boils down to a challenge to a well-intentioned teacher to balance one student's needs against those of the rest of the class -- and her own needs as well. A central problem in this case is the need to establish trust and maintain consideration for all in a discussion class.

Mood

This is a rather difficult case because it includes distressing images -- like the pictures of the crippled former athlete in his wheelchair and the blind woman with her seeing-eye dog. Discussion participants may identify with some of their pain, or perhaps feel kinship to the frustration of the beleaguered teacher. Some may recognize or even share the bitterness of the disabled student or feel fellowship with the courageous blind advisor. To prevent the seminar from becoming overly depressing, the discussion leader might underline participants' comments that highlight the universals that underlie these details.

Suggested Uses

This case discussion should broach the infinitely complex question of responsibility. On the face of things, Frank Edgerton is an obvious victim. He needs protection. But of what sort? What must Paula Wilson do to help him? These questions will probably find several evolving answers during the discussion. Perhaps what Frank needs most from Paula is something to trigger _self_-discipline. She must modify his behavior in the hope that he will eventually control himself.

This issue -- call it discipline -- may take a fair amount of class time to explore, and its implications should be investigated as thoroughly as possible.

One practical problem for the instructor will be to fit this complex discussion into the allotted time. If the case is to be used in an earlier section of a syllabus, when the issues are largely action-oriented and less philosophical because the participants haven't built up a bank of experiences with teaching cases, then it will probably be advisable to spend more time on the (A) and (B) cases, leaving the (C) case and its reflections for a brief ending section, suggesting that the participants ponder Paula's conclusions on their own.

If, on the other hand, the case is going to be discussed relatively late in a course, when the participants have experience and expertise at seeing complex implications, the discussion leader might reverse the emphasis and try to stimulate a

This teaching note has been prepared as an aid to instructors in classroom use of the case series "The Handicapped Heckler" (A) 9-384-192, (B) 9-384-193, and (C) 9-384-194.

thorough discussion based on the lessons of the whole unfolding situation, with special emphasis upon the implications inherent in the (C) case. What <u>should</u> Paula have learned from this experience?

Conflicts, Sensitivities

Needless to say, if there should be a handicapped person in the seminar, the leader will have to use special tact in preparing and directing the discussion. Should the handicapped person be singled out and asked to provide special insights into Frank Edgerton's point of view? Perhaps contacting that participant in advance with a direct inquiry would be advisable. If this is not possible, the discussion leader will have to "read" the handicapped person's reactions with care and sensitivity during the discussion. Is the participant, like Frank Edgerton, bitter? Does he or she interrupt or try to dominate in an unhealthy way? If so, the discussion leader, like Paula Wilson, should treat the student with polite but brisk firmness, making it clear that this case, like any other, is for everyone. If, on the other hand, this material embarrasses the participant, the discussion leader should attempt to protect him or her by stressing those comments that make it clear that the handicapped student in the case has genuine rights as well as responsibilities, and that any teacher dealing with such a student must make a special effort to find the best way to help that person grow and adapt. The object is to project benevolence without condescension -- not an easy task!

Teaching Objectives

This case presents an unusually dramatic opportunity to guide teachers who have focused largely on their own needs and professional goals to empathize with their students. It also offers the chance to expose and complicate a few facile stereotypes of educational interaction. What is the best way to offer genuine assistance to a student who inspires (but may not want) pity? What is the difference between sympathy and pity? In various guises, the unusually demanding student who destroys a discussion class's delicate rapport, pops up often in the career of almost every teacher.

As always, this case discussion will benefit from the wider references and personal experiences of the participants. The leader should, however, take care to probe for the basic issues behind these incidents in their pasts. What did the participants learn, in the long run? What

further and, perhaps, different lessons might the other participants have drawn?

The "Blocks" of Analysis

It is always useful to begin with the separate characters in a case and examine the constraints within which they must work and the goals they may hope to achieve. What can Paula lose, or gain, here? What about Frank? What about the rest of the class? What is inescapable in their situation? What can be changed?

1) First and foremost, Frank Edgerton's handicap and its implications must be considered. Why is he there? What can he gain from going to college? Without dwelling overly long on a painful subject, one must ask, "How might Frank feel?" 2) The teacher's <u>responsibility</u> to Frank follows naturally from the consideration of the first topic. 3) Having tagged responsibility as an issue, one should push this issue further: What is Paula's responsibility to the rest of the class? What is her responsibility <u>to herself</u>? 5) Some inescapable elements in this situation are the physical setup of the university and the classroom. What can Paula do about the noise, and the ugliness? How do they affect her efforts to run a discussion group whose subject is poetry? 6) The organizational environment seems equally inimical. Paula is one of forty full-time members in a department that serves many hundreds of students annually. How can such a situation promote understanding?

Preparing for the Discussion

Opening Speaker; Backstop

This choice will depend more on where in the syllabus one places this case than on any obvious intrinsic qualities of the participants. The teacher is female; the problem student, male. This might determine some of the selection of opening speaker and backstop. As noted earlier, if a handicapped participant happens to be in the group, the discussion leader will have to judge carefully whether to single that participant out as an "expert."

The Discussion Questions

After the (A) case has been read, the following questions can be addressed:

1. [To the opening speaker]: Would you start us off on an analysis of the critical elements in the situation facing Paula Wilson?

This question requires a selection of the critical elements. Are these environmental (impersonal school, cumbersome administration, depressing physical facilities), or do they stem from the personalities and situations of the involved participants? (Both aspects merit consideration, but the opening speaker is likely to emphasize one variety of constraint over the other.) Attention is likely to focus quite quickly on Frank Edgerton. What sort of difficulty does he really present? The hard-nosed view of Frank might be to consider him merely as a discipline problem (which he is). Whatever his reasons, he behaves abominably. He must mend his ways or leave. Others -- most participants, probably -- will find it difficult to be tough on Frank. His plight is too pitiful. Why add to his pain by rebuking or rejecting him? He has special needs. In a way, his disability protects him: many would allow him a certain freedom to misbehave because he is suffering. But is this right? Should a miserable person be allowed to make others' lives less comfortable? The discussion should pay attention to these points.

One would hope that the first speaker would draw the seminar's attention to Frank. With luck, he or she might also mention the needs and rights of the other students and the teacher. Don't the students deserve a seminar in which they can speak without fear of interruption or insult? Doesn't the teacher deserve to see her efforts to provide a pleasant, helpful experience to the students bear fruit? She is under personal and professional stress. Why should a student -- any student -- make her life more difficult?

2. [To the backstop]: Perhaps you could help direct our attention to some of the constraints in this situation -- environmental facts of life that these people all had to deal with.

Such a pointed question will probably elicit a fairly specific answer. In this case, it is reasonable to consider the unpleasantnesses of Paula's teaching situation factually and fairly briskly. The room is awful -- ugly and noisy and not designed for discussions. The social situation is antithetical to the development of a community of students: most of them commute; there are far too many of them in far too many classes with no effort made to offer them opportunities to form learning groups. And, finally, the teachers work in extremely large departments with offices scattered who-knows-where. And they, too, commute. There seems to be little opportunity, from any point of view, for warmth.

The question will probably arise: What can one do in this situation? There will be many answers, all partial, many tentative, many impractical, some perhaps helpful. Paula might have organized a social gathering early in the term, although one can imagine -- given commuting schedules and students working part time -- that scheduling a casual, friendly event would pose great difficulties. Failing that, she might have tried to gather students for informal meetings in small groups. If that didn't work, she might have encouraged them -- perhaps with personal notes or telephone calls -- to come and speak casually with her during office hours. Paula mentions that when students did come for conferences, she hesitated to ask them how they felt about Frank's interruptions because it was her policy "to avoid talking behind students' backs." It might be useful to ask the discussion participants if they agree with this point of view. Could she have gotten some legitimate and useful information by drawing other students out on the subject of Frank? If so, how best might she have phrased her questions?

3. What dynamics do you see developing in this seminar?

There is a range of possible responses to this question. One can see the seminar functioning reasonably normally within a bothersome set of constraints (many teachers have endured seminars like this one), or one can see something genuinely pernicious brewing. Between these two poles, there is a large gray area. The seminar is limping, but it hasn't collapsed. Paula does not mention a significant falling-off of attendance, nor does she complain that the students have ceased to prepare their assignments. But the discussion -- the heart and soul of this educational process -- is withering. We see Paula, throughout the (A) case, trying to encourage her students to talk. But Frank's derogatory outbursts -- painful, no matter how one excuses his motives -- always derail the discussions.

At first, the class tries to ignore Frank's rudeness. But, during the next few sessions, the interruptions proliferate to the point where Paula describes their effect as devastating. "The other students always became very quiet when he did this" she states. This sort of silence is the death of a discussion. Every teacher who has been confronted by such a "black hole" knows how excruciatingly difficult it is to crawl out of it, dragging the participants along as best one can. In Paula's case, every time she succeeded in getting a few students to volunteer their comments again,

Frank was likely to take one of his potshots at the speaker.

Discussion on this point -- the dynamics of the seminar -- is likely to include many shades of reaction but little or no actual disagreement. It is difficult to imagine anyone evaluating Paula's seminar on pastoral and satire as a picnic for anyone concerned.

4. **What options are available to Paula to improve this state of affairs? What are some risks she might take? How might she win? How might she lose?**

This section of the discussion should be freewheeling, since its function is to air as many options for action as possible. Many avenues are open to Paula. She might, for example, continue to do nothing in class to squelch Frank, and let the situation work itself out. After all, these are college students, not nursery school children; they have to learn to work together, no matter how uncomfortable the initial situation. Why should Paula assume responsibility for the whole situation? To this end, Paula might try to encourage the students to organize themselves to improve their own learning experience. Perhaps one of them might take Frank aside, privately, and request that he try not to interrupt in class. Why can't the students take the initiative? Why don't they do so in many classroom situations?

Most likely, there will be discussion participants who disagree with the idea that Paula can escape the responsibility for trying to improve this situation. The leadership, they will argue, is hers -- any teacher is, de facto, the final authority in the class and the person most liable for its atmosphere.

Paula's students seem to assume that she, if anyone, will address the difficulties. The (A) case tells us that "no one complained to her [Paula] about his [Frank's] behavior." This seems to have been an oddly reticent group of students. Perhaps they were just too preoccupied with the rest of their lives to find time to complain. Or some innate reluctance to seem like "stool pigeons" guaranteed their silence. Or the school was so alienated they expected little from it. At any rate, Paula was left isolated in this situation. She had only her own observation of the class's deterioration to spur her to action. It is characteristic of what we know of this school that her attempts to find out more about Frank Edgerton met with little initial success. Despite Frank's unmistakable presence, no one Paula knew could tell her a thing about him. In short, the option of gathering information for a decision presented difficulties.

Paula could also have chosen to drop Frank from the seminar. This would have been a drastic solution to the problem, but it would have had the benefit of removing him as a threat to the others. One might guess that Paula would be least likely to adopt this course of action because she comes across as gentle. There may well be some discussion participants, however, who espouse this idea. After all, being asked to leave the class permanently -- losing the credit and having to make it up -- would make it quite clear to Frank that his actions had consequences. Frank has chosen to attend college; he probably wants a degree -- validation from the "normal" world. Shouldn't he abide by its conventions?

There are also other ways in which Paula might have gotten tough with Frank. But doing so would have required her to break her own formal teaching contract. She had allowed Frank freedom to interrupt and insult from the very first time he had done so. By the time this had occurred repeatedly with no protest from Paula, he would have been justified in considering the arrangement fairly permanent. But, still, an unworkable, destructive contract ought to be abrogated. Paula has the option to break her permissive contract. A question then arises: Should she warn Frank that this is about to happen? If so, how should she deliver the warning? One might argue that a maximum of drama might be salutary. She could come down hard on him, and in public. But this would entail a risk. Given his bitterness and tendency to verbal abuse, he might burst out with some very upsetting remarks. In this case, everyone would be hurt. On the other hand, he might collapse psychologically, and telegraph through body language (pale face, bent head, clenched fists, perhaps even tears) that Paula had really hurt him. This possible reaction would be quieter but scarcely less painful than an outburst.

At this point in the discussion, it might be advisable for the leader to emphasize the point that Paula's predicament is complex. She has no crystal ball to predict Frank's reaction or the class's. She wishes to improve things, but cannot know the best way to do this. She has to operate with insufficient information in a situation where genuine damage is possible. Everything she might do entails some sort of risk. This is a typical quandary for a teacher.

5.   What do you think Paula ought to do?

This is the predictive question, coming, as it does, before the distribution of the (B) case that will reveal what she <u>did</u> do. The discussion leader should encourage participants to recommend strategies for Paula, noting for future reference which contingents are "hard-nosed," and which are more "softhearted." It might be useful, in the remaining sections of this discussion, to instigate some debate between these two factions, with a view to getting each side to see and appreciate -- if not adopt -- the other's point of view.

*   *   *

After the (B) case has been read:

1.   Paula delayed action until she had sought information and advice. How do you assess this decision?

Paula indicates her main reason for delaying: she was afraid. Some participants might wonder why. Shouldn't a teacher go ahead and give a student a mild rebuke if that rebuke is truly for the student's -- and the class's -- benefit? The unpleasant question of pain is inescapable here. Is learning always pleasant? Should it be? Should we refuse to change our unacceptable behavior because we have become comfortable being obnoxious? If pain is inevitable, how should the educator feel about inflicting that sort of pain? What are the bounds within which this discipline must be kept and what sort of pain is it not proper to inflict? The practices of flunking students or expelling them for clearly inappropriate behavior might be mentioned here as analogues. Surely, one ought to flunk a student whose work is either virtually nonexistent or patently below the lowest standard. But flunking is painful. Is it the teacher's responsibility to spare the student that pain? Or is it the student's responsibility to produce acceptable work in order to avoid the pain of failure? What about students who are genuinely incapable -- for whatever reason -- of doing acceptable work? How can one concoct a legitimate learning experience for them? Must one hurt them by saying quite honestly that their work is poor?

The implications of this area of questions are broad and by no means simple to unravel. Pain seems to be inescapable in much of the educational human experience, as Gragg tells us in his two seminal arti-

cles. The problem is to contain it and give it a productive, healthy creative outlet in enhanced competence and self-control. Without resorting to unnecessarily harsh tactics, Paula has to try to provide some sort of discipline for Frank because he seems unwilling (perhaps unable) to abide by the general conventions. The hope would be that by doing so, she would show him that from that point on, it is going to be his job to discipline himself. The very word <u>discipline</u> is distasteful to many -- it smacks of Dickensian boarding school cruelties -- and can indeed lead teachers to inflict useless injuries, either in the form of unfairly severe grades, unjust expulsions, or the milder-seeming but very painful form of sarcasm. These unjust and counterproductive excesses are by no means rare among teachers, and this is a good place for the discussion participants to exchange opinions on these subjects. The discussion leader may find this section intense, possibly interlaced with many personal experiences with difficult students or sadistic teachers. The challenge would be to channel these personal experiences into a consideration of basic principles. How can one recognize the occasion for firmness? How can one distinguish reasonable, helpful firmness from negative, injurious rigidity?

Paula chose to play for time. Probably her hope was to escape the necessity of doing anything at all. Many of us would react the same way. But Paula's wish was not granted. The situation did not improve by itself. Her students did not try to help their colleague to adjust. The buck was passed to Paula. Her instinct to turn to more experienced colleagues for advice seems to have been a sound one, and, in fact, it produced -- although not immediately -- a good result: she found the Office for Disabled Students. Some discussion participants will have made the connection between Paula's decision to gather more information through university channels and her discovery of the helpful advisor. This is the ideal point to use as a transition to the central episode of this case: Paula's interview in the Office for Disabled Students.

2.   What do you think of the advice she received from the woman in the Office for Disabled Students?

It would, of course, be a waste of dramatic impact to ignore the advisor's blindness. She represents a successful adjustment to a devastating handicap. It is extremely significant that Paula does not at first realize that the woman is blind. Not only has the woman learned to converse gracefully with sighted people -- even adopting their mannerisms -- but she expresses herself in terms that imply that she identifies with members of the "normal" world. She is an administrator; she gets about with the aid of a seeing-eye dog (this implies a great degree of independence), and she counsels adjustment for Frank: "Handicapped people have to live in the real world like everybody else."

It is impossible to separate the advisor's suggestion (that Paula "get tough" on Frank) from her own handicap and successful adjustment to it. A severely handicapped person probably must learn self-discipline in order to participate as fully as possible with the rest of the world. This process must involve a great deal of pain -- and innumerable triumphs over despair when the process seems cluttered with obstacles and setbacks.

It is unlikely that there will be much disagreement with the woman's advice. She is a living example of its success. But the sensitive discussion participants of the class may point out that it is unfair to saddle Paula with the sole responsibility for "re-educating" Frank. Yes, she has chosen education as a career, but perhaps she didn't bargain for this. Paula prepared to lead discussions of nature poetry and satire. Instead, she is being asked to be a behavioral therapist to a paraplegic. Must she?

3. **What do you think of Paula's reprimand to Frank? What effect would you expect it to have?**

Another cliffhanger. By this point in the discussion, few people are likely to criticize Paula for putting Frank down in class. For one thing, his behavior hurt the rest of the class, and there is an obvious point in letting them see that Paula has decided to put an end to Frank's rudeness. For another thing, the discussion participants realize that Paula has been influenced by the advice and example of the advisor in the Office for Disabled Students.

Where there may be divergence of opinion is in consideration of the way Paula chose to confront Frank. Her words, delivered "calmly," are somewhat oblique. She avoids actually criticizing Frank with any of the terms that some of us might have wished to use -- "rudeness," or "impoliteness," for example -- and then she gets up and, it appears, deliberately turns her back on him. Is this a symbol of the rejection -- and anger -- that she has shied away from expressing verbally? Or is it just a way to play for time (a tactic she often chooses, we have seen) and not face his first reaction? Perhaps she is assuming that he will be upset, shocked, perhaps furious. And she wants first of all not to see this, and second of all, to give him some time to cool off. In any case, she turns around when she reaches a physical position that symbolizes authority -- standing at the board in a class where all the students are seated. Then, she looks at Frank to see what her mild -- but probably shocking, because unexpected -- rebuke has done to him.

Discussion participants' expectations of what this rebuke did will probably match their own approaches. The "stricter" members of the group may well say that Paula was much too soft on Frank. She merely asked him to address his colleague's point more precisely. She should have said something like, "Speak politely or keep your mouth shut, please!" Frank, they may argue, should be grateful that she has put up with his bad manners this long. Some sort of put-down was long overdue.

Others might pay more attention to the fact of Frank's handicap and its psychological ramifications. Despite his desire to attend college and get on with his life in some fashion, he is not normal. Perhaps his spinal injuries have created unavoidable mood swings. Perhaps Frank will burst into furious, ashamed tears. Or perhaps he will scowl, turn his wheelchair toward the door, and leave the room. Or perhaps he will retort with something far ruder than he has produced thus far. Or perhaps he will simply cave in. Most people will probably think it unlikely that Frank will accept her rebuke meekly and mend his ways.

The point of these exercises in prediction is not to train legions of seers but rather to underline the multiplicity of potential outcomes of any classroom interaction. We all have to realize that any remarks we make to students may produce unexpected results -- possibly painful, possibly far more positive and desirable than we might have dared to hope. There is an inescapable element of uncertainty in everything we do, and the classroom is a heightened arena for this phenomenon.

*   *   *

After the (C) case has been read:

1. **Did Paula do the right thing (and why, or why not)?**

This is a springboard question to the more important issues broached by the second question of this section -- the issues that symbolically expand the material to include a broad cross-section of classroom experiences. Did Paula do the right thing? Participants will have to assess her action by Frank's response and the long-term effects the episode had on the seminar. Frank's response was surprisingly mild. The unexpected happened. He swallowed the rebuke. Paula made him blush, not explode in rage or fury. Perhaps we may assume that blushing -- a social emotion -- indicates that he realized quite clearly that the rebuke was just. He had been acting childishly.

Paula's symbolic gesture of staying at the board for a few moments -- retaining the position of authority and command in a classroom before rejoining the group -- signaled that she was willing to accept Frank's reaction as his superior, but also to work with him and the rest as a colleague. The students seem to have taken her cue. We are told that one of them picked up the discussion, and the class continued.

Paula noticed an improvement in morale almost immediately. Members of the discussion group may question this "instant fix." How many situations in real life improve so quickly? Yet Paula asserts that this was so, and she is our informant. We gather that Frank did not reform completely. He interrupted a few more times, but Paula continued her new policy of squelching him, and "soon his interruptions ceased." In fact, it seems as if he may have learned to adjust; we read that he actually participated in discussions a few times instead of just interrupting. The "cynical cast" to his contributions, one may argue, indicates that these were honest thoughts, candidly expressed -- for Frank Edgerton seems to have been genuinely bitter. But his willingness to join the discussion group as a participant rather than a spectator implies that he may have learned a bit of trust.

If one thinks that Paula did not do the right thing, there may be several reasons for this. Perhaps she delayed too long, losing valuable time for the other students and exposing her credibility to steady erosion. Perhaps she should have forced the students to solve their own problems (or not solve them: their choice!) -- but in any event realize that they were responsible for their own learning experience. Or perhaps she was too public in her actions, taking too big a risk. She should have rebuked Frank privately. We know, for example, that he always arrived in the classroom early. She could have come very early and seized the opportunity for an impromptu, private conference with him on the unpleasant subject of his interruptions.

2.   **What is your appraisal of the lesson about leadership that Paula mentions learning from this experience?**

The proponents of "free will" for students will probably criticize Paula for intervening. Others will applaud her decision, though perhaps lament its lateness. Still others may say that Paula missed the point. Leadership is inescapable for a teacher. It is implicit in the position. The teacher sets the curriculum, leads (or at least organizes) the discussions, and, of course, assigns the grades. Pretending that students are completely responsible for their own experiences in such an unequal situation is hypocrisy. But Paula fails to mention what the goal of her leadership was. Her actions show that she knew this quite well: she acted to establish a climate of open inquiry in the seminar -- that atmosphere of trust without which discussion learning is impossible.

Another symbolic implication of these events emerges less clearly than the right of all students to be protected from the belligerence of a disaffected member. But Frank Edgerton, with his handicap, has something of the perplexing, intrinsically unsettling aspect of any "outsider" working under a disadvantage in a group. Be that outsider a female in a male environment, a member of a racial, ethnic, or religious minority, or a foreigner with obvious language problems, that outsider's difference from the rest of the class may hamper his or her performance and integration into the group -- particularly if teamwork is a necessary goal. It is truly difficult for such outsiders to cooperate fully, however well-intentioned they may be. It would seem obvious that they deserve special help from the teacher. But this help must be offered with tact, respect, and sincerity.

Another interesting factor to emerge from the whole range of experiences this three-part case series presents is the exaggerated influence of the teacher's behavior on the students. We observe the seminar group following Paula's lead almost instinctively. When she shies from confronting Frank, they are all cowed because she is cowed. As soon as she assumes a more assertive role, they relax and stop fearing Frank. The students dare to present their ideas only after Paula shows that she will no longer tolerate discourtesy. Perhaps this is a point we all should ponder.

The Handicapped Heckler

Researcher's Perspective

Applicability of the Case

This case focuses on a sympathetic teacher confronting a deeply upsetting paradox: a belligerent, handicapped student whose aggressiveness cannot be separated from an instantly apparent, painful vulnerability that inspires a certain protectiveness. The unsettling details of the case -- wheelchair, ugly classroom, socially fragmented student body, increasingly rattled teacher, and, finally, the blind administrator with her seeing-eye dog -- provide melodrama that ought to produce an engaged discussion. In short, this case is a "grabber."

This researcher finds many universally recognizable features in the case, even though some of its particular elements might seem parochial. True, the seminar's subject is literary and somewhat rarefied; the young female teacher is under unusual personal stress; and the student's disability is uncommonly severe. Nevertheless, the dynamics at work in "The Handicapped Heckler" make it an "everyman" case. The class's primary material -- poetry -- invites a teaching style appropriate to all sorts of case method discussions because the documents under study are open to many valid interpretations. Accordingly, the teacher tries to help students find and support their own opinions, preferably by appreciating and challenging each other's interpretations. This goal is common to all teachers who wish to stimulate open, honest discussion. The damage the handicapped student inflicts upon the class's willingness to take risks could have been the work of any truculent misfit. And most of us can identify with the teacher, both in her human vulnerability and generous desire not to cause pain.

Some Basic Observations

1) The teacher needs to gain objectivity and control her instinctive urge to pamper the handicapped student. A clear assessment of the needs of everyone -- including herself -- in this situation will show her that she must "get tough" with Frank.

2) Any teacher faces the challenge to balance responsibility to an individual student's needs with those of the group. The difficulty of finding this balance is obvious here. Furthermore, the balance point is never constant.

3) It is essential to make the distinction between empathy (a true, imaginative understanding of another's feelings that can lead to consideration) and pity (sometimes an uncomfortable, distracting, even alienating emotion that can lead to avoidance).

4) There is genuine difficulty in dealing fairly with the severely handicapped without patronizing them, whether their disability is physical, or emotional, or both.

5) It is this researcher's abiding fascination to observe how the instructor's prominence in the classroom almost invariably creates a mirroring effect. Unconsciously, students imitate teachers. In this instance the teacher goes from pity to something approaching fear of the handicapped student. Observe her class's self-confidence and willingness to take a corresponding nose dive. The lesson here is not as uncomplicated as it might seem. Given Paula Wilson's situation and basic decency, who among us would have taken an early opportunity to rebuke Frank Edgerton?

6) Helpful criticism is difficult to offer without offense. How could Paula prevent psychological injury to Frank once she had decided to confront his rudeness?

7) Once Paula had decided to rebuke Frank for his unacceptable behavior, she had also taken a step toward violating her own clearly permissive contract with him.

This commentary on "The Handicapped Heckler" was written by Dr. Abby J. Hansen, research associate, in collaboration with Professor C. Roland Christensen for the Developing Discussion Leadership Skills Seminar. Its objective is to help instructors in the development of their own teaching plans for this case.

What are the implications of this? How should she have framed her unexpected rebuke? Should she have tried to get him into a private conference? Should she have telephoned? Written a note? Gotten some third party to meet with the two of them?

8) Operating issues in this case exist on at least two levels. First, the specific: How should one treat a disabled student? What background information should one have in each case? Where can one obtain the appropriate information? What should one do with it? Second, the general: What should one know about <u>any</u> student? How can one identify potential problems and, once identified, do something about them within an appropriate sphere of influence? And last, at what point in a course can one decide that some behavioral problem is chronic and won't evaporate by itself?

9) The environment -- or setting -- plays a vital role in this case. These events occur in a state university where, we gather, the instructors and most students commute to class. There seems to be no community: no one knows anyone else there. This might have a beneficial side, from Frank Edgerton's point of view: there is no tightly knit society to ostracize him. But it seems a cold, impersonal place. The irony of discussing nature poetry, which often celebrates the most touching moments of human experience (love, creation, natural beauty) in a classroom as noisy and grim as the one Paula Wilson had to use must have been painful at times. Given an alienating institution, what can an instructor do to provide warmth?

Summary

In brief, this researcher finds "The Handicapped Heckler" an appealing case to open discussion on some essential questions of leadership and the teacher's complex responsibility to students. The very intensity of the disturbed student's pain suggests that the discussion participants will recognize his genuine need for help. Also, the teacher's obvious good will and basic competence make her an attractive character with whom to identify, both in her desire to do the right thing and her initial confusion about what that right thing might be.

The French Lesson

Teaching Note

Special Features

"The French Lesson" will probably inspire a discussion that moves swiftly. It will very likely involve little clarification of case content, and the participants will probably furnish similar experiences and present opinions about the case characters with facility. The discussion should, ideally, also offer many opportunities to reflect on some basic teaching issues, but this desirable turn of events will depend largely on the discussion leader.

Like all minicases, "The French Lesson" should generate a participant-focused discussion. This means that the discussion leader should prepare to use participants' comments to guide the group into complexities that the case implies rather than states. Achieving this will call upon the skills of listening, probing for subtleties, and illuminating the emerging structure of the discussion with periodic summaries.

This particular minicase describes a college-level French class in which the teacher, meaning to be kind, quietly asks a hesitant student if he has studied the day's lesson. The gesture backfires to produce intense embarrassment and damaged rapport with the whole class. The strength of this case is the multiplicity of deeper issues that underlie such an apparently simple interchange.

Mood

The case is relatively light in tone. The teacher insults a student, to be sure, but the insult is unintentional and the damage it inflicts on the student's self-esteem and status, while real, is not catastrophic. Nor is the injury to the whole group's rapport with the teacher irreparable. Other cases in our syllabus take up far more painful issues: racism, sexism, unsettling outbursts in class, for example. "The French Lesson," by contrast, is low-keyed.

Suggested Uses

Because of its accessible material and light tone, this case makes a good ice-breaker. Coming after more dramatic, emotionally draining cases, "The French Lesson" might seem anticlimactic. Its strength is that it can get participants talking without fear of exposing personal weaknesses by over-identifying with a severely troubled case character.

Another reason for using this case early in a workshop or seminar syllabus is that it crystallizes a very basic issue of classroom philosophy: respect. The instructor in this case -- Bert Peters -- explicitly tries to accord students respect because he thinks this encourages them to learn.

This issue should be pointed out, ventilated, and returned to throughout the discussion and the teaching seminar (or workshop) as a whole.

Conflicts, Sensitivities

As we have noted, "The French Lesson" contains no concealed land mines for the unwary discussion leader (although unexpected sensitivities in the members of the group are always possible).

Teaching Objectives

This case focuses on a teacher's well-meant efforts to balance his responsibilities toward a less-talented student and a generally apt, enthusiastic class. It is, basically, a kindly case. Since its central issues are responsibility and respect, it presents a splendid opportunity for the discussion leader to act as a classroom model, applying the very principle under discussion: respect. There are many ways to do this. Acknowledging participants by name, speaking with courtesy, consciously maintaining a physical posture that communicates attention when participants speak,

---

This teaching note has been prepared as an aid to instructors in classroom use of the case "The French Lesson" (A) 9-384-066 and (B) 9-384-067.

and making eye contact with members of the group when they listen as well as speak -- all these contribute to creating an atmosphere of respect. It often happens during our seminars that a participant will notice what the discussion leader is doing and will call attention to it. If this occurs, so much the better. It should lead to further discussion of ways to demonstrate and convey respect.

The "Blocks" of Analysis

If you happen to find the mnemonic device of breaking a discussion case into analytic "blocks" appealing, this is a good case on which to practice the technique. This writer usually tries to extract approximately six or eight rubrics under which various points may be logically grouped. I then write these, with brief (almost shorthand) references to supporting data in the case, on a single sheet of paper -- to be kept constantly in view during the discussion. This device provides a snapshot of the terrain and helps the leader remain oriented as the discussion moves freely. It also helps provide clues for new directions by giving an almost instant reading of which areas have been covered and which have not.

The basic elements of "The French Lesson" are simple and brief enough to be covered during a normal seminar session. One "block" might be case characters. The instructor might, for example, direct attention to Bert Peters and his student, Jack Sothern. What do we know of them? What do our intuitions suggest? What are some implications of their bearing, words, implied attitudes? One should also consider the class as a whole -- the way the students and teacher interact: another "block." Furthermore, what is the physical setup of the room? How does Bert Peters move? What are some implications of these details?

And how does Bert use humor? How does his dramatic flair affect the class as a whole? How does it affect Jack?

One should also pay attention to the dialogue, which is brief but suggestive. How do people speak in this case? What do their words imply? What tone do they use? What diction (kinds of words) do they use? All of these details may lead to more general considerations of basic issues. "The French Lesson" presents the discussion leader with a clear opportunity for asking the participants to examine, or at least consider, many constituent elements in the learning environment that often go unremarked in a denser, more complex case.

My own study of this minicase discerns a manageable set of blocks, besides characters and environment: humor in the classroom; balancing responsibility to a single student with responsibility to the whole class; rapport; teaching contract; and the subtleties of expressing respect. (All of these are especially relevant to the early days, of course -- although they pertain to the whole of teaching as well.)

The elusive but pervasive issue of "chemistry" might also constitute a discussion block. In this writer's estimation the two major characters are disharmonious. Bert is a high-energy teacher whose style reflects his talent and enthusiasm for his subject. Jack is a less-gifted student, especially inept at this particular kind of learning, with a potential for resistance and even disruption in the classroom. The others in the group come across as a unit with a common denominator of relatively high aptitude and a generally congenial acceptance of Bert's teaching style. So, the principal tension occurs first between Bert and Jack, but it then spreads to the class as a whole (tension usually does). The result: a general rise in counterproductive nervousness. The group should devote attention to this situation and try to suggest ways to identify and improve it.

Preparing for the Discussion

Opening Speaker; Backstop

Our general practice is to ask two participants to open the discussion. This employment of an initial double-call serves several purposes. First, it signals cooperation to the group as a whole, saying, in effect, that this is a seminar in which the long-winded "star performances" that bore and annoy the nonperforming seminar member will be avoided in favor of collaborative efforts. Second, asking two participants to open provides the discussion leader not only with twice as much material to probe, but also with insurance: if the first speaker fails, perhaps the second may present more usable material.

In this case, the protagonist is a young man, the subject is French grammar, and the students are undergraduates in a liberal arts institution. Some participants might find this situation unfamiliar. In the interests of signaling that this seminar will encourage participants to identify with characters in diverse situations, the leader might ask a woman from a discipline other than foreign languages to open the case. This done, it would signal another set of positive values -- equality and cooperation -- to ask a male to function as backstop. The backstop's task usually is fairly loosely assigned. He or she is asked to "fill out" and comment on the first speaker's remarks, helping the class find direction for further investigation.

Typically, in our seminars, the backstop avoids direct challenge to the first speaker. Even when he or she presents basically contradictory information or opinions, these usually emerge cloaked as agreements. The discussion leader should stress that the first two speakers are opening the territory for exploration. They are not providing an exhaustive analysis.

(At this point, let us hasten to assure any novice teachers that even if the two opening speakers <u>do</u> appear to bring up all the points the leader has prepared, this is not cause for despair. The seminar need not end there, some ten minutes after it has begun! On the contrary: the simple mention of a point should not be confused with a thorough discussion of it. It is the discussion leader's task to pose open-ended questions <u>based on</u> the points, invite participants to disagree if they feel this is appropriate, and press for further applications.)

Another consideration in the choice of a pair of opening speakers might be their location in the room. Choosing a participant far to one's right might suggest asking another participant seated far to the left to backstop, thus symbolically enclosing the whole group in the arc of attention. In any case, it would be extremely ill-advised to choose participants seated side by side or too near each other. In the first place, if they are seated together they might be friends and particularly averse to contradiction. This would guarantee a bland opening. In the second case, having two speakers seated very near each other would close the focus of the discussion, eliminating most of the participants from the arena of action.

The question of whether to ask for volunteers is always worth considering. Particularly in the early days of the seminar, when participants and leader are all relative strangers, inviting volunteers to open has the advantage of letting the group know that the leader will not try to impose too much structure on their discussions.

The disadvantage is that the seminar will begin with presentations from the more aggressive, attention-hungry members of the group and impose some rejection upon the shyer participants.

The Discussion Questions

Before we begin to consider possible responses to these questions, let us mention that it is generally our practice to make the first calls (pose the first two questions) before presenting a few minutes of introduction and "housekeeping details" (schedule changes, references to secondary readings, written assignment deadlines, and the like). We ask the first speaker to take the time to think about his or her response while the introduction is in progress. Then, after the introduction, we put down our notes, turn in a conversational way to the first speaker, and informally rephrase the first discussion question. The symbolic implication of this gesture is twofold. First, we are trying to convey a feeling of ease along with a moderately colloquial style of speech -- no need to grope for elegant expressions and, in the process, get tongue-tied. Second, we are saying, "I've put down my notes; now the time has come to pay attention to <u>your</u> reactions, not mine."

The discussion leader should keep in mind that a philosophical assumption underlies these actions: the belief that Bert Peters's desire to accord students respect in the classroom is the most essential element in this case. Not only should the discussion leader try to draw the group's attention to this issue, but he or she should reflect on it personally. It is useful to ask yourself whether you agree with Bert. Do you, too, take pride in "putting students at their ease"? If so, how do you do this? Relaxation is by no means an uncomplicated goal. How much is desirable? How can one encourage the right degree of relaxation? Do relaxed students really perform better? What settings are more relaxing than others? And how can a teacher recognize when relaxation has turned to slackness? (Concomitantly, how can one reintroduce a healthy tension when this occurs?) These open-ended questions -- all implied in the primary case material -- give "The French Lesson" the potential for stimulating genuinely helpful thought about the whole enterprise of teaching.

Let us now consider the discussion questions, in the order given, with our primary focus being ways in which the discussion leader may capitalize on partici-pants' comments to suggest directions of discussion that will expose as many of the gray areas as possible. Let us stress again that in these cases there is no specific correct conclusion; there are virtually endless subtle ramifications of all points, and these can be "played" in a number of ways. It will always be valuable to ask the group for further implications, or assump-tions, or even fantasy scenarios based on analytical points made from the case. All of these exercises will not only help provide depth for the analysis, but also furnish a healthy redundancy that may drive some points home for members of the group who are either more leisurely in their pace of thought, or perhaps accustomed to different methods of intellectual analysis than infor-mal group discussion.

Each of our questions might produce a response somewhere on a spectrum that often stretches between two poles -- ex-treme approval of the central case character and extreme disapproval. The discussion leader's task is to devise questions that will nudge the group into providing some inter-mediate points on this spectrum.

*   *   *

After the (A) case has been read, the following questions can be explored:

1.   **What's going on here?**

This should be the question directed to the first speaker. It could produce a simple rehearsal of the facts in the case -- devoid of interpretation of the motives and the forces the speaker sees exerting their powers in these events. The question's intended thrust is analytical, but it is meant merely as an opening to an exami-nation of constituent elements. Given a highly wrought, extremely abstract presen-tation, the discussion leader should make a mental note to ask, later on, the seminar participants to backtrack a bit and turn their attention to describing the event and the people involved. The spectrum of response on these questions, thus, might range from simple repetition of facts to elaborate abstractions. The discussion leader's object would be to try to introduce the missing element -- for both are neces-sary to a complete discussion.

Another answer to "What's going on here?" might address itself to the teacher's personality. One participant might say, "A talented teacher is trying to run an ener-getic, exciting class despite the dullness of the lesson's content: French grammar." Another participant might read the situation quite differently and say, "A nervous, sharp-tongued prima donna teacher is hogging the limelight and intimidating his students with humor." Neither point is necessarily correct or incorrect. Either -- or both -- should lead to deeper considera-tions of the implications of pacing, humor, and the teacher's responsibility to be sensitive to student's reactions to his or her style. Faced with a seemingly opposed set of responses like the above, the discus-sion leader should not hesitate to ask for further ways to view the situation. If these are not forthcoming, he or she might appropriately introduce a few.

2.   **What would you advise Bert Peters to do?**

Answers to this question will be condi-tioned by the drift of the discussion. Should Bert apologize? (Perhaps not. If not, why not?) If he ought to apologize, first of all, why? Secondly, how? (Should he apologize in class? Privately? In writ-ing? In a formal or informal setting?) The discussion leader's task in this section of the discussion is to try to get participants to examine the assumptions that underlie each piece of advice. For example, if one suggests that no apology is necessary, is that because a teacher's dignity would be compromised by apologizing to a student? What elements constitute a teacher's dig-nity, then? If one thinks the apology should be public and involve the rest of the class, what does that imply about one's view of the teacher-student contract?

Almost invariably, seminar participants find it amusing to match their predictions and advice with the actual events that succeeded the decision point of the (A) case. Here, those who recommended apolo-gizing will find themselves vindicated by the reality of the situation, but the "hardliners" may well take exception, asserting that while Jack Sothern says he always prepares but lacks language apti-tude, he is just taking advantage of his teacher. He actually was not prepared, and now he's trying to make Bert feel guilty, in hopes of cadging some preferen-tial treatment.

*   *   *

After the (B) case has been read, the following questions can be stressed:

1. **Did Bert Peters do the right thing?**

Bert decided to treat the issue privately. He made his contact with the student informal -- choosing neither to send him a written apology, nor to summon him to his office for a personal conference. What are the ramifications of this course? What would it signal if the teacher had treated this incident more formally? What would it signal if he addressed it in front of the other students?

Some participants may note Jack Sothern's whiny tone in the reported phone conversation and point out that the student seems to be taking the opportunity to make retribution for having been insulted. Bert Peters seems to accept the student's statements at face value and take pains to adopt a conciliatory mode of reaction. Is this appropriate? Is the teacher groveling, letting the student get away with too much? What about Jack's assertion that "I'm not good at languages?" Does a student's lack of talent in a specialized field put an increased burden upon the teacher?

2. **How do you explain the effect of the initial incident upon the class as a whole?**

Again, the range of interpretation will probably hinge upon attitudes toward Bert Peters's teaching style. If one is "student-centered," one might say that Bert had been keeping the whole class in a state of nervousness by his movements and jokes, and Jack Sothern's slightly asocial gesture in leaving the class and then returning in a state of obvious upset focused a great deal of the anxiety that the other students were probably feeling but concealing. The opposed point of view is that Jack Sothern's actions were babyish. He spoiled not only his teacher's good mood, but everyone's. Embarrassment -- particularly when it is given physical form in a gesture such as leaving the classroom (presumably with a pained facial expression) -- is catching. The other students might well have empathized with Jack. He performed poorly in class, so the teacher stood right by his chair and singled him out to question his preparation. What an insult! It is customary in language classes for teachers to stand while the students remain seated (except to walk to the chalkboard occasionally). This physical disparity automatically reinforces the teacher's potential to intimidate. (In this section of the discussion, it will be profitable for the discussion leader to refer to the "blocks" which encompass issues such as rapport, teaching contract,

humor, and the separate personalities of Bert and Jack.)

3. **What were some of the ways Bert Peters was creating the classroom atmosphere?**

This is a straightforward question that should elicit answers that pay attention not only to the physical arrangement of the room -- desk chairs in a "U" that allowed students to see each other, yet focused attention on the teacher as he moved freely around the central space -- but also on Bert's use of humor and what little data we have about his gestures (he pretends to eat the chalk, and points to the students -- sometimes by surprise -- to trigger their participation). In short, Bert is a self-conscious, theatrical sort of teacher, who communicates a desire for the spotlight and a personal preference for laughter and quick pace.

It may well be noted at this point that we have no information about whether Bert ever asked this group how they wanted to proceed, or announced at the outset what sort of pace he expected or what classroom mood he hoped to evoke (another instance of the virtually ubiquitous "one-sided teaching contract"). The question of the value of "spontaneous buoyancy" (Bert's term for his favorite classroom mood) may also occur at this point. What, indeed, is the effect of spontaneity on learning? Is there value in running a slow-paced class? How can a teacher gauge the pace, how alter it, how evaluate its effectiveness?

4. **What were some of the problems facing Bert Peters in the long run?**

Many seminar participants will answer, "Restoring good feeling." This reply will probably find few dissenters. But Bert also faced another decision: What to do about Jack Sothern? Bert had to make an evaluation of the student's problem: Was he untalented, lazy, truculent, or perhaps truly incapable of performing acceptable, college-level work in French? Is it fair to make a genuinely slow student participate in a class populated by talented students? How important is homogeneity in a class? Are the criteria different in language classes?

Another way to approach this question is to wonder whether this might be a good time for Bert Peters to engage in a bit of self-appraisal. Are his jokes intimidating students? Is he moving too fast around that "U"? Is he startling students by abruptly pointing his chalk at them and expecting them to spew good, grammatical French? Should he try to modify his classroom pace according to the students' developing needs? What cues should he look for (besides laughter) to gauge the class's mood?

5.   **What underlying issues does this case focus for you?**

It is to be hoped that the seminar group will come up with new and stimulating issues to consider, but the set that this researcher has assembled -- respect, humor and its dangers, homogeneity, rapport, the teaching contract -- are a reasonable starting point.

Some seminar participants may well have experienced similar incidents in the classroom, either as students or teachers. It would be well to ask the group to give some thought to the underlying issues of this interchange, should they be presented.

Most important for the discussion leader to remember here is the unlikelihood of achieving thoroughness or impressive depth in this part of the discussion. The case is not the sort of emotional "grabber" that is likely to trigger deep, passionate, or profound thought during the discussion period, and the order of the discussion questions happens to place this section last. Final elements on teaching plans tend to be short-changed. The discussion leader's task, thus, is to try to sustain the group's interest with all sorts of cues -- verbal and physical -- which indicate that this discussion of principles should be pursued after class, either in company or in one's own mind.

The discussion leader would be well advised to wrap the session up with a brief summary of some of the questions the group has posed and finish with a further question to ponder privately: "What have we learned from Bert Peters's mild blunder and what does it mean for each of us in our own teaching?"

The French Lesson

Researcher's Perspective

Case Informant's Comments

Bert Peters reflected: "This incident still fascinates me in a horrible sort of way because of the shock I felt when my intended kindness to Jack Sothern backfired. I meant well, but nonetheless managed to insult him publicly -- which is not something I like to do, although I know some teachers who not only don't mind it but even positively enjoy it. To me, this episode showed that questioning a student's preparation in class creates a no-win situation. You're either saying, 'Aha, caught you unprepared, you lazy bum,' or 'Well, if you did prepare, you're so dumb it didn't do you any good!' Neither implication can do anything but embarrass the student in front of his peers."

Bert also perceived a personal loss stemming from the incident: "The class got edgy and stayed that way for a surprisingly long time," he observed. "I paid a price in damaged goodwill, and rapport is worth something, especially in a foreign-language class where people are already guaranteed to be nervous about sounding foolish in public when they make their inevitable mistakes. My strained relations with Jack spilled over and dampened the whole class's enthusiasm, making it necessary for me to work extra hard to restore good relations. The damage was subtle, but real."

Researcher's Comments

We don't see much of Bert Peters in this case, but his teaching style shows energy, confidence, and humor. He also seems to value those qualities and encourage them in his students. In the terms of this teaching seminar, he sets a onesided contract -- making him the sort of high-energy teacher who can deeply intimidate a less-talented student. For those who absorb unfamiliar material more slowly than most of their peers, energetic instructors can be terrifying. Jack Sothern appears to be of this sort. Given Bert's intention to spare his students public embarrassment over their failures, Jack presents a teaching problem: how can Bert include him in the class exercises without sacrificing pace and mood?

Bert sets his fast pace in many ways, verbally and physically. By having the students arrange their desks into a U-shape, he creates an audience for his own theater-in-the-round performances. He moves fairly quickly -- one assumes -- and carries a piece of chalk to use as a pointer and stage prop, as well as writing implement. Sometimes he proceeds student-by-student in his invitations to participate; sometimes, not. He is, thus, unpredictable, and that is bound to create tension. Bert flings questions at his students almost like a juggler tossing flaming Indian clubs to his partner. He launches each question with a laugh, thus focusing a great deal of heat on the student who must catch it without killing the laughter or breaking the fast pace. Bert's own superior command of material and personal fund of nervous energy set a tone that he finds comfortable. Doubtless many of his students also find it congenial, but Jack Sothern certainly does not.

In the situation as we have outlined it, Bert is using his position (physical and metaphorical) to reinforce his leadership. However benevolently he uses his power in the classroom, he is, nonetheless, inflicting a style on his students -- apparently without their consent. Most teachers do the same. When this method works, it goes unnoticed. But here, however, Bert faces a mismatch between student and style. He has only two basic options for improving the situation: change the student or change the style. How can he change the student? He can, perhaps, move him out, transfer him to the jurisdiction of a teacher with a less-threatening style. He can,

---

This commentary on "The French Lesson" was prepared by Dr. Abby J. Hansen. Its objective is to help instructors in the development of their own teaching plans for this case.

perhaps, arrange a private contract with Jack and forgo calling on him in class entirely. Perhaps he can change the whole basis of their contract and arrange some sort of private "Independent Study," in which Jack focuses on reading and writing French and relinquishes his efforts to learn to speak the language. (In cases of genuine lack of aptitude, such as learning disabilities or varieties of dyslexia, this might be the only successful course of action.)

Bert Peters's own comments show valuable insight. After reflecting on this incident and its implications, he decided to avoid this sort of confrontation with students in class -- even on issues that seem fairly trivial, like one evening's grammar lesson. There seems little question in Bert's mind that he should have spoken to Jack privately. Bert focuses our attention on one of the inescapable facts of teaching: the inequality of power in the classroom that magnifies everything the teacher does, from moving around the room to raising or lowering the voice, to inquiring about a student's preparation. In the classroom, thus, singling a student out -- either for praise or blame -- causes genuine tension. Praised, a student can begin to worry: What did I do right? How can I repeat this performance? Will this magic rub off? Blamed, a student can be so embarrassed that he or she gives up the desire to improve. The effect on the others in the classroom will also, most likely, be negative. Hearing a fellow student praised, they may feel envious; hearing him blamed, they may feel both empathetically embarrassed and implicitly threatened -- wondering when the insult may land on them.

Another aspect of classroom dynamics that surfaces in this brief interchange is the ubiquitous phenomenon of emotional contagion. People catch each other's moods and the enclosed atmosphere of the classroom is a hotbed for this sort of infection. In this vignette we see the highly charged, comic energy of a classroom turn into negative tension that spreads from the insulted student to the rest of the class and then to the teacher himself.

Bert Peters's one-sided, implicit teaching contract with this class seems to have included clauses stipulating humor, a fast pace, and talent. Not all of his students, however, were capable of fulfilling these demands, and his contract, unfortunately, made no allowance for these students. Recognition of the situation and some sort of renegotiation would seem to be in order.

I Felt as if My World Had Just Collapsed!

Teaching Note

Special Features

A three-part case, "I Felt as if My World Had Just Collapsed!" contains some of the protagonist's general reflections based on an upsetting incident, but deals mainly with a classroom crisis and its possible implications. All three parts should be read, for the long-term outcome is not clear until the (C) case. The setting is "a typical New England women's college" (a phrase that would irk the protagonist, Sue Roper, intensely). The teacher is a woman, and so are all her students. The subject is advanced Spanish Conversation. Special care should be taken to prevent these particulars from limiting the discussion because the underlying issues of this case include racism, trust, control of the classroom, the effectiveness of modeling ethical values, and crisis-management -- all issues with universal applicability.

The case is particularly rich in description of the teacher's feelings. Sue Roper speaks of her intense misery and sense of failure when she found herself stymied in "her" classroom by a remark she considered racist. Her honesty and commitment make it easy to empathize with her. This openness and the issue of racism itself allow participants to get involved with this case quite readily.

Mood

Sue "still shakes" when she recalls these events. A long-time social activist, she recoils at the possibility that racism could have cropped up in a class she was leading. Like-minded discussion participants will share her agony. Others of a more skeptical ilk may accuse her of hypersensitivity. If both opinions (and the spectrum in between) appear in the discussion, controversy may accompany them. As with most episodes of human interaction, the true significance of what really occurred will retain its essential mystery. Did Carrie, a white student, balk at working with Sarah, a black student, out of blatant, reckless racism? The teacher assumed so, and still feels certain she was right. But Carrie denied it, and we will never know. The discussion leader should prepare to explore the ambiguities, exploiting the participants' involvement to first encourage close attention to the case details, and then a lasting appreciation of the limits of any teacher's perceptions and power (particularly under conditions of stress).

Suggested Uses

In this researcher's opinion, this is a reasonably advanced case whose details bring out important questions of methodology and philosophy. Sue Roper is an experienced teacher with a clear idea of her multiple purposes and sufficient expertise to know how to arrange things to serve her ends. Neither a beginner nor a jaded old-timer, she blends innocence and experience in a way that can stimulate wide-ranging discussion, partly because Sue's behavior seems contradictory at times. A committed liberal, she behaves autocratically in the classroom and feels almost violently betrayed when a student seems to differ from the values she labors so hard to impart. For reasons like this, the case requires advance preparation (unlike a minicase, for example), and should be read in advance of the discussion. "I Felt as if My World Had Just Collapsed!" could be scheduled according to its content -- say, in a workshop dealing with classroom crises, or the place of moral issues in teaching. It could also fit into a segment of a longer teaching unit in which the introductory issues -- like establishing a contract, setting a classroom mood, creating a learning group -- have already been broached and the group is ready to work on a more advanced level.

Sue's challenges are those of the experienced teacher. Having done many things "right" for a long time (even win-

---

This teaching note was prepared by Research Associate Dr. Abby J. Hansen as an aid to instructors in the classroom use of the case series "I Felt as if My World Had Just Collapsed!" (A) 9–383–171, (B) 9–383–172, and (C) 9–383–173.

ning several teaching awards), she finds herself completely derailed by a student who breaks from the norm of unquestioning, polite compliance with the teacher's directions. Sue assumes that the teacher can create the classroom's emotional climate almost singlehandedly, and that modeling moral qualities is a virtual guarantee that the students will pick them up. If a student violates Sue's moral code, that must mean either that Sue has made some obscure but fatal error or that the student is willfully refusing to cooperate. The challenge to the discussion leader is not only to elicit these poles of interpretation but to get the group to color in the gray area between them.

Conflicts, Sensitivities

The first word of the (A) case is "Racism!" This, of course, poses an obvious challenge. How can the discussion leader protect any "minority" participants from embarrassment during the discussion of this case? One obvious answer is not to single them out for "expert" testimony unless they clearly signal their desire to present a specialized viewpoint. Another way to cushion the issue -- appropriately, in this researcher's opinion -- is to lay early stress upon the wider issues like perception, challenge to authority, breach of contract, and morality in classroom process. Many participants have tended to shrug off as minor the central incident in this case because they have experienced or witnessed far less ambiguous incidents of prejudice. The discussion leader should be prepared to handle potentially disturbing anecdotal material if the participants present it. If the discussion is being conducted in a predominantly white institution, the blacks in the group can hardly fail to have some personal reactions to this case, but if they choose not to reveal these during the discussion, it would be best not to expose them to potential embarrassment by pointedly soliciting their comments.

The "Blocks" of Analysis

The following rubrics occur to the researcher as convenient segments into which to divide the topics of discussion -- simply for purposes of providing a rough map of the terrain by which the discussion leader may remain oriented during the free give-and-take of the actual conversation.

1. *Setting.* Note the school, its popular reputation, what we know of its actuality, and the classroom itself.

2. *Characters.* What information do we have about the teacher, the two key students, the rest of the class?

3. *The course.* First of all, does a language class involve special teaching problems? What about the composition of the class? How does Sue Roper seem to approach the course?

4. *Operational issues.* What sorts of tasks does Sue assign her students? How does she lead the group? In other words, how does the class operate (perform the assigned tasks)?

5. *Contract.* Sue sets the usual one-sided contract with her students. In her case, it seems to be a highly personal, emotionally charged one. What does she offer the students, and what does she expect in return?

6. *Control.* How does Sue lead the group? Where do you place her on a spectrum from authoritarian to laissez-faire?

7. *Establishing a good classroom atmosphere.* What does Sue seem to be doing to encourage her students to feel comfortable with her and with each other? How does she try to promote the "right atmosphere" and what does she think that atmosphere should be?

8. *Modeling.* Sue seems to place a great deal of faith in modeling values (openness, acceptance) as a means of imparting them. To what extent does she succeed? How reliable is this technique?

9. *Questions.* Several of Sue's quoted questions are really disguised commands. What are some of the subtle functions of questions -- and how do these vary by phrasing, tone of voice?

10. *Responses.* Note that Sue's greatest problem in this crisis is how to respond. When Carrie refuses to work with Sarah, Sue feels all eyes are on her, waiting for her to do something. What options does she have? What are some of the ways teachers can respond in the classroom, and what are their implications?

11. *Limits of influence.* How much control does a teacher really exert over students? What are some of the limits of that control?

12. *Protection.* The issue of protecting the weak is always embedded somewhere in the teaching situation. The question of

who, exactly, needs protection and how best to protect them is often far from simple to answer.

13. Interpretation. This dovetails with response. Sue Roper interprets Carrie's remark as racist. Is this the only possible interpretation?

14. Responsibility. Closely allied with the issue of protection is the question of responsibility. Who is accountable for what happens in the classroom? What are the reciprocal rights and responsibilities of teacher and students?

15. Timing. This relates to the issue of response. How much time can a teacher allow to pass before making some sort of response to a situation that he or she considers unacceptable? Is swiftness of response a virtue or a mistake? What about delay as a tactic?

These topics neither exhaust all the possibilities in this case, nor segment it with perfect neatness. It will be noted that some of them overlap. Nonetheless, the discussion leader who uses these -- or some logical breakdown of the issues in this case -- will ease the burden of staying oriented during the sometimes associative ebb and flow of discussion.

Preparing for the Discussion

Opening Speaker; Backstop

This case presents no particularly knotty problems in the choice of a first speaker. Sue Roper is a woman, rather liberal in her social views, and a teacher of Spanish at a New England women's college. The usual considerations apply: to start "from strength," one might call on a participant with a similar profile, at the risk of beginning the case on too limited a note and allowing teachers from other disciplines to assume at first that the problems of teaching Spanish are unique and not transferable to their disciplines. To avoid this, one could select an opening speaker with a very different profile from Sue Roper -- perhaps a male teacher of science -- and ask him to concentrate on those elements of Sue's predicament that are human and universal. Balance is a reasonable criterion for selecting the backstop. If one has asked a woman somewhat like Sue Roper to open, one might choose a male backstop -- and vice versa.

The Discussion Questions

Foreword. This case can be taught with emphasis on either the operational (action-oriented) or the theoretical (principle-oriented) aspects of teaching. The discussion leader must decide whether to stress and amplify questions related to what Sue Roper did (or might have done) to create the atmosphere she wanted and inculcate morality as well as good Spanish conversational skills in her students, or to stress questions that probe the situation and raise basic issues such as control, influence, modeling of values, and teaching style. This note will provide both sorts of questions and consider possible answers. Varying our frequent practice, we will begin with an operational question and then broaden the discussion to include analysis and theoretical considerations.

*   *   *

After the (A) case has been read, the following questions can be addressed:

1.   [To the opening speaker]: Could you start us off with a recommendation to Sue? Speaking as a friend of hers, what would you advise her to do at the end of the (A) case?

Responses to this action-oriented question will vary according to one's approach to the whole situation. The discussion leader should be alert for clues to the speaker's basic orientation in order to assure that other points of view also emerge. One's reply will tally with one's attitude toward the inculcation of morality in the classroom. What is Sue Roper's real mission in this Spanish class? What is her most basic, most inescapable responsibility -- to teach Spanish conversation skills, or to teach ethical values?

If one agrees with Sue that morality is the bedrock of true education and its teaching is the instructor's most abiding, most important responsibility, one may very well recommend forcing the issue of racism. Sue has two extreme choices: she could stop the class, confront Carrie's racism, declare this behavior unacceptable, and demand that Carrie work with Sarah. Or -- on the other end of the spectrum -- she could "roll with the punch," pretend nothing had happened, assign Carrie a different partner, and swallow her own fury. The discussion group should mention as many middle courses as possible.

While many find the classroom the ideal arena for moral education -- and the teacher's responsibility an essentially moral trust -- others may differ violently. Not everyone equates teaching with preaching. Why should a superior grasp of Spanish language and literature certify Sue as an ethical model? Some might assert that the teacher's highest duty in the classroom is to avoid partisanship and refrain from abusing the intrinsic influence of the teacher's position.

On the side of moral modeling, participants will recommend a variety of responses that may include delivering a speech on racism to Carrie, giving a general speech to the whole class, demanding a personal apology to Sarah, and buying time -- if only to formulate a more effective strategy for confronting the issue of racism in class at some future date.

On the other side, some participants may express lack of sympathy for Sue Roper's whole approach to teaching. She deliberately introduces personal details of family life, embraces "openness" and "honesty" and expects her students to reciprocate in kind. Some teachers espouse objectivity, neutrality, purely intellectual (rather than emotional) content, and a certain mystery about their private lives.

2.   [To the backstop]: What would you select as the most important factors in the whole situation?

This extremely broad, open-ended question could lend itself to considerations of the setting (women's school, conventional classroom with movable desk-chairs), the racial composition of the class, Sue Roper's personality, approach, and reputation, or the material of the course. The discussion leader should be prepared to work with whatever the participants select as paramount -- suggesting the remaining elements for consideration during the rest of the discussion.

Let us begin with the personalities of the principal characters as they are given in the (A) case. Sue Roper dominates the description, partly because she is the case informant, and partly because she is an eloquent, lively, intense person. Her self-description is extremely apposite: a civil rights activist, who "consciously" models moral values in the classroom in line with her "conviction" that "teachers shouldn't shy away from moral issues," she asserts that she "doesn't hesitate to reveal" herself and that, to her, there is nothing more personally offensive than racism.

Added to this, we have a description of Sue's office (to which the discussion leader might refer in class if no participant mentions it): the room is cluttered with colorful objects (sombreros, toys, posters, shawls), notes for several projects, and many people. What attracts these people to Sue? Is her warmth unusual at Greenwood College? Despite Sue's emotional intensity, she does not seem to function purely on instinct in the classroom; she plans, theorizes, and works out tactics to achieve her pedagogical purposes.

Our data on the involved students are a great deal thinner. The offending student, Carrie Draper, is "a rather quiet white girl from Ohio, a sophomore interested in European art history." The "insulted" student, Sarah Hawley, is "a black girl from Washington, D.C.," a junior majoring in economics. We know that both girls have "shown strong language skills," and that Sue, who encourages social mingling in her classes, has not previously seen them speaking together.

What can we guess from these few details? Possibly, the white student comes from a wealthier background: art history is a less practical major than economics. We have no way of knowing what previous experience either student has had with members of other races. In any case, we may gather that the two students have different interests, and they are not members of the same graduating class. Also they are clearly not friends. It is even possible that there may be some sort of grudge between them. This is a conversation class, but Sue has not seen them in conversation: are they intentionally avoiding each other? Proponents of the "live and let live" school of teaching may point out this possibility. Sue Roper has an interventionist teaching style. People of a more self-contained inclination might say that, having noticed that these two students had not spoken together, Sue should have refrained from pairing them (at least until she had privately raised the possibility with them to see if it provoked painful grimaces).

Another significant factor in the situation is certainly the school itself. Greenwood College for Women is suburban, almost a hundred years old, and generally considered "predominantly white and middle class." The case notes the college's "significant efforts to recruit minority students." Is this a sign that minority students would not expect Greenwood to be hospitable without special prompting? At the time of this incident, 75 out of 800

Greenwood students were "officially classified as 'minorities.'" That's less than 10%; and we should bear in mind that the term <u>minorities</u> includes several racial and ethnic groups besides American blacks like Sarah. It seems reasonable to assume that students like Sarah felt conspicuous and outnumbered on this campus.

In the opinion of this researcher, the single most important factor in this situation is the teacher's highly personal style. Sue mentions that she deliberately introduces opinions into the classroom, creates assignments to break up cliques she perceives, and tries to get students of different backgrounds to befriend each other. In her extracurricular time she is something of a crusader for racial equality. Sue is not a woman to accept the world as she finds it, and her forthright nature expresses itself in an interventionist teaching style. As a teacher Sue seems to fall closer to the "controlling" than the "directing" end of the spectrum -- the difference being one of subtlety. She is friendly, warm, and cordial, but she gives orders. Her description of the exercise that provided the background for this upsetting incident shows her assuming most of the responsibility for what occurred in the classroom. She had "begun to prepare some students for their next task," in which she would "pair" them according to her own priorities (although her system may have seemed arbitrary to the students).

At this point in the (A) case, Sue shows a certain dissociation from the process. Having directed this exercise for several years, she can fly on automatic pilot. Instead of observing the students' responses to her orders, she delivers a "standard speech" and does not look intently at their reactions. One important element of the situation might be Sue's momentary inattention. This was, after all, a routine classroom assignment that had never triggered any particularly unpleasant scenes before. Why should she have scanned the students for danger signs? We gather that Carrie had never given any warning of unusual recalcitrance or deviation from the social norms of the college. But there does seem to be some irony in comparing Sue Roper's extremely accepting social philosophy with her directive method of leading the class and anger at Carrie for resisting.

When this issue -- Sue's classroom style -- is raised, it might be useful to brainstorm a bit. What other techniques might she have tried, to accomplish her purpose? For example, she might have invited the students to choose their own partners for classroom dialogues with the stipulation that she -- or some recording secretary chosen by the class -- would be responsible for making sure that every student had spoken with every other member of the class by the end of the semester. Such an approach would have given at least the illusion of free choice, within a clear framework. In this system, Carrie might have postponed working with Sarah, but not avoided it, and the postponement might have given her time to perform her task more graciously.

3.   **What is at stake at the end of the (A) case?**

This question is a lead-in for the (B) case, which reveals what Sue Roper did in response to Carrie's shocking refusal to work with Sarah. There are, of course, several viewpoints from which to answer this question. At the end of the case, we find Sue Roper feeling shell-shocked by what she is certain was a racist remark. She describes herself as "positively sick." But she is trapped in front of a class of fifteen Greenwood students; five of them are black, and one of them -- Sarah Hawley -- is the victim of what Sue calls "a stunning slap in the face." Sue has to maintain her dignity. The other students have not "dared look at Sarah"; we do not know if they are looking at Carrie. But the teacher remembers "feeling them watch me to see what I'd do." What is at stake for Sarah Hawley, whom Carrie has just rejected as a partner because "we're . . . we're not in the same dormitory"? (One's reaction to this will depend on one's interpretation of Carrie's remark. Is she hastily wallpapering a rabidly racist remark? Might she have some other reason for balking at working with Carrie -- whose language skills, we have been told, were as good as hers?) Also very important is the question of what is at stake for Carrie. If her remark <u>was</u> racist, what consequences can she expect? If the remark was innocent, what price will she pay for having been misunderstood?

The most striking character in this configuration is, of course, the teacher, to whose intense misery we have extensive testimony. Having carefully constructed a socially healthy microcosm in her Spanish Conversation class, Sue feels personally betrayed, sick, and shocked when Carrie refuses to get up and sit beside Sarah and begin to plan a small class presentation with her. To Sue, her authority as a teacher and moral model is clearly on the line; her orders have been defied. But in her opinion, there is also much more at stake: her whole world. The discussion leader should ask some probing questions on this point. In what sense is the classroom a "world"? And who rules it? How does the teacher control this little planet? In what way (if at all) does Carrie's uncooperative reaction reflect upon Sue's leadership?

Finally, we must consider the other students. How might the other minority students in the room have felt? What about the "non-blacks"? At the very least one would expect embarrassment on every side, and a great deal of sympathy for Sarah. We can also probably count on feelings of intense discomfort. Any breach of social norms will produce a general squirm. Racism aside, Carrie's refusal to cooperate with Sue's polite request was quite enough to produce an undercurrent of tension in the class. One wonders, however, whether the other students in the room immediately and unequivocally interpreted Carrie's words as racist, and whether they -- like Sue -- felt that their tacit contract to accept and trust each other had been brutally violated.

*   *   *

After the (B) case has been read:

1. **Sue seems to have acted on instinct -- most of us do under fire. What do you think of her response?**

The participants should take a close look at Sue's movements -- "I turned back to Sarah," she says, adding these words: "Please take out your minidrama so you can see which one you and Carrie will perform." In a sense, Sue has symbolically rejected Carrie by turning away from her. She has made her physical gesture (of solidarity) in the direction of the injured party -- Sarah -- and seems simply to be ignoring Carrie's refusal as if it were so ludicrous that it could not possibly be taken seriously. Sue's actual words are a repeated command. In the mouths of teachers, polite questions beginning with "Would you please" are generally orders -- as students learn, almost as early as they learn to brush their teeth. (To demonstrate this subtext of command we have Sue's report of her accompanying thoughts: "Damn it, there's no way I'm going to let Carrie get away with this sort of behavior in my class!" One could hardly ask for a clearer statement of determination.) Participants will react to Sue's actions and words in ways that tally with their sympathy for her and

her point of view. If they, too, consider Carrie's refusal to work with Sarah as racist, and find Sue's social mission in the classroom appropriate (or even noble), they will either applaud her for standing firm or suggest that she might have gone much further in the direction of confrontation. Perhaps she could have turned toward Carrie -- with a stinging rebuke. On the other side, participants who think Sue has overreacted, or who differ with her directive style of managing the undergraduates, will say that she should have backed off, bought time, and let the situation cool off.

In discussing the (B) case, the leader should note that Sue's response took a while to develop. Only after repeating her words to Sarah did she turn back to Carrie and begin to argue: "It doesn't matter if you aren't in the same dorm. . . . There's absolutely no reason you can't work together." What is the effect of this direct refutation of Carrie's stated reasons for refusing to work with Sarah? Participants may applaud its comprehensiveness or disapprove of it because it brings the teacher down to Carrie's level, exposing her to charges of "protesting too much." Sue seems to be overwhelming Carrie with advice, and her statement that there is "absolutely no reason you can't work together" is a risk. Perhaps there is some reason, something that should be aired only in private. How can Sue know? Is she treading on thin ice by insisting that these two students work together? (At this point in the case, there's no way to tell.)

2. **What about Sue's concern with "the larger sense" of the problem?**

As the class hour progressed, Sue intentionally tried to dissociate her boiling feelings from her public behavior. Carrie did get up and walk across the room to sit beside Sarah, and Sarah permitted her to do so without demanding an apology or creating any sort of public stir, but Sue continued to stew over the larger implications of the incident. It is interesting to note that Sue's self-control seems to have paid off, for she got through the rest of the class without incident (despite her private agonizing), and the two girls did perform their minidrama in class a week later.

The discussion leader should draw attention to their performance. Is there, perhaps, something suspicious about its "innocuousness"? What significance is there in the fact that the two students chose Sarah's script, and that the content of that script was conventional, to say the least? And what about the grade (B+) Sue awarded both students for this bland performance?

The central issues to discuss in this section of the case are those of responsibility, public versus private confrontation (what would have happened if Sue had stopped the class to accuse Carrie of blatant racism?), and, finally, the overarching question of the larger implications of this incident.

3. **Should Sue have let the matter drop after the girls performed their minidrama in class?**

Again, there will be a spectrum of response. Answers will range from "certainly" to "certainly not," depending upon how pernicious people consider the initial incident. Those who share Sue's orientation -- or who have become more sympathetic during the discussion -- may argue that the classroom is truly a microcosm, and the teacher's duty included publicly labeling and rejecting clearly unacceptable behavior. Some will say that a flimsy excuse like Carrie's so obviously masked pure prejudice that only a cowardly teacher would have let her get away with it (and Sue did not). On the other hand, some participants may cling to their skeptical view of the prospects for success of Sue's social mission. A classroom is just another room, they may say. Students do not surrender their free will or their prejudices at the door. Whatever sort of modeling a teacher may choose to do still leaves them room to demur and disagree. Furthermore, some might argue, the responsibility for protecting Sarah should really rest with Sarah herself. Shouldn't Sue have allowed her the privilege of seeking Carrie out privately and demanding an apology? Some may also argue that Sue's passing thought of alerting a black dean (Cynthia Wilson) was an excellent idea. If anyone has the clear mission to guard Greenwood's minority students against racism, surely it is Cynthia Wilson.

4. **Given that Sue felt obliged to pursue the matter, how would you have advised her to do this?**

There are several courses of action Sue might have taken. She might have called each student to her office for a private rehash of the incident and, in Carrie's case, an explanation. She might have called them in together to make it clear that she expected them to learn to work together -- as a lesson in cooperation

as well as Spanish conversation. She might have taken the weekend to plan a cool-headed, well-reasoned speech on racism for the whole class. She might have telephoned Dean Wilson to ask what similar incidents had occurred on campus and how these had been treated. Or she might have lodged some sort of formal complaint with Carrie's dean and asked for an official reprimand.

Certainly, whatever course of action Sue decided upon, the prime ingredients to improve this situation had to include time and information (they usually do).

It would be valuable to call for discussion of Sue's compulsion to take some long-term action. The students had complied with her initial request and performed their assignment together. Wasn't that enough? Did Sue feel unsatisfied because of her personal sensitivity to racism? Or is there possibly some broad issue of institutional responsibility at stake? Can one extrapolate from a teacher's permitting a hint of racism to drop in class unremarked and unchallenged to an institutional personality? If black students are permitted to be insulted in class, what does this mean for the institution? And what does it mean for the larger society that holds such an institution in generally high esteem? Putting yourself in Sarah's shoes, how might you have felt when Carrie balked at having you as a working partner, and then only grudgingly agreed to team up with you?

The discussion leader should take care to assure that participants do not brush Sue off as a knee-jerk liberal, just as they should not leap to brand Carrie as a racist.

*　　*　　*

After the (C) case has been read:

1. **How do you appraise Sue's report of her conferences with the two students?**

Carrie, it seems, stubbornly denied any racist content to her remark even though it had struck Sue (and, apparently, many other students in the class) as patently prejudiced. Is it possible that Sue lost an opportunity to educate Carrie, letting her animosity show and inspiring feelings of defensiveness? Accusations usually breed denials and rationalizations (often quite creative ones). What tactics might Sue have adopted to relax Carrie, find out what she really meant by her refusal to work with Sarah, and ascertain whether actually going through with the assignment had done anything to change her views?

Sarah, on the other hand, seems to have relaxed with Sue -- not surprisingly, given Sue's reputation for friendliness and helpfulness to black students. In fact, Sarah's attitude, as Sue reports it, confirms Sue's assumptions about the implications of Carrie's remark in class. Her words might be stressed and offered for consideration to participants who have been espousing the "tempest in a teapot" approach. Sarah applies the microcosm/macrocosm model here, and associates the incident with larger structures: There is racism at Greenwood, she says. Everybody knows it; nobody really fights against it; and some teachers actively promote it. In this interview, we note that Sue truly assumes an advisory position and offers Sarah some responsibility for improving her own situation: "Sit with Carrie . . . make conversation . . . you can't always expect other people to assume the burden of friendship," she says.

The discussion leader should try to emphasize this passage, citing it if no participant does. For this is a true nugget of instruction. In this part of the case we see Sue focusing on the larger implications of the incident and trying to help her student learn to solve her own problems. Carrie has objected to the black students' cliquishness (which is, no doubt, the result of their fear of rejection). Sue tells Sarah to break away from her black friends and make a few overtures to people like Carrie. Multiply this several hundredfold and more interracial friendships might indeed take root at Greenwood. Sue seems finally (in this case, at least) to have grasped the sad truth that she cannot protect her students all the time. They have to learn to protect themselves and, further, help lay the groundwork of structures (wider friendships, for example) that will extend the protection throughout society.

2.   **What about Sue Roper's feelings that Carrie had "duped" her and that she, the teacher, had "somehow failed the group"?**

This question carries deep implications in the realms of contract, more modeling, and responsibility -- all of which should have been touched upon in the discussion. But these are enduring problems; they should be reconsidered often. Sue learned a bitter lesson of the limitations of her power to create atmosphere and control the classroom dynamic. Some teachers try to stuff information into students' heads and

feel frustrated when they absorb it incorrectly (or not at all). In Sue's case, the lessons she wanted to inculcate were emotional and ethical, and her technique was double-barreled: she both instructed her students openly, and created assignments to force them out of their social ruts. She also assumed that modeling a system of values and practicing emotional honesty would inspire exactly those qualities in her students. The questions are: Has she failed? What is success? Can one look for instantaneous results in teaching? How can one measure students' moral progress?

Needless to say, these questions have no simple answers, but they are, in the opinion of the researcher, essential.

Exhibit 1

I Felt as if My World Had Just Collapsed! (A)

Study Questions

1.   What is most significant about the principal characters of this situation?

2.   How does the school's atmosphere affect the main incidents?

3.   How do Sue Roper's assumptions affect her teaching?

4.   What is the greatest challenge Sue faces at the end of the (A) case?

5.   What should she do?

Exhibit 2

I Felt as if My World Had Just Collapsed!

Discussion Questions

After the (A) case has been read:

1.   [To the opening speaker]: Could you start us off with a recommendation to Sue Roper? Speaking as her friend, what would you advise her to do at the end of the (A) case?

2. [To the backstop]: What would you select as the most important factors in the whole situation?

3. What is at stake at the end of the (A) case?

*   *   *

After the (B) case has been read:

1. What do you think of Sue's response to Carrie's unexpected refusal to cooperate?

2. What about Sue's concern with "the larger sense" of the problem?

3. Should Sue have let the matter drop after the two girls performed their minidrama in class?

4. Given that Sue felt obliged to pursue the matter, how would you have advised her to do so?

*   *   *

After the (C) case has been read:

1. How do you appraise Sue's report of her conferences with the two students?

2. What about Sue's feelings that Carrie had "duped" her and that she, the teacher, had "somehow failed the group"?

I Felt as if My World Had Just Collapsed!

Researcher's Perspective

Among the usual "who, what, where, when, how" of the typical analysis, I consider two factors -- the <u>where</u> and the <u>who</u> -- by far the most important in this particular set of incidents. Despite its official policy to recruit minority students, Greenwood College for Women comes across as a conservative, upscale institution, preppy, Ivy League, and exclusive. Such an environment, with its traditional social homogeneity, would seem somewhat uneasy for at least two of the important characters in this case -- Sue Roper and Sarah Hawley. Sue's emotional forthrightness and outgoing approach to teaching seem out of step with the generally muted, reticent sort of style one associates with places like Greenwood (at least traditionally). Sarah Hawley, Sue's student, is a black girl from Washington, D.C. The (C) case tells us that Sarah's background is working-class, and she, herself, thought of leaving Greenwood until her parents persuaded her to stay.

Sue Roper portrays herself as an activist for racial equality, unusually sensitive to the feelings of minorities, and extremely zealous in protecting their interests. (One gathers that she is not, herself, a member of a group usually termed a "minority" under the Affirmative Action Statutes, so the question of condescension or "white guilt" may come up in discussion.) In any case, Sue has other characteristics that mark her as unusual, perhaps <u>sui generis</u>, in a "New England women's college." Her personal warmth and outgoing, honest, almost confessional style of teaching set her apart, and the case shows us her effusive, expressive gestures (she "pushes" the very word <u>racism</u> away from her physically, for example). Her office is another clue to her personality. It is friendly in its clutter, full of inviting, almost childlike objects (sombreros, posters, toys) that she uses as audio-visual aids. Even more important, her office is full of people -- students, fellow teachers, and friends. This copiousness seems almost an objective correlative for some aspects of Sue's personality: she surrounds herself with bright, playful objects and a variety of people (while many college teachers opt for neat bookshelves and as few people as possible to interrupt their private thoughts).

We also note Sue tapping a pencil nervously (first page of (A) case) as she speaks to the researcher. She is a volatile woman, we gather -- used to expressing powerful emotions physically and verbally, and also used to having people like and respect her for this quality. (Her office would not have been so full of colleagues, students, and friends if her style had not attracted them.)

Let us turn to the other important characters in this case -- Sue's students. We know a good deal less about them because Sue is the case informant; we must be content with her impressions of them. Carrie Draper, a sophomore, is a white girl from Ohio, and a student of European art history. What does this tell us? Perhaps we may infer a degree of affluence in her Midwestern background from her declared major in European art history, which is not a subject that one takes in preparation for a lucrative career. We also know that she has "strong language skills," but not any stronger than Sarah Hawley's (her black colleague). Not until the (C) case do we learn a few more things about Carrie. Confronted with a direct accusation of racism, she flatly denies it. But Sue Roper follows this information with some behind-the-scenes gossip she has heard about Carrie: apparently Carrie had been assigned a black roommate at the beginning of the semester, but had arranged to have the assignment changed. Why? On this point we have no information. Carrie herself makes two negative statements about

---

This commentary was written by Research Associate Dr. Abby J. Hansen for the Developing Discussion Leadership Skills and the Teaching by the Case Method seminars. Its objective is to help instructors in the development of their teaching plans for this case.

blacks at Greenwood College: they are cliquish and they play loud music in the dorms.

About Sarah we have only a bit more information. She is a junior from Washington, D.C., proficient in Spanish, and an economics major. Her purpose in remaining at Greenwood despite some misgivings about the place (where she thinks racism is so embedded that nobody notices it except those who suffer from it) is to become "upwardly mobile," and enter the job market with a prestigious degree in economics. In other words, Sarah is doing her best to improve her socioeconomic status. To Sarah, Carrie's instinctive and rude public rejection was obviously racist. "I know Carrie didn't want to work with me because I'm black," she says, and goes on to tally Carrie's feelings with the whole background of Greenwood culture: "There's plenty of racism at Greenwood." "One teacher assigns a textbook that describes blacks as inferior. If the teachers are racist, what can you expect of the students?" Sarah thus comes off as a sensitive person under family pressure to endure the sometimes bruising rejections implicit in the culture of a basically alien environment.

Interestingly, each of these girls feels that the other wants nothing to do with her. Carrie finds the black girls cliquish (which implies hostility to non-blacks like herself) and alien in their musical tastes. Sarah, on the other hand, finds the dominant culture at the school shot full of racism, and includes at least one teacher in her assessment. Such mutual distrust cannot fail to have its effect in the classroom.

The issue of trust (or its opposite) brings us back to Sue Roper again -- for trust is one of her most cherished values. In the (C) case, Sue cites trust when she explains why she continued to "feel distant from Carrie," who, she thinks, had "deceived" her. What form had this deceit taken? "A betrayal of trust." To Sue, the fact that Carrie had "openly rejected Sarah" in class (even though she did later rescind that rejection and publicly accept Sarah as a working partner) constituted a violation of faith. "I still feel that Carrie duped me," says Sue. To dupe someone is to fool them, to conceal the truth from them, to lie. Sue seems to think that Carrie sneaked her intrinsic racism into the classroom and sat in silent cynicism as Sue openly proclaimed her liberal views and confided her deepest feelings about the necessity for social equality. Then Carrie took the first opportunity in class to reveal

her true colors. ("Wham!" says Sue. "She openly rejected Sarah.") This seems overstated.

In my opinion, the private content of Carrie's rejection, "I'm not going to work with Sarah," will forever remain a mystery to us. Only Carrie can know what really motivated it, if her subsequent rationalizations have not clouded the truth, even for her. We do know that the reason she gave ("We aren't in the same dorm") might or might not have had something to do with race (the black students chose to live apart). It might have had more to do with accessibility.

It seems surprising that the initial incident with all its potential for true, lasting hurt, blew over with relative gentleness. Sue stood her ground, and -- without stopping the class for a passionate address on the subject of social acceptance or the utter perniciousness of racism -- made it clear that "there was no way" Carrie was going to get out of working with Sarah. Sue stuck to practical details as she argued her point with Carrie: the girls could meet in the student union, or they could talk on the phone. (This seems considerate.) Leaving the volatile and potentially devastating issue of racism aside in a class that is 30% black seems to embody the better part of diplomacy. Had Sue stopped the class for an impromptu speech on racism, I believe the black students would have felt not only rejected and singled out for special treatment, but also condescended to by their non-black protectress. These feelings would have been not only extremely painful (rejection always hurts) but also "infantilizing."

In sum, I find the actual course of action that Sue Roper took to deal with this situation to have been the best, given the circumstances. In this, I disagree with Sue, herself, who "still feels I failed the whole group and I failed myself" for not confronting the issue instantly.

In any teaching case, the question of long-term success or failure is always complex. What lesson did Sue's action teach her students? Perhaps one could say that her self-control under pressure was educational. Certainly, the students must have known Sue well enough to realize that Carrie's initial rejection of Sarah had shocked and upset her deeply. Second, she decided to postpone any confrontation of the issue until after the two girls had worked together in class and completely fulfilled the original terms of her assignment. In other words, Sue insisted on exercising her classroom prerogative of making assignments as she thought best and requiring that the students perform them. In this we see another side of Sue's personality that I think extremely apposite, for a certain directive quality distinguishes her teaching style. Her personal intensity seems to be powerful enough to envelop the students in a charged emotional force field -- one that they enter either because they agree with her values and inclinations or because they are drawn into her vortex by sheer energy.

Sue seems aware of her ability to create a unique emotional climate in the classroom. Her fifteen years of teaching experience have certainly not been lost on her. On the contrary, she has learned a great deal of sophistication in controlling the class. She knows how to speak to students. She knows what kind of body language to use to involve and include them in the classroom process. She also knows how to create assignments that will give the illusion of turning the classroom over to them -- pairing them in teams, for example. But she really continues to hold all the cards. Her overarching purpose is indisputably benevolent: she wants to break up cliques in order to widen students' social horizons and, at the very least, expose them to a variety of conversational styles. But her assumptions about the true power of any teacher to impart basic values seem to be inflated. Can one always transmit social values by modeling them? What about students' private right to disagree, to find the teacher's values untenable, even to consider the teacher ridiculous? Does a teacher who notices disagreement on a student's part have the right to feel duped, cheated, thwarted, betrayed? To what extent can a teacher monitor the impression he or she makes on a student's mind and heart?

A further caveat I would add to these considerations is the possibility that Carrie did learn a lesson about racism. She performed the team assignment successfully with a black partner, and it can hardly have escaped her attention that her partner's command of Spanish was equal, if not superior, to her own. Also the girls chose Sarah's, not Carrie's, dialogue to memorize and present. I wouldn't put too much emphasis on Carrie's evasiveness in confer-ence with Sue, because Sue's hostility must have been apparent to Carrie, and defensiveness is not a favorable soil in which to nurture honesty.

It is possible that Carrie did, in fact, blurt out her initial remark from racist motivations, but the ensuing emotional turmoil -- Sarah's hurt feelings and the teacher's obvious shock -- may have horrified her sufficiently to prevent her from making a similar remark again. Unless we assume that Carrie was some sort of monster (she seems to have been quite an ordinary student), she can hardly have failed to regret her own remark. Perhaps having made it and then realizing she would have to live it down was lesson enough for her.

To my way of thinking, this case provides a lesson in humility for teachers. Sue Roper came to this Spanish class with fifteen years of teaching experience, solid credentials as a crusader for social equality, and an extremely engaging teaching style. But all of these positive factors did not prevent disaster. Sue faced the limits of her power to create the sort of classroom atmosphere she valued. And she faced the ineradicable recalcitrance of human nature. Despite Sue's heroic efforts to model certain values, Carrie let slip an unfortunate remark of the very sort Sue most detested. But Sue's self-control and instinctive realization that direct confrontation would only exacerbate the painful situation seem to have been laudably tactful reactions. They pointed the way to a long-term solution to the problem in which Sue's initial requests were successfully met. In the long run, she finally took her opportunity to discuss the event privately, calmly, and in some depth with its two protagonists. The art of teaching can never be sufficiently mastered to prevent all unsettling reversals, but the realization that tact, above all, must be invoked to contain them can help teachers through the initial few moments after a shock, when the temptation for hasty, emotional reaction is almost overwhelming. Her actual classroom behavior was protective in the best sense, and avoided hurting either Carrie or Sarah. As Sue herself puts it in the (B) case, "When a teacher humiliates a student, it shows the teacher's weakness, not the student's."

Part II   Professional School Teaching Seminar

Professional School Teaching Seminar

Introduction

James F. Moore

This note is designed to support a discussion leader's stewardship of a seminar for instructors teaching in a professional school milieu. Case method teaching is a rich and complex craft. The materials that follow represent an attempt to explicate that craft, to promote dialogue about teaching, and to articulate some key elements in the practice of discussion leadership.

Background

As our society becomes more complex and the influence of professionals more widespread and powerful, a better understanding of professional practice is increasingly important. As Donald Schön puts it in The Reflective Practitioner:

We are in need of inquiry into the epistemology of practice. What is the kind of knowing in which competent practitioners engage? How is professional knowing like and unlike the kinds of knowledge presented in academic textbooks, scientific papers, and learned journals? In what sense, if any, is there intellectual rigor in professional practice?[1]

This kind of understanding may be particularly difficult to obtain because, as Schon says, universities are generally committed to "a view of knowledge that fosters selective inattention to practical competence and professional artistry." At the same time, practitioners often resist close analysis of their work, invoking a "mystique of practical competence":

When people use terms such as "art" and "intuition," they usually intend to terminate discussion rather than to open up inquiry. It is as though the practitioner says to his academic colleague, "While I do not accept your view of knowledge, I cannot describe my own. . . ." These attitudes have contributed to a widening rift between the universities and the professions, research and practice, thought and action. They feed into the university's familiar dichotomy between the "hard" knowledge of science and scholarship, and the "soft" knowledge of artistry and unvarnished opinion. There

is nothing here to guide practitioners who wish to gain a better understanding of the practical uses and limits of research-based knowledge, or to help scholars who wish to take a new view of professional action.[2]

A better understanding of professional practice should help us both in improving current performance and in transmitting skills from the adept to the novice. A continuing human task is to pass on the fruits of experience from one generation to the next. The problem of professional succession has historically been solved by apprenticeship, but that approach has several important limitations: knowledge can only be transmitted in face-to-face relationships over long periods of time, and unless students serve multiple apprenticeships they have little means to compare alternative approaches with the same professional challenges. Thus in most fields the attempt has been made to codify professional knowledge and make it systematically teachable -- hence, the impetus to establish professional schools.

The transmission of professional knowledge requires the creation of new relationships and new modes of analysis, description, and teaching. Close, collaborative relationships are needed between researchers and practitioners -- relationships built around the twin aims of understanding and improving professional practice. In addition, one must develop ways of describing and analyzing practice that capture its important dimensions and assist in teaching its essential features.

For over seventy-five years Harvard Business School has been deeply involved in just this sort of effort, directed toward understanding administrative practice. From the beginning, it was recognized that conventional modes of academic research and teaching were not generally well suited to the study of administration and that it would be necessary to invent alternative methods. Over the years a variety of approaches has been tried, and the unconventional nature of the School -- as seen from the perspective of the academic community -- has sometimes made it controversial.

1. Donald A. Schön, *The Reflective Practitioner* (New York: Basic Books, 1983), p. viii in Preface.
2. Ibid., p. vii in Preface.

Perhaps the most notable achievement of the School is the development of the case method in its modern form. Research is carried out by examining the practice of managers in a variety of settings. This requires an unusual relationship between university-based researchers and practitioners. Both must work together to examine what the practitioner does and how it might be improved. This research attempts to understand not only the tools and techniques that help practitioners be effective, but also the recurring problems that require managers to exercise judgment and take creative action.

The results of these inquiries are embodied in case descriptions of actual managerial situations. The situations are chosen and described so as to simulate for the reader the problem situations faced by managers. These cases become the focus of discussions about the nature of practice. Students are encouraged to identify the factors they believe are most crucial in a particular situation, the action the manager should take, and the generalizations that can usefully be drawn from the case -- building on both the classroom discussion and their own professional experience.

Though the case method is not a universal panacea, it has been a tremendously effective way to organize research and teaching about administrative practice. Its very effectiveness, however, has presented a difficulty for the Business School. Case method teaching -- including the conduct of research, the development of cases, and the organization and teaching of discussion courses -- is itself a professional enterprise requiring judgment and artistry. The School has had to develop not only modes of teaching about administration, but ways to pass on the art and craft of case research and teaching.

For most of the School's history this task has been accomplished principally by apprenticeship. Though this method has been effective within the School, it has all the limitations of apprenticeship in general. In particular, it has been difficult for the case method to spread to other institutions. Gradually, recognition grew that it was important to make a systematic attempt to understand and pass on the School's own professional practice of graduate education.

This task was first addressed when the School set up a program under the direction of Andrew Towl, a member of the faculty, to teach about the case method. This program, which was established in 1955 and continued for ten years, had a

good deal of success, particularly in stimulating the writing and use of cases at other schools. However, the art of case discussion leadership proved more resistant to diffusion. The nature of teaching practice seems more elusive; moreover, with good cases, the very interest of the content may have the effect of diverting attention from the process of teaching.

To address this problem, Andrew Towl and Thomas Graves, then assistant dean of the Harvard Business School, began a series of forums at which experienced case instructors were asked to speak about teaching. Though these continued with some success for several years, it was clear that, given the complexity of the art of discussion leadership, more needed to be done. Out of this effort, Professor Roland Christensen launched what grew to be a major enterprise aimed at better understanding the artistry of case discussion leadership. He established, in close collaboration with the Harvard-Danforth Center for Teaching and Learning, a yearly seminar on case teaching as well as a similar effort for the faculty of the Harvard Business School and its sister professional schools.

Building on this effort, Chris and I decided to embark on a new enterprise. Drawing on my background in the study of professional practice, we would work together to articulate, for a wider audience, the skills required to teach teachers about case method teaching. This effort took more than a year of close cooperative work. The resulting teaching notes, I hope, will convey key perceptions and skills involved in case method teaching and make possible a much broader dissemination of the method.

Seminar Goals and Working Plan

A central aim of our seminar is to foster an appreciation and understanding of the art of discussion leadership, and especially of the subspecies known as case method teaching. Good case discussions are profound educational events which achieve ends seldom reached by other methods. Some believe that the ability to lead such discussions is a rare and essentially unteachable gift. Others regard case discussions as glorified bull sessions and believe that leadership requires only patience, tolerance for student opinions, and (it is implied) little concern for academic rigor.

The seminar experience is intended to counter both of these views by helping participants define and examine the factors that contribute to effective discussion leadership. We wish to show that discussion leadership is a sophisticated ability, but one that is intelligible and can be developed through a close consideration of discussion situations and the broadly predictable challenges they present. To do so, we create a setting in which instructors can come together as colleagues to discuss their work, and to examine a selection of cases and questions that highlight key dimensions of discussion teaching.

The seminar is organized around themes we believe central to discussion teaching: establishing and managing the instructor-student learning contract; the critical skill requirements of questioning, listening, and responding; working out the balance between controlling versus directing the discussion; and exploring the basic operating "conundrums" that create difficulty for instructors dealing with handicapped students, problems of student apathy, and grading written and in-class participation.

The cases used in the seminar all describe actual situations. Though this seminar and these cases were originally designed for use at the Harvard Business School, we soon found that the issues raised have much wider applicability. Our colleagues from medicine, design and architecture, government and education have found participation in this seminar valuable. In fact, the central issues in discussion leadership are relevant to nearly all professionals who must manage group discussions of important and complex problems. This includes a spectrum from board chairmen to leaders of scientific and design teams.

In addressing each case, seminar members are asked to explore what is going on (i.e., to diagnose the case), what action should be taken, and what generalizations may be made. The relative emphasis on these three types of thinking changes over the twelve weeks of the seminar. We begin by stressing diagnosis; after several cases we move to a concentration on planning for action; and, finally, we shift to generalization. This modulation is accomplished principally through the strategic choice and sequencing of discussion questions, as described in detail in the "Suggested Process Plan" section of each teaching note.

Our initial emphasis on diagnosis is intended to help participants develop more complex views of situations that may initially strike them as simple and transparent. As seminar members compare their various perspectives, they come to recognize how their views of teaching situations are shaped by their own often unexamined assumptions. An early emphasis on diagnosis also helps develop norms and values that make the seminar more effective. It is important to encourage wide participation, attention to the details of the case text, accurate listening, respect for a diversity of opinion, and a willingness to explore the assumptions and implications of various views of the case. Focusing early seminar sessions on diagnosis helps establish these norms, since many people can be simultaneously "right" -- even if only partially so -- on diagnosis. Different diagnostic interpretations tend to be complementary, whereas different action plans are often mutually exclusive. Thus, discussions of action planning are often highly involving and full of conflict -- and, while exciting, could produce more heat than light if undertaken early in the seminar, before a firm basis of trust and mutual respect has been established among participants.

Our goal in the seminar is to produce better practitioners, not scholars, of teaching. An unremitting emphasis on diagnosis enables participants to develop a complex and articulated view of teaching situations, but may not help them turn their insights into effective action. Thus, as the semester progresses, we use strategic questioning to turn the attention of the group to action planning: we ask participants what they would do if they were in the shoes of the case protagonist. Seminar members begin to project themselves into the case situations, identifying with the players. Since participants' suggestions for action are often mutually exclusive, discussion often becomes spirited at this point. But, if the early meetings have established a fundamental respect for diversity -- and for each other -- such disagreements will seldom become contentious or disrespectful. These middle sessions are occasions for experimenting with high, emotional involvement -- teaching for the "gut" as well as for the intellect.

We conclude the seminar on a reflective note, asking participants to compare their philosophies of education with those presented in the cases. This emphasis on generalization gives members an opportunity to integrate and summarize for themselves the meaning of the seminar. Such reflection seems important in helping participants link the seminar discussions back to their teaching situations.

Creating the Setting

Virtually any institution of learning includes instructors who would like to get together to discuss their teaching practices. The basis for a teaching seminar may well be just such an informal group. Though this seminar has evolved into a course with a formal structure, it is in essence a group of colleagues, largely self-managed, who come together voluntarily to share their common questions and insights about teaching.

Whether such a group flourishes, once established, seems to depend upon a variety of factors. Some of these factors are relatively difficult to control, such as the institutional climate or the participants' personal chemistry (though the teaching notes in this manual do include suggestions for "Building the Seminar Group"). But, in our experience, the ultimate success of the venture depends to a surprising extent on several seemingly mundane factors which are relatively easy to control. For example, it is important to have a regular, convenient time and meeting place, so that members can adjust their schedules and count on that time together. Because we like to discuss only one case a week -- to give participants a chance to digest each one -- we typically meet for an hour and a half on twelve consecutive Wednesdays or Thursdays. If participants find it hard to make time to read and prepare each case in advance, sessions can be scheduled for two hours, with the first half-hour devoted to individual reading. In either case, we have found that a midweek, late-afternoon meeting time is about the only one for which our participants can consistently be available. Other arrangements have also been tried with success, however. For example, one can meet for three whole-day sessions, perhaps on consecutive Saturdays, discussing three or four cases per day. Alternatively, one can create a shorter seminar, perhaps meeting only once or twice for a few hours, considering one or two cases each time. Limited seminars of this type can be quite valuable; a suggested mini-seminar is found in Part III of this Instructor's Guide.

The room should be comfortable, and chairs should be arranged so participants can easily see and hear each other. Our own preference is for chairs arrayed in a nearly closed semicircle, with the instructor seated at the front of the room, only slightly separated -- perhaps by a low table -- from the rest of the group. It often helps to invite participants to come 15 to 30 minutes early to meet each other, shift gears, and prepare for the discussion.

Because many institutions (even those of higher education) tend to devalue teaching, it is good to hold the seminar in a room with prestigious and pleasant associations, signaling that here, at least, teaching and teachers are held in esteem. It can be a plus if the seminar is sponsored by the dean of the faculty or another academic officer, and also if the group includes well-respected faculty members (as long as their presence does not overshadow others). Conversely, the worst possible situation would probably be one in which instructors were "sent" to the seminar for remediation. Our faculty seminars have included deans of our own and other professional schools, as well as senior professors.

A seminar that includes deans and senior faculty need not be led by someone of equivalent institutional rank. Because the primary learning in the seminar results from confronting the cases and key issues in teaching, and from entering into dialogue with one's peers, the instructor certainly need not be the group's most experienced or expert member. It should be someone who is interested in the art of discussion teaching and in the articulation of what goes on in the teaching and learning process. We have seen several seminars successfully conducted by less-senior people. In fact, we hope the seminar design and cases will prove useful to groups who have no case method experience whatever but wish to explore the method.

When both junior and senior faculty members participate in the seminars, the younger people often fear that a spurious evaluation of their teaching will be made on the basis of their comments in the seminar. We find it best to deal with the issue early on. The seminar is a place to explore ideas, which inevitably involves exposing some biases and blind spots. Moreover, participants may sometimes wish to take extreme points of view in order to test their implications and/or to stimulate the group by playing devil's advocate. If such ventures are not made safe for the participants, the seminar as a whole will suffer. In our experience it is important that senior members (including the convenor) consciously approach the seminar as a place to learn, and make an effort not to evaluate their junior colleagues' teaching on the basis of comments made in the discussions. In addition, we believe that discussion contributions should be considered privileged communications, not to be reported to others beyond the group.

Quick judgments can be misleading, in any case. We know of one seminar group, for example, in which a participant made himself so thoroughly difficult, by constantly taking controversial and counter-intuitive stands, that the convenor privately asked him to restrain himself for the sake of the group. But subsequent conversations with students in his home institution revealed that he was widely considered to be one of the most demanding and effective teachers there, and one of the best loved.

Using These Teaching Notes

As each of you will have your own personal preferences regarding how best to teach a case, there are a variety of approaches to the development of supporting teaching notes. As you have noticed, my colleague Abby Hansen has developed a format somewhat different from mine. She sometimes adds to our traditional teaching note a personal commentary identified as the Researcher's Perspective. But our objectives are the same: to be of assistance to you as you prepare to lead a teaching seminar session.

Our own approach is to put aside the teaching note (with the exception of the study questions which we use as the basis of our preparation) until after we have read the case several times and formulated our own spontaneous response. Then, as we compare our reading of the case with that of the author of the teaching note, and later with those of the other seminar members, we are better able to recognize our own characteristic perspective on the teaching situation. Thus, we reinforce our own roles as learners as well as instructors or convenors. In addition, considering the case without special preparation helps us get a sense of how it will strike seminar participants, and can make it easier to understand their responses in the discussion.

Only when we have formulated our own response to the case do we turn to the teaching note, which provides suggested discussion questions, a process plan, and a representative analysis of each case.

The teaching notes in this manual represent an attempt to engage the reader in a conversation about teaching. While the art of case method teaching defies precise analysis, it can be observed -- and key

elements can be abstracted, discussed, and taught to others. Thus, in these notes, we have made a special effort to make explicit a format that helps focus attention on the crucial _process_ dimension of case method teaching, as this is reflected both in the cases themselves and in our handling of the discussions. Although my colleague Abby Hansen uses a slightly different format, we have both strived for a consistency that makes it easier to compare cases and to see how they fit together into a coherent whole.

My teaching notes are divided into six major parts. First, an introduction briefly states the main theme we highlight in our discussion of the case. This theme is further developed in our discussion questions for the case and in our sample analyses.

The second section of each teaching note summarizes the case in terms of six dimensions that we find important in understanding teaching-learning situations: (1) the institutional context, (2) the course itself, (3) the instructor, (4) the section, (5) the teacher-student relationship, and (6) the critical incident facing the instructor. This section is primarily a heuristic to help instructors organize their thoughts on the case, in preparation for teaching. Particularly for longer cases, it provides only a focused outline of the case situation. Few supporting details from the case text are listed. The seminar leader needs to examine the case text and note supporting evidence; discussion of the case will provide an opportunity for participants to identify more of these details and to note their significance.

Over the course of the seminar, we vary our emphasis in the six dimensions noted above. In general, our early cases emphasize individual characteristics of the instructor, especially as these influence the teacher-student relationship. At the middle of the course, the cases focus more on the nature of particular incidents, in the context of overall teacher-student relationships. Cases used in the latter part of the course have a mix of emphases, but a central feature is typically the institutional context in which the teaching takes place.

The third section of the teaching note consists of study and discussion questions. These constitute our primary teaching plans, for case teaching is a question-driven approach to education. Study questions can be handed out with the case for participants' use in preparing for class. Discussion questions are used by the instructor in preparing for the class and for guiding the case discussion when appropriate. In preparation to lead a discussion, we often write both open-focused questions which elicit a broad range of participant responses, and more precisely targeted probes which can be used to highlight themes of special importance.

Next, we suggest a process plan for teaching. Based on the discussion questions supplied, this plan outlines our approach to teaching the case, points out the contingencies we have come to expect, and suggests a general course of action. We encourage instructors to create their own versions of the process plan, adapted to the needs and strengths of the participants with whom they are working.

The fifth section offers a usage note on each of the discussion questions, indicating how and why each one might be used, and also an analysis of the issues. The analysis incorporates our best reflections about the case situation, but it is not intended to be definitive. To avoid foreclosing a variety of points of view, we recommend that the instructor consider carefully his or her own analysis of the case before reading ours.

Finally, the teaching note concludes with suggestions for using the particular case discussion as a means of developing the seminar as a learning group. Instructors who are experienced in organization development, and especially in team building, may find some of this material familiar. Our suggestions take into account both the nature of the case material and the point in the seminar at which we typically use the case. Reading several of the teaching notes in sequence may give an impression of the life cycle of a typical seminar (at least our view of it) and raise some interesting questions about the group processes that underlie effective teaching.

Of course each of the cases covered here are far richer than our notes can convey. Our interpretations are necessarily limited and partial. We hope each of you will feel free to challenge these points of view and refresh, with your own perspective, the ongoing discourse about teaching. An openness to new ideas is fundamental to case method teaching. Participants in your seminar, like the biblical archetype of the stranger or messengers, bring new and vital truths. You will soon want to develop your own teaching notes as you develop familiarity with the seminar program.

Some of the teaching materials for this Professional School Seminar have already been included in Part I of this Instructor's Guide and therefore are not repeated in this section. Hence, in following the order recommended for this Professional School Seminar Program (as outlined in the Part II table of contents), please refer to Part I for those materials.

Ernie Budding

Teaching Note

Introduction

"Ernie Budding" focuses on the first case-teaching experience of a young man who has just completed his Ph.D. and is now an instructor in a required first-year course for MBA students.

We tend to use this case series as the third or fourth in our seminar on case method teaching, since it focuses attention on the critical issue of the teacher-student learning contract. This working agreement represents the rules of the game for instructor and participants. The contract has both a formal, verbal aspect (e.g., guidelines for attendance, preparation, evaluation methods, and classroom operating conduct) and an informal, nonverbal (or behavioral) aspect.

The learning contract evolves over the course of the semester and is negotiated both overtly and covertly between instructor and students. The evolution and negotiation of a learning contract is central to the "Ernie Budding" case series.

In our syllabus this case series usually follows the "Henry Jasper" case which addresses questions about learning contracts. "Henry Jasper" explores how a learning contract becomes set over the course of a semester. It highlights the degree to which such contracts are negotiated and established without the awareness of the participants, and it points up some of the dangers encountered when the instructor is not aware of the contract he or she is setting with the students.

In discussing "Ernie Budding," we explore in greater depth the different sorts of contracts an instructor can make with a section, and the ways in which contracts can be negotiated and renegotiated. In this case situation, the instructor consciously chooses to alter the contract as his teaching goals and understanding of the section's needs change.

More than the preceding cases, "Ernie Budding" presents detailed information about the instructor's question and response style -- a powerful aspect of the learning contract. In our syllabus, "Ernie Budding" is usually followed by "Assistant Professor Graham and Ms. Macomber" and a series of other cases further highlighting issues of question and response style in case teaching.

The first three cases of "Ernie Budding" -- (A), (B), and (C) -- deal with the situation in a section as it develops during an academic year. As detailed below, we generally teach this as a "prediction case." That is, we hand out (A) and (B) in advance, and then discuss them in class -- asking participants to predict the results of Ernie's actions in (B). After they have made their predictions, (C) is handed out and read quickly by the participants; then the class continues with a discussion of the actual outcome.

The (D) case, presenting Ernie's reflections as he looks back on the year of teaching, is often handed out at the end of class for the participants to read at their leisure. It can also be used in a subsequent discussion centering on instructional philosophy. For such a discussion we often pair it with "Class on World Hunger (B)," which contains similarly philosophical reflections by another case method instructor.

In summary, the present case emphasizes the degree to which section needs and teacher learning goals may change over time, and how an instructor can respond to a changing situation by intentionally renegotiating the learning contract. In addition, it points up several important aspects of changing a contract, including:

1) the difficulty of realizing when a contract is not working and needs to be modified;

2) the complexities of actually negotiating

This teaching note was prepared by Dr. James F. Moore, in collaboration with Professor C. Roland Christensen, as an aid to instructors in the classroom use of the case series "Ernie Budding" (A) 9-381-038, (B) 9-381-039, (C) 9-381-040, and (D) 9-381-041.

a change (in particular, when the instructor tries to alter the contract unilaterally); and

3) the importance of the instructor's willingness to depart somewhat from a personally preferred style of teaching and learning, in order to respond to the needs of the section.

Case Summary

In our teaching seminar, which includes participants from many areas of study and teaching, we have found that those from outside the Business School often find some aspects of "Ernie Budding" initially confusing. In our introduction to the case, we usually acknowledge this problem, and during the discussion try to stay aware of points at which clarification or explanation might be helpful. For example, the case contains many terms from the world of manufacturing management; participants may also be unfamiliar with the unusual structure of the Bay curriculum and the separation of the student body into large sections. In the following notes we have tried to alert the instructor to some of the unique features of Bay.

The Institutional Context

The case takes place in an MBA course at Bay Area Graduate School of Management. Bay is a pseudonym for a large, highly selective business school with a case-based curriculum. The institutional details are important in this case, because Bay eschews the familiar course and semester format. Instead, the first-year class of MBA students is divided into approximately 10 sections of 80 students each. Each section is assigned an amphitheater-shaped classroom in which the students assemble daily at 8:30 a.m. for the first of three classes, each lasting 80 minutes. The instructors move among the various sections' classrooms.

Because each section stays together and is taught by several instructors, each develops a reputation with the faculty -- and several faculty members can discuss the general progress of a given section. By the same token, students see how their section operates with a variety of instructors, and thus can more easily compare instructors and their teaching approaches.

All first-year courses are required. Courses are of varying lengths, with some running the entire year and some less than one semester. In addition, one course -- the one Ernie Budding is teaching -- has a split-schedule design -- that is, it meets for three months at the beginning of the term (September to November), then (except for one class meeting) takes a long break until February, when a normal schedule is resumed.

The Course

Ernie Budding is teaching Manufacturing Management (MM), a technically oriented course. As Ernie puts it:

> Most students come to Bay to specialize in finance or marketing, but MM is required. It was clear to me that many of the students . . . were uncomfortable with the material, for it teaches a way of thinking that was foreign to most of them. Inventory policy, aggregate planning, scheduling -- few were familiar with these concepts.

The Instructor

Ernie is apparently well liked by the students. Perhaps because he resembles them in many respects, he is able to establish rapport with the section very early in the semester. Twenty-eight years old, unmarried, and looking like a student, he is described as enthusiastic, extremely energetic, and active -- always moving around the classroom as he teaches.

Many clues in the case indicate that Ernie is highly individualistic, and does not prefer group activity. This may help explain why he is not initially sensitive to the implications of the change in section behavior over time, and why he is uncomfortable with more open modes of teaching. For example, he says he was drawn to teaching by the "independence" of the role. He describes himself as very much involved in sports, and names a series of individual -- not team -- sports. He comments that he is very competitive, but likes to compete against himself rather than other persons. In addition, Ernie apparently does not have previous experience with the case method, either as a student or as an instructor. His academic background at Berkeley and Carnegie Tech has been discipline-based.

He chose the Carnegie program because its quantitative orientation would supply a rigor that he wanted. "Rigor" is a key term for Ernie. As he defines it, "Rigor is a matter of reasoning, accounting for everything in a problem." He also notes, "I feel dissatisfied about data that come to me with loose ends. Generally, I look for order and logic in the presentation of material." Not surprisingly, then, his initial approach to teaching is relentlessly logical and ordered.

Implicitly, Ernie seems to think of rigor as an unpleasant but vital discipline -- generally learned by subjecting oneself, as a student, to demanding instruction. There is something stoic about his search for rigor. As a teacher, he is demanding and tends to interpret slowdowns in student performance as "sluggishness" and as evidence that the class is "slipping."

The Section

The section consists of 80 first-year MBA students -- a group described by the instructors as the "brightest, hardest working, and liveliest" of all the first-year sections. Ernie calls it a "wonderful section, very highly motivated," and notes that during the first three months "their preparation exceeded my recommendations."

Each Bay section elects one of its members as an "educational representative" who serves as a liaison between the students and the faculty. In Ernie's section, Arlene Allen has this role.

Ernie names several students as particularly strong performers. One of these -- Harris Pauley -- is a principal in the student-teacher classroom interaction reconstructed in the case text.

The Teacher-Student Relationship

"Ernie Budding" is by far the longest case text used in our seminar. Its length is due largely to its focus on the evolution of a teacher-student learning contract over many months. In this teaching note we have taken the events of the case based on data available in the text and more systematically organized them than in the text itself. Moreover, our outline includes both implicit and explicit inferences about cause-effect relationships in the sequence of events.

The (A) case covers the first three months of the course, the single meeting during the winter, and the first month and a half of the second-term meetings (which begin in late February). During this period Ernie's style is highly directive: the students are expected to follow closely his logical ordering of the material as he directs the discussion and considers in turn a series of predetermined conceptual "blocks" of material.

The students' participation is closely controlled; their role is primarily to supply important facts relevant to the unveiling of Ernie's analysis. The nature of the contract is determined relatively unilaterally by Ernie, who does not consciously vary it.

Meanwhile, there are indications that the section's needs and abilities are changing. Ernie notices "a slight difference in [the section's] general attitude and performance when I met them briefly in January." By the second term the students had become "more confident and less willing to be led," and the section "developed into a stronger social unit with different operating modes in class."

Concurrently, the emphasis of the course material is shifting from quantitative analysis to strategic planning, which requires a more integrative, imaginative, and synthetic style of thinking from students (as opposed to purely analytic thinking). A less directive style of teaching might give students the appropriate amount of "air time" in class to develop and present more complex, integrative understandings.

During the period covered by the (A) case, Ernie does not respond in any systematic way to these developments. He attempts to maintain the same contract he began with.

The students seem to become increasingly uncomfortable with the contract. A variety of clues in the case suggest that they are withdrawing from voluntary participation in the contract, and sometimes actively resist the status quo and signal their desire for a new contract. For example, although the group is talented and at first seemed highly motivated, performance drops off. Game playing becomes a problem, with the section playing pranks, indulging in a "buzzword" game during a discussion, "triaging" their course participation and controlling output in order to help the slower students, and reacting wildly to a short electrical blackout.

One might interpret these occurrences as signals that the contract should be renegotiated. Instead, Ernie sees them as indications of a slacking off in response to demands for rigor. The (A) segment of the case ends as he considers whether to reprimand the section.

In the (B) case, Ernie delivers what he calls a "formal reprimand." When he has finished, Ernie reports, "you could have heard a pin drop. It felt like a scolding, and they seemed as chastened as first- or second-graders." Ernie also comments, "I had felt extremely uncomfortable lecturing a section of adults as if I were their parent -- after all, I was younger than some of the students -- but I also felt I had a responsibility to uphold standards."

Though Ernie is interested in exhorting the section to do higher-quality work, he focuses his reprimand on the use of buzzwords and on poor performance in opening up case discussions. His policy has been to "cold call" (that is, call without warning) students to make such openings. He expects that the student will then present an organized, detailed analysis of the case.

Following the reprimand, students perform well in the remainder of the class. Afterward, Ernie "collars" six to twelve students to ask their reactions to his speech. Some agree that buzzwords have become a problem. Others challenge his policy of cold-calling. Ernie is surprised that the students missed what he thought was his main point: the importance of quality performance. It is significant that he does not pursue these conversations further to discover in more detail how the students are experiencing the section and what they think an appropriate learning contract would be.

The (C) case begins with the first class session after the reprimand. Ernie expects that performance will be excellent. Instead it is dismal, with many students saying they are not prepared to lead off the discussion. The person who finally leads off is able to describe the case situation but cannot give an analysis. Ernie is shocked and annoyed. He "tightens the reins" further, emphasizes the quantitative over the qualitative aspects of the case, and even forces some calculations.

The (C) text exposes us to the students' views for the first time. Arlene Arden, the educational representative, reports that the students are alarmed by Ernie's angry response during class. Moreover, they are having difficulty meeting his demands and expectations. (In effect, she is saying that the students object to the learning contract he is trying to maintain.) As Arlene puts it:

People still liked him at this point. The problem with our relationship with him was that at first -- at the beginning of the year -- we just loved being told how things went. By the middle of the second semester, though, we all felt calmer, more confident about casework. We didn't want to be led anymore, but he was still leading. It seemed as if we were all on a forced march. I decided I'd better go and have a talk with Ernie on behalf of the section.

Arlene calls on Ernie. She reports the students' reactions, says that there is a great deal of tension in the classroom, and asks that Ernie relax his demanding, directive teaching style somewhat. Ernie responds that "standards must be maintained." But he is sensitive enough to understand that the tension in the classroom is making learning very difficult, and he decides to try to reduce the strain. He states that he will continue to expect students to "lay out cases," but will not cold call and will "step back further" from the discussion and let students set the direction. And he will not insist that the discussion proceed in order through his conceptual blocks of material. In short, he agrees to alter certain elements of the contract.

Ernie begins the next class with "a speech in which I announced a new, relaxed approach and called for volunteers. There was silence at first, and I was afraid that no one would open the case -- but finally, Arlene raised her hand. After her opening, the case went smoothly."

Ernie reports that the course ended very well:

The buzzwords didn't disappear, but they were bolstered by explanations. The level of analysis remained high. My student evaluations were almost uniformly good, and the students thought that my change at the end was distinctly for the better. Giving up cold calls seems to have gone all right. I don't know if I lost rigor. Maybe it's a trade-off; how much do you buy by going through a logical structure -- A, B, C, D -- versus letting it come out A, D, E, C, B? Maybe it's all right as long as all the pieces are there.

The (D) case, which we seldom use during class discussion, continues Ernie's reflections on a variety of related themes, including his overall questions about learning contracts with students, the possibility of intimidating students with an aggressive teaching style, and his own evolving teaching style. He concludes with his thoughts about the grading system used at Bay, and the pranks students played on him (as they do on most instructors at Bay).

A Note on Study and Discussion Questions

Typically we prepare at least two sets of questions for use with each case. The first group (see Exhibit 1) consists of study questions, and can be handed out with the case for participants' use in preparing for class. The discussion questions (see Exhibit 2) are used by the instructor of the seminar in preparing for, and guiding, the case discussion.

Instructors must decide how directive the discussion questions should be. In teaching "Ernie Budding," for example, we want to call attention to several key features of the situation described in the (A) case. We hope participants will note that the section's capabilities and preferred style of learning are changing, that Ernie is trying to maintain an unchanging and very directive learning contract, and that he is largely unaware that the development of the students is rendering his contract less acceptable to them. We have designed, and often use, a series of probing questions that direct attention to these features of the case (see optional probes in Exhibit 2).

Or, the instructor can take a more open-focus approach, supplemented by the use of directive probe questions. Open-ended discussions give the participants a better sense of discovery. Even when they arrive at the observations and conclusions to which the instructor had planned to lead them, they have made genuine discoveries and added their initiative as a key ingredient in the discussion. Participants (and the instructor!) tend to find these sorts of discussions much more exciting and engaging.

Further, only open discussions offer participants a chance to practice articulating what each of them sees as the important considerations, problems, and issues raised in the case situation. It is typically only in more open discussions that participants demonstrate and discuss with each other their own synthetic, integrative thinking. In our judgment the capacity for such integrative, "problem-finding" thinking is crucial for an effective case method teacher. It is through practicing and developing such thinking that participants learn to transfer their learning in the course to new situations they will encounter in their own teaching.

Thus as the seminar develops and the participants become more capable and confident in analyzing teaching cases, we increasingly encourage them to articulate their own approaches to understanding the cases. Of course we still try to guide the "controlled spontaneity" of the discussion. But we try not to program too tightly in advance the general direction taken by the

discussion. We want to be alert to participant initiatives -- and to those serendipitous times when the participants discover an angle the instructor had missed!

Thus we prefer to use a relatively open discussion outline combined with skillful questioning and response to encourage the development of participant initiatives. For example, we use selective calling, "bridging" between comments, the insertion of summaries at key moments, and direct questioning of participants to guide the discussion in appropriate directions. The use of questions and responses -- which we consider a key skill in case teaching -- is examined in more depth in "Assistant Professor Graham and Ms. Macomber" and the cases that follow in our syllabus.

The discussion questions presented in Exhibit 2 reflect the sort of open outline we might use in discussing "Ernie Budding." The discussion probes included with Question 1 can be used to lead participants more directly to some of the features that seem central to understanding the case. For all discussion questions, we have provided detailed notes below.

Closely targeted discussion probes may turn out to be not appropriate to the discussion that emerges in class. But formulating and considering how to answer such questions can have great value for the instructor in preparing to teach the case. They help him or her walk through the case in depth, and become sensitive to potential themes that may develop in discussion. Thus while we tend to be cautious about using directive questions during a discussion, we find it very valuable to prepare and consider such questions in advance.

A Suggested Process Plan for the Case

Overview

"Ernie Budding" is a long case series. We tend to use two full cases and part of the third in class. After a discussion of the (A) and (B) cases, which were read before class, participants are asked to predict the results of Ernie's reprimand. The (C) case is then handed out and read. Predictions are compared with the actual result reported, and the implications of the new information are discussed.

With a case series of this length, it is important to move discussion along briskly. Thus we tend not to linger too long with each set of major questions. Rather, we allow ourselves to leave a few loose ends in each subdiscussion, in order to cover the central aspects of the case.

The (A) and (B) Cases

The first two cases sketch the events leading up to and including Ernie's reprimand to the section for its deteriorating performance. Our overall thrust in teaching "Ernie Budding" is to encourage diagnosis rather than action recommendations. Our first discussion question asks participants to identify the central features of the situation and Ernie's fundamental problem. As the discussion proceeds, we encourage participants to alternate between considering features of the situation and trying to define the key problem.

The instructor can use two types of response tactics to help this discussion succeed. First, he or she can encourage participants to clarify the significance of features of the situation by asking fairly pointed questions (e.g., What are the implications of Ernie's directive style? What effect does it have on the section? What are the implications of the long break between segments of the course?). In addition, the instructor can use the chalkboard to organize participants' comments as they are made. For example, situational features that occur early and late in the term can be listed separately. In this way the instructor can unobtrusively guide participants to discover that Ernie's fundamental teaching situation changes over the year.

Second, the instructor uses his or her responses to move the discussion back and forth between description of the situation and definition of the problem. To move away from situational factors, the instructor can ask, "All right, given all this, what seems to be the central problem facing Ernie?" To shift back to the situation, one can ask participants what has contributed to the development of that problem. For example, one can ask, "Why is this problem developing? What is it about the situation that has led to this problem?"

As we see it, the basic problem is a breakdown in the learning contract. Sometimes the section arrives at this diagnosis fairly early in the discussion. An inexperienced instructor may find it unnerving to have the case "cracked" so soon, and may be uncertain what to do next. This problem bears examination.

First, it should be noted that early diagnosis is a common occurrence. Like

the members of Ernie Budding's section, participants in the seminar will be getting "smarter" by this third case discussion, and thus are already primed to discover problems in the learning contract. In addition, the case is fairly straightforwardly focused on the contracting issue; unlike "Henry Jasper," it contains no alluring red herrings.

Second, our purpose is not simply to have participants discover that teacher-student learning contracts are important, but to help them understand more deeply the range of phenomena and the dynamics involved in such contracts. Thus our discussion need not stop with the identification of the problem, but can continue on to explore the meaning and dimensions of learning contracts, the implications of contract breakdown, and the factors involved in negotiating, renegotiating, and maintaining such contracts. Merely identifying the problem is like opening a door, or turning a corner, into a whole area of discussion. This area can be entered simply by asking the respondent to develop his or her point. Or one can ask if others can expand on the point. The section as a whole can be urged to articulate their own views of what is important in such contracts.

This brings up a general issue that we believe is critical to effective case teaching -- whether that teaching is being done with participants in the teaching seminar or with students in another setting. That issue is: when a key point has been raised in discussion, the instructor must not assume that the whole section has either understood it or realized its significance. While we sometimes compare analyzing a case to solving a mystery, the analogy holds only to a degree. Quite often our aim is to use case discussions to help participants learn to work with a key concept -- such as "learning contract" -- and to gain a feel for its profundity and dimensions.

Even very experienced instructors can easily make the mistake of thinking that a case has been cracked when a student first raises a key point. To the instructor who has read and considered them, cases often take on a transparency that is not obvious to the students. Some of the dangers of prematurely assuming that a section has comprehended a point are dramatically illustrated in the next case in our syllabus, "Assistant Professor Graham and Ms. Macomber." In our experience the section needs to work with a significant point -- and often even move away from it, to return later -- before its significance is appreciated. The most profitable section meetings are often those that explore the significance of a key point, rather than simply discovering it. Thus when participants have identified Ernie Budding's problem as the breakdown of his unchanging, directive learning contract, we encourage them to explore the point in greater depth.

We are also interested in encouraging participants to reflect on why Ernie is not aware of this problem. Therefore, when and if we feel that most section members have an understanding of the basic problem, we often change the focus of the discussion by asking, "Why does Ernie use this style of teaching, and why doesn't he see the need to change his contract?" This line of questioning encourages the participants to reflect upon how teaching style grows out of the personal experiences and personal values of an instructor. Further, it helps them realize how difficult -- and important -- it is for instructors to go beyond their starting points in teaching to understand and respond to the ongoing, changing teaching situations they face.

For the (B) case, our questions encourage participants to examine Ernie's speech, discuss its appropriateness to the situation, and speculate on its effect on the section's performance. Generally a range of opinion is expressed, and the views follow from participants' diagnosis of the situation. Typically, some participants support the reprimand as a risky and/or unpleasant but appropriate step, while others see it as a heavy-handed gesture that misses the point -- which is to rebuild an active relationship with members of the section. After some brisk discussion of these predictions and their links to the diagnostic hypotheses from which they are derived, we hand out the (C) case.

The (C) and (D) Cases

To save class time, we typically ask participants to read just the first part of the (C) case. This early portion describes the section following the reprimand, and demonstrates its apparent ineffectiveness. The (C) case should give pause to participants who, like Ernie, predicted success, and the new information challenges everyone to reassess his or her diagnosis of Ernie's situation. It is at this point in the discussion that participants generally recognize the problems inherent in Ernie's insistence on establishing the contract unilaterally.

If there is time, we ask participants to read and discuss the remainder of the (C)

case, which illustrates a negotiation between Ernie and the section's representative, and then between Ernie and the section as a whole. (The latter negotiation is conducted largely through behavior in the next class.) The (C) case also gives Ernie's impression of the result over the next meetings. Thus it provides a useful vehicle for discussing how learning contracts can be renegotiated.

The (D) case can be used to stimulate discussion of the general issues raised by the series. We generally find it most useful to encourage participants to read this after the central issues have been raised and explored in class. Then the (D) case becomes a continuing stimulus to thinking about the issues.

Special Features of the Case Text

"Ernie Budding" is the longest case series in our syllabus. We find it helpful to warn participants in advance that they should allow somewhat more time than usual to prepare for the discussion. More important, the discussion itself must be moved along quickly to ensure that at least (A), (B), and (C) are discussed. We recommend that the instructor plan in advance the approximate time to be allocated to each segment, and give some thought to how the discussion transitions should be handled.

Despite its length, our experience is that this case series stimulates relatively focused discussion centered on Ernie's teaching style and learning contract (in sharp contrast to "Henry Jasper," which can elicit a variety of powerful and divergent discussions). This centripetal tendency seems largely due to the way "Ernie Budding" is written. By and large, the information presented pertains directly to the core issue, and there is very little material to stimulate an alternative focus.

This series examines closely the interaction between instructor and students. With direct data about the interactions, participants can more concretely understand the facts of the situation. We find it valuable to call the participants' attention to the details of Ernie's classroom question and response style. This sets the stage for our next few cases, which focus on question and response and examine small sequences of interaction between instructors and students.

Finally, because the (A) and (B) cases consist primarily of direct quotations from Ernie about his experience with the section, they amount to a representation of Ernie's perceptual world as he tries to deal with his teaching task. As readers of the case, the seminar participants have virtually the same information as Ernie. More precisely, the (A) and (B) cases give them the information to which Ernie is paying attention, plus the snippet of classroom interaction. A central point of the case discussion, as we encourage it, is the discovery that Ernie does not have enough information to assess his section's progress and mood, nor is he asking the most relevant questions of the data he does have. It can be useful to call seminar participants' attention to the restricted viewpoint of the (A) and (B) cases. This lead can encourage them to explore what other information they might want to have if they were in Ernie's shoes. Such a line of thinking can lead to a discussion of how instructors can get information about the mood and learning progress of their sections, and how students are interpreting their interactions with the section and experiencing the teacher-student learning contract.

Notes for the Discussion Questions

1. **As a friend and colleague of Ernie Budding, could you please help our seminar group understand the situation confronting Ernie Budding at the end of the (A) case?**

   a) What do you see as the one or two critical factors contributing to his current situation? What features of the situation are important to note in sizing up this situation?

   b) Given these elements of the situation, what is the problem?

Usage Note

This broad question sets the stage for the rest of the session. As discussed in the process plan above, we encourage participants to work back and forth between identifying relevant situational factors and trying to articulate the central problem.

Analysis

Participants typically point to the following features of Ernie's situation:

a) Ernie is using a very directive teaching style: he leads the class on a very short leash through his own tightly ordered analysis of each case.

b) Because he relies so much on leading questions, organized in a logical sequence, students who want to contribute to the discussion must guess his line of reasoning and anticipate its unfolding. Their thinking must become closely attuned to his, and they are given little room to develop their own independent lines of thought.

c) Ernie's personal epistemology centers on his understanding of "rigor," which to him means precise, comprehensive, ordered analysis of situations. Ernie believes his own ability to be rigorous was sharpened by submitting himself to a quantitative program during graduate school -- a program which ran counter to his inclinations. He seeks to impart this same quality of rigor to his students, and he appears to be doing so by enforcing a disciplined teaching process which may run counter to their inclinations.

d) The instructional situation changes over the course of the year. The students' instructional needs, abilities, and, most important, their desire for structure appear to be changing. They seem to be seeking a more open, less directive contract, which would allow them to do more synthetic thinking. Further, they are learning to function as a group (as shown by the pranks and triaging), and thus are capable not only of coordinated learning, but also of coordinated resistance and rebellion.

The course subject matter is changing, too, moving from material designed to elicit relatively mechanical applications of concepts and techniques to material that calls for high-level strategic thinking. This sort of thinking is better pursued and displayed in a more open discussion format than that used by Ernie.

e) Ernie is attempting to maintain a unilaterally imposed teacher-student learning contract with the section. Though he seems to be aware of other teaching styles, he apparently does not realize there are other, more negotiated ways to establish a learning contract.

f) Section members do not seem to like Ernie's contract nor are they willing to acknowledge its legitimacy and submit to it. Instead, they are rebelling against Ernie's contract, both passively and actively.

g) Ernie is not aware of the situation. Ernie senses some resistance to his teaching style, and thus to the contract, but he does not see that this may keep him from accomplishing his teaching objectives. Further, he does not seem to realize that he needs to change the unilateral way in which the contract is being maintained. Viewing the section's behavior as a sign of laziness and a shirking of rigor, he does not consider interpreting these signals as attempts to renegotiate the contract, or as signs that the contract is inappropriate to the present situation.

h) Ernie believes that the section is "slipping" and that externally imposed sanctions may be needed to reinforce discipline and encourage high performance.

The discussion of critical features can be developed by employing the optional probes listed in Exhibit 2. By asking participants to compare Ernie's understanding of the situation with that of a typical class member, and with their own, the instructor can help them recognize key factors in the breakdown of communication about the learning contract. They fairly quickly realize that Ernie defines the problem as "slipping" or slacking off, while his students probably define it some other way, and that there is no direct explicit communication between them that would permit the negotiation of a mutually agreeable contract. This line of discussion should help participants identify the breakdown of the learning contract as Ernie's fundamental problem.

Participants tend to feel the central problem is a breakdown in something in the teacher-student relationship. Some will call it "respect"; others will talk about the implicit contract. Our response is often to ask the participants to articulate what they mean by "the elusive term 'respect.'"

In so doing, they will often describe several aspects of a successful learning contract. In addition, they may express different views about how learning contracts should be established and maintained, and what kinds of contracts are desirable. These different approaches can be discussed, with the instructor encouraging participants to clarify the distinctions (as well as similarities) between the different approaches, and to explore the strengths and weaknesses of these alternatives.

In our judgment the central problem illustrated in the case is that Ernie is trying to retain an unchanging and unilaterally imposed contract with a section whose instructional needs and desires have changed. The problem persists because Ernie is unaware of it, since he misreads the signals from the section. He appears to believe that the section's pranks, nonperformance, and use of buzzwords are signs of resistance to an appropriate and appropriately negotiated contract. He might better read these as signals that the contract is not being voluntarily maintained by both parties, and needs to be examined and perhaps renegotiated.

The longer he tries to maintain the unchanging contract unilaterally, the more the section resorts to active and passive resistance. Thus the section's performance and compliance with Ernie's directives continues to decline.

2.   Why didn't Ernie see the need for a change in his contract with the section?

Usage Note

This question is used to turn the seminar's attention away from the central problem and toward the reasons for Ernie's failure to recognize it. Participants typically identify a variety of features about his background, training, and personality that may underlie his particular teaching style. The key generalization we encourage the participants to discover is that a new instructor's teaching approach is often based primarily on his or her background, personal style, and values -- and may have little or nothing to do with the present teaching situation. One of our aims in teaching this case is to heighten participants' sensitivity to their actual situations as they develop their approach to teaching.

Participants tend to hear this question, initially, as a call to identify factors in Ernie's experience that lead him to use his particular style. We support this reading of the question at first, and work during the discussion toward the general point that most new instructors (and many experienced ones) develop their teaching approach without paying enough attention to the situation in which they are teaching.

Analysis

Some of the factors in Ernie's experience that participants identify as important contributors to his present teaching style are:

a) He has little experience with the substantive content of the course. Thus he tries to control the discussion and keep it within limits within which he knows he can be competent.

b) Ernie apparently has not been exposed to question-based teaching, or case method teaching. Given this lack of experience with effective alternative approaches, he may be justifiably reluctant to vary his style.

c) Perhaps because this is his first term as an instructor, he appears not to have considered the development of the students and the section in his process plan for teaching. Thus he was not attuned to the possibility that students' development might call for a change in instructional style.

d) Perhaps because he is new to the substantive material of the course, he does not seem to realize that the shift in pedagogical aims in the second term has implications for teaching style. The early segment is designed to show students a variety of tools of analysis, and familiarize them with the concrete conditions and the common terms of the world of manufacturing management. The second half is designed to let the students build on this foundation and move into synthetic, strategic thinking. In our opinion such thinking is best expressed when students are relatively free to structure their approach to the material and their actual presentations during the class discussion, and are given an opportunity to understand and critique each other's approaches, thus learning by making comparisons.

e) Ernie tends to see the problems presented by the cases as solvable by one or at most a range of ordered solutions. Hence the "conceptual blocks" he uses in teaching and also, perhaps, his failure to see the value of letting the students discuss and compare their approaches to the MM problems. In our judgment, Ernie is too confident that there is one best solution to each case. This seeming lack of appreciation for the complexities of actual situations may be the result of his own highly analytical training, his limited academic experience with manufacturing management issues, and his lack of any actual experience dealing with manufacturing problems on the shop floor.

f) It appears that Ernie attributes his own academic development, and thus by implication his current success, largely to the externally imposed discipline he experienced in his graduate program at Carnegie-Mellon. He tries to give the students the pedagogical gift he himself received: "rigor." He interprets the students' signals as a slacking off from the demands of rigor and decides, for their own good, to intercede to force them to submit again. Thus he is unable to see the students' behavior as a sign that an appropriate and pedagogically helpful change in the learning contract is needed.

g) Participants may note Ernie's taste for highly demanding individual sports. This proclivity, combined with his academic rather than manufacturing background, may indicate a lack of experience working with groups. Thus he may not have developed his sensitivity to group process. As a result it may simply not occur to him to stay alert to group signals, and to question his first interpretations, considering alternative explanations and paths of action.

3. **How would you describe Ernie's teaching style?**

Usage Note

It may not be necessary to ask this question directly during the discussion -- particularly if the group has quickly picked up and explored the issue of learning contracts. However, this question and the two that follow are helpful in focusing the seminar discussion on how a learning contract is expressed in and maintained by a teaching style, and how a teaching style is embodied in a particular way of using question and response.

To move the discussion toward question and response, we often urge participants to describe the nature of Ernie's teaching style in detail. We ask them to draw upon the data in the case -- for example, the snippet of class interaction presented in the (A) case.

Analysis

Our own assessment is that Ernie's style is highly directive. Its dominant feature is that the students must learn to guess Ernie's train of thought, and supply facts at the appropriate times to support the unfolding of Ernie's argument. The classroom dialogue included in the (A) case makes it clear that Ernie's queries, while leading, do not lead precisely enough so that students can always guess what he is pulling for. This, we suspect, makes the game both risky and mildly exciting, and allows some students to shine by showing themselves particularly adept at anticipating Ernie's line of thought.

Ernie's teaching style is part of his overall learning contract with the section; it is unilaterally set by Ernie (to the best of his ability) and places him in a dominant, directing role, with primary responsibility for analyzing the case and presenting the result.

4. **What are the advantages and disadvantages of this approach -- in terms of student learning?**

Usage Note

This question is used to turn attention from Ernie's style itself to its impact on the students (i.e., its effectiveness).

Analysis

In our opinion, the central advantages of Ernie's approach are:

a)   By learning to understand and anticipate Ernie's thinking, the students learn a language and basic techniques of approaching manufacturing management problems. To the extent that Ernie's analyses are strong, the students will probably learn something useful through this process of mimicry.

b)   The directive, leading style of teaching provides a clear and relatively risk-free role for the students, particularly after they have mastered the basic concepts in the field. Thus the students probably at first feel quite relieved to slide into this directive contract. It probably helps alleviate their anxiety at being new MBA candidates who are not yet confident of their ability to analyze and discuss cases.

The disadvantages are that the students are prevented from practicing their own integrative, imaginative, and synthetic thinking. They do not get an opportunity to present and discuss with others their appraisals of complex and ambiguous situations, to make plausible diagnoses of situations, and to present plans for action that they have created and to which they feel committed.

A further disadvantage is that the role the students practice in the classroom is quite different from the real-life role for which they are preparing: that of the general manager. This point is central, in our view, because we are committed to professional education that simulates fundamental elements of the situation for which students are being prepared. Properly conducted, case method teaching offers many opportunities for students to try out the role of general manager.

5.   Why does Ernie Budding use this instructional style?

Usage Note

This question brings the participants back to exploring Ernie Budding and what he brings to this teaching situation. Probable responses to this question parallel those listed earlier under Question 2, and

we refer the reader to that list. The purpose of this question, once again, is to highlight the ways in which instructors can overlook important aspects of their teaching-learning situation by being too much influenced by their own preferred styles of teaching, their own intellectual talents and traditions, and their desire to avoid chaos and lead a tightly controlled classroom.

*   *   *

Following a discussion of these five questions, we suggest that attention turn to the (B) case and Question 6.

6.   How effective do you think Ernie's speech was? What, if anything, does he do now -- or has he dealt with the problem?

Usage Note

This prediction question often builds participants' involvement in the discussion, since they are asked to take the personal risk of committing themselves to an action recommendation.

We offer two suggestions for fielding responses to this question. First, the discussion leader may want to press participants to identify the diagnostic assumptions behind their judgments of whether Ernie's reprimand will be effective. This ties the discussion of intervention back to the earlier discussion of the key factors and the central problem in the situation. Second, if participants believe that Ernie's reprimand will not be effective, they should be asked how they would respond. This encourages the seminar members to consider the range of alternative actions available to instructors faced with problems like Ernie's.

Analysis

We might appraise Ernie's reprimand as follows: If the assumptions that underlie his analysis are correct, then the reprimand may be effective. Ernie appears to assume that the students tacitly agree that they are in class to submit to externally directed rigor, and that they believe Ernie's sort of rigor is appropriate to their learning goals. Further, Ernie appears to assume that the students feel he has a legitimate right to set the learning contract unilaterally. If these assumptions are not correct, Ernie's reprimand is unlikely to evoke a new commitment to high-quality work. Instead, the result is likely to be either resentful submission or continued rebellion and/or passive resistance.

In our judgment Ernie's assumptions do not fit the reality very well. As an alternative to the reprimand, it would be helpful for him to try to discuss the educational process within the section directly with at least some of the students. Perhaps it would be most appropriate to talk with the educational representative, but he could also speak to any section member he has come to know and trust. Unfortunately, he does not seem to have built relationships with the students that would allow him to make ongoing tests of the suitability of the contract. Thus, he has little established access to them now.

At this point in the discussion, participants may become somewhat polarized, with one faction wanting to give all the power to the students, while others support Ernie's reprimand. It may be useful to raise this dispute to the general level by asking, "Are there any ways to negotiate a contract while at the same time maintaining one's power and legitimate authority?"

7. **What is his contract with the section now?**

Usage Note

This question brings participant attention back to the overall learning contract. By implicitly assuming that Ernie's reprimand will change the contract, it emphasizes the evolutionary nature of such tacit agreements.

Analysis

In our judgment, the information provided in the (B) case does not allow the reader to be sure of the nature of Ernie's new contract with the section. An assessment of the contract would require more in the way of student comments, and/or reports of the relationship between Ernie and the section in the following class. (Both kinds of data are included in the (C) case.) If Ernie's intervention is effective, he will have expanded his directive role to include a parenting, disciplinarian aspect. Thus his contract with students will become even more directive and unilateral. On the other hand, if his intervention is not effective, he will have little if any contract with them at all.

8. **More generally, how do you know when to change a contract? How do you change it?**

Usage Note

This is the fundamental question of the discussion, in that it encourages participants to move from Ernie's case to their own experience, and begin to articulate some general guidelines for maintaining a productive learning contract.

Analysis

In our opinion, the keys to knowing when to change a contract are first to stay in communication with the section members, and second to try to anticipate changes in the learning situation that might render the learning contract obsolete.

To stay in communication, instructors must try to develop informal channels of communication with the students (e.g., meeting with a few students for a beer after class, and/or talking informally with them after the class and during breaks). In addition, they must learn to read the covert behavioral signals the section sends. For example, Ernie's students' pranks were partly a signal which he failed to read.

Changes in the learning situation can often be anticipated. Curricula and course content are modified, and individuals and groups develop over time, particularly with effective teaching. These developments often require changes in teaching style, and thus in the learning contract.

*   *   *

If there is time, the (C) case can be handed out to let participants know what actually happened. We normally suggest that the participants read only the first two sections of the (C) case during discussion time (through "A Student's View of the Salinas Walnut Case"). The following questions can then be used to guide discussion.

Alternatively, the (C) case can be given to participants at the end of the discussion period, to be read at their leisure. The questions can then simply be mentioned as the (C) case is passed out, in order to stimulate further thinking.

9. **Why didn't the reprimand work? And why did the discussion of Salinas Walnut go so poorly?**

Usage Note

This question calls the participants back to the consideration of their basic diagnoses of the situation. Most will modify their earlier positions to some extent on the basis of the new data. Those who thought Ernie's reprimand would be effective will probably be somewhat shocked, and will often begin to reconsider not only their reading of this case, but also their approach to teaching.

Analysis

In our judgment, the reprimand did not work because Ernie's assumptions about the students were not correct. The students are not willing to submit to his discipline, and they do not find it helpful to their development. Thus, he cannot get them to accept the legitimacy of his unilateral control, or the superordinate goal of attaining rigor Ernie-style.

We believe the students' lack of preparation for the Salinas Walnut case discussion may have been a form of resistance. Their explanation -- that no one in the class realized that a particular sort of calculation would "solve" this particularly difficult case -- is not plausible. After all, this is by all accounts a very bright group of students who have a history of high performance and intensive preparation. And they had already been introduced to the type of calculation required.

10. What does Ernie do now?

Usage Note

This question turns the seminar's attention to action. It lets participants explore their own ideas before they are influenced by reading about what Ernie actually did.

Analysis

Ernie needs to open up some channels of communication with the section members. Now that his plan has failed, and he has some sense that his assumptions about the section are incorrect, he must develop some way to find out what is really going on. Thus he might, for example, talk with the educational representative to ask her perspective on the problems of the section. Or if he has developed some rapport with individual students, he could perhaps talk with them.

Second, he might discuss the situation with another faculty member. The ideal person would perhaps be a trusted colleague who will not be judgmental, but who can help Ernie rethink the situation.

Third, he must develop a new hypothesis about what is happening in the section, and about how to relate to the section as its instructor. He may have to reconsider his teaching style and manner of leading the discussions, and do some new thinking about learning contracts.

Fourth, Ernie must consider how to renegotiate a new contract. Is he going to do so unilaterally? If not, how is he going to open up the negotiation? Should he do it with the entire class, or with the representative? How can he conduct a truly bilateral negotiation? (Just giving in to the section would represent another form of unilateral contracting -- this time student-directed.) And how should he deal with what has already gone on? How should he respond to it? Should he acknowledge the problems of the past, or should he simply try to correct them and go on, without comment?

*   *   *

After participants have read the entire (C) case, one can ask:

11. What do you think of Ernie's response to Arlene's visit?

Usage Note

This question directs attention to how the negotiation was actually carried out, and invites participants to consider in detail the process of negotiation.

Analysis

In our judgment Ernie's response was effective. He articulates his perspective to Arlene, but he also listens to hers. And he decides to try a compromise. The negotiation is carried off in two stages. First, by listening to Arlene seriously, as well as presenting his own views candidly and clearly, Ernie takes the first steps toward renegotiation. Second, while he definitely maintains his prerogatives as instructor, he states his willingness to experiment with changing his teaching style. During the next section meeting, the contract negotiation is carried forth on the behavioral level. Ernie begins by "announcing" his new approach, which may seem a unilateral approach. But his announcement is really simply an opening offer. When Arlene volunteers to speak, and the class as a whole joins in the discussion, they signal at least tentative agreement to the new contract.

While Ernie does not completely come around to our view of the limits of his style, he moves quite a bit and he begins to explore the strengths and weaknesses of various approaches to case teaching. In fact, it may be just as well that Ernie did not go farther in a collaborative direction. Some instructors, at such a turning point, might tend to move to the other pole -- toward a totally nondirective teaching style and/or a very open, collaborative negotiation of the contract. In our judgment, the section would probably find it difficult to adjust to such a radical shift, which would also clash with Ernie's natural or rather well-learned style. We thus think it probably was wise for him to move just part way in terms of opening up the negotiation.

12. **Teaching this section raised a number of questions for Ernie Budding about the nature of effective teaching. What questions does reading about it raise for you? Have any of you had similar experiences?**

A variety of questions are raised by this case. Perhaps the most important are:

a) What are the strengths and weaknesses of more and less directive questioning?

b) How can you read a section, and know when a contract needs changing?

c) How can you change a contract and/or renegotiate one?

d) If you are not going to use a directive question and response style that forces students to guess your thoughts, what should you do? (This last question moves us into the subject of "Assistant Professor Graham and Ms. Macomber," the next case in our syllabus.)

Suggestions for Building the Seminar Group

By the time we come to "Ernie Budding," in the third or fourth meeting of the seminar, our section-building goals have evolved somewhat. In the first meeting, we encouraged wide participation -- to establish a pattern of high involvement and to learn as much as possible about the participants and their ways of approaching case discussion. We also tried to model good listening skills. In the second session, we began to build the seminar group's capacity to carry on a dialogue with a sense of common purpose. We tried to refine the behavioral norms guiding discussion, subtly emphasizing mutual respect, and encouraging courtesy and the use of each others'

names when speaking about previous contributions.

In this third meeting we continue to emphasize the development of group norms that support effective dialogue. We still encourage analysis more than action recommendations, to emphasize the complexity of the case teaching process and to highlight the many possible perspectives on the same situation. Moreover, talking about diagnostic issues helps build group cohesion, while discussion of action recommendations may prove divisive.

In the "Ernie Budding" discussion, participants are asked to make some suggestions for action, but we try to restrain their prescriptive exuberance in two ways. First, through our questioning we encourage participants to ground their recommendations in an explicit statement of the supporting analysis. Second, we provide an immediate "reality check" on their thinking. Participants' recommendations are initially solicited in the form of a judgment of the likely effectiveness of Ernie's reprimand. The (C) case then presents them with the actual outcome. This sequence helps participants appreciate the difficulties involved in taking action and achieving predicted outcomes. The lesson is further reinforced by the fact that Ernie's intervention is not effective.

Our goal in this discussion is to help participants see that it is not necessarily easy to read situations clearly and straightforwardly, and that the effect of one's actions can be quite different from what one expects. Making action recommendations is a tentative, chancy business, and should be grounded in analysis.

During this week in the seminar we also try to emphasize that we are working as a team: as a group of professionals we are coming together to explore our questions about teaching. We believe that this image of the seminar task helps to reduce competition and defensiveness, and to create an atmosphere in which participants can share their deepest concerns and most precious insights.

The cooperative, group-oriented image of the seminar task can be promoted in a variety of ways. It is essential that the seminar instructor model respect and openness during discussion, and insist that respect be shown by others. The instructor's phrasing of questions can also underscore the cooperative nature of the task. For example, "Can you please help us understand the situation confronting Ernie

Budding?" sets a different tone from "What is your personal opinion of the situation confronting Ernie Budding?"

Finally, through our phrasing of questions and responses, we encourage participants to see themselves as supportive colleagues of Ernie Budding. Thus we ask, "As a friend and colleague of Ernie Budding, can you please help us understand. . . ?" The subtle instruction embedded in the question phrasing establishes a tacit identification and empathy with Ernie. We believe this helps reduce the participants' tendencies to be judgmental, and increases their willingness to generalize from the case situation to their own experience.

Overall, our aim in the first few sessions of the seminar is to produce a group whose norms support open exploration of questions about teaching. Participants should be able to expect that their contributions will be heard and respected, as well as searchingly and critically examined.

Once the group coheres around these values -- and in our experience this happens within a few weeks -- we can let it become more autonomous in its functioning. At that point we will turn more of our attention, as instructors, to the strengths and weaknesses of individual seminar participants. And we will begin to consider how we can shape the seminar meetings to address the particular educational needs of the participants.

Exhibit 1

Ernie Budding

Study Questions

The (A) case:

1. What is your appraisal of the situation confronting Ernie Budding as of the end of the (A) case? How does Ernie see the situation? How might a member of the class explain the section's behavior?

*   *   *

The (B) case:

1. What is your evaluation of Ernie's speech?

2. How do you interpret the class's reaction to his comments? Would you, as Ernie Budding, take further action before the next class?

Exhibit 2

Ernie Budding

Open-Focused Discussion Questions

1. As a friend and colleague of Ernie Budding, could you please help our seminar group understand the situation confronting Ernie Budding at the end of the (A) case?

    a) What do you see as the one or two critical factors contributing to his current situation?

    [or]

    What features of the situation are important to note in sizing up this situation?

    (Optional probe): How does Ernie see the situation? How do the section members see the situation? How do you see the situation?

    (Optional probe): What is Ernie's teaching style? What are the pluses and minuses of such a style? [These questions can be introduced here, or saved for use as outlined below in Questions 3 and 4.]

    b) Given these elements of the situation, what is the problem?

    [or, somewhat more provocatively]

    How did this good section turn bad?

2. Why didn't Ernie see the need for a change in his contract with the section?

3. How would you describe Ernie's teaching style?

4. What are the advantages and disadvantages of this approach -- in terms of student learning?

5. Why does Ernie Budding use this instructional style?

* * *

Following the above discussion, we suggest that attention turn to the (B) case, with:

6. How effective do you think Ernie's speech was? What, if anything, does he do now -- or has he dealt with the problem?

7. What is his contract with the section now?

8. More generally, how do you know when to change a contract? How do you change it?

* * *

If there is time and if the seminar participants want to know what actually happened, the (C) case can be handed out. We normally suggest that the participants read only the first two sections of the (C) case during discussion time. These contain the discussion of the Salinas Walnut Compa-

ny, and "A Student's View of the Salinas Walnut Case." After participants have read this much, Questions 9 through 12 can be used to guide discussion.

Alternatively, the (C) case can be given to participants at the end of the discussion period, to be read at their leisure. The questions can then simply be mentioned as the (C) case is passed out, in order to stimulate further thinking.

9. Why didn't the reprimand work? And why did the discussion of Salinas Walnut go so poorly?

10. What does Ernie do now?

* * *

After the entire (C) case has been read:

11. What do you think of Ernie's response to Arlene's visit?

12. Teaching this section raised a number of questions for Ernie Budding about the nature of effective teaching. What questions does reading about it raise for you? Have any of you had similar experiences?

Bill Jones

Teaching Note

Introduction

"Bill Jones" describes a case method instructor facing what he sees as a potential racial incident in his class. It draws attention to the critical role of listening in the classroom. Without careful listening, students simply can't get their points across. Its importance increases enormously when 80 section members are trying to converse.

Moreover, attentive listening is one of the most powerful ways we know to communicate respect; it is much more effective than praise. As such, it helps set a climate in which students feel willing to discuss their best insights, deepest concerns, and most difficult questions. As Rogers and Farson have written:

> When people are listened to sensitively, they tend to listen to themselves with more care and make clear exactly what they are feeling and thinking. Group members tend to listen more to each other, become less argumentative, more ready to incorporate other points of view. Because listening reduces the threat of having one's ideas criticized, the person is better able to see them for what they are and is more likely to feel that his contributions are worthwhile.

Not the least important result of listening is the change that takes place within the listener himself. Besides the fact that listening provides more information about people than any other activity, it builds deep, positive relationships and tends to alter constructively the attitudes of the listener. Listening is a growth experience.[1]

In our syllabus, this case generally follows "Assistant Professor Graham and Ms. Macomber," which emphasizes ways to direct discussions by using questions, including planned questions. "Bill Jones," in contrast, focuses on the unpredictable dimension of case discussions, and the need for sensitive listening and quick creative thinking to turn apparent crises into opportunities for teaching and learning.

Case Summary

"Bill Jones" is divided into two parts and is generally taught as a prediction case. Before class, students read and prepare an analysis of the (A) case which describes the incident and gives background information. After some discussion, the (B) case, describing Bill Jones's response to the incident, is handed out in class, read, and discussed.

The Institutional Context

The case takes place in an MBA course at Metropolitan Business School. Metropolitan is a pseudonym for a large, highly selective business school with a two-year, case-based curriculum. The incident occurs in an elective course that is part of the second-year curriculum. While first-year students are assigned to sections and remain with them throughout the year, the second-year program allows students to choose their courses so that they encounter a different group of classmates in each course.

The Course

The incident occurs in a labor relations course that is being taught for the first time. Bill has 90 students (about 10 more than the hypothetical maximum) in his section. Students apparently find the case material very stimulating, and Bill's class

1. Carl R. Rogers and Richard E. Farson, "Active Listening," *Organizational Psychology: A Book of Readings*, 3rd edition, ed. D. P. Kolb, I. M. Rubin, J. M. McIntyre (Englewood Cliffs, N.J.: Prentice-Hall, 1979), p. 170.

This teaching note was prepared by Dr. James F. Moore in collaboration with Professor C. Roland Christensen as an aid to instructors in the classroom use of the case series "Bill Jones" (A) 9–378–038 and (B) 9–378–039.

has had exciting discussions and periodic open conflict.

The Instructor

Bill Jones is an energetic young associate professor -- a former college football quarterback and Phi Beta Kappa member -- who brings to class a booming voice, a great deal of enthusiasm, and a quick wit. He was hired directly out of graduate school -- with no postgraduate work experience -- to teach on Metropolitan's Production and Operations Management faculty. Bill has six years' case teaching experience at Metropolitan, including four in his department's first-year MBA course and two in a course he had designed himself on management of nonprofit organizations.

Bill was asked by his department chairman to help design and teach this course, which is outside his area of expertise. Bill knows little about labor relations and has not worked in the field. He was apprehensive about the project -- given his limited background -- but he accepted. From the case data we can infer that a tenure decision is imminent for Bill. He is an associate professor and has been at the school six years. Thus, he may have felt forced to take the teaching assignment, and he probably feels under great pressure to succeed at it.

Bill is a Southerner -- an Arkansas native with a Tulane bachelor's degree and a Ph.D. in economics earned in 1970 from the University of Texas. Seminar participants often point out that racial turmoil was widespread in the South during Bill's youth, and it is likely that racial issues hold a special emotional charge for Bill.

The Section

Though courses in production and operations management at Metropolitan had traditionally been a male domain, Bill's section includes 12 women.

Several students are introduced in the case text, among them the following:

Dave Young, who Bill thinks represents "a somewhat radical point of view about labor policy," is 27 years old, has a B.A. in economics from the University of Wisconsin, and has worked with Cesar Chavez's United Farmworkers Union and with the California State Department of Labor as assistant to the secretary.

Paige Palmer is a recent graduate of a well-known eastern women's college where she majored in art history. She came directly to Metropolitan where she has done well academically, though her in-class comments are viewed as naive by some of her more experienced classmates.

Fred Wilkens is a Stanford engineering graduate with bachelor's and master's degrees; he worked for Hewlett-Packard for two years before coming to Metropolitan. Fred is the only black student in the section. Initially, he does not participate in class discussions, and acknowledges to Bill that his priorities lie elsewhere. Bill asks him to contribute to discussions anyway and Fred begins to do so.

Jim Casey has worked four years with General Motors. The text provides little more on his background, but does note that Jim is somewhat conservative politically, and is appreciated by his classmates as a bright, articulate person who often draws on his General Motors experience to contribute interesting insights and anecdotes.

The Teacher-Student Relationship

There is little information in the text about Bill's style of discussion leadership. It appears, however, that he follows a laissez-faire approach, allowing students great freedom in their responses to his questions. In addition, he appears to enjoy conflict in the classroom, and perhaps elicits it by calling on participants with predictably opposed views.

Throughout the first half of the semester, discussion had been quite spirited. Bill believes that part of the excitement was due to the diverse opinions and experiences of section members regarding issues in labor relations.

The Incident

The incident takes place near the middle of the semester, during discussion of a case about a General Motors experiment with the use of worker teams to assemble automobiles. GM research had shown that younger workers were far more discontented with traditional production jobs than older workers, and were generally less productive. In the assembly plant where the experiment was carried out, the labor force was 60% black, with almost all of the black workers under the age of 40. The older workers were mainly white.

Opening comments in Bill's class address the issue of estimating the cost of assembling cars by the team method. Jim Casey, the former GM employee, suggests that the experimental team is not representative of other workers, and probably is made up of "rate busters" -- that is, employees who are willing to work harder and faster than average.

Bill Jones does not reply to this comment, but calls on Paige Palmer, who is sitting next to Fred Wilkens. Paige says, "Well, I disagree with Jim; I don't think the workers could be 'rate busters' because three of them are black, and. . . ."

From the case: "At that moment, the entire class gasped. Fred Wilkens shot back in his seat so that his chair seat banged loudly; his fingers tensely gripped the desk. A hush fell over the classroom. Most students looked down at their desks; others stared at Paige in disbelief. Paige did not finish her sentence; an icy silence prevailed in the room. Fred . . . slowly gathered his papers . . . and . . . turned . . . as if to leave the classroom. Dave Young began to rock back and forth in his chair in an agitated manner." The (A) case ends without indicating Bill's response.

In the (B) case, we learn that Bill assumes Paige has almost made a racist comment, and that she is now ashamed of her slip. Bill responds by walking over to Fred, putting his hand on Fred's arm and apologizing for Paige. Fred nods his head back at Bill, as if to signal agreement and acceptance. Bill then turns back to the class as a whole and continues the case discussion, apparently without referring directly to the incident again.

A Note on Study and Discussion Questions

Typically we prepare at least two sets of questions for use with each case. The first set (Exhibit 1) are study questions, and can be handed out for participants' use when preparing the case before class. The discussion questions (Exhibit 2) are used by the instructor of the seminar in preparing for class and in guiding the case discussion when appropriate.

Our discussion questions constitute a "question-based teaching plan," which gives the instructor a general direction to pursue, but is not so restrictive as to prevent the students from developing their own alternative interpretations of the case. In this way, we encourage the participants to structure their own approaches to understanding the case situation. Through careful use of questioning and response, we then manage the ensuing discussion to encourage the development of the partici-

pant initiatives that emerge. That is, we use selective calling, "bridging" between comments, the insertion of summaries at key moments, and direct questioning of participants to move the discussion in potentially profitable directions.

The discussion questions we have provided reflect an open outline typical of one we might use in discussing "Bill Jones." In exploring this case, we wish to focus attention on the importance of instructor responses to student initiatives. Sometimes we underline this point by using a particularly response-oriented teaching style in our own leadership of the class discussion. Thus, our teaching plan features relatively broad, open questions, and the use of probes, bridging, and other response techniques to shape and deepen the discussion as it emerges (in contrast to the intensely question-oriented plan we use for "Assistant Professor Graham and Ms. Macomber" -- a case which emphasizes the role of questioning rather than responding).

For all discussion questions, but not for study questions, we have provided detailed notes in the "Analysis" sections.

A Suggested Process Plan for the Case

Overview

Our overall aim is to help the participants become more conscious of the complexity of listening and responding to students during a case discussion. The art of case method teaching lies largely in the skillful use of questions, listening, and responses. In "Assistant Professor Graham and Ms. Macomber," we emphasized the use of questions. In the present case, we move into the domain of listening and response -- a much more complex topic.

With questions, the instructor has a certain amount of control. A teaching plan can be based on sequences of questions organized into either a linear or a branching, contingency-based design. With enough questions written down in your notes, you'll never be without something to say. Listening to student statements is much more complex. The content of these statements is unpredictable. Assertions and retorts often come in a rapid-fire series, and the instructor must listen and respond continually throughout the class period.

The key to discussion leadership is listening. It is difficult to respond effectively to something one has not heard.

Experienced discussion leaders listen for the content, logic, and consistency of a statement. They listen to the relationship between the present comment and those that have preceded it, looking for emerging themes that could provide ways to connect various insights. And they listen with an ear to the future, seeking opportunities to move the discussion toward potentially profitable areas. Good discussion leaders also try to attend to the needs of the individual student -- challenging at some times, protecting, supporting, and encouraging at others -- looking for ways to help the individual student have an important learning experience.

Given effective listening, the range of potential responses is enormous. One can say nothing; this will be interpreted as a comment of sorts. One can write on the board. One can restate, paraphrase, highlight, and/or comment on some aspect of the student's statement. The student can be questioned or simply encouraged to say more. One can ask other students to comment, either on the matter at hand or on the statement just made. One can move the discussion down the path it has been following, or one can redirect it. All this may be done in words, but can also be done with simple gestures.

All teachers encounter dozens of opportunities for skillful listening and responding every day; it is our experience that we fail to meet these challenges more often than we succeed. But we hope that we will succeed at many of the most important moments. We believe that even really superb teachers are on target only about one in three times.

To help seminar participants sharpen their abilities in these areas, we concentrate the case discussion on how Bill listens to and interprets Paige's comment, the nature and impact of his response, and the range of alternatives he might have used.

We begin discussion of the (A) case by asking what the problem is. There are a number of good responses to this question, and we encourage participants to explore different ways of conceiving the problems in Bill's situation. The most obvious problem is the potential racial incident. A more important problem, some participants may suggest, is that Paige does not finish her comment. Although the class seems to have felt she was making a racist remark, no one really knows what Paige might say if she finished. We feel this point is crucial, and we do all we can to encourage the seminar to mull over the class's lack of listening,

and the various ways Paige's comment might be completed. In addition, some participants believe Bill's teaching style is a central problem and has contributed to the development of a crisis.

We then move to discussion of what Bill Jones should do. A wide range of alternatives are usually suggested, which helps expand participants' sense of possibilities. We press each person to make a commitment to a particular course of action, perhaps personalizing our question by asking, "Imagine you are now caught in this situation. What are you going to do?" This approach helps participants feel the urgency of the situation and appreciate the difficulty of choosing effective responses to complex, fast-developing situations.

We usually spend about half the class session on the (A) case, dividing this time about equally between diagnosis and consideration of action. However, our allocation of time depends, in part, on when the seminar picks up the point that Paige has not finished her comment. If the implications of this observation are not discussed in response to the (A) case, we move ahead more quickly to (B) and raise the issue during that phase of the discussion. After the (B) case has been handed out and read, we first ask <u>what</u> Bill did, and <u>why</u>. In discussing this question, participants build a detailed understanding of Bill's response with particular attention to his presumptions, the rapidity with which he moved in, and the controlling nature of his interventions. They also distinguish between his conscious thoughts about Paige's motives and the situation facing him and the possible unconscious reasons for his actions. For example, many participants feel that his actions may have emerged more from a felt need to control the situation than from a considered pedagogical strategy.

Next we examine the consequences of Bill's intervention, particularly for Paige, who we feel is potentially the most misunderstood and vulnerable participant in the case. This shift in focus underlines the influence of instructor listening -- or lack of it -- on students' experience, and emphasizes the potential for harm in prematurely conceived and insensitive responses. Finally, we ask participants once again to consider how they might have handled the situation, thus linking the previous analysis back to action, and emphasizing once again that effective teachers must be able not only to analyze their situations, but to act with commitment.

Notes for the Discussion Questions

1.   **What is the problem here? What went wrong?**

Usage Note

Participants' responses to this broad diagnostic question are likely to identify levels of problems -- some obvious, some more subtle. We try to help them see connections between their comments, thus highlighting the main problems presented in Bill Jones's class.

Analysis

Perhaps the most obvious problem, and the one that is usually identified first, is that a racial incident may be about to occur in the classroom. It appears that members of the class have interpreted Paige's comment as racist and offensive, and are reacting to the event in a variety of ways. Fred Wilkens looks as if he is about to leave the room, Dave Young is agitated, and most of the other class members are looking down at their desks in silence.

In fact, however, Paige has not finished her statement. The class's interpretation of her meaning and her motives is based on only the first part of an incomplete sentence. While it is clear that her statement will deal with racial material, it is not certain that it will be offensive.

When discussing this point, we have sometimes asked participants to suggest some possible endings to the sentence. For example, the case text indicates that younger workers are less productive on average than older workers, and that the plant's black workers were almost all less than 40 years old. Thus, Paige might have intended to say, "I don't think the workers could be 'rate busters' because three of them are black, and thus probably young. And we know that the young workers tend to be more dissatisfied with their work and less productive." While this may not be a very strong argument, it is not necessarily a racist one either.

Our central concern in teaching this case is the importance of letting students be heard, and of listening closely to their statements before taking action in response. Thus, the fact that Paige has not finished her statement is most crucial. After that observation has been made by several participants, we often ask participants to explore it further -- perhaps by brainstorming alternative endings to the sentence or by considering how Bill Jones might have made it possible for Paige to finish. However, we usually do not underscore the point the first time it is raised -- particularly if this occurs in the first two or three comments -- for to do so can signal to the section that "this is the point of the case" and discourage the development of other important insights. In addition, the fact that one or two students have grasped a point does not mean that most students share the insight. In our experience, the class as a whole is best able to learn if the instructor waits until several students have raised the point before underlining and encouraging its development.

A less obvious but very important problem is Bill's style of managing the day's discussion. The case text provides no evidence that Bill uses questions or responses to shape and control the discussion. Rather, it appears that he calls on one student after another, following the drift of the discussion and exercising control primarily by choosing who would speak next.

Selective calling on students is a useful way of shaping a discussion. Some students open discussions well; others are masters at summary. Some students raise the emotional heat and involvement of discussions; others cool them down. Some are more practical, while others shine at theoretical analysis. An instructor can pick students when their strengths are needed by the class. And by contrast, an instructor will sometimes help students develop breadth by asking them to contribute in ways that are uncharacteristic for them individually. However, if an instructor limits him- or herself to this mode of discussion leadership, a great deal of control is given up. If Bill has been operating in this way, it may have contributed to the volatility of the situation by allowing a relatively free-wheeling discussion to develop.

Moreover, Bill's choices of student participants do not seem to be based on a very detailed analysis of the needs of the class or of individuals. Rather, his choices appear to be based primarily on predictions of conflict. On the day of the incident, Bill "anticipated a lively discussion particularly between Jim Casey, who . . . was fairly conservative, and Dave Young." Bill's comments throughout the case suggest that he equates success with exciting discussions that include clamorous student participation and open conflict.

Experienced teachers in our seminar sometimes wonder aloud whether Bill is succumbing to one of the great temptations of case teaching: the routine creation of drama for its own sake. Case materials are usually designed to be emotionally as well as intellectually stimulating. Add to this the intrinsic excitement of conflict, particularly for the more aggressive students, and you have a mixture that makes it relatively easy for a case teacher to create dramatic classes upon demand. Some students love them, and so do many instructors.

However, our experience has been that too much drama leads to game-playing. The more aggressive students adopt stock roles -- the class radical, the class conservative, the feminist, the anti-feminist -- and create predictably polar analyses of each case. The lead players and the rest of the class soon learn to avoid the more tedious, confusing, complex, tentative thinking that leads to less predictable but often more profound insights. In a section that is playing games, careful listening declines because it is unnecessary. As long as most persons play their parts, the discussion remains shallow and easy to follow.

From painful experience with our own indulgence in classroom theater, we have discovered that it can create problems for individual students as well as for the class as a whole. The instructor becomes a director, calling up each part when he or she feels it is dramatically appropriate. Unfortunately, the same players tend to lead in discussion after discussion, and become typecast in their roles. Their original purpose in taking the class -- to grow and change and broaden their repertoire of analysis and action -- is too easily forgotten. By the same token, less aggressive participants are relegated to the audience. As spectators, they soon become bored by the predictability of the show.

This trap is particularly tempting in the first weeks of the term. The undifferentiated mass of students begins to take form, and the characteristics of individual students become clearer. It suddenly becomes possible to direct the discussion through selection of students, and having this new element of understanding and control is a heady experience. It is altogether too easy to forget that one is seeing how students have decided to present themselves, not who they really are. More time must elapse, and more trust be developed, before they will show their real cares, concerns, and deepest insights.

2.   What should Bill do now?   Why?

Usage Note

This question asks the seminar to consider action. A variety of actions will be suggested, depending upon the seminar members' readings of the problem, and their approaches to resolving them. We do not pull for any particular choice, but rather press the participants to clarify what they think needs to be done, how it should be accomplished, and in what order steps should be taken. We are particularly interested in having them set priorities and define a plan for the first moments following Paige's comment.

Analysis

In our judgment, the top priority is enabling Paige Palmer to finish speaking. At the same time, it is important to get Fred Wilkens to stay in his seat, at least until she is finished. Both aims could perhaps be accomplished by quickly gesturing to Fred -- catching his eye and motioning for him to pause just for a moment -- and asking Paige gently to "please go on."

We believe both students will probably comply with these kindly signaled requests. Although emotions are running high, the instructor derives considerable social power from his or her formal role, and a stronger intervention might be overwhelming. Fred is described as basically a shy person, slightly built and studious -- seemingly not the type to challenge the instructor's authority at such a moment. Paige has a more direct reason to continue, for it is the only way she can make her point and perhaps redeem herself with the other section members.

Once Paige has finished, new decisions must be made. In our opinion, it is unlikely her comment will prove to be racist. But if it is, one way to handle the situation is for Bill to ask her to examine the assumptions her statement is based upon, thus exposing to scrutiny the unfounded inferences that underlie such stereotyping. Racism is a way of thinking, and it can be discussed and analyzed profitably in the classroom -- as long as the students' (and instructors') emotional reactions can be contained.

We would not suggest simply throwing the ball to another student, as Bill is apparently in the habit of doing. With a section already primed to create dramatic conflicts, such a move could lead to truly damaging personal attacks on Paige. After an analytical exchange with Paige, Bill might involve the rest of the section by asking a student to comment on his or her reactions to Paige's statement. The choice of respondent would be very important here. We suggest a student who is basically kind, and tends to be able to see various viewpoints and bridge them. Such a person might be able to verbalize some of the feelings of the class, thus making them discussable, without attacking Paige and/or provoking more emotional reactions in the section. We would not call on either Dave or Fred initially. Fred is particularly vulnerable -- being the only black in the room -- and might feel very much put on the spot. Dave's aggressive manner and emotional intensity make it unlikely that he could contribute constructively to the early moments of such a discussion. Fred, and perhaps Dave, could be brought into the discussion at a later point.

We believe it is much more likely that Paige's comment will not be objectionable. Bill then faces other choices. He can continue the case discussion by ignoring the potential incident. Or he can focus the section's attention on its own reactions to her comment. To some extent, his decision must be based on his estimate of the section's readiness to become self-reflective, as well as his own ability to lead such a discussion profitably. We feel, however, that something very important may have been revealed by the reaction to Paige's comment, and it requires some action by Bill, either immediately or in the near future.

The section's response is symptomatic of two possible problems. First, its members may not be listening attentively to each other's statements; they may have gotten into the habit of quickly forming a general impression of a comment and reacting immediately on that basis. If such poor listening is widespread, it can devastate case discussions. It needs to be corrected. Second, Bill and the section members do not appear able to discuss racial issues effectively. This lack of capacity to discuss a truly controversial issue also suggests that the section may have been playing games, and that the "open conflict" Bill noted has been mock conflict over issues that had little immediacy for the students.

More important, the inability to discuss issues involving race is a serious weakness at both the section and individual levels for people who are studying labor relations. Race and racism are important factors that must be dealt with in modern labor relations. Future managers, especially those going into either production management or labor relations, need to learn to discuss such matters routinely and rationally.

If Bill seizes the opportunity, the class's reaction provides a wonderful chance to make discussable both the importance of listening closely -- rather than stereotyping a speaker -- and the awkwardness that section members (and most people) feel when discussing issues of race -- particularly when both blacks and whites are present. Such a conversation might go a long way toward helping these future managers become more effective in dealing with these important labor relations issues.

Bill might start such a discussion in a variety of ways, either just after Paige finishes or after a short period of case discussion had allowed students to calm down and gain some perspective on the incident. Bill might say, "One thing I noticed a few minutes ago, and I think provides us with an important opportunity for learning, was the strong response of various class members to Paige's mention of the race of the workers in this case. Can anyone see how our reactions might relate to problems that are important in labor relations?"

This statement strongly reaffirms the central aim of the course -- to learn about labor relations -- and puts a discussion of the class's reactions clearly in the context of that aim. Further, it asks students to make an analytical connection between their reaction and these aims, thus encouraging initial replies that are more intellectual than emotional. Such an approach helps students develop some reflective distance from their own reactions, and makes volatile issues more manageable. Questions inviting a more personal exploration can follow later if that seems desirable. For example, Bill could ask, "What was your reaction, [student's name], and what did you learn from that?"

*   *   *

The following questions are used after the (B) case has been read by participants:

3.   What did Bill do? Why?

Usage Note

This question asks the seminar to examine the sequence of Bill's assumptions and actions. We usually teach the case by asking for a detailed, sequenced, play-by-play recapitulation. We want the participants to take this particular response apart to see how it is constructed. In our judgment, the steps Bill takes are not idiosyncratic; many of us might do much the same thing under similar pressures.

Analysis

Bill assumes that he knows Paige's and Fred's thoughts and feelings without being told. He takes very strong action to keep Fred in his seat, and he speaks for Paige to Fred, making an apology. Then he resumes the case discussion, apparently without further direct reference to the incident.

Key points include the following:

a) Bill acts quickly, while Paige is still trying to speak.

b) He makes quick and damaging attributions about Paige's comment and her intentions -- that she had made a racist comment (when in fact, she had not finished her sentence) and that the comment was made accidentally: "He realized that Paige Palmer had not meant to say what she had." That is, Bill immediately assumes he knows her thoughts. He does not wonder what she was going to say or what she meant and he does not ask her for a clarification or even allow her to finish her sentence.

c) He walks directly toward Fred -- a very dominant move for a discussion leader to make, particularly an ex-football player facing a shy, slightly built student. He puts his hand on Fred's arm -- an even more dominant gesture. In most case classrooms, instructors never touch students at all. And Bill completes this sequence by looking directly at Fred -- also an intimidating action in this context.

d) Rather than asking Fred how he feels, Bill assumes he can read Fred's mind: "Fred, I know you're hurt and you're probably angry . . . you can't even know how badly she feels. . . ."

e) Speaking for Paige, Bill makes what amounts to an admission of guilt and an apology: ". . . she didn't mean to hurt you and she didn't mean to say that. She's probably never felt worse in her life."

f) Looking over at Paige (seated next to Fred), Bill sees that she is flushed and apparently on the verge of tears. Bill chooses not to respond to her directly.

g) Fred also looks at Paige and nods his head slowly at Bill -- perhaps to signal agreement (the case is ambiguous on this point).

h) Bill does not reply, but instead immediately calls on another student to continue class discussion. Bill appears to assume that the incident is now closed, not only for Paige and Fred, but for the rest of the class members. The case text gives no indication that he considers the reactions of the other class members or thinks of checking with them directly to find out how they are thinking and feeling about the situation. Bill apparently resumes the discussion by signaling another student to carry on. There is no information in the text to suggest that Bill poses a specific question, or gives much thought to the best way to direct the discussion in the minutes after the incident.

Why does Bill act as he does? His reaction seems to be to manage the crisis by controlling the participants and suppressing potential conflict. He perceives a potential problem, quickly sizes up the nature of the problem, and takes forceful action -- an effective strategy for a football quarterback, but probably not for a discussion leader.

Such reactions are virtually instinctive in situations that are perceived as crises, and cause problems for nearly all professionals who work with other people -- teachers, managers, shop stewards, supervisors, and even counselors and labor relations experts. This is why training programs for managers often emphasize learning how to listen. Such programs are also helpful to instructors, and we find we need to remind ourselves periodically not to jump to conclusions, to listen carefully and inquire directly to test our assumptions, and to restrain our tendency to try to overcontrol others in situations of potential disagreement.

Like the section itself, Bill has perhaps not yet developed a capacity to discuss controversial issues -- or at least the issue of race -- comfortably. His own discomfort appears to drive him to act as he does. Yet he enjoyed earlier dramatic class sessions with their periods of open conflict -- perhaps he, too, has become comfortable with mock conflict, rather than with authentic discussions of difficult and personally relevant concerns.

As many participants have pointed out, Bill's background in the South during a time of intensely painful racial conflict may have left him gun-shy about this particular issue. It may be that he can discuss other controversial issues with less difficulty, but that this particular matter "touches all his buttons." We have found it valuable -- as case discussion leaders -- to ask ourselves whether we are particularly sensitive to certain issues. Most discussion leaders have some areas of special sensitivity, and many find it valuable to work consciously to improve their ability to discuss these particular issues.

4.   What are the implications of his particular response to this situation? What result is it likely to have?

5.   Do you agree with this approach? Why or why not? How else might Bill have handled this situation?

Usage Note

These questions, which overlap in their effect and can be combined or used in sequence, draw the seminar's attention forward to the impact of Bill's intervention.

Seminar groups vary in their responses at this point. Some have reached an early consensus that Bill's approach was overly controlling; this question then evokes a kind of "working session" on alternative approaches. In other instances, a sizable group of participants may insist that Bill's action was warranted. In our opinion, this perspective deserves to be heard, but it is important to examine explicitly the assumptions on which it is founded (e.g., that such issues are too explosive for the class to handle; that this intervention "protected" Paige).

If enough participants support Bill's intervention, the discussion may get bogged down if the instructor tries to achieve consensus before moving on to consider alternative approaches. At some point, we believe it makes sense just to move on, without waiting for agreement. One way to make the transition is to say, "Holding aside for the moment our support for Bill's approach, how else might this be handled?" and then call on a few participants who are known to disapprove of Bill's intervention.

Analysis

Bill's response has several damaging implications. First, it signals to the section that questions of race cannot be discussed in class. This is a particular problem in a class on labor relations, since racial problems constitute one of the fundamental problems of the field.

Second, his intervention implies that Paige was making a racially objectionable comment, and that she is guilty primarily of a "slip" by making the comment in public. This stereotypes Paige in the worst possible light. His reading of her has special weight because he is not just a student in the class, but is the professor in charge -- the expert, and the official judge of student contributions.

Though we have little data about the effect of the incident on Paige, we can make some plausible guesses. The immediate pain and frustration of being so forcibly misunderstood could be tremendous, and might lead her to decide to contribute much more cautiously in future discussions. In addition, she probably feels humiliated and angry at having been labeled a racist in front of Fred and the other members of the class. Already handicapped by a reputation for naivete, she will have still greater difficulty in the future in trying to overcome the effect of this negative stereotyping.

Third, some students will probably realize -- either immediately or later -- that Paige was at best interrupted and more likely misunderstood and prevented from making a correction. They will interpret Bill's intervention as a sign that he cannot be relied on to help them should they be misunderstood by the class. This, in turn, may discourage some students from making controversial comments in class.

Fourth, Fred and the other members of the class are reinforced in their tendency to jump to conclusions when listening to other students. Bill misses an important opportunity to show them the importance of listening carefully. Learning to listen more effectively would increase students' ability to profit from future case discussions -- not to mention from conversations and discussions throughout their lives. In a labor relations course, such a lesson is particularly relevant.

Fifth, Fred's manner of handling this situation is tacitly affirmed. We do not have direct data on how Fred was coping with the situation, but it appears that he made a quick presumption of guilt and became angry enough to leave the room. This sort of response will probably not be to Fred's advantage in the long run and when Bill affirms it as appropriate, he deprives Fred of an important opportunity for learning. As the only black student in the room, Fred is in a vulnerable position, and it would probably be unwise to thrust the lesson on him directly. But if Paige were allowed to finish, and if the class were then asked to analyze their reactions, Fred might also realize the need to develop his ability to listen and manage his feelings when racial issues are discussed.

There are many other ways in which this situation might have been handled, and each time this case is discussed, participants suggest insightful new ways to approach it. In general, we believe that the incident can, with skill and luck, be turned into a valuable learning experience for the entire class. Our thoughts on one way in which this might be done are included in the notes for Question #2 earlier.

6. **What questions does this raise for you as a discussion leader?**

Usage Note

This question asks seminar members to generalize from Bill Jones's situation. We tend to encourage such discussion increasingly during the semester, in order to provide opportunities for participants to identify wider issues raised in the cases, and to make explicit connections between the case situations and their own teaching practice.

Analysis

Participants in the seminar have identified a variety of questions raised by the case. Some of the most interesting include:

a) In this case, like the earlier cases, there is little evidence that the instructor had planned for the process of his or her discussion. Why is that? How can one do such planning?

b) Why is listening so difficult? How can instructors train themselves to listen more effectively? How can case discussion leaders promote careful listening in their sections?

c) What are an instructor's special responsibilities to the students who are in a racial or ethnic minority in the classroom?

d) How can an instructor prevent scapegoating and stereotyping of students within the classroom, particularly when students make themselves vulnerable by taking risky, controversial, or easily misunderstood positions?

Suggestions for Building the Seminar Group

By the middle of the term, when this case is normally used, we expect that the seminar members will have built enough trust in each other and in the overall process to permit deeper dialogue. The instructor may want to pay special attention to sharpening his or her own listening skills and making sure that seminar members are taking the time to hear each other.

At this point in the term, we begin to make two important shifts. First, we work to increase the involvement of the participants in the discussion process. Though greater involvement often means heightened emotional intensity, we try simultaneously to increase the quality of our listening in order to avoid stereotyped game playing. As pointed out in Teaching by the Case Method:

Discussion dialogue can develop at three levels. At the first level, students explore a case problem by sorting out relevant facts, developing logical conclusions, and presenting them to fellow students and the instructor. The students discuss someone else's problem; their role is that of a commentator-observer in a strictly classroom-academic mode.

The second level of discussion may be stimulated by assigning students executive roles in the case situation under discussion. Their comments tend to reflect their sense of the organizational and personal circumstances of the company managers whose "robes" they wear. Their analysis and recommendations embrace both academic logic and specific company dynamics. When the role-playing session is complete, the section resumes a regular case discussion pattern, but the dialogue usually is more firmly rooted in practical realities. The section has moved away from the external observer's role toward that of an involved corporate officer.

The third discussion level is reached when students, on their own initiative, project themselves into the case situation. The classroom and business situation meld together, with the students vicariously acting as the firm's executive group, albeit a quite large executive group. Problems are not discussed as abstract topics, but as issues inextricably bound up in a manager's career circumstances. Student comments reflect a personal commitment to the arguments they advanced. This level of discussion comes as close to real life as can be achieved in an academic situation. Learning opportunities, and risk, are high for all involved.[2]

We build involvement by using cases that raise more powerfully engaging issues. In "Bill Jones," for example, the issues of race, racism, potential classroom explosions, and an instructor moving strongly to dominate the discussion process all feed a more emotionally charged discussion. In addition, as instructors, we use response techniques that encourage students to project themselves into the case. For example, we might ask a particular student, "What would you do if you were Bill Jones?" or, "How would you feel if you were Paige Palmer?" Instead of simply accepting his or her response, we might ask, "Would you really?"

The movement toward greater involvement is also promoted by spending a larger part of the discussion on questions of action. To invent and evaluate courses of action, the participants must project themselves more deeply into the case situations. In the early classes of the term, we spend about 90% of the seminar time on diagnosis, i.e., on understanding the situation facing the protagonist of the case. At this middle period in the term, we shift to spending about 50% of the time on diagnosis, and 50% on discussing actions that might be taken.

The use of prediction cases also generates challenge as participants select action plans, knowing that the latter part of the case sequence will contain information that will support or undermine their approach.

At this phase in the term, we also begin emphasizing generalization. We want to encourage participants to articulate the wider issues that link all of the cases, and help them begin to apply some of their insights to their own teaching. We ask, for example, "What questions does this case raise for you in regard to your teaching practice?" "What do you think is the central issue raised by this case?" "Have any of you ever experienced a situation like the one described in 'Bill Jones'? What happened? How did that situation affect you?" "Given that you had that experience, what was it like for you to read 'Bill Jones'?" We try to save at least the final minutes of the session for discussions stimulated by these questions.

Exhibit 1

Bill Jones

Study Questions

The (A) case:

1. What is your diagnosis of the situation at the end of the case? What went wrong?

2. What response should Bill make? To whom?

Exhibit 2

Bill Jones

Discussion Questions

After the (A) case has been read:

1. What is the problem here? What went wrong?

2. What should Bill do now? Why?

*   *   *

After the (B) case has been read:

3. What did Bill do? Why?

4. What are the implications of his particular response to this situation? What result is it likely to have?

and/or,

5. Do you agree with this approach? Why or why not? How else might Bill have handled this situation?

6. What questions does this raise for you as a discussion leader and case method teacher?

---

2. C. Roland Christensen, *Teaching by the Case Method* (Boston: Harvard Business School, 1981), pp. 14–15.

Kurt Jacobs

Teaching Note

Introduction

This case describes an outburst by an MBA student in the classroom of a senior faculty member and experienced case discussion leader. The key issue in "Kurt Jacobs" is the role of instructor responses in the classroom. In discussing this case, we focus on action planning -- for while the problem facing Professor Brett is relatively clear-cut, he has many options for action and only moments to make a critical choice.

As in considering "Bill Jones," we emphasize the complexity of listening and response, given the rapid-fire and essentially unpredictable nature of a classroom discussion. The situation in "Kurt Jacobs," however, also involves crisis management and response under very unusual conditions.

Compared with earlier cases in our syllabus, this case contains very little information about the institution, instructor, and substantive content of the course involved. Instead, readers simply share the experience of Professor Brett as he encounters Kurt Jacobs over the first eight weeks of the course, during the minutes leading up to the incident, and at the outburst itself.

Case Summary

The Institutional Context

Although the school is not identified in the text, this case takes place at Metropolitan Graduate School of Business Administration, a large, highly selective business school with a two-year case-based MBA curriculum. The incident occurs in a required second-year course.

The Course

Business Policy is a 13-week capstone course whose cases require students to integrate what they have learned throughout the program. Like most courses at Met, it is taught by the case method, and half of a student's grade is earned in classroom work. Students can sometimes arrange to submit written reports or other alternative work in place of class contribution, particularly if participation is prevented by medical or psychological difficulties.

The Instructor

The case text provides little information about Professor Brett. He is an experienced discussion leader, and though the case does not make this point, he is a senior member of Metropolitan's faculty.

The Section

With 98 students, Section A is almost 25% larger than a typical second-year class. Though many of the students probably know each other from other classes and from their first-year sections, they probably do not share the deep sense of a common experience and understanding of each other's styles that characteristically develop in the first-year program.

Several students are mentioned in the case text: Kurt Jacobs, the pivotal character, is atypical of the section in being older (age 31), married, of German nationality, with a background in a German technical institute. He appears to be socially isolated from the other students: he sits alone, his relationships with section members are courteous and formal, and he does not appear to chit-chat with other students before or after class. He seems to have a condescending attitude toward his peers (in his meeting with Brett he refers to them as young "students" whom he will help to learn) and also toward in-class discussions ("There is so much rubbish, just rubbish, in all classes here -- yours, too."). In a meeting with Professor Brett, he is marked-

This teaching note was prepared by Dr. James F. Moore in collaboration with Professor C. Roland Christensen as an aid to instructors in the classroom use of the case "Kurt Jacobs," HBS Case No. 9-376-094.

ly abrupt and unwilling to engage in dialogue. Kurt is active in a university religious club -- an interest he shares with Bob Anderson, another section member -- and is a Christian fundamentalist. This is a minority religious/ethical orientation at Metropolitan.

Bob Anderson is apparently a friend of Kurt's. Like Kurt, Bob is 31, has a technical background, is married and lives in the same married students' housing development, and is an active member of the university's religious club to which Kurt belongs.

The Student Association representative for Section A is mentioned in the case but not identified by name. He or she is apparently willing to talk candidly with Brett about Kurt, supplying background information on Kurt's social situation.

Millicent Wyeth ("Mil") is described by the student representative as "liberated." At a section social event in the first year, Kurt had tried to use biblical quotations to convince Mil that the proper role for women is the "traditional" one. Mil had responded in an "extremely spirited way," suggesting that Kurt should at least try to "crawl into the Dark Ages."

Mike Healey is a recognized academic leader of the section. Tom Mooney is his roommate and sidekick; Mooney's wit and insight have often turned routine discussions into "sparkling, high-interest, productive, class sessions."

The Teacher-Student Relationship

Professor Brett first became concerned about Kurt's silence during the early weeks of the course. In the fourth week, Brett sent a personal, handwritten note that complimented Kurt on his written work but expressed concern about his lack of participation in class, and suggested meeting to discuss the situation.

Kurt quickly scheduled a meeting, arrived promptly at the appointed time, and explained that he came to class prepared, followed the discussion, but did not feel comfortable talking in large groups. Furthermore, he expressed some disdain for the level of discussion in his courses. He assured Brett that when he did have something worthwhile to contribute, he would speak. Having finished what he wanted to say -- and apparently without waiting for Brett to reply -- he excused himself abruptly and left.

For the next four weeks Kurt's performance in class continued in the established pattern. Though he seemed very well prepared for class and followed the discussions, he remained silent. He showed interest only when the class discussed questions of ethics and morality in corporate and personal decision making.

Professor Brett found out more about Kurt by observing him and by discussing him with the student representative. He noted that Kurt seemed socially isolated, except for his relationship with Bob Anderson, and had strong religiously based beliefs, as evidenced by his confrontation with Millicent Wyeth.

On the day of the incident the class was discussing the Heublein case and whether a company that had been successful in the liquor-vodka market should enter the beer market. After about half the class time had been spent in a relatively dull discussion, Mike Healey spoke up, offering a convincing analysis and recommendations. The class became somewhat more involved, though the discussion still seemed tedious to Brett.

At this point, Tom Mooney, a class jester and friend of Mike Healey, broke in with a series of humorous recommendations. Brett chose not to cut this off, and other members of the section joined in what Brett perceived as a humorous game.

The Incident

At this point Kurt Jacobs stood up and walked into the open area of the classroom amphitheater -- the area reserved for the instructor and never entered by students unless invited. His face flushed, his arms close to his body, and his fists clenched, he turned and faced the section -- and delivered an intense three- to four-minute harangue. Supporting his argument with biblical references, Kurt chastised the other students for the immorality of their suggestions. He concluded by turning and looking at Brett, saying "Professor. . . ." When Brett stood frozen, Kurt said again, "Professor."

The case text ends at this point, and discussants are asked to explore the response options available to Brett.

A Note on Study and Discussion Questions

Typically we prepare at least two sets of questions for use with each case. The first set (Exhibit 1) comprises study questions, and can be handed out for participants' use when preparing the case before class. The discussion questions (Exhibit 2) are used by the instructor of the seminar in preparing for class and in guiding the case discussion when appropriate.

Our discussion questions constitute a question-based teaching plan which gives the instructor a general direction to pursue, but is not so restrictive as to prevent students from developing their own alternative interpretations of the case. In this way we encourage the participants to structure their own approaches to understanding the case situation. Through careful use of questioning and response, we then manage the ensuing discussion to encourage the development of the participant initiatives that emerge. That is, we use selective calling, "bridging" between comments, the insertion of summaries at key moments, and direct questioning of participants to move the discussion in potentially profitable directions.

The discussion questions we have provided reflect an open outline typical of one we might use in discussing the "Kurt Jacobs" case. For all discussion questions, but not for study questions, we have provided detailed notes in the "Analysis" sections.

A Suggested Process Plan for the Case

In our seminar, this case heralds a shift in the design of our teaching plans. In the early discussions we emphasized analysis of the case situation, holding off from action planning and generalizing. With "Kurt Jacobs," we begin to emphasize action planning, with diagnostic analysis used primarily to argue for or against particular lines of action. In addition, we now begin allowing much more time for generalizing, so that participants can think more broadly about the issues raised by the cases for their own teaching practice.

In the early sessions we are teaching participants to appreciate the hidden complexity and significant patterning in situations. Our experience is that the most common mistake made by participants early in the term is to assume the case situations are simple and the problems presented obvious. They have a strong tendency not to question their first interpretations. As instructors, we counter this tendency by emphasizing diagnosis and highlighting both the variety of initial interpretations made

by participants, and the complexity of the situations when they are understood more fully. In this we feel a kinship with Louis Agassiz as he is described in "Louis Agassiz as a Teacher" (reprinted in Teaching and the Case Method).

By the midpoint of the seminar, however, the participants may develop a tendency to focus exclusively on analysis, in isolation from action planning. At the extreme, this separation can lead to paralysis of action. That is, participants can learn to see complexity and implications everywhere, and become agonized at their inability to devise actions that are perfect from every perspective and for every possible development. To counter this tendency, it seems necessary for participants to develop a kind of habitual courage (an optimistic fatalism?) that enables them to size up a situation, devise the best plan they can, and then take committed action.

To teach the linking of analysis to action planning, we use a discussion plan that leads off with a call for action recommendations. This ensures that the participants will formulate decisions about action, and reminds the seminar that the goal is informed, effective action, and not simply analysis. Their analyses are discussed -- with rigor and attention to detail -- in the context of justifying and evaluating plans.

We begin this discussion by briefly calling attention to Professor Brett's predicament: a crisis situation, involving an emotional and confrontational outburst from a socially isolated student. The student breaks the established norms of behavior in the classroom, and challenges the class's and Brett's moral integrity. We encourage the seminar to examine the implications of the situation and consider what Brett will need to accomplish in his response.

Next we ask the seminar to consider what response Brett should make. With this question we establish the central thrust for the discussion, which will be guided by the image of a decision tree. We ask first for Brett's broad options -- the trunk and main branches of the tree -- which include calling the class off, responding directly to Kurt, or asking a class member to respond to Kurt. Then we ask seminar members to pick one of these main choices and explain in more detail how they would proceed, and why.

In this phase of the discussion we encourage participants to project themselves into Brett's situation and to spell out in detail how they would cope with Kurt's outburst. At the same time we ask them to justify their plans with reasoning based on information in the case. As the discussion proceeds, participants develop a deeper appreciation of the situation, while simultaneously linking this analysis to action planning.

We conclude this discussion by giving participants a substantial opportunity to work together to generalize from this case. We ask them to create links with other cases, and to make connections to their own experience. While we try to allow some time for consideration of wider issues in nearly all case discussions, we particularly encourage the seminar to spend a substantial amount of time generalizing from their discussion of "Kurt Jacobs." This is the concluding case in the section of the course concerned with questions, listening, and response. By now, participants have considered quite a range of cases and are glad to have an opportunity to try making sense of them as a whole.

To underline the completion of the first phase of the seminar, we may conclude the session with a few summarizing comments, highlighting some themes identified by participants and offering some thoughts of our own about links among the cases discussed so far.

Notes for the Discussion Questions

1. **What makes this response situation especially difficult? In managing this predicament, what might be some of Professor Brett's aims? Why?**

Usage Note

This question asks participants to appraise the crisis and note how different it is from standard classroom situations. The question reinforces our central teaching emphasis that everything one does as an instructor needs to be grounded in an understanding of the specific situation.

Analysis

Normally an instructor formulates his or her response primarily on the basis of the substantive content of a student's comment. The instructor pays close attention to the logic of the argument, to implicit assumptions, and to the implications of the student's conclusions. The instructor may choose to probe the assumptions or implications of a comment, may simply ask the student to expand, or may ask other students to comment on the statement. If similar content has preceded it, the instructor may highlight the connection. If the instructor wishes to move the discussion in a particular direction, he or she may underline a particular aspect of the comment -- and ask the class to develop the point further. Thus most of the instructor's attention is normally focused on substantive content.

However, other information is available to the instructor and may be used in formulating responses. For example, the student's tone of voice, pitch, and gestures signal his or her emotional state. When emotional tone is flat, the instructor may want to raise involvement by personalizing the questions and pushing the students to project themselves further into the roles of the actors in the case. When emotional tone is persistently high, an instructor may wish to cool the discussion by asking more abstract, analytical questions, thus creating distance between the students and the case material.

And finally, through both content and tone of voice, the student communicates his or her overall stance toward the instructor, other students, and the material being discussed. The student may be respectful or sarcastic, compliant with the demands of the instructor or resistant. In general once the instructor-student contract is establshed, students stay within appropriate limits, treating each other and the instructor with courtesy even when vigorously disagreeing, and complying with the broader rules of classroom etiquette. When a student does violate the norms of the section, usually a subtle reaction of displeasure or discomfort -- either from the instructor or from other students -- brings the offender into bounds.

The conditions under which Professor Brett must act, however, are far from normal. He must manage an outburst by a student who has dramatically violated several classroom norms: Kurt has interrupted the flow of discussion, walked into the center of the arena, and chastised the section and -- by implication -- the instructor. Thus his stance becomes a major factor in determining Brett's response.

Kurt's clenched fists, flushed face, and dramatic speech show that he is intensely disturbed by what has been happening in the classroom. Brett probably cannot tell to what degree Kurt has control over himself at this time. Thus Kurt's emotional state is also a major factor in Brett's decisions about his response.

Finally, the substantive content of Kurt's comment is dramatically discontinuous with the preceding discussion. He appears not to realize that the class has been jesting and creating an impromptu parody of typical discussions. In addition, his comment runs counter to typical classroom remarks in several important ways. First, rather than commenting on the case, either in seriousness or in jest, Kurt comments on the behavior of the section. Second, his argument raises issues of morality rather than effectiveness. Third, his logic is built on the premise that in matters of morals the Bible is the final authority. Consequently it is less important for Professor Brett to deal with the substantive content of Kurt's outburst than to respond to his stance vis-à-vis section norms and to his emotional condition. In our judgment Brett's first priority must be to regain control of the section and reestablish classroom norms, while calming Kurt or at least avoiding antagonizing him further.

Beyond these immediate aims, Brett must get the section to return to the course agenda, without simply sweeping the incident under the rug. In addition, he will wish to protect Kurt from becoming a class pariah, while also signaling to both Kurt and the others that such outbursts, regardless of content, are not appropriate in class. Ideally, Brett will want to help Kurt become more constructively engaged in the learning activities of the course, if this is possible. And finally Brett will want to exploit the opportunities for teaching and learning opened up by this incident.

2. **What general options for response does Professor Brett have now? Please hold off on detail at this time, and just sketch his broad choices.**

Usage Note

This question asks the seminar to generate a simple decision tree, concentrating first on the major forks and branches.

Analysis

There appear to us to be three major immediate options, each of which leads to other choices that must be made. First, Professor Brett can respond to Kurt Jacobs directly. Second, he can ask members of the class to respond. Third, Brett can call off the class.

Responding directly to Kurt allows Brett more control over the situation than if he asks a class member to respond. In addition, with the enormous social power of an instructor, he might have a better chance of getting Kurt to comply with his wishes. But a direct response would be a further violation of the established classroom contract, substituting teacher-student interaction for the prevailing norm of student-to-student dialogue. And it has the further disadvantage of prolonging the confrontation between Brett and Kurt. It is possible that, instead of diminishing the conflict, a direct response could cause Kurt to harden and escalate his resistance.

If Brett decides to act directly, he must then choose whether to respond to the obvious manifest content of Kurt's speech (as he would to a normal contribution in class) or to the latent emotional content. There is a danger in responding to the substantive content. Not only is it discontinuous with the rest of the discussion, and based on premises not generally shared within the course, but in his present emotional state, Kurt is probably not able to respond coherently.

On the other hand, if Brett chooses to base his response on Kurt's emotional condition and stance, what should he do? How does one respond to a person in intense emotional disarray?

A second possibility is to ask a class member to respond to Kurt. This move would reestablish the classroom pattern of dialogue between students, with the faculty member moderating. It might also help to create dialogue between Kurt and the other students, thus reducing his isolation. A major risk of this strategy is that the instructor cannot determine the student's response. Thus there is some chance that a very unhelpful response will be made -- such as a verbal attack on Kurt.

If Brett decides to ask a class member to respond, further choices ensue. He may ask a specific person to comment, or simply pose a general question to the class and pick a respondent from those who volunteer. He may ask the respondent to comment, or he may ask a specific question. In the latter case, he must choose a question from an infinitely wide range of possibilities.

A third major option is to call off the class. This has the advantage of taking Brett quickly off the spot, and gaining him some time to think. However, it has three major disadvantages, and we consider it a last resort to be used if the other two approaches fail. The first disadvantage is that it would break his contract with the other students to provide them with a full discussion session. Some might object and not wish to leave if the section is dismissed. Brett would then be faced with a double insurrection.

Moreover, dismissal might signal to the section members that the incident is more serious than it really is. Kurt's outburst might then become "the event that was SO wild it shut down the section." Finally, calling off the session would eliminate Brett's opportunity to manage the class's interpretation of the event by how he handles the situation. Instead the students would draw their own (perhaps angry, perhaps confused) conclusions and by the time Brett saw them again, their reading of the event would be well established.

If Brett calls off the class, his use of the time between this session and the next becomes crucial. He must decide when and how to talk with Kurt, and if, when, and how to talk with the rest of the class members.

3. **Which would you select? How would you proceed? Why?**

Usage Note

This question, which we regard as central to our discussion, moves the seminar from consideration of general options to designing specific lines of action. Participants must deepen their analysis of the situation as they evaluate the merits of various plans. We encourage this by mixing <u>how</u> and <u>why</u> questions -- thus forcing a careful reexamination of the case in the context of action planning.

Analysis

Obviously, a wide range of responses could be made in this very complex situation, and none will be assuredly right or wrong. But because the better responses will be grounded in a sensitive appreciation of the situation, our analysis will examine in detail several features of the situation and their implications for action.

The case text indicates that Kurt is socially isolated and does not seem to have the interpersonal ability to break out. He finds it uncomfortable to speak in any class and rarely does so, he sits alone, and he doesn't socialize before and after class. In his meeting with Brett, Kurt is abrupt and displays an unusual degree of condescension toward both his classmates and his professor.

Though schools like Metropolitan pride themselves on the diversity of their students, Kurt is farther from the norm than most. He is older, he is married, and rather than living in Metropolitan's dorms (which are the scene of much social activity), he lives in a married students' housing complex. Moreover he is German, with a technical background (in a school where many of the students have general business backgrounds); he is a Christian fundamentalist; and in classroom discussions he is apparently more engaged by issues of corporate and personal ethics than efficiency and effectiveness.

Overall, it seems safe to conclude that Kurt's view of the world differs profoundly from that of most of his peers. This in itself would not necessarily be a liability for Kurt or for the section. Students with unusual backgrounds and perspectives often enrich the life of the school and have a successful educational experience themselves. However, Kurt's social isolation and condescending attitude are likely to preclude the dialogue that is vital to such valuable learning opportunities. This problem is indicated in his brusque meeting with Brett and in his heated confrontation with Millicent Wyeth. Both interchanges seem to have been memorable but not enlightening.

On the basis of this diagnosis, we believe that a central teaching problem is how to help Kurt out of his isolation and into meaningful dialogue in the classroom situation. Kurt probably needs both help and some encouragement or pressure to genuinely listen to the views of others. He also probably needs assistance in finding appropriate and effective ways to make himself heard in the Metropolitan environment. This help might come from Professor Brett and/or other students, and might occur either in or out of class. It might also be valuable for Kurt to work on communication issues with a counselor or religious leader.

For many readers, Kurt's problem is obscured by the more dramatic issue of classroom control. Kurt has usurped the instructor's position and challenged his ethical legitimacy. In a sense he has hijacked the classroom to get attention for his concerns. The hijacking itself requires immediate attention.

In addition, concern for Kurt as an individual must be balanced against other competing demands, including responsibilities to the whole section. Until the moment of the incident, Kurt's isolation was more of a problem for him than for the section as a whole, and it is easy to see why this problem stayed on Brett's back burner during the early weeks of the term. Even now that the problem has erupted in the classroom, priority must be given to staying with the educational agenda of the course as a whole.

Finally, it is uncertain how much headway can be made with Kurt, given his demonstrated inflexibility and the effect of the incident itself. His relationship with the section is in danger of becoming irreversibly polarized. If his resistance or his instability increases, professional counseling or psychotherapy may be needed. It is not the instructor's role to do psychotherapy with students.

And yet, if real (and respectful) in-class dialogue can be achieved, it is likely to benefit both Kurt and the other section members. Encouraging such communication is one of our most central aims as case method instructors. In case discussions we foster multiple points of view and work to strengthen the section's capacity for respectful consideration of differences of perspective and judgment. In responding to Kurt Jacobs, we believe it is crucial to keep this goal in mind. While it is important to reestablish control over the situation, and to signal clearly the inappropriateness of Kurt's manner of expression, it would be very detrimental to Kurt and the section to take action that diminishes the possibility of future dialogue. Kurt's outburst has certainly violated the classroom norms of respectful discussion moderated by the instructor. But to silence him forcefully, for example, or to allow other students to attack him, would also violate these norms. Ideally, a way will be found to use this incident to increase, rather than decrease, constructive communication between Kurt and other students.

A second important feature of the situation is the conflicting interpretations of the section's "game playing." To the professor it was a harmless way of letting off steam, as well as a welcome relief during a tedious discussion. With the exception of Kurt, most of the students seem to have agreed. However, there is no information in the case text about what the nonparticipating students thought of the banter, and it is possible that some of them found it objectionable but simply decided not to intervene. Kurt -- much to the surprise of the instructor -- not only found the situation objectionable but saw it as a

symptom of deep ethical and spiritual irresponsibility, and felt compelled to interrupt the game and chastise the section and instructor.

Kurt does not seem to understand that the section has been jesting. As a socially isolated foreign student, he may find it difficult to pick up subtle verbal and nonverbal cues in conversation. He would find parody -- such as that which has occurred in the classroom -- particularly hard to identify, since much of the humor arises from the very narrowness of the line that separates the parody from its "straight" original. Even if Kurt understands that the section has been joking, he may still find the comments objectionable -- especially given fundamentalist beliefs regarding blasphemy.

Kurt's reaction to the section's game playing underlines the degree to which his view of the world differs from that of other members in the class. Somehow Brett and/or the class members need to ensure that, at minimum, Kurt realizes that they were joking. Even so, the job of bridging between Kurt's view of reality and that held by most students is likely to be difficult. Such bridging will probably have to be done explicitly, by highlighting the misunderstanding and talking directly with Kurt about the differences between the two views.

An additional problem is that Kurt is extremely upset. In his present emotional state he is unlikely to be able to particpate in a rational discussion of his beliefs and values. Given his behavior, Brett may well wonder if Kurt has become seriously unstable. It is wise to deal with him carefully to avoid provoking him further.

The reactions of the other students also need to be anticipated. The major threat to classroom control may lie in their reaction to Kurt, rather than in his outburst itself. Kurt is an unpopular classmate who has spoiled their game, attacked their moral integrity, disrupted the class, and violated section and school norms. In addition he holds minority religious views and is attempting to force them on the section. Though some students will probably see his vulnerability, and others may be embarrassed for him, there will probably be students who are quite angry at Kurt. In our opinion it is very important to protect Kurt from verbal assault by these students. Such an attack could be damaging to Kurt, and might signal to other class members that Brett cannot protect students with unpopular views. Further, there is much wisdom in the adage that after the hanging, the scoundrel becomes a martyr. A verbal assault on Kurt could raise sympathy for him and polarize the class into camps supporting and opposing him.

How then should Professor Brett respond? For clarity we break the problem down into three parts: what Brett should do in the moments immediately following the outburst; in the minutes following; and before the next class. We emphasize that the following remarks are merely suggestions, and that all our projections of outcomes are at best informed speculations. We offer these to stimulate your answers, not to foreclose other options.

Immediately after the outburst, Brett needs to reemphasize and reestablish classroom norms, while not further upsetting Kurt. One possibility is for Brett simply to remain silent, turning his gaze away from Kurt and/or physically moving over to the side of the room. In this way Brett diminishes his psychological contact with Kurt, thus reducing the possibility of further confrontation between them. The hope is that the silence will become too much for Kurt to bear, and that he will decide to resume his seat. Brett can then return to his normal discussion leadership stance, having regained immediate control of the class.

One seminar participant who had been trained in counseling and crisis intervention suggested that Brett acknowledge Kurt's feelings, his courage, and the importance of his point of view for the discussion. It often helps a disturbed person regain control of himself if a person he is confronting neither agrees nor disagrees with him, but instead communicates respect and understanding by acknowledging the disturbed person's strong feelings.

For example, Brett might say, "You seem to be extremely upset by this discussion, Kurt. I also imagine it took a great deal of courage for you to confront the entire class in this way. Though I don't agree with your point of view, I do value hearing from you and would like to make it more possible for you to be heard." The expectation here is that Kurt will feel relieved and affirmed by having his experience recognized and acknowledged by the instructor, and will relax. Building upon the rapport established in this way, Brett can then ask Kurt to go back to his seat so that the discussion can continue in a more orderly fashion.

If Brett is unable to regain control of the classroom through such measures, he might more forcefully ask Kurt please to take his seat. In the extreme situation that Kurt maintains the confrontation and refuses to sit down, it might be necessary to dismiss the class and give full attention to managing Kurt.

Assuming Brett can regain control of the classroom within the first few moments, he must then decide how to carry on. One option is simply to reopen the preceding case discussion, implicitly asking the class to disregard the incident. This has the risk of isolating Kurt further. In addition, it means that the class's first direct responses to Kurt will occur after the session -- at a time when Brett cannot influence or even observe them.

Asking someone from the section to address Kurt has the risk of allowing a verbal attack. However, this approach has the advantage of reinforcing the section norm of dialogue between members and of connecting Kurt with another student and thus beginning to reduce his isolation. Brett can influence the interchange both through his choice of a respondent and by the particular task he sets for this person. Because of the possibility of an angry reaction toward Kurt, we believe it is crucial to keep control of the situation by asking a specific question of a specific student.

We would call on someone we believe has the capacity to address Kurt directly and humanely -- someone who could sense Kurt's vulnerability and isolation, and who could perhaps appreciate Kurt's courage as well as his foolhardiness. This person might be another foreign student who could empathize with Kurt's cultural isolation. Another possibility is calling on Kurt's friend, Bob Anderson, who can be expected to understand Kurt's position and has his confidence. We also assume that Bob has been able to understand the perspective of the "game players" in the incident, and can thus act as a translator and bridge. Calling on Bob also involves some risk, however, since he might feel intense pressure to side publicly with Kurt, and could thus become isolated with him, further polarizing the class. It is hard to define in the abstract who should be picked; our choice would probably be guided more by our intuitions and instantaneous reading of faces than by any specifiable criteria.

Perhaps the worst choice would be to call on the game players. They are the section members most directly attacked by Kurt, and are likely to be angered. In addition, Kurt may view them as ringleaders of just the movement and values he deplores, and may see talking with them as an opportunity for further crusading.

No matter who is chosen to respond to Kurt, the question posed and the manner in which it is delivered are very important. It is important to signal to the respondent, and to the class as a whole, that their most caring and creative help is needed to resolve the difficult situation facing the section. Thus we might ask if the student could "help us out here" by responding to Kurt. Our hope would be that he or she could somehow communicate respect for Kurt, while at the same time helping him see that the class had been playing a game and meant no harm by it. Assuming some sort of rapprochement is achieved -- even if only a slight movement in that direction -- we would be satisfied. At least a positive direction would have been established, and instructor support for it clearly communicated.

If time remains in the period, we might conclude by returning to the agenda of the course, thus emphasizing its importance. We might, for example, make a few summarizing points about the Heublein case and its relation to other cases in the series.

4. **What would you do before the next class?**

Usage Note

This question directs the seminar's attention to the sometimes forgotten possibilities of responding outside of class. A great advantage of talking with students out of class is that they often feel less formal and less anxious to protect their public image, and thus sometimes are willing to be much more candid with the instructor. In addition, one can meet students in a variety of locations, including neutral places not "owned" by the professor -- e.g., a local bar, a street corner, a student lounge. This can put the student on a more equal footing with the instructor -- again sometimes promoting more candor and less defensiveness.

Analysis

In our judgment it is important to contact both Kurt and the section's informal leadership. We want, first of all, to assess Kurt's emotional state -- in order to know how to respond to him in the future -- and

to refer him for professional help if he appears unstable. In addition, we want to begin the process of linking him back into the section. This will involve explaining to him the game-playing circumstances from the perspective of the other section members, letting him know that the students were jesting and the suggestions were certainly not meant seriously.

We would offer Kurt an opportunity to make his views known in a forum where they could be heard and would not disrupt the class. In this way we would support a presentation of diverse views -- one of our fundamental aims in case teaching. For example, Kurt could write a memo to the section, which would be duplicated and distributed (this is something that is done with some frequency in sections, and thus it would not seem abnormal); or he could call an out-of-class meeting to explain his position; or we might let him lead off the next class to explain his position. After supporting Kurt's right to express his views, we would remind him (rather gently) that his outburst was disruptive, and indicate that we hope it won't happen again.

In addition to talking with Kurt, we would approach the section's informal leadership -- e.g., Mike Healey. Our primary purpose would be to enlist these students' support in keeping the class going: helping case discussions run strongly, and avoiding any section actions that would further isolate or offend Kurt. It would be helpful to try to get them to see Kurt's vulnerability rather than his disruptiveness, and to take it upon themselves to help the community renew itself, and perhaps even incorporate Kurt and his views into its range of acceptable experience.

5. **What wider questions are raised by this case?**

Usage Note

This question asks participants to generalize from this case, thus encouraging connections to their own experience as well as to the other cases used in the seminar. When a seminar member raises one of these questions, we usually ask him or her to try to answer it -- and then ask if others would like to respond to that question or jump in with one of their own.

Analysis

Participants often mention a variety of questions raised by this case. To stimulate thinking and demonstrate just a bit of the range, six such questions are listed here, along with very brief sample reactions. It should be noted that any of these questions can also be used by the instructor as probes -- if probes are needed to stimulate or broaden the range of discussion.

a) Has anyone in the seminar had a similar experience? How did you manage it? On the basis of your experience, do you have any lessons you could share with us?

This question draws a variety of interesting responses. It can be helpful if the instructor asks the participant who shares an experience to say explicitly how his or her experience is similar to Brett's. In this way the general theme is articulated and emphasized.

b) We urge instructors to be sensitive to the students and to their points of view. Why didn't Brett pick up on Kurt's signals? Should he have? What might Brett have done to prevent the incident, anyway?

To use managerial terms, the instructor's span of control is terribly large. Brett probably had responsibility that term for two sections of 80 to 100 students each. Though he did notice Kurt's signals to some extent, he did not devote a great deal of time to following through. There is no reason to assume either malice or negligence on the part of Professor Brett; it was simply that he had little time available and other students seemed to have more pressing needs.

In our experience, instructors seem to spend most of their out-of-class time with two sets of students: those who are failing the course or doing very poorly -- and thus need help simply staying afloat -- and the very talented and involved students who can benefit from extra tutelage. The students in the middle who, like Kurt, are clearly capable of managing the course material but do not shine with interest are -- rightly or wrongly -- left more to their own devices. This raises another question: how should instructors allocate their scarce out-of-class time?

It is unclear whether Professor Brett could have prevented the incident, but he might have taken more initiative in reducing Kurt's isolation. Several possibilities come to mind. He could perhaps have responded to Kurt's visible interest in the ethical questions raised by cases by asking Kurt to comment on them in class, or to write supplemental reports on these issues in lieu

of class participation. This might have made Kurt feel more listened to, and less alone and isolated in his concerns. Brett might also have talked with Kurt's friend, Bob Anderson -- who appears to be more integrated into the section -- about ways to involve Kurt. This might have led to some suggestions, and at the same time would have sent an indirect message back to Kurt about his participation.

c) Kurt seems to have wanted a special contract with Brett. Should he have one? Should instructors make special arrangements with students? If so, in what situations?

Kurt seems to have wanted a special contract that would absolve him of the need to participate with the rest of the students, except when he felt it important to instruct them as a superior. By not directly challenging Kurt -- either in class, after class informally, or during the abrupt meeting in his office -- Brett gave his tacit consent, if not exactly approval, to a special contract with Kurt.

This contract unfortunately increased Kurt's isolation from the class and decreased his opportunities for learning. Such a contract does not seem to be in his long-term interest, and as instructors we would probably not make one were we aware of it. In general our policy is to make special contracts only if they will increase a student's involvement and opportunities for learning. For example, some students find it virtually impossible to speak in class. Forcing them to do so simply makes no sense. In these cases we allow them to remain silent, but ask that they write supplemental analyses of the cases. In this way their involvement is increased.

d) What about humor? Should you keep the students' noses constantly to the grindstone, or allow humor to emerge? Should an instructor allow game playing in class? How much, and at what points? When and how should he or she step in to stop such gaming?

In our experience sections need a bit of relief from time to time, and humor and gaming definitely have their place. Usually humor emerges from the section and need not be artificially promoted by the instructor! In addition to relieving tension, humor can enhance creativity by expanding the range of thinkable options -- and can sometimes lead to new and unique solutions to problems. In this way classroom gaming can be similar to exercises in educational programs designed to increase creativity, such as Synectics.[1]

e) In replying to a student's comment, when should you respond to the latent emotional content, in addition to the manifest content?

It seems to us important to be aware of both the manifest and the latent content. This point is discussed more fully in the notes for Question #1.

f) What connections do you see between the issues and questions raised by this case, and questions raised by previous cases? Do we seem to be identifying any common themes, or common conundrums?

A major theme is the importance of the teacher-student learning contract. From "Bill Curtis" through "Henry Jasper" and "Ernie Budding," we have been highlighting the importance of the web of often unspoken mutual expectations that give order to life in the classroom and whose undoing leaves perplexity and confusion.

A second common theme has to do with students who seek special contracts -- a theme that joins "Henry Jasper" with "Kurt Jacobs." A third has to do with crisis management and the essentially unpredictable nature of case discussions. This issue arises in "Henry Jasper" and "Bill Jones," which both deal with managing a shocking and fast-breaking, emotionally volatile situation. A fourth theme is the importance of questions and responses -- a topic highlighted by "Assistant Professor Graham and Ms. Macomber," "Bill Jones," and "Kurt Jacobs."

Suggestions for Building the Seminar Group

In our syllabus this case is discussed just after the middle of the term. By this time the teacher-student learning contract is well established and seminar participants trust each other and respect divergent as well as convergent views. Hereafter we make three shifts in our management of the discussion process. First, we put less emphasis on case diagnosis per se and more on options for action. Since action plans must be carefully justified, participants still put a great deal of effort into diagnosis. But now their diagnostic work must be more directly integrated into the consideration of options for action. Moreover, the emphasis on action encourages participants to project themselves into the cases -- learning more

about how these situations feel to participants, and committing themselves deeply to their choices.

Second, we spend much more time on generalization. This lets the participants integrate their learning across cases, as well as link the cases to their own experiences.

Third, in our process planning as instructors we pay less attention to the group dynamics of the seminar and more to the experience of individual participants. By this time in the term the seminar usually has become a highly self-maintaining social system, and our efforts -- at establishing and maintaining norms, at correcting problems that come up in sessions -- are much less important to the group discussion process. The section usually begins to feel quite different to us: beginning a class now seems like stepping into an ongoing process rather than one we must rev up each session.

This leaves us free to focus some attention on the learning needs of individuals. For example, if a participant has not spoken, we may now try to help that happen. Or if a member is very good at case analysis, but not so strong on action planning, we may start pressing him or her to speak about action planning. In this way participants are encouraged to develop in the areas where they lag.

Exhibit 1

Kurt Jacobs

Study Questions

1. What response options are open to Professor Brett as of the end of the case? Which would you believe most appropriate? Why?

2. What should Professor Brett do in the next minute? The next few minutes? Before class meets again?

3. Compare the "Ernie Budding," "Assistant Professor Graham and Ms. Macomber," "Bill Jones," and "Kurt Jacobs" cases. How are they similar? What are the implications for a section instructor?

---

1. W. J. J. Gordon, *Synectics* (New York: Harper & Row, 1961).

Exhibit 2

Kurt Jacobs

Discussion Questions

1. What makes this response situation especially difficult? In managing this predicament, what might be some of Professor Brett's aims? Why?

2. What general options for action does Professor Brett have now? Please hold off on detail at this time, and just sketch his broad choices.

3. Which would you select? How would you proceed? Why?

4. What would you do before the next class?

5. What wider questions are raised by this case?

[The following probes can be used if desired]:

a) Has anyone in the seminar had a similar experience? How did you manage it? On the basis of your experience, do you have any lessons you could share with us?

b) We urge instructors to be sensitive to the students and to their points of view. Why didn't Brett pick up on Kurt's signals? Should he have? What might Brett have done to prevent the incident, anyway?

c) Kurt seems to have wanted a special contract with Brett. Should he have one? Should instructors make special arrangements with students? If so, in what situations?

d) What about humor? Should you keep the students' noses constantly to the grindstone, or allow humor to emerge? Should an instructor allow game playing in class? How much, and at what points? When and how should he or she step in to stop such gaming?

e) In replying to a student's comment, when should you respond to the latent emotional content, in addition to the manifest content?

f) What connections do you see between the issues and questions raised by this case and previous cases? Do we seem to be identifying any common themes, or common conundrums?

The Section Just Took Over: A Student's Reflections

Teaching Note

Introduction

This dramatic case centers on a discussion that turns into an angry shouting session, undermining the tight control usually maintained by the instructor. The content of the outburst revolves around the ethics of a controversial marketing plan, and thus "The Section Just Took Over" is often read as a case about the challenges of discussing ethical questions in class. We believe, however, that the explanation of the explosion lies less in the particular content of the day than in the instructor's excessively controlling teaching style. This sort of style can prevent a section from developing the capacity for real dialogue, including the ability to consider truly conflicting points of view. Thus we try to use this case as an opportunity to explore the vital issue of freedom and control in case teaching.

We usually use this case in the final phase of the seminar on case method teaching. By this time in the semester, the major themes of the seminar (e.g., rapport, the teacher-student learning contract, questioning, listening, and responding) will have been introduced. In the remaining classes we consider a variety of special but recurrent problems of teaching, while reviewing and further exploring the central themes of the course.

In this phase of the course we feel free to adapt the selection of cases and the focus of case discussions to the emerging needs and interests of the group. Yet in our experience certain issues tend to recur from year to year; virtually all participants, for example, are concerned about how to deal with apathy, quiet students, insubordination, cheating, requests for counseling, and administration and/or student pressure to modify grades. During these final class sessions, we encourage seminar members to generalize from the cases, articulating their own teaching philosophies as well as making concrete connections between the seminar discussions and their own teaching practice.

Case Summary

"The Section Just Took Over" is brief, and thus lends itself to use in a variety of situations, including those -- such as workshops -- where participants have limited preparation time. It is an exciting, engaging case, described entirely through the eyes of a student who was present but relatively uninvolved in the incident. Unlike many of the other cases in our syllabus, "The Section Just Took Over" includes little background information about the institutional context, the course, or the protagonists. The heart of the text is a characterization of the instructor's style of managing case discussions, as seen through the eyes of the student casewriter, and the account of the blowup itself.

The Institutional Context

This case takes place in a required, case-based course in the first year of the MBA program at Southeastern. Though the text gives little information about the nature of Southeastern's program, we can infer that it includes only a few case-based courses. (The casewriter observes that the incident took place in one of the school's few amphitheater classrooms -- that is, the type suitable for case teaching.) The case provides little additional information on Southeastern or its MBA program.

The Course

The case involves an incident in a case-based course in marketing policy, which is described as a key first-semester MBA course.

This teaching note was prepared by Dr. James F. Moore in collaboration with Professor C. Roland Christensen as an aid to instructors in the classroom use of the case "The Section Just Took Over," HBS Case No. 9-379-007.

The Instructor

Associate Professor Kenneth Webster is described by the casewriter (a first-semester MBA candidate) as a "case method instructor <u>par excellence</u> -- the professor who was always in perfect control." According to the casewriter, most of the first-semester students were awed by Webster's ability to control a case discussion tightly and precisely. Following an apparently memorized teaching plan for each class, Webster was "able to needle students into corners, only to lead them out again when the time was ripe, by getting someone to dredge up three numbers to 'crack the case.'" Webster invariably concludes each session with a "brilliant five-minute windup" presenting his views on the essential lessons to be learned from the day's case.

The Section

The section consists of first-year, first-semester MBA students, with presumably little case discussion experience. We are given little information about the un-named casewriter. Three other students -- Kay Woodward, Bob Kinney, and Harry Jones -- are identified by name. The casewriter believes that Kay has had little business experience, and he has heard that she has deep convictions on social issues. Before the day of the incident, she had not spoken in Webster's class.

The casewriter believes that Bob Kinney had been an investment banker for a number of years. No other background information is provided. Harry Jones is described as one of the older students in the section, and a former divinity student.

The Teacher-Student Relationship

The hallmark of Professor Webster's approach is instructor control of the discussion process. Though he says he tries to "combine class discussion freedom with a logical, scientific, and disciplined approach to marketing problems and solutions," there is little evidence of freedom in discussion. Webster controls the content, working from a hidden outline and invariably presenting a prearranged summary at the end of each class. More important, he tightly controls the discussion process -- smoothly leading students into and out of traps, guiding them toward the key recognitions that "crack" the cases, and managing the discussion timing so precisely that the students marvel at his ability to do so without visibly glancing at the clock.

This pattern of control apparently began with the early sessions of the course, and has continued unchanged to the halfway point in the term when the incident takes place. There is no report of overt resistance to this control (as, for example, was experienced by Ernie Budding in a previous case), although on the day in question class performance was poor and could be construed as passively resistant. A poor opening contribution had been followed with further comments that were noticeably "slow in coming." Professor Webster "kept slugging away" though "his disappointment . . . was clearly visible in his frequent gazing around the room during students' comments." As the session continued, the casewriter noticed a lack of continuity developing between Webster's questions (presumably predetermined by his teaching plan) and students' comments. This may indicate that the students were trying to pull the discussion in some direction other than the one Webster had in mind -- to the extent they could wrestle free of his control.

The Incident

On the day of the incident, the class is discussing a complex case about "the marketing of birth control pills in an underdeveloped country by a large, multinational drug company." Up to this point in the semester, the course has apparently emphasized individual techniques of marketing analysis and practice. This case is the first to present students with a complex, multidimensional marketing problem.

At about the halfway point in the discussion (presumably classes are about 80 minutes long), Kay Woodward takes the floor and argues that the discussion has bypassed important ethical issues raised by the case. Bob Kinney snaps back that "that's not really the main issue here. . . . I didn't come here to learn what I'd missed in Sunday School. . . ." The classroom erupts in chaos as students argue among themselves.

Though Professor Webster makes several attempts to quiet the class, the bedlam continues for many minutes until Harry Jones commands the class's attention and argues that Bob's objection was out of line. Harry asserts that ethical issues should be discussed in class because, as future managers, the students must be prepared to deal with these questions when they arise in actual management situations.

Taking advantage of the order produced by Harry Jones, Professor Webster regains command of the class and asserts that Kay's question was inappropriate because ethical concerns are personal matters to be discussed outside of class. The casewriter reports that "No further 'social-ethical' questions were raised in [Webster's] marketing course that semester."

A Note on Study and Discussion Questions

Typically we prepare at least two sets of questions for use with each case. The first (see Exhibit 1) consists of study questions, and can be handed out with the case for participants' use in preparing the case before class. The second set (see Exhibit 2) is made up of discussion questions, to be used by the instructor in preparing for the case discussion, and in guiding the case discussion when appropriate. For all discussion questions, but not for study questions, we have provided detailed usage and analytical notes.

A Suggested Process Plan for the Case

In past discussions, we have found that this case draws energy not only from the power of the text but from the ethical issues to which the protagonists allude. That is, several seminar participants often become exercised about the issues of birth control, multinationals in the third world, and religious authority -- and whether or not these issues are directly discussed in the teaching seminar, they give added emotional charge to the case.

Our general plan is to play counterpoint against the natural focus of the text on ethics and ethical issues. We find that without strong direction, the group will gravitate toward a discussion of the appropriate role of ethics in the classroom and ways of handling ethical issues. While these are very valuable questions, we wish to take participants farther into the issue, so that they can see that the question of handling ethical issues is part of the broader question of developing a section's capacity for deep, emotionally involving, and diversity-respecting discussion.

We try to accomplish this with an intense focus on diagnosis in the case, and with a series of optional probes (Questions 2 through 4) that call attention to various features of the situation that help determine how the ethical issues are received. These features are the particular nature of Kay's comment, Professor Webster's style of discussion leadership, and the teacher-student relationship that is evolving in the section.

Once we have established the problems with Webster's overcontrolling style, we ask participants to consider what forces might push Webster or any young instructor to use such an approach. This question helps seminar members to sympathize with Webster's difficult situation, and to realize the forces in their own practices that pull toward a similar style.

We continue the discussion with an extensive consideration of action alternatives. First, participants discuss how it might have been possible to respond to Kay and Bob more constructively. This discussion calls upon seminar members to consider crisis management and the handling of unexpected and emotionally driven comments. Second, participants consider alternatives to Webster's overall style of discussion leadership.

Finally, we ask participants to consider the more general issues of freedom and control in case teaching. They are invited to review the range of discussion management techniques presented throughout the seminar, as well as to explore their own broader personal philosophies of freedom and control in case teaching.

Notes for the Discussion Questions

These notes parallel the suggested discussion questions presented in Exhibit 2. For each question a brief note is provided about the pedagogical intent and use of the question. In addition, for each question we have provided our best attempt at a reasoned response. These analytical responses represent our current thoughts on the matters raised, and are provided primarily to aid the instructor in preparing for a discussion of the case. As such, they are intended to sensitize him or her to key issues in the case. We do not regard these responses as the definitive solutions to the questions raised by the case. "The Section Just Took Over," like other cases, can be profitably analyzed from a variety of viewpoints -- and a variety of actions could be usefully taken in situations like that described in the case. We hope each new discussion will provide new insights of value to both the discussion participants and the discussion leader -- and we can say with gratitude that this has been our experience in leading discussions of this case and others in the seminar.

1. **What is your diagnosis of this situation? Why did the explosion occur? What is the central problem posed by this case?**

Usage Note

This broad opening question allows the seminar members to range widely in their diagnostic thinking. As the session proceeds, we use discussion management techniques, such as bridging and selective reinforcement of comments, to encourage participants to see the case not as an illustration of the explosiveness of ethical issues, but rather as an example of how such issues may become explosive when they arise in the context of a particular sort of instructor-student dynamic.

Analysis

The immediate problem is that the section exploded into the worst of uncontrolled discussions. But why has this happened? Some participants may suggest that ethical issues of the type raised by Kay simply tend to be explosive. While this is in one sense true -- birth control, exploitation of women, the activities of multinational corporations in third world countries are all questions of great current controversy -- our experience is that, properly handled, each of these issues can be respectfully and profitably discussed in case classes.

The central problem, in our view, is that a number of factors have converged to create a class with almost no capacity for open, spirited, self-managed discussion of issues of great felt importance to the students. This is a serious deficiency in a case-based course, for the value of the method derives in large part from just such discussions.

The students -- individually and as a group -- appear to have developed little capacity for open exploration of differing perspectives. A very important part of the case method experience is that students learn that disagreement is all right -- indeed, that it is through reasoned, trenchant dialogue that new insights can be created and learning can occur. Over the first term or so, students learn to value differences of opinion, and greatly increase their tolerance for healthy disagreement and even spirited conflict.

The members of Webster's class do not seem to have learned this lesson yet. Neither Kay nor Bob shows tolerance for diverse views. On the contrary, they both react defensively, thus feeding the class's anxieties and triggering a free-for-all.

It is perhaps not surprising that the class does not have a capacity for disagreement. The students are relatively new to case discussions. Webster's class is apparently one of the few conducted in this manner at Southeastern, and the students are only halfway through their first semester. Thus they have had little experience with open discussions. Further, if we can believe the casewriter, the cases examined so far in Webster's course have apparently concerned relatively circumscribed marketing questions, thus not affording great latitude for interpretation -- or for differences of interpretation. Finally, Webster has not made his class a place where real disagreement is valued. On the contrary, his contract with the students is that they must try to guess his view of the case -- and any deviation from that view is apparently treated as evidence that the student has not grasped the point of the case.

Kay introduces her point in a provocative, challenging manner that increases the likelihood of a defensive reaction from other members of the class. Moreover, the class already appears to be chafing under Webster's close rein. Thus the opportunity for an explosion may be experienced by the students as a welcome relief from his control. Both of these points will be discussed in more detail below.

The following questions can be used to deepen the diagnostic discussion:

2.   **What is it about the nature of Kay's comment that made it so difficult for others in the class to handle?**

Usage Note

Focusing on the way in which Kay raised her objection helps seminar members understand that it is not necessarily ethical issues per se that are explosive, but rather the incendiary way in which they may be introduced. This insight suggests that there are more and less skillful ways to raise controversial issues in discussion -- and that an important objective for students and instructors may be to learn how to introduce difficult concerns and questions in ways that maximize productive, respectful, and rational discussion.

Analysis

Kay does not simply raise ethical concerns about the marketing plan described in the case. Rather, she attacks the integrity of the class for not identifying these concerns earlier, accusing them of "avoiding" (rather than simply missing) these issues. She states that "this company's marketing plan should strike everyone's conscience as being highly unethical, even immoral" -- in effect indicting those who did not find it so. Her language is emotionally charged and provocative -- comparing the company to cases in The Ugly American and asserting that it is dedicated to immoral activities in the pursuit of "almighty profit."

Kay could have raised the same issues without accusing her classmates of immorality for not discussing them sooner. Had she done so, she might have found a good deal of support for at least some of her points. Further, had she simply avoided the use of highly charged, virtually taunting language, her comment would have had a better chance of drawing reasoned rather than defensive responses from those who did not agree.

3. **Could the explosion have been predicted? Why or why not?**

Usage Note

This question shifts the focus from Kay and the nature of her comment to other situational factors. Again, we wish to help participants see that the explosion did not result simply from the content of the comment, but probably from a convergence of factors. We tend to manage discussion a bit at this point in order to selectively reinforce comments that draw attention to Webster's way of handling the section and how this may have set up conditions that favored an explosion.

Analysis

In our judgment some cases raise issues that are more sensitive than others, and an instructor should be alert to the possibility that an emotional conflagration could develop in class. To some extent, what issues are hot depend upon what controversies are active in the world at large at any given time. In the United States during the 1970s, women's issues, the role of multinational corporations in the third world, and to some extent birth control were all major issues of controversy among university students. Thus Webster should probably have realized the potential for deep differences of opinion in the class, for defensiveness and polarization, and therefore for comments like Kay's and Bob's.

On the other hand, it is in the nature of case discussions that one often cannot predict when an emotionally charged issue will surface. As one participant in the seminar wrote, "Emotions can run high over

such unlikely subjects as monetarism versus Keynesianism, and market share versus cash flow." The case method instructor must be ready, to some extent, to deal with surprising outbursts whenever they occur.

In the case of Webster's section, certain other factors might have led an outside observer, if not to predict an explosion, at least not to be surprised that one occurred. Chief among these is Webster's tight control over the section, and the intimations of resistance seen in the passivity of the class on the day in question. This issue will be discussed in the analysis for the following question.

4. **What is it like to be a student in Kenneth Webster's class? What is his contract with the students? How has it been communicated?**

Usage Note

This question emphasizes Webster's role in creating a situation that invites an explosion. Further, it asks participants to examine in some detail the nature of his working relationship with the students, and how he maintains it. If much of this material has come out in previous discussion, there may be little need to ask this question.

Analysis

Webster's contract is, perhaps unfortunately, quite clear. The students are to spend most of the class session trying to guess his analysis of the case, while he alternates between prompting them to supply relevant details, and trying to lead them astray. In the final few minutes of the class Webster will dramatically point the students to a key insight, and then will summarize for them the important (for Webster) lessons of the case.

Webster communicates this contract in a variety of ways. He informs the class that his analysis is the "right" one by preparing a graphic summary before the session on a hidden chalkboard -- and concluding the class with a dramatic unveiling and explication. He keeps a close rein on discussion, leading students toward the "discovery" of his analysis. When students go off track, he doesn't follow; rather, his and their comments simply become less connected -- apparently until the students return to Webster's line of thinking. One seminar participant characterized Webster's approach as follows:

Professor Webster believes there is

an Easter egg buried in every case and that the students' job is to find it. He brings the egg with him to class wrapped in his class notes. Then, before the students arrive, he hides it behind the mechanical chalkboard, and draws a map of the garden it is hidden in for all to see. Whenever students get "warm" too soon, he shoos them into a "cold" corner. Then, when the class is almost over, he drops bigger and bigger hints until "Surprise!" -- the most unlikely student finds the egg. Finally everyone oohs and aahs as he spends the last five minutes taking off the silver paper for all to view the fearful symmetry of the egg revealed.

Though the case contains little direct evidence of students' reactions to this game, one wonders if they weren't beginning to look for an opportunity to express their own sense of direction. The participant who wrote the Easter egg account of the case thought so:

One day, instead of an egg, he brings a pill to hide. But, alas, the students are growing tired of the game. After looking in several different places, they begin to give up looking for so difficult a prize. Professor Webster doesn't give up though. When someone suggests one part of the map which is clearly not warm at all, he just tries another student, and then another. . . . Just as everybody is getting fed up with the guessing game, Kay Woodward says, "I don't think we should be playing hunt-the-pill at all! I think we should choose our own game."

Pandemonium breaks out. Some students say, "No. We came here to play the teacher's game." Others begin talking all at once about the different games they would like to play -- but no one can seem to agree. Finally the teacher tells them they have been very naughty. They can play any game they like after school, but in his class only hunt-the-pill is allowed. And so the class went unhappily ever after. . . .

5. **Why does Ken Webster behave so as to stay "on top of the class"? What situational or personal circumstances might encourage such an approach? What are its benefits and liabilities?**

Usage Note

This is a more reflective question, and asks participants to mull over factors that can draw any instructor into the trap of

trying to overcontrol a section. This question helps participants not only to understand others, but also to consider the pulls toward overcontrol in their own teaching.

Analysis

The case includes little information about Webster, and we wish to avoid psychoanalyzing him. It is worth noting, however, that overcontrol is a particular problem for new instructors. Many of them are used to thinking in terms of lectures -- and thus preparing a sequence of ideas ("answers") they feel they need to be transmitted to the students. If these ideas are not transmitted, the inexperienced instructor often feels the students are being cheated.

The remedy for this problem seems to involve thinking in terms of questions, issues, or themes that one wants one's students to examine rigorously. A body of knowledge consists of not only a set of standard techniques, but also a set of questions -- often unappreciated by the novice -- for which the standard techniques are working answers. From this perspective, each case becomes an opportunity to challenge students with a series of important questions -- leaving primarily to them the task of working out responses to these questions.

A second reason instructors sometimes seek excessive control is insecurity about their role and authority in the classroom. This can be a particularly difficult problem for new instructors, who may be virtually the same age as their students -- and who may feel slightly illegitimate in the new role of professor. With luck, a bit of successful teaching experience will remedy this sort of insecurity. In most universities, professors -- even junior professors -- are accorded enormous respect and social power by the students. Once the new instructor experiences this, he or she can often loosen up and evolve a more open, interactive teaching style.

A third common reason for overcontrolling involves the instructor's insecurity about the subject matter. Open discussions sometimes move beyond the instructor's expertise, and this can be upsetting to new instructors, particularly those who are asked to teach courses outside their primary areas of competence. Fear of going beyond one's competence may also be an important reason why many instructors shy away from discussion of ethical issues: they do not know of any systematic way to consider such matters, and they feel out of their depth in attempting to do so.

There appears to be no simple solution for this problem. We take it as axiomatic that an excellent teacher must understand the subject matter and have an appreciation for how the content is best learned. In the multidisciplinary sort of teaching that lends itself best to the case method, there is probably no substitute for wide experience and learning: the more, it seems, the better.

Often, however, a teacher can do an adequate job without a full mastery of a field if he or she understands the process aspects of discussion leadership and is interested in fostering critical thinking in students (i.e., by stressing the need to use evidence appropriately, to make assumptions explicit, and to draw out the implications of arguments). As will be described below, ethical issues in particular can be handled effectively by instructors who are not trained in moral philosophy. What seems to be required is an insistence on respectful, rational discourse among students, and a willingness to press students to sharpen their arguments and examine their assumptions.

6.   **How might Webster have better handled Kay's comment? Or Bob Kinney's? What learning opportunities exist for them? For the class? How would you facilitate such learning?**

Usage Note

Though the case text does not pose an action question, participants find it valuable to consider how one might respond constructively in a similar situation. The discussion may focus on either how to respond to Kay or Bob Kinney, or how to respond to Harry Jones and the entire class after the full explosion. In our judgment it is more useful to discuss how to respond to Kay and/or Bob, because the resulting discussion pertains to a relatively common and very important problem -- particularly with students who are new to the case method: How does one respond to student comments that are emotionally driven, provocative, and (in Bob's case) insulting to another student?

Analysis

As soon as such an incident occurs, it becomes virtually impossible -- at least for the moment -- to continue with any prearranged teaching plan. Our first priority -- perhaps paradoxically, given our contention that Webster has been overcontrolling -- would be to maintain control of the discussion. This would probably require stepping in quickly and firmly to engage Bob and respond to his comment before the class can erupt. By figuratively positioning ourselves between Bob and Kay, we would hope to defuse the conflict and take command of the subsequent interchange.

Kay and Bob may be able to learn a great deal from this incident -- both about the process of learning in a discussion class and about the content of their comments. On the process side, both students (as well as other members of the class) need to increase their ability to cope with differences of perspectives in their classmates. In our judgment Bob has violated a central norm of case discussions: that one must show respect for other persons in the classroom. The instructor should respond to this violation, sending a clear signal to Bob and the rest of the class that this is unacceptable behavior. Only in this way can we assure that the norms supporting open discussions are reinforced rather than weakened by this incident.

Kay's attack on the class is also counterproductive though, in the opinion of many participants, not as damaging as Bob's. Kay would probably benefit from being pressed to separate her core argument about the case from the fireworks of her presentation, and it would be good if she could realize how differently the two can be experienced. Probably the latter aim is too optimistic, but by asking her to clarify her position, the instructor can probably get her to disentangle the argument.

Once some decorum has been reestablished, we would strive to get both Kay and Bob to explore the assumptions and consequences of their positions. Their comments could then become the stimulus for further analysis of the case. Several approaches are possible. For example, Kenneth Goodpaster, a professor of business ethics at Harvard Business School, made the following suggestions during one of our seminars, in response to this request:

Instructor: Could you -- as somebody who teaches students to discuss difficult ethical issues all the time -- give us some sort of first steps? Because for most of us it is frightening. We know that we're waltzing on a minefield.

Goodpaster: First I would try to elicit Bob's implicit ethical position -- to peel back the onion for a while to see exactly what kind of value judgments are the premises of his remark. That in itself would demonstrate to Kinney that ethical issues are relevant, because there must be some ethical premises behind his conviction here.

Then I'd shift ground back to Kay. There are two things that struck me about what she said. First, she was appealing to the potential harm and danger in marketing these drugs. Then she was appealing to religious authority. Those are two radically different kinds of ethical arguments. I would display that to her and ask her which one she thought was more crucial here.

In this way the class would begin to see that ethical arguments are not just emotional explosions, but have some structure. They can be taken a lot farther than most people realize. But it would have to be part of your class preparation. Webster should have thought through these things.

In addition to this approach, there are a variety of other ways in which Kay's comment could be made the basis for further discussion of the case. For example, one could ask a member of the class, "Is Kay's query a useful one? Why or why not?" This would allow a discussion of the issues, of their appropriateness to the class, and perhaps of Kay's manner of raising them -- but a discussion moderated by the instructor, not a free-for-all.

One could also turn the question into a corporate role-playing exercise, asking another student, "If you were the director of marketing for this corporation, how would you react to Kay's comment? Why?" This would demonstrate the relevance of at least considering Kay's type of concerns. Finally, one might work with the class's disagreement about the appropriate place for such concerns, and ask, "Where should we discuss ethical issues in business? Where do we do it now? Where should we do it at this school?"

7.   Could such an incident have been prevented? How?

Usage Note

This question asks participants how they might handle a case course throughout the term in order to prepare the ground for the productive discussion of controversial issues. As such, it opens up a broad

discussion of case method teaching, often (depending upon the seminar) focused on how to handle emotional issues and ethics, and more broadly how to direct but not overcontrol a section.

Analysis

In our experience, sections have distinctly limited capacities for tolerating diversity in discussion. It is the job of the case method instructor to build that capacity, particularly during the first weeks of the term. Of many possible methods, three stand out for us as particularly important. First, the instructor needs to model respectful appreciation for student comments that reflect diverse perspectives. Particularly during the first sessions of a course, the instructor can help seminar participants to see the links between seemingly disparate contributions, and thus realize that consideration of a variety of opinions will build a richer view of the case. One small hint we have found helpful: in early sessions we tend to emphasize diagnosis rather than action planning, for the value of multiple perspectives is easier to appreciate during analysis of situations. In contrast, action planning often leads to conflict because many of the participants' suggestions will necessarily be mutually exclusive. Therefore, we tend to deemphasize action planning until the section has become respectful of its own richness.

Second, the instructor must insist that all student comments be treated with respect and given a fair hearing. Students may need to be reminded that comments that first seem naive or misdirected may later seem insightful. In any case, mutual respect must be an ironclad rule of the section, and one that the instructor does not hesitate to enforce when necessary.

Third, students need to be helped to see that the way in which they make a comment often influences how it is received. They need to be encouraged to avoid provocative, taunting language. Comments instead need to be made clearly and forcefully, but without the additional "spin" that communicates scorn or hostility. The possible exception is humorous banter between group members who are on good terms -- but even this can be misunderstood and seems best avoided except on rare occasions.

As these norms and values are adopted, most sections develop an increasing capacity for genuine difference. Students test the water and, finding it safe, begin to join the discussion with their deepest insights and concerns. In talking about teaching, people often emphasize what one can control in a discussion. It is just as important to reflect on what one cannot control. An instructor cannot control the interests of the students, their true involvement in discussion, or their willingness to contribute their most precious insights. Individual students alone make their choices about how deeply they will become involved. In our experience, a major factor in this choice is the degree to which the students feel that their individuality -- that is, the diversity of the section -- is protected and valued by the instructor and other students.

8. **What techniques can you use to encourage a section to achieve general discussion objectives without subjecting the students to the sort of controlled lockstep pattern Webster has chosen?**

Usage Note

This question builds upon Question 7, asking participants to consider the more general issue of how to manage a case discussion effectively. Discussion may focus on philosophical considerations -- centering on the need for both control and freedom in the discussion process -- as well as to a concrete discussion of directorial techniques available to the case method instructor.

Analysis

Throughout this note and others in the series, we have presented a variety of techniques for managing the controlled spontaneity of the discussion process -- ranging from the design of question-based teaching plans to the use of bridging, selective reinforcement, and summaries to shape the content of discussion. A more concrete discussion of freedom and control might include the consideration of when and how to use these techniques. We will not provide such a review here, but will instead comment briefly on the overall stance of case method instructors.

Case instructors generally put a premium on student involvement and initiative, and accordingly try to maintain a great deal of classroom freedom to encourage a variety of contributions. But this freedom is most valuable when the 80 or so students of the section are focused on a common set of questions. Only then can diverse comments be integrated, and a rich synergy emerge. Thus, in the service of

productive freedom, the instructor exercises considerable control over the questions, if not the answers, under consideration by the section.

Moreover, the free interchange of a case discussion cannot continue without mutual respect and listening. Thus the successful instructor seeks to control the process of the discussion -- and the norms about communication in the group -- in order to support its higher freedom. These matters bear underlining in a discussion of freedom and control in teaching.

However, these observations neglect another important dimension of case teaching: openness. Case teaching aims to involve the students deeply in the issues raised by the cases. It is often most successful

when students, on their own initiative, project themselves into the case situation. The classroom and business situation meld together, with the students vicariously acting as the firm's executive group, albeit a large executive group. Problems are not discussed as abstract topics, but as issues inextricably bound up in a manager's career circumstances. Student comments reflect a personal commitment to the arguments they advanced. This level of discussion comes as close to real life as can be achieved in an academic situation. Learning opportunities, and risk, are high for all involved.[1]

This sort of involvement, which requires so much openness on the part of the students, tends to require a corresponding openness on the part of the instructor. This openness is difficult to describe. It does not necessarily mean that instructors must share their views on the case, though they may wish to do so. Rather, it seems to involve an emotional openness, a certain willingness to care about the matters being discussed, a willingness -- on the part of the instructor -- to make this particular moment in this particular discussion the object of his or her total attention.

The instructor is in a certain sense willing to look foolish for the sake of, and for the joy of, the discussion. He or she becomes willing to risk admitting that the discussion process really matters. Under these conditions students seem to feel freer to come out from behind their masks and explore their true concerns.

---

1. C. Roland Christensen, *Teaching by the Case Method* (Boston: Harvard Business School, 1981), pp. 15–16.

Student involvement requires that the participants take intellectual and social risks. It is often difficult for the instructor to appreciate the degree of jeopardy experienced by the students. Students are deeply submerged in a powerful and often very judgmental peer culture; they have very little power except their social standing; and they are confronted in discussion with questions that are -- by design -- new and difficult for them. Under such conditions we believe an instructor's willingness to take a bit of emotional risk can go far toward building rapport and creating a safe climate for the genuinely hazardous activity of engaging important ideas.

Suggestions for Building the Seminar Group

At this time in the life of the seminar, we assume the group has become a working forum. If not, we try to help it become one. But assuming it has, we focus on helping individuals strengthen their areas of relative weakness, so that they will be able to combine analysis with action, and abstract, reflective thought with personalized, committed thought. Thus we may press members to experiment with ways of thinking in which they are less accomplished.

Second, we want the seminar to be able to use these final cases to explore issues that it defines as important, so we look for emerging themes and use our skills to highlight and clarify them, even when these issues are tangential to those in our teaching plan. The theme of freedom and control may appear here in our handling of the process of discussion. At this point in the term, we hope that the seminar will be quite self-managing, and thus we may shift our stance in order to give it more freedom.

In some sense our relationship to the process of the section (in contrast to the substantive content) can be understood through the metaphor of the orchestra conductor. In the early sessions we operate a bit like a conductor at rehearsal, guiding and teaching the seminar members to develop a particular discussion style or process. By the middle of the seminar series, the group has created a style, with the instructor conducting. In the later sessions we may sometimes want to put down the baton and just appreciate the process of discussion. Under some conditions we may even join in the substantive discussion, almost as if the conductor -- now enjoying a self-managing orchestra -- were to slip in and play a few notes on his or her favorite instrument.

Finally, we wish to help the seminar members to integrate and apply what they have learned throughout the term. This process can be facilitated by comparing the present case with those discussed earlier, noting similarities and differences; by reminding the group of comments made in previous sessions that bear on the matters at hand; and by recalling for the seminar the positions previously held by particular people, and asking these participants for their current thoughts on the issues in question.

Along with this linking of cases and discussions, we also encourage seminar members to generalize from the work of the seminar. This can be facilitated in several ways. We may ask members who have had experiences similar to those in the case -- for example, those who have dealt with distressed students, requests for help, and cheating -- to share their experiences and insights with the group. We may also ask members to talk about the general questions about teaching that the discussion raises for them. Finally, we may ask directly how a participant might apply in his or her teaching the insights expressed in the discussion. In all these ways, we begin the process of building out from the concerns of the seminar into each participant's teaching practice. And it is there, of course, that we ultimately hope the participants will find the seminar of value.

Exhibit 1

The Section Just Took Over

Study Questions

1. The case researcher comments, "I keep thinking about the class; it poses so many tough questions for me." What questions does this case raise for you?

2. Could the "explosion" have been predicted by Professor Webster?

3. How might he have responded to Kay's comment?

4. Should Professor Webster have presented his views on the ethical issues in the case to the class? Why didn't he?

5. From your teaching experience (or observation of instructors as a student), what philosophy, techniques,

and/or methodology appear to be most useful in working out a balance between (a) <u>freedom</u> for the section to explore ideas of significance to them, and (b) sufficient instructor <u>control</u> to prevent nonproductive discussion sessions?

Exhibit 2

The Section Just Took Over

Discussion Questions

1. What is your diagnosis of this situation? Why did the explosion occur? What is the central problem posed by this case?

The following questions can be used to deepen the diagnostic discussion:

2. What is it about the nature of Kay's comment that made it so difficult for others in the class to handle?

3. Could the explosion have been predicted? Why or why not?

4. What is it like to be a student in Kenneth Webster's class? What is his contract with the students? How has it been communicated?

5. Why does Webster behave so as to stay "on top of the class"? What situational or personal circumstances might encourage such an approach? What are its benefits and liabilities?

These last three questions turn the discussion toward action planning and generalization:

6. How might Webster have better handled Kay's comment? Or Bob Kinney's? What learning opportunities exist for them? For the class? How would you facilitate such learning?

7. Could such an incident have been prevented? How?

8. What techniques can you use to encourage a section to achieve general discussion objectives without subjecting the students to the sort of controlled lockstep pattern Webster has chosen?

The Section Was Mine to Lose

Researcher's Perspective

[Note: No teaching note is available for this case; however, the following "Researcher's Perspective" has been written to aid instructors in developing their own teaching plans.]

Structural Insights to Dynamic of This Case

More than anything else, the phenomenon I call "mirroring" accounts for the pivotal events in this case. Ed Sherman seems to be imbued with nervous energy. Is it coincidence that nervousness comes to Ed's classroom style (he moves around a lot) and has apparently spread to most of the class. This is not to say that nervousness is inescapably negative. One of Ed Sherman's problems is how to find a comfortable place on the spectrum between laxity and tension, both for himself and his section. Perhaps he enjoys tension. Perhaps some of his students do, too, but surely, all eighty-odd of them do not! Meanwhile, before Ed has found this elusive balance point, we see him and the section suffering. It is striking that in several places in the case, Ed and Hayes Latham (the ed rep) use almost identical words or images. Both speak of stomach-knotting nausea (Ed referring to having conquered that feeling before teaching a class of difficult material, and Hayes citing a student who experienced the same feeling before Ed's classes because he found them so intimidating). Another mirrored image is that of claustrophobia. Ed felt shut in with this group of students, but it is Hayes who describes Ed striding up the classroom aisle to enclose the whole group symbolically by shutting a sliding panel in a door -- the only access to the outside in the windowless room.

Second, one sees the usual power struggle in progress. Ed Sherman seems extremely concerned with establishing and maintaining authority in the classroom.

"If you let up in October, will you pay for it in May?" he muses. His attempt to run a tight ship in the early weeks of the semester has, apparently, created recalcitrance in the students, who are already tense because of heavy workloads and the new, threatening, high-pressure atmosphere of business school. Ed uses humor to keep the students in line, and he also bolsters his authority with unconsciously condescending gestures -- writing down latecomers' names, for example. What Ed doesn't realize is that his intellectual power has already impressed this group sufficiently. Hayes Latham states that Ed's command of the elusive marketing concepts impressed the students so much that it intimidated them (a word that Ed would like, no doubt). But Ed feels the need to hold the reins because, unlike most Bay instructors, he lacks business training and experience and has no background to call on but the previous year's experience with this material, a Ph.D. in Sociology, and a few years of liberal arts teaching.

Some Salient Issues

There are many intriguing discussion topics embedded in this case. A good discussion group, with enough time and preparation to explore them, could discover hours' worth of issues; for example, sensitivity in the classroom, the use and abuse of humor, self-management, the value of colleagues' advice, and the establishment and maintenance of authority are just a few. Some suggestive passages include: Ed's well-intentioned "grilling" of Margaret Peters and its effect on the members of his Marketing section, the importance of his professional background, the effect of his previous year's elation and subsequent disappointment with his teaching recommendations, Ed's futile search for clear advice from experienced colleagues, and Hayes Latham's role in all the events of this case. (Does Hayes foment, assuage, or merely convey the section's discontent?)

This commentary was written by Dr. Abby J. Hansen, research associate, for the Developing Discussion Leadership Skills and the Teaching by the Case Method seminars. Its objective is to help instructors in the development of their own teaching plans for this case.

One should also pay attention to the larger picture. Ed has been handed a daunting task by the administration that hired him. He works at a real disadvantage because he lacks significant business training, and he does seem to be constitutionally prone to extreme tension. Is he the right person for this job? One might argue that a man like Ed could not resist the challenge to change fields and compete in the arena of a high-powered business school, but that this sort of competition might ultimately cause him pain, even injury (extreme, prolonged tension can literally kill). What criteria should the hiring committee apply in cases like his? (At this point it should be noted that we are leaving the character "Ed Sherman" aside for a moment to raise a basic issue of staffing policy.) The case seems to show Ed Sherman thriving on tension. At the end of this case he has mastered the situation. He feels fine. Nonetheless, things might have turned out badly.

A glance at his personal background shows a powerful source of Ed's tension. He is the only son of aging parents, and his father is in poor health. As ill-luck would have it, just when Ed reaches a frustrating impasse with his Marketing section, his father also lands in the hospital with a case of exhaustion that might prove fatal. Ed -- who is close to both parents and whose success is no doubt a source of pride to both of them -- now must worry not only about himself and his relationship with Section VI, but also about his father. One also imagines that part of his drive to succeed is rooted in an understandable desire to continue to please his parents, who have no other children upon whom to focus their emotional energy. (These sorts of dynamics are, of course, present in all human interactions, but the rare candor of this case informant gives us hint at one source of his drive. Filial duty can be a powerful spur to success, but also a powerful source of depression in case of failure.)

The Incident

The event that definitively exposes the rift between Ed Sherman and Section VI seems minor at first. Charles Finch arrives unprepared, gets called on to present an opening analysis, lamely pretends he is ready, and finally gives up, murmuring "I pass." Painful, but not an unheard-of-scene at a large business school. But there are complications to this particular "pass." First, Ed had told the students to inform him privately before class if they had not prepared. Second, Charles had actually approached Ed before class, but concealed the fact that he wasn't prepared. Third, after being asked to open the discussion, Charles had shuffled pages of notes on his desk, causing Ed to assume that Charles was simply looking through his papers to locate his Marketing analysis. This assumption prompted Ed to make a mildly sarcastic joke ("It's the Royal Foods case, Charles") by which he meant to imply "Charles, I'm so sure you're prepared that I'm willing to joke with you publicly and pretend I think you're so unprepared you don't even know what case we're doing today." In fact, the students must have known by now that Charles really wasn't prepared, so they took Ed's joke as a twist of the dagger. On his side, Ed took Charles's attempt to stall as a personal affront -- a public challenge to his right to set the rules for this Marketing class. Ed was also annoyed at the clumsy start all this created for the discussion, irritated by Charles's charade with the fake study notes and, given that this case occurred on Friday afternoon and everyone was probably tired and anxious for the week's work to be over, probably just generally edgy.

What must have particularly upset the students in the class was Ed's response. He mentions that, when Charles surprised him by passing, he made sure to smile as he asked Charles (extremely politely) to come and see him in his office. Given the context -- Ed's habit of writing down names of latecomers and the section's growing nervousness with him -- the smile could hardly have been persuasive, and the polite invitation must have sounded about as friendly as a subpoena. Furthermore, "come to my office" carries unavoidable, condescending connotations of grade school. It must have seemed like just another attempt to infantilize the students. Hayes Latham's comments make it apparent that the other students realized Charles was culpably unprepared, but they sympathized with him, not Ed, because they all felt the day might come when they would show up unprepared and try to fake their way through a class discussion. Students at large business schools often play by the odds, not by the rules. During busy times in their lives, they come to class unprepared, silently praying they will not be asked to open the discussion. Their tactic on such occasions is to listen for a while and then contribute some synthetic point based on others' analyses, thus giving the impression that they know what's going on.

No wonder Hayes describes the section as watching Charles squirm and thinking, "My God, this could happen to me!"

The Aftermath

The six days between this deceptively minor contretemps and Ed Sherman's next meeting with Section VI are both a grace period during which Ed has time to plan his next move and a time of torture in which the little wounds inflicted on all sides fester. Several events occur during this period. Charles does come to Ed's office hours, but the interview is a failure. Ed practices official inflexibility to bolster his authority. He is not interested in why Charles wasn't prepared. He simply reiterates that Charles broke a rule and got caught. Period. Charles, on the other hand, is obsessed with explaining why he didn't prepare: his car was towed the night before the Royal Foods case, and he had an extra assignment due the same day for another class. Charles, like Ed (like everyone) has a personal life that matters to him and sometimes conflicts with his work. But Ed considers the irritations of Charles's life irrelevant. At best, they are insufficient excuses for failing to warn Ed that he hadn't prepared. One might imagine that Ed was less offended by the "pass" than Charles's paper-shuffling routine, a feeble subterfuge that probably irritated Ed because it led him to make a joke that backfired -- and humor is a serious business to Ed Sherman. One guesses that he really hates his jokes to go awry.

Examining the weekend's events, we first see only Ed's increasing agony. Then Hayes comes into full play, shuttling back and forth between meetings with the section and phone calls to Ed, relaying his impressions of each party's position. Hayes labors under the usual ambassadorial constraints; speaking for a heterogeneous group of people, he speaks in a plural voice that is, at best, approximate. A group of eighty people can hold no single, simple opinion about an instructor. Nonetheless, Hayes manages his difficult role with apparent success. He sees it as his task to get Ed Sherman to relax his choke-hold on the section and to realize that some things he has been doing have created painful tensions.

Ed's initial attitude to the "Charles Finch episode" is irascible. Annoyed at the student, he tries to dismiss the whole thing from his mind as a minor irritation. But when Hayes presents the affair in a different light and reveals that it has triggered widespread "discontent" about Ed, the situation takes on a new hue. Ed is now feeling injured: his rules have been broken, he has been put into an embarrassing position, yet the students are angry at him! How infuriating!

The next section of the case involves yet another issue: Ed, who is stewing about his endangered relationship with Section VI, now seeks advice from several quarters. Once again, his candor enables us to see several aspects of his situation. Some of his colleagues endorse his irritation with Charles and his fairly stringent treatment of this infraction of the "no pass" rule. His lawyer does the same. A business school colleague supplies a piece of advice: do something appropriate to your personality to defuse the tension -- perhaps open the next class with a joke. Yet another senior colleague gives utterly ambiguous advice: don't let the wounds fester; confront the issues -- but on the other hand, beware of saying things you may regret. Ed now faces a dilemma: Should he take any advice? If so, whose? Should he speak to students? If so, which students? How many? How can he reestablish rapport with Section VI? How can he deflate this whole incident? How can he tell the students that he wants to run a tight ship, but does not want to seem petty or inhuman? How can he change bad feelings into good? Ed seems to equate loss of face with apology, and apology with humiliation -- one of his worst nightmares. But on the other hand he clearly recognizes the need to give ground and lessen the section's tension, and, in turn, his own. Both have, apparently, by now, reached nearly clinical dimensions.

The passages in the case where Ed Sherman describes his feelings during those six intervening days between the first meeting on the Royal Foods case and the second are a tribute to his forthrightness. He presents his acute personal discomfort for our scrutiny. What we see is a triple crisis, involving image, power, and projection. Ed now realizes that he fears the section just as much as it fears him. He thinks the students are bellyaching and misjudging him, and no doubt tearing him apart in their secret meetings. They, on the other hand, think he's just uptight. There is little charity but some justification in both positions. Such is the polarizing nature of confrontation. The balance of power here tips toward Ed Sherman. He can attempt to ease the situation by adjusting his behavior. The central questions are: How shall he change, and how shall he communicate this change to the students?

Remarks on the (D) Case

Ed's account of the next class is strangely compact. Almost miraculously risen from his sickbed, his laryngitis conquered, Ed dons a red plaid vest and "works the crowd" like a politician or a comedian. He is using his sense of humor to get him out of this scrape. He does not address the situation directly, but rather relies on Hayes's manipulation of the grapevine to convey the message that Ed has agreed to stop writing down latecomers' names. Ed does not turn the class meeting into an open gripe session. He depends on performance: his attire (apparently good mood) will be the lever to turn the whole situation around. Oddly enough, this seems to work!

Still, Ed's testimony matches Hayes's, and these are all we have to go on. At the end of the case, Ed's teaching evaluations turn out extremely well, possibly because as the year wore on, the section got used to his hyperbolical, sardonic sense of humor. Or perhaps the improvement came because Ed showed himself willing to participate in the system -- to work through the ed rep and make concessions to the students. Ed displayed flexibility. The class reciprocated with gratitude. No doubt there are teachers at Bay who do not cooperate with ed reps' suggestions and who make Ed look like a teddybear. We note that Hayes is perfectly aware of Ed's stagemanaging of the next class meeting. Ed chooses a student of manifest competence to lead this class (not taking chances on another "I pass"), and relies on his calculatedly buoyant manner and bright vest to signal an end to the estrangement. Symbolism seems to triumph.

It is interesting to look at the footnote to these events -- Hayes's congratulatory note to Ed. Hayes meant it to formalize the end of the students' quarrel with their instructor and compliment Ed on his sensitivity. Ed, on his part, found it depressing because it meant that the students were continuing to judge him -- whereas judgment, in his opinion, should rest with him. After all, who's grading whom? (A question to ponder, for all teachers.)

One final issue that this case raises, at least for the researcher, is the ownership of the classroom. The incident where Ed marches up the aisle to close the shutter on the door seems very suggestive. Hayes tells us the students felt invaded. By walking all the way up the long aisle, far from the teacher's desk, past the seats where the shyest students hide as far from the teacher as possible, he penetrated their territory. Both teacher and students feel proprietary about the classroom. In all human interaction, one faces, of course, a multiplicity of perceptions. Everything that happens between two or more people registers on several consciousnesses -- "belongs," in a sense, to each person involved. Surely teaching is no different. The classroom, with its simultaneous learning and teaching, cannot "belong" to any one person. In other words, the section was never really, in Ed's words, "mine to lose."

Trevor Jones

Teaching Note

Introduction

"Trevor Jones" concerns a teacher's attempt to help students understand the emotional side of human problems described in a case. Without announcing his intentions, the instructor engages the class in a role-playing exercise that he hopes will give them a feel for the pain of losing a job and/or causing others to lose their jobs. The role playing has an extremely powerful effect -- more than the instructor intends, and more than the students find valuable or humane. The emotionally bruised students become extremely hostile toward the instructor.

The case raises concerns about both the technical and the ethical aspects of using role playing and other involvement-increasing techniques in the classroom. It calls attention to the great power of the instructor's position -- a power that can be abused, even when the instructor has the best of intentions.

"Trevor Jones" also calls attention to the problem of dealing with students who are unwilling to speak in class, particularly when the general instructor-student learning contract calls for a great deal of verbal exchange. And the case reemphasizes the importance of being sure that both instructors and students know clearly what their contract is, and respect it.

Further, the case asks participants to consider when it is constructive for an instructor to use his or her power to force students to confront difficult issues, and under what conditions such force is humiliating and constitutes an abuse of power. In "Trevor Jones," the instructor accidentally crosses this line and loses the trust and respect of his students. Seminar members are asked to consider how the instructor can make amends in such a situation and regain students' trust. The

more general question is how instructors can recover from their mistakes.

This case is used in the final phase of the seminar on case method teaching. By this time in the term the major themes of the seminar (e.g., rapport, the teacher-student learning contract, questioning, listening, and responding) have been introduced. Thus we allow the seminar to range beyond these concerns and follow its own emerging interests.

By this point, a great deal of trust and respect has usually developed among participants who have come to know each other's views quite well. Under such conditions we feel free to encourage higher levels of emotional involvement and personal risk taking, and may use cases that can arouse strong, often contradictory, feelings and spark intense debate. "Trevor Jones" is such a case. Participants can learn a great deal from experiencing the often surprising power of their felt commitments. By reflecting on the sources and implications of their views and those of others, they gain deeper insights than could probably be achieved in any other way.

Case Summary

"Trevor Jones" is an exciting, provocative case that usually stirs intense discussion. Though the case contains little information about the institutional context or the course, the school is identified as New Dominion, a pseudonym regularly used in these cases for a large, case-oriented graduate school of business. The case text contains a good deal of background information about the professor, Al Vinceberg, and includes sketches of the two key student players, Trevor Jones and Bob Smith. The bulk of the case, however, is devoted to a careful, play-by-play description of a dramatic classroom incident. We are given

This teaching note was written by Dr. James F. Moore in collaboration with Professor C. Roland Christensen as an aid to instructors in the classroom use of the case "Trevor Jones," HBS Case No. 9-380-016.

Distributed by HBS Publishing Division, Harvard Business School, Boston, MA 02163. Printed in U.S.A.

no information beyond the perspective of the casewriter, a student in the section. In particular, we do not know the thoughts and feelings of Jones, Vinceberg, or Smith.

The Institutional Context

This case takes place in a required course on organizational behavior in the first year of the MBA program at New Dominion. Little other information about the institution is provided in the case, but it is described in some detail in a note by Dr. Abby Hansen called "Background Information on a Graduate School of Business Administration" (found in Part III of Teaching and the Case Method).

One institutional feature not mentioned in the case probably figures importantly in the events that occur: At New Dominion, first-year MBA students spend the entire school day in assigned sections of 80 students each. The section members remain in the same place while instructors rotate among classrooms to conduct the various courses.

Social cohesion within the section is typically quite strong, and is encouraged by New Dominion through a variety of means, including section-based intramural sports, other section social events, and the election of section educational representatives and section secretaries whose job is to keep sectionmates in touch with each other after the first year.

Since the incident takes place in a course that begins after Christmas, we can assume that the section members know each other well -- at least within the classroom setting -- and have become a close working group. This familiarity helps explain both the other section members' general awareness of "how Trevor is," and their support for him.

The Course

Organizational Behavior (OB) is a required first-year case-based course dealing with the "human problems of administration." The first-year program at New Dominion mixes courses of different lengths and different starting dates. OB is one of the shorter courses, with only 30 meetings (probably three per week) rather than the more typical 50.

OB cases contain little quantitative data, which many students probably find a relief after the heavy "number crunching" in the fall courses. Some students may see OB as too soft to be taken seriously, and

the casewriter describes Vinceberg as knowing that "some of his colleagues were having discipline problems with their sections."

The Instructor

Al Vinceberg is probably an assistant or associate professor, though his academic rank is not mentioned in the case. His academic training is in sociology, and his central interest is in research on what is currently termed "macro-organizational behavior" -- that is, the effect of overall organizational structures on performance. This research has been his consuming interest during his five years at New Dominion.

Vinceberg is described as having little interest in psychology or group dynamics, and though he finds the confrontation inherent in case teaching stimulating, he wishes he could share more of the complexities of his research with the students. These two observations suggest he is probably not very much interested in the complexities of teaching and learning, or in the dynamics of the discussion process.

A tall man with a dominating voice and manner, Vinceberg apparently likes confrontation, and is described by one of the section's informal leaders as "blunt, aggressive, and demanding." The student also observes that, in Vinceberg's class, "you often knew what he wanted you to say and you went right along."

Though Vinceberg tends to drown out the students, he apparently tries to treat them as individuals and can listen to them on occasion. Yet he has not established real rapport, trust, and open, comfortable communication with the students. "I got the feeling he liked us and liked our section. Yet we never felt close to him. I didn't ever feel like just going to his office for a chat and I don't think others did either."

The Section

The section consists of first-year, second-semester MBA students who have had time to develop a good deal of social cohesion and to evolve their own style of case discussion. The section's educational representative reports that its "general atmosphere was friendly and tolerant. We weren't a dog-eat-dog section like many of the others. Individual differences were respected and even encouraged."

Students are assigned to sections at

New Dominion in such a way as to balance ages, sex, management experience, and geographical background. Three students are singled out in the case text. We have little information about the (unnamed) casewriter. Bob Smith is described as a member of the large "male, white, conservative group" -- an ex-Navy officer, probably older than many of the students, who plans to run his own business after graduation. His nickname is "Mr. Middle America." Smith is described as one of Professor Vinceberg's stars -- one who likes Vinceberg's educational approach, and who is in turn liked by the professor.

Trevor Jones is a young student -- 25 years old -- from Wales. Though apparently socially comfortable outside of class with most of the students in the section, Trevor "tended to mix primarily with those from the U.K. and the Commonwealth." He comes from a working-class background and has a "burning desire to succeed at New Dominion" in order to "put a seal of approval on his career to date and free him for good from any social origin slurs."

Most strikingly, Trevor never speaks in class: he finds himself unable to argue for his views, and apparently is afraid of making a fool of himself and being humiliated, though he masks this fear in a general condemnation of case discussions as unreal and irrelevant. He has persuaded instructors to accept this behavior by going to speak with them privately and establishing special contracts with them. The other section members apparently do not object, although the casewriter notes that Trevor "was sometimes scathingly critical of his fellow students and teachers when he felt they made themselves look ridiculous in class."

The Teacher-Student Relationship

Vinceberg is a dominating presence in the class -- respected but not really liked. He tends to telegraph his views to the students, and to reward those who agree with him.

Of particular interest is his contract with Trevor Jones before the incident. Trevor has met with Vinceberg and apparently believes he has established a contract allowing him not to speak in class. If such a contract was in fact mutually arranged, then Vinceberg's calling on Trevor on the day of the incident constitutes a clear breach of the agreement. Both Trevor and Bob Smith seem to see the situation this way.

Trevor and Vinceberg may have misunderstood each other, however. The case contains no direct data about their earlier meeting -- an unfortunate deficiency, for we suspect that Al Vinceberg may not have agreed to Trevor's request. Rather, he may have followed the common approach of trying to be encouraging and supportive by agreeing to let Trevor wait for a while, and join in when he felt more comfortable. When Trevor never did join in, Vinceberg may have decided it was time to press him. The rapport that Vinceberg and Trevor achieved with each other while talking about Trevor's father's background may have been interpreted quite differently by each player. Vinceberg may have assumed that Trevor had begun to loosen up, and thus might soon be more comfortable speaking in class. Trevor seems to have assumed that the rapport signaled agreement by Vinceberg that Trevor need not participate in discussions.

The Incident

The incident happens during the sixth session of the course. The class is to discuss the case of a paternalistic company -- the only employer in a small, closely knit town -- which had gone into decline and was forced to dismiss workers. The focus of the case is on ways to evaluate employees in order to determine who should be let go.

Professor Vinceberg strides into the room, establishes order, and calls upon Trevor Jones to begin the discussion by "laying out the case" -- that is, summarizing its content and key points and suggesting an initial approach to resolving the problems raised.

Trevor speaks for about five minutes, making a poor showing. Al Vinceberg asks the class to evaluate Trevor's performance through a show of hands. After about two-thirds of the class "hesitantly" indicate that Trevor has done a poor job, Al spins around to Trevor and says, "Your colleagues don't think you've done an adequate job. You're fired!"

Trevor, apparently stunned, leaves the room. Vinceberg continues the class discussion, "seemingly unconcerned"; but when Trevor does not return after a few minutes Vinceberg abruptly sprints after him, then rejoins the class alone and tries to continue the discussion. There is considerable tension in the section, however, and no one will speak. Even after a coffee break, Vinceberg cannot get the discussion moving. Finally, he suggests that the class talk about what had happened in order to "clear the air." He acknowledges that he had not expected Trevor to react as he did and asks for students' help in rebuilding their relationship, which he sees has been badly damaged by the incident. One of Vinceberg's best and favorite students then shoots back, "I'll tell you what I think. As far as I'm concerned you're nothing but a son-of-a-bitch for doing what you did. You know what Trevor is like. You know he doesn't talk in class. Calling on him was wrong. And what came after was worse -- much worse. In my book you're a son-of-a-bitch."

This attack appears to stun Vinceberg, and the class seems universally hostile to the professor.

A Note on Study and Discussion Questions

Typically we prepare at least two sets of questions for use with each case. The first set (Exhibit 1) consists of study questions, and can be handed out with the case for participants' use in preparing for class. The second set (Exhibit 2) is a series of discussion questions for use by the instructor in preparing for the case discussion and in guiding the discussion. For all discussion questions, but not for study questions, we have provided detailed usage and analytical notes.

A Suggested Process Plan for the Case

Because it deals with the volatile issues of rejection, betrayal, manipulation, and abuse of power, this case can stimulate highly emotional, even polarized discussions. Thus we do not use it until the seminar has become a coherent group of mutually respectful, trusting colleagues. Taught in the latter part of the seminar sequence, the case is an excellent stimulus to discussion and has provided some of our most memorable sessions.

On the surface this is a case about the use, and misuse, of role playing and other involvement-stimulating techniques in the classroom. Though the case provides no direct information about Vinceberg's intent, it seems clear to most readers that he was pursuing a pedagogical strategy of showing rather than telling -- that he hoped to demonstrate dramatically the pain experienced by all parties when a member of a close working group is fired. Of course Vinceberg's attempt goes seriously wrong,

raising a series of questions about how (and how not) to use role playing and how to recover from teaching disasters, particularly when one has lost the trust of the students.

"Trevor Jones" can also stimulate discussion of an even more fundamental issue in teaching. Many instructors feel that learning is best promoted when students perceive their teacher as a trusted, caring, and generally predictable guide who does not subject students to unnecessarily painful experiences. On the other hand, good teachers often sense a need to shake students out of their complacency and to force them to confront difficult issues of professional practice, which may mean putting them in uncomfortable positions. It can be difficult to promote this kind of learning while still maintaining the students' trust. The issue, then, is how to balance and integrate these two dimensions of teaching.

It sometimes seems that these dimensions require fundamentally different approaches to students -- one calling for care and nurturance, the other for confrontation and "tough love." In the heat of face-to-face teaching practice, instructors often find these two stances contradictory and even mutually exclusive. Educational philosophies also seem to polarize around this question, with some advocating caring, accepting relationships with students, and others arguing for confrontation and challenge. While our judgment is that these two approaches are best blended, such an integration will not come easily, but requires -- for most of us -- conscious awareness and deliberate effort.

"Trevor Jones" tends to polarize responses along the dimension of care versus confrontation, and thus can provide an excellent opportunity for participants to develop a more sophisticated understanding and integration of the two approaches. Many seminar members initially see these two approaches as polar opposites rather than elements to be balanced. To the extent that they believe a teacher's fundamental role is to be a trustworthy guide, seminar members often react angrily to Vinceberg's actions. From this perspective, he has violated his contract to provide the section with a predictable range of classroom experiences; he has betrayed both Trevor and the other students. One participant of this persuasion wrote:

Using a strategy of enlivening case issues by "firing" students would have been extremely dangerous even if Al had known the section well. Deliberately breaking an understanding with a student (or permitting Jones to believe there was such an understanding) was also very wrong. These two serious errors of judgment were compounded by Al's choice of Jones (caused by his ignorance of the students' backgrounds and personalities, caused in turn by his teaching style). . . . To Al, Jones may have been the only student sure to perform badly enough that his lesson plan would work.

Once these important mistakes had been made, there was nothing Al could do to retrieve the situation. He recognized quickly that he had blundered -- though it would have been difficult not to, given the dramatic departure and nonreturn of Jones. To [Al's] credit, he was quick to admit his fault, although, again, he first prevaricated by attempting to bring down the tension level merely by taking a short break and starting the class again. Having been forced into a corner by the continuing hostility, Al then . . . took the first steps toward creating a genuine understanding with the class. He was fortunate that he had a section with enough spark in it to fight back . . . and to thereby almost force him to take a more open and constructive approach.

Other participants may emphasize the instructor's responsibility to challenge students: to help them confront their own assumptions and behavior, and to grow through responding to experiences that simulate the complexities -- and even the emotional agonies -- of real-world decision making and action. This second conception emphasizes the need for "tough love" in teaching, to force students to confront the difficult issues involved in managing other people. As another participant in the seminar wrote:

When I first read the Trevor Jones case, I agreed with Bob Smith's diagnosis. Professor Vinceberg was an SOB, no doubt about it. What he had done to Trevor Jones was sadistic and humiliating. There was, and is, no defense for that kind of behavior by anyone dedicated to teaching.

I still believe that, but [another seminar member's] insightful comments opened up a new perspective for me on Vinceberg's behavior. Vinceberg discovered a very effective and emotionally **riveting** way of teaching this particular

case. He made a group of relatively conservative, middle-class business school students really understand "the gritty realities of every day, blue-collar work life." For a few minutes, the students in his section felt the same powerful anger and resentment that the workers in the paternalistic Southern factory experienced after one of their number was fired.

While I concede that Vinceberg's techniques were wrong -- especially not informing Jones of his plan -- the success of the role playing was extraordinary. If it had been done properly, Bob Smith -- Mr. Middle America -- could have come away with a much deeper insight into one of the realities of blue-collar life: namely, the rage and feeling of helplessness that follows a violation of trust, even if that violation was in the "best interests" of the rest of the workers. For a few moments Vinceberg had cut away from his students their complacency and detachment, and made them vulnerable to real learning.

Upon reflection I would admit that my sympathy for the role playing in this case stems largely from my own limited personal experience with Harvard undergraduates. Last year I was struck by the seeming detachment with which my students could discuss such topics as the Cold War, American slavery, and Nazi Germany. I confess to growing tired of this detachment, to their unwillingness, as Harper Lee wrote in To Kill a Mockingbird, "to walk around in another man's shoes, and see the world as he does." A Danforth Center [for the Improvement of Teaching] counselor, while viewing a tape of a tutorial dealing with slave codes, commented that my students seemed to approach the material in a completely impersonal manner, as though they were talking about last year's tax legislation.

That bothered me a great deal. History for me is a matter of the heart as well as the head. While I recognize the value of cool, dispassionate analysis, I also want my students to care about history as well as to read it. I want them to be able to understand and at times identify with the human beings they encounter in their study. Maybe that's why I was attracted to Vinceberg's goal, if not his methods. Unwittingly and unintentionally, he had broken through the limits of his students' backgrounds and prejudices, and helped them walk around in someone else's shoes.

Discussion of this case is often characterized by great sweeps of shifting emotion, as participants wrestle with their feelings about Al Vinceberg, Trevor Jones, Bob Smith, and the overall situation. Anger toward Al Vinceberg is especially prominent. Passion and condemnation of Vinceberg are not problems in themselves, but they can swamp discussion if not tempered by thoughtful reflection. Thus, while for many cases we choose discussion questions designed to stimulate involvement and emotional commitment, here we pose questions that we hope will encourage reflection.

Early in the session, moreover, we use questions that encourage empathy and identification with Al Vinceberg, in order to enrich the consideration of his actions and to balance the tendency for some participants to condemn him out of hand.

We begin with the broad diagnostic question of what happened and why, inviting seminar members to take a reflective, analytic approach to the case, while allowing them freedom to express (and if necessary vent) their feelings toward the protagonists. The next two questions ask participants to speculate about Vinceberg's motivations for initiating the role playing and for choosing Trevor Jones. The hope is that, by putting themselves in Vinceberg's place, seminar members will develop empathy and understanding for his position.

Questions 4 through 7 move the seminar from analysis to action planning, but do so very gradually. Moreover, the questions emphasize analysis and evaluation of action, rather than involvement and commitment. To maintain an external perspective, we ask "What do you think of Vinceberg's response -- asking for process evaluation by the members of the section?" (not "If you had been Vinceberg, how would you have responded to the tension after the coffee break?"). Thus we hope to maintain a reflective attitude toward the case.

The high involvement typically stimulated by the case tends to pull discussion toward the specifics of the situation and away from generalization. But since we believe that we learn most by moving back and forth between the general and the specific, we try to call the seminar's attention to the broader questions raised by their deliberations. To this end we often use six probes, which are included as Questions 8 through 13 in the list of discussion questions. These questions can also be used to conclude the discussion.

Those that ask seminar members to generate guidelines for role playing (Questions 11 and 12) often provide a particularly effective conclusion.

Notes for Discussion Questions

These notes parallel the suggested discussion questions presented in Exhibit 2. We have briefly indicated the pedagogical intent and use of each question, and provided our best attempt at a reasoned response. These analytical responses represent our current thoughts on the matters raised, and are provided primarily to aid instructors in preparing for discussions of the case by sensitizing them to key issues. We do not regard these responses as the definitive solutions to the questions raised by the case. "Trevor Jones," like other cases, can be profitably analyzed from a variety of viewpoints, and a variety of actions could be usefully taken in situations like that confronting Al Vinceberg. We hope each new discussion of the case will provide new insights of value to both the discussion participants and the discussion leader -- and we can say with gratitude that this has been our experience in leading discussions of this case and others in the seminar.

1.   **What happened? Why? What key factors contributed to the problem?**

Usage Note

This broad diagnostic question encourages the section to identify the variety of factors that contributed to the "mess" described in the case. The openness of this question allows participants to vent some of the strong feelings that may have been aroused by the case. But we avoid phrasing the question in a provocative manner (e.g., "We've heard from Bob Smith in the case; now what do you think about this situation?"). The somewhat abstract, evaluative stance encouraged by the question helps participants put a counterbalancing measure of reflective distance between themselves and the case.

Analysis

By calling on the usually silent Trevor, and then without warning tricking the section into evaluating one of its own members and "firing" him, Vinceberg has violated his implicit contract with both Trevor and the other students. It seems likely that Trevor concluded after his meeting with Vinceberg that the two of them had agreed that he need not speak in class.

This understanding was probably not shared by Vinceberg -- but even so, calling on Trevor violated Trevor's perception of the contract. Thus Trevor is likely to feel both confused and betrayed simply because Vinceberg has called on him.

Moreover, since the expected range of course experiences clearly does not include expelling students from the classroom for mediocre performance, the firing constitutes a further violation of the implicit contract between Trevor and Vinceberg -- and will probably make Trevor feel further betrayed and abused.

Whatever their feelings about Trevor's being able to avoid speaking in class, the other students appear to know that this is his pattern, and assume that he has made a contract with Vinceberg to maintain it. When Vinceberg calls on Trevor, they no doubt also feel confused at the apparent contract violation, in addition to feeling sympathetic to Trevor in his vulnerability.

Subsequently Vinceberg tricks them into publicly condemning their peer -- something they are not normally asked to do and that runs against the norm in virtually all student cultures. They probably then feel guilty because they have violated their own standard and joined in the humiliation of their sectionmate. Their anger naturally builds as they quickly realize Vinceberg has manipulated them into this action.

In summary, the students are likely to perceive that Vinceberg has violated his implicit contract with the students, tricked them into doing something beneath their ethical standards, and publicly humiliated one of them. Since the section members have little experience with Vinceberg and do not find him particularly personable, they are not likely to trust his good intentions and give him the benefit of the doubt on this mistake. Instead, they will probably conclude that Vinceberg cannot be trusted, and that if he is willing to pick on poor Trevor Jones, then any of them could be his next victim.

An additional factor is Trevor's possible status as a class maverick. Many sections (and indeed most groups and organizations) include one or more members who deviate in some harmless but highly visible way from the general norms of conduct. These individuals often come to symbolize for others a certain independence of spirit which is admired. Perhaps the more conforming students derive a small vicarious pleasure from seeing someone act out contrary impulses. In any case, an

instructor who humiliates or attacks such a person may be perceived as attacking the spirit of independence in the section. Such an action can quickly alienate the other students, and Vinceberg's firing of Trevor may have had this effect.

Vinceberg is difficult to confront, because of his imposing presence and his power (70% of students' grades will depend on his subjective rating of their in-class performance). Moreover, by initially ignoring the situation, Vinceberg signals that he does not wish to discuss it. The pot boils until finally -- at Vinceberg's invitation -- it explodes.

2. **What do you think might have been Vinceberg's reasons for using role playing? What was he trying to accomplish?**

Usage Note

This question encourages participants to see the situation from Vinceberg's perspective and to develop empathy for him. It helps the seminar bear in mind that Vinceberg may be a well-intentioned person who has made an honest mistake, rather than a brute. It also helps participants realize that they too might make a mistake in predicting how a section will respond to an intervention.

Analysis

Vinceberg may have been trying to stimulate the high level of student involvement that often marks successful case discussions and case courses. Discussion dialogue can proceed on various levels. At the first level, students are purely observers, commenting on someone else's problem in a strictly classroom-academic mode. A second level of discussion may be stimulated by assigning students roles in the case situation under discussion. Their comments then tend to reflect their sense of the circumstances of the company managers whose robes they wear. When students step back into their own normal classroom mode of operation after a successful role-playing exercise, their perspective has moved a little closer to that of an involved corporate officer.

The third discussion level is reached when

> students, on their own initiative, project themselves into the case situation. The classroom and business situation meld together. . . . Problems are not discussed as abstract topics, but as issues

inextricably bound up in a manager's career circumstances. Student comments reflect a personal commitment to the arguments they advance. This level of discussion comes as close to real life as can be achieved in an academic situation. Learning opportunities, and risk, are high for all involved.[1]

Al Vinceberg may have been trying to achieve Level 3 involvement in his case discussion. The case requires students to consider the task of evaluating employees for possible dismissal -- an emotionally arduous experience for most managers. Vinceberg may have felt that a Level 1 discussion could not give the flavor of the central human dilemmas involved in such situations. Thus he may have chosen an intervention that would bring the situation to life in the classroom -- not realizing the possible harm that could be done by a poorly planned and executed attempt.

3. Why might he have chosen to call on Trevor Jones?

Usage Note

This question too is intended to make participants consider the possibility that Al Vinceberg had good intentions in what he was doing.

Analysis

Participants tend to mention two possible reasons for selecting Trevor. First, Vinceberg may have realized that Trevor -- unprepared to speak and caught off guard -- would do poorly in the recitation and thus be a good candidate for the role of the fired worker. We think it unlikely that Vinceberg would be so insensitive to Trevor's needs as to act on this perception. But the other students, whose trust in Vinceberg has been destroyed, may well put this interpretation on events.

We believe that, in Vinceberg's original plan for the class, the decision to call on Trevor may well have been unconnected to the decision to use a role-playing exercise. Al may have thought that this case would provide a good opportunity for Trevor to make a contribution to the class. Although we do not know what actually happened in the meeting between Vinceberg and Trevor, Vinceberg may have assumed that Trevor would eventually participate but merely hoped to wait until he was comfortable. In view of their conversation about Trevor's father's experiences in the declining British steel industry, Al may have thought that Trevor would be especially well prepared for this case and that his contributions might help the class understand the painful realities being described. Thus Al may have decided to call upon Trevor for his potentially positive contribution.

Even taking this charitable view, it is difficult to justify Vinceberg's calling upon Trevor to lead off. Opening the class is a particularly stressful task, even for those who are more experienced at contributing in case discussions. It would have been more appropriate, in our judgment, to wait until the discussion had developed, and then to ask Trevor to comment upon the substance of the contributions so far. Nevertheless, participants should recognize that Al may have had a basically positive reason for calling on Trevor.

Whatever his thinking about Trevor, Vinceberg may have independently planned to introduce the role-playing exercise at whatever point in the discussion seemed most appropriate. After Trevor's dismal performance Vinceberg may have made a quick and ill-considered decision to use it then -- perhaps out of irritation at Trevor's rambling contribution, or perhaps simply because it struck him that he had been presented with an example of poor performance that would enable the role play to "work" if introduced immediately.

Instructor errors of this type seldom spring from a conscious desire to hurt a student. Rather, they generally result from quick moves made during the heat of teaching without considering crucial features of the situation. An intervention as risky as this one, which raises feelings most people find very difficult to deal with, should not have been undertaken without very thorough advance planning. In our judgment Vinceberg should have (1) selected his "victim" very carefully, picking someone with a good deal of personal resiliency and a strong standing in the section, (2) asked his or her cooperation in advance, (3) made contingency plans to abort the role play if it seemed to be getting out of hand, and (4) debriefed the section immediately after the incident, letting students understand his educational intent and giving them a chance to share and sort out their feelings.

4. At the end of Bob Smith's outburst, what are the critical tasks facing Al Vinceberg?

---

1. C. Roland Christensen, *Teaching by the Case Method* (Boston: Harvard Business School, 1981).

Usage Note

This question begins the shift to action planning, while continuing to counterbalance strong feelings in the seminar by encouraging reflective distance.

Analysis

First, Al needs to keep the class from completely blowing up. If dialogue breaks down now, Vinceberg will lose an important opportunity to begin to reestablish a working relationship with the section, and will probably have a much harder time later on.

Second, Trevor Jones needs to be protected from further humiliation.

Third, and very important, Al must work to establish mutual trust between himself and the section members. Trust is basic to an instructor's ability to communicate with and lead a section, and without it good teaching is nearly impossible.

5.   **What do you think of his response -- asking for process evaluation by the members of the section?**

Usage Note

This question continues the gradual movement toward action planning, while maintaining a somewhat detached perspective.

Analysis

In our judgment Al Vinceberg's most difficult and crucial task is to regain the trust of the section. Students trust instructors who are open and fair, and who avoid humiliating them. Al's approach, which is to admit his failure and ask for student reaction and assistance, has the advantage of being open, of admitting culpability (and thus being fair), and of helping to undo the humiliation of Trevor and the other students by losing face himself.

However, Al's response comes much too late. Immediately after the firing and even before Trevor left the room, Vinceberg could have opened up and allowed the class to see his intentions. By trying instead to conduct classroom business as usual, Al has caused two problems. First, he has reinforced the impression that he is insensitive to the feelings of the students and thus given them more reason to be angry at him. Second, he has put them in the position of stewing in these feelings without being able to confront him. Now the risk is much

greater that, when he does open up and cede control to the section, there will be a complete blowup -- a shouting session of the type inaugurated by Bob Smith.

6.   **After Bob Smith's outburst, what are the alternatives open to Al Vinceberg?**

Usage Note

This question asks participants to suggest alternative ways to handle the difficult problem of a hostile blowup when a student's ire is justified. Like the preceding questions, it still encourages reflectiveness rather than involvement -- though it sets the stage, finally, for the involvement-raising question "What would you do in this situation?"

Analysis

Al Vinceberg has several options. He could attempt to return to the case discussion, although that could probably not be sustained. Or, he could call off the class, either immediately or after apologizing once again. If he takes this tack, the crucial questions are: What should he do before the next class session, and how should he begin the next class?

Most likely he will try to continue the discussion of the incident itself, since he has asked for feedback; adjourning the class might, in this context, look like a further attempt to squelch the expression of student feelings. He can respond to Bob, or he can ask for other comments. If he chooses to respond to Bob, he must decide how to do so. If Al asks for other comments, he can do so with a general query, or he can call on specific students. Over the course of the ensuing discussion, Al will need to develop a process plan, if he can, to guide his attempt to regain authority while at the same time beginning to restore trust.

7.   **What would you do now, and why? [Optional probes: What would you suggest Al do before the next class? What might he do at the beginning of the next class?]**

Usage Note

Finally, this question asks directly for action recommendations. Rather than asking what Vinceberg should have done, we take what has happened as an unfortunate given, and ask participants how they could make the best of the situation. The intent of this question is once again to encourage identification with Al Vinceberg and his predicament, rather than simple condemnation.

Analysis

Now that the discussion of the intervention and of Vinceberg's performance has been opened, it seems unlikely that it can be closed. Thus we would probably proceed with it, hoping to rebuild credibility and a working relationship with the section. Though it is difficult to plan for such a discussion, the following points seem important. First, we would not want to get into a shouting match with Bob Smith, and thus would try hard to remain calm and poised during his blast. After he finishes, we would probably respond directly to him, in order to gain some control over the situation (others are unlikely to jump in while we are locked in interaction) and to begin to reestablish two-way communication. Since a good deal of Bob's rage is probably due to the frustration of not being able to speak earlier, we would borrow a technique from crisis intervention counseling and "validate his feelings" -- that is, show him that we have heard and respect his anger. This could be done by simply saying, "I think I can really understand how you feel, and if I were in your shoes I probably would feel the same way."

If another student now starts in, we might handle them similarly. However, it seems more likely that the room would fall silent for a moment after Bob finishes, as the students collect their thoughts. We might then call on another student, asking for his or her thoughts. Calling on a specific student has two advantages. First, we can choose the student. We would probably try to find one who is clearly angry (we don't wish it to appear that we are trying to suppress dialogue) but with whom we have established trust, and who is known to be able to keep a clear head under pressure. This would increase the chances that his or her comments would be constructive. Second, by calling on a student -- even one who is so agitated it seems he or she will jump in momentarily anyway -- we begin to reestablish our control over the process of the discussion.

During the ensuing discussion we would keep several aims in mind. We would want to remain open, in order to reestablish communication and trust. We would want to regain control over the process of the discussion. At the very least, we would want to determine who speaks, and if possible we would begin to ask specific questions in order to establish control over the substantive direction as well.

Over the course of the discussion we would continually emphasize the overarching goal of developing a constructive working relationship that can make the rest of the semester's work a success. This is a goal the students will subscribe to, and focusing on it should lead the dialogue into more constructive channels.

Students can learn a great deal from the incident itself. If possible, we would point out that the feelings generated by the role playing and subsequent events are like those that arise in real life when retrenchment and dismissals are necessary. But it could be important not to raise this interpretation too early, lest it appear that we have not fully appreciated the ill effects of the incident and are merely hastening to return to the point of the original role-playing exercise. The students are unlikely to agree that the cloud has a silver lining until they are sure we have experienced the darkness everywhere else. Ideally, this interpretation might be made by a student, and/or noted by the instructor at the beginning of the following session as a way to bridge between these events and the case content of the course.

The following probes highlight some wider issues raised by the case, and can be interspersed in the discussion wherever they seem appropriate. We often use them when they help make explicit an issue already raised in a participant's comment. No separate usage notes are provided, as these questions all function in much the same way. Each question moves the discussion toward greater generality, but also focuses consideration on a particular issue, creating opportunities both to consider general guidelines and philosophy and to examine similar situations in the participants' experience. Since increasing generality usually has the effect of cooling emotional involvement, these questions can be used to manage the level of involvement when desired.

8. **How can an instructor deal with section members who contribute little or nothing verbally?**

Analysis

There are probably as many ways to help students who do not participate verbally as there are instructors. One approach we favor is to give them more structured support for their contributions.

For example, we would avoid asking low contributors very wide, general questions -- at least initially. Rather, we may try to use more specific questions, perhaps asking for help with a particular point, and/or a response to a previous contribution. In addition, we often assign special roles to low contributors, perhaps asking them (probably privately, before class) to monitor the first part of the day's discussion, and give a summary to the class at the halfway point, or to be part of a panel of contributors.

We also find it helpful to ask students to exercise the subskills of participation. For example, during the first weeks we often ask all members of the section to attend not only to the content of their sectionmates' contributions, but also to the way in which each contributor thinks -- his or her style, biases, strengths, and so forth -- and to consider how to respond to the person, as well as to the point, when addressing the question being discussed. This is a particularly good practice for low contributors, for it helps them to think of their prospective comments as rejoinders in a dialogue rather than a performance. In general, such students find participation easier when they feel less on stage, and when their comments can be directed toward a specific person or viewpoint.

To strengthen analytical skills, we may allow participants to submit written analyses of cases for reading and comment, without grade, by the instructor. Such work, completed before a given case discussion, warms up the students and often increases verbal contributions in class.

Learning from cases requires in-class engagement, including actively synthesizing ideas and testing them in dialogue with other students. As case method instructors we believe all should share in the benefits of this experience. For those who cannot make their contribution verbally, we may substitute written forms of communication, but we still try to design an experience that will come as close as possible to that of the other students.

For students with bona fide problems that seem beyond our corrective intervention, we will sometimes allow written papers to substitute for in-class participation. These papers are to be short, but of high quality, and submitted at regular intervals. Sometimes their substance may be a reaction to the in-class discussion, and in such instances we may ask that the student allow us to distribute the paper to the section.

9. Al Vinceberg used class participation to determine a large part -- 70% -- of each student's grade. Do you think this was wise? Why or why not?

Analysis

In case-based courses it is standard to award 30% to 50% of the grade on the basis of class contribution. In our experience this system puts great pressure on students to perform in class, and helps to ensure preparation. Assigning a weight of less than 30% to participation can lead students to conclude that the case discussions are unimportant, and to put their energies elsewhere.

Basing 70% of the grade on participation seems to us extreme, and probably unwise for several reasons in any but a public speaking or debating course. Assigning participation grades is ultimately a very subjective process; the instructor has a great deal of power, while students who feel unjustly evaluated have little opportunity for appeal. Weighting participation so heavily gives Vinceberg so much power that fearful students may adopt classroom strategies designed to satisfy him rather than maximize their learning. The casewriter, for example, notes that Vinceberg "tended to shape and guide the discussion to the point where . . . you know what he wanted you to say and you went right along."

Too much emphasis on classroom participation can have several sorts of negative consequences. Since grades are based on subjective evaluations by the instructor, an impression of arbitrariness and unfairness can easily develop, undermining trust between students and teacher. Students typically become resentful of the instructor's authority and/or begin playing games in order to conform to the instructor's position (as they perceive it).

This latter response causes communication between students and instructor to break down, with the result that the instructor cannot determine the students' genuine interests and concerns or track their progress in learning the material. Students become much less willing to risk being wrong or to become personally involved in their responses to the case. So while participation, as measured by number and length of comments, may remain high, involvement is likely to decline to practically nothing.

10. What is the proper place of confrontation and challenge in teaching?

Analysis

This question, which defies simple answers, can be valuable in focusing attention on the need to manage the level and manner of confronting students. Helping students to see the limits of their present understanding is a central task in all teaching. The question is who should do this, and how such confrontations can be managed so that they result in student learning rather than humiliation.

We believe it is essential to create a learning situation in which (1) the instructor confronts the students by asking them to respond to difficult questions that, at least occasionally, raise profound issues not easily resolved, (2) student responses are examined carefully and critically -- by the students themselves whenever possible; and (3) better responses are rewarded, while incomplete or even clearly mistaken responses (assuming they are the result of sincere engagement with the case material) are understood to provide valuable contributions to the section's learning process.

A great deal of the power of case method teaching lies in the questions posed to the students. Ideally, students are forced to confront difficult issues of professional practice -- issues that cannot be resolved in any simple or final way. Students usually have not asked themselves these questions, at least not in a clearly articulated way. Formulating responses is a genuine challenge, and confronts each student with his or her limits of knowledge and experience.

We see the creation of such confrontation as a primary responsibility of the case method instructor. It is his or her job to raise central questions, and to insist that the students attempt to answer them. Sometimes students resist a question -- perhaps imagining they are answering it while actually skittering off on a tangent. In such instances the instructor restates the question, driving it home and insisting that it be answered. Rather than objecting to such pressure, students usually appreciate the challenges of difficult questions, and rise to meet them.

Responding to the students' answers is another matter. In our opinion, it is not a primary job of the instructor to critique students' contributions, at least not in class. This, rather, is the task of the section as a whole. In this view we seem to differ from Vinceberg, who is described as having "strong ideas about what his students should know . . . [often interrupting] class discussion to summarize with lectures on points he felt to be important." While we are not averse to stating an opinion from time to time, our primary allegiance is not to "points" or answers, but to questions. Thus we are much more apt to interrupt class discussion to ask a key question than to summarize an answer.

Beginning case method instructors are often concerned about how to handle poor student contributions. They may assume that if they don't catch a problem, no one will. Quite the contrary. If section members are encouraged to talk with each other, and not simply respond to the instructor, they will usually demonstrate considerable skill in sniffing out the weaknesses in each other's arguments.

As instructors we will usually correct factual errors made during the early laying out of the case -- for otherwise these have a way of skewing the later discussion -- but we try to do so as unobtrusively as possible. Once the basic facts of the case are on the table, and the key questions have been introduced and apparently understood, we seldom comment directly on the content of the discussion. Indeed, a key reason for using the case method is to teach critical thinking in a group context. Thus the development of the section's ability to examine the arguments presented is one of our primary tasks as instructors.

This process of critical thinking can be encouraged in a variety of ways. One can simply ask for students' comments about an argument just made, or a particular line of reasoning. Generally the section members will find it stimulating to be given responsibility for critical appraisal of contributions. The instructor's primary task is then to help them learn to disagree with tact and sensitivity as well as clarity. The instructor may sometimes feel like a boxing referee, insisting that the fight be fair -- though most sections require no more than an occasional buffering of sharp-edged comments and the encouragement to maintain a certain lightness and a caring sense of humor in the rough-and-tumble of discussion.

We find that the process of discussion is profoundly affected by the section's overall attitude toward "mistakes" and apparently weak comments. We promote the attitude that all sincere comments (and even many of the humorous asides) are potentially grist for the mill, and may be refined by the section into more complex, sensitive, and powerful insights into the case material. Comments that at first seem weak often reveal facets of the case not yet taken into account by the section; they may provoke a better articulated presentation of opposing points of view and frequently contain seed ideas that will be developed later into effective responses. At the very least such contributions illustrate common traps and pitfalls presented by the material under consideration.

When such an attitude toward contributions prevails, students are more apt to work for effective answers without feeling crushed when the section points out weaknesses in their analyses. Though an instructor cannot always succeed in creating this sort of section process, there is much that can be done to foster its development. The instructor can demonstrate an appreciation of diversity, making it clear that any view -- if soundly argued and supported -- will be well received. He or she can show special interest in contributions that buck the tide in discussion -- comments that counter premature consensus. When a student becomes isolated -- apparently the only one holding an unpopular but defensible view -- the instructor can step in to support it.

In these ways the instructor fosters dialogue -- or more properly, perhaps, dialectic -- in the classroom. The discussion becomes less a guessing game (with the instructor judging the responses) and more a genuine working conversation. At best, the level of confrontation is very high, while the level of hurt feelings is quite low.

11. Are there some ethical principles that should guide role playing? If so, what are they?

Analysis

Role playing creates an extraordinary situation in the classroom, one that can powerfully enhance student learning. But the use of this technique should be guided by some ethical principles. Though we do not wish to lay down the ten commandments of role playing, the following suggestions, derived from our experience and that of past seminar participants, seem to make sense.

In general, the well-being of one individual should not be intentionally sacrificed for the learning of the group. Humiliating or otherwise injuring a student (or, for that matter, an entire section) is not an acceptable price to pay for section learning -- and in the long run will destroy the trust necessary to continued discussion teaching.

Role playing creates a situation of potentially high emotional stress. Since each individual responds differently to such conditions, the instructor should think carefully about who should be chosen as protagonists in the play. Those who seem

emotionally or socially vulnerable should be avoided.

Special care should be taken with any role-playing situation that might arouse feelings of rejection -- either the experience of being rejected, or the experience of rejecting someone. Such feelings are particularly difficult and painful for most people to handle.

Finally, in many role-playing situations it may be necessary to gain informed consent, particularly from any proposed victim. One of the central problems in the present case is that Trevor was a totally involuntary victim. This issue is complex, however. Many of our finest discussions shade almost imperceptibly into Level 3 involvement, and much of the potency of the learning situations comes from the participants' initial lack of self-consciousness that they are responding in any other than a "real-life" situation. Stopping to get informed consent as involvement rises would break the flow of experience and introduce an element of self-consciousness that in our judgment would significantly reduce learning.

We do not wish to trick students, and in the Trevor Jones incident we believe that informed consent, particularly from Trevor, should have been obtained. But we do believe an instructor should feel free to enhance involvement without giving specific advanced warning.

Perhaps the best way to handle this matter is to provide a general, rather than specific, warning. That is, at the beginning of the term the instructor may wish to discuss the value of occasional high-involvement situations, pointing out that he or she will take pains to protect the students involved, and preparing the section members to understand these events before they occur. Then, over time, one can gradually increase the use of such techniques, so that their judicious use becomes a part of the implicit as well as explicit teacher-student learning contract, and understood and accepted. Part of Al Vinceberg's error was that he used a very powerful intervention early in the term and in a section where similar experiences had not (as far as we know) occurred previously.

By the same token, when using an intervention that might be experienced as trickery, one may wish to issue a general warning just before the specific case discussion. This can be as simple as a statement such as "Today's case provides an exceptional opportunity for role playing and similar kinds of experiences -- and as you participate today you might want to be prepared for something of that sort."

12. What process issues are relevant in using role playing?

Analysis

We have found it useful to keep several points in mind when using role playing and similar sorts of interventions. First, instructors often underestimate the impact role playing can have in the classroom. Though the instructor is often concerned that the students will not get into the roles, the more common problem is that they cannot get out of them when the simulation is over.

One should be especially wary of role-playing exercises that are designed to stimulate feelings of loss, betrayal, and rejection. Such experiences may have their place in some sorts of training programs, but they must be used with extreme care, and usually only by instructors with psychological training.

One should plan ways to abort or cool down the role playing during the process if it becomes necessary. For example, one can identify points at which the exercise can be stopped early -- working out alternative ways to discuss the experience if it must be terminated before the originally intended completion point.

Role playing is not an effective learning tool unless the students reflect upon their experiences. Simply having an experience is not generally helpful; they also need to take in-class time to think about it. The instructor should devote as much effort to planning the reflective portion of the exercise as to designing the simulation itself. This "debriefing" can be structured very much like the flow of a case discussion. One can ask students to think about what happened, what problems came up, and how they were handled and might have been handled. Suggestions for alternative actions can sometimes be played out, thus extending the role playing and allowing students to experiment with new behaviors.

The simulation should normally be discussed as soon as it is completed. A prompt debriefing enables participants to separate themselves from the roles they have played; otherwise they may feel stuck in the role and overwhelmed by the emotions evoked by the situation. Prompt debriefing also allows participants to ex-press feelings stimulated by the exercise, which might otherwise boil up at less helpful times in the following discussion -- as seems to have happened in Al Vinceberg's class. Expressing these feelings in the context of the debriefing also serves an important pedagogical purpose, because it helps participants to become conscious of and learn from their emotional responses. And an early debriefing ensures relatively accurate memory of what went on, and promotes more detailed analysis.

Debriefing generally works best when the central protagonists are first asked to share the thoughts and feelings evoked by the simulation. They are the ones who have taken the risk of exposing themselves to their classmates, and it is they who have potentially the most to learn from reflecting on their actions and feelings. Thus we almost always start with them, listening carefully to what they are experiencing and focusing our instructional effort on helping them benefit from the experience.

Moreover, the protagonists are often left a bit socially vulnerable -- particularly if they have played unsympathetic characters -- and may be emotionally overwhelmed. Letting them speak right away as themselves helps to remind the observers of who the protagonists really are, and also helps the protagonists establish reflective distance from their feelings. Moreover, it allows them to criticize their own inadequacies before outsiders do -- thus helping them reassert their own competence and reducing their tendency to feel attacked when weaknesses are later discussed by their classmates.

13. How can an instructor recover from his or her mistakes?

Analysis

There are many answers to this question, of course, and no answer that will fit every situation. One rule of thumb is to admit errors early, establish that one's objectives are the same as those of the class (i.e., to foster students' learning and skill development), and go on from there. Usually students are forgiving, particularly if the instructor's overall track record is good and they have reason to expect that he or she can learn from mistakes, and over the long haul of the semester teach them well.

Suggestions for Building the Seminar Group

At this point in the term the seminar has usually become an effective forum, with a highly developed ability for self-management. In this situation, the instructor's attention can turn to providing special learning opportunities for the participants, for example by creating occasions for individual members to contribute in ways that differ from their previous patterns, or by using cases, like "Trevor Jones," that raise potentially volatile emotional issues.

Finally, at this point in the term we may invite some discussion of the seminar's own process. Usually this is done at the close of the day's discussion, perhaps by asking participants to compare the present session with the previous one. In general we avoid such process discussions earlier in the semester, because they tend to create too much self-consciousness and impede the normal development of the group's discussion capabilities. But at this late phase, the seminar's modes of operating are so well learned and habitual that they are unlikely to be disrupted -- and the increased self-awareness that comes from discussing the process can be quite interesting to participants.

"Trevor Jones" provides an excellent opportunity to explore the nature and dynamics of highly emotional discussions. In many of the previous cases the discussion questions were used to create emotional involvement as a counterbalance to participants' tendency to respond on a purely intellectual level to the situations portrayed. With "Trevor Jones" the situation is reversed. The case material itself tends to stimulate a great deal of passionate discussion, and the questions are by and large designed to stimulate reflection and somewhat generalized analysis.

By adjusting the degree to which the discussion is allowed to follow its own course (rather than focusing on the pre-planned questions), the instructor can to some extent modulate the level of emotional intensity in the seminar. It can be interesting, both to the teacher and to participants, to vary the range and note what happens near the extremes. Too much intensity can sharply reduce the number of participants involved in the discussion, as typically only a few members will be comfortable contributing in that atmosphere. In addition, the intellectual caliber of remarks is likely to drop off, and the comments may become more stereotyped and viewpoints artificially polarized. On the other hand, a very high level of abstraction can create a discussion that feels artificial, as participants find it necessary to suppress their feelings in order to conform to the predominant tone of the discussion.

An interesting way to end the discussion of this case is to ask participants to comment on how the session felt to them, and perhaps to compare it with the previous meeting. This works well if the seminar session has been particularly lively, and provides an opportunity for the section members to reflect on their responses to a highly emotional discussion. The seminar leader may also call attention to his or her use of questions to manage the intensity. This raises the important topic of how to manage involvement, and can lead to an interesting discussion in its own right. Allowing the seminar to focus on the leader's actions may also stimulate participants to learn by reflecting more generally on how the instructor has conducted discussions throughout the seminar.

Exhibit 1

Trevor Jones

Study Questions

1. What is your diagnosis of the situation? What happened? When? Why?

2. What does Professor Vinceberg do immediately? Later?

3. More generally, under what circumstances is role playing an effective involvement technique? What are the key decisions an instructor has to make when deciding to use role playing?

Exhibit 2

Trevor Jones

Discussion Questions

1. What happened? Why? What key factors contributed to the problem?

2. What do you think might have been Vinceberg's reasons for using role playing? What was he trying to accomplish?

3. Why might he have chosen to call on Trevor Jones?

4. At the end of Bob Smith's outburst,

what are the critical tasks facing Al Vinceberg?

5. What do you think of his response -- asking for process evaluation by the members of the section?

6. After Bob Smith's outburst, what are the alternatives open to Al Vinceberg?

7. What would you do now? Why?

The following probes highlight the wider issues raised by the case, and can be interspersed in the discussion wherever they seem appropriate. We often use them when they help make explicit an issue already raised in a seminar member's comment.

8. How can an instructor deal with sec-

tion members who contribute little or nothing verbally?

9. Al Vinceberg used class participation to determine a large part -- 70% -- of each student's grade. Do you think this was wise? Why or why not?

10. What is the proper place of confrontation and challenge in teaching?

11. Are there some ethical principles that should guide role playing? If so, what are they?

12. What process issues are relevant in using role playing?

13. How can an instructor recover from his or her mistakes?

Class on World Hunger

Teaching Note

Students in the "Class on World Hunger" confront their instructor with a dramatic in-class prank. This case sequence, which we ordinarily use toward the end of our seminar on case teaching, contains leads to a wide range of issues. A central question is how an instructor can maintain authority without stifling students' initiative and voluntary contributions in the classroom. And when the instructor's authority is challenged by student behavior (for example, by tardiness or pranks), how can he or she recover without slipping over into authoritarianism?

The case also raises many other important issues. For example, what difficulties face young instructors making the transition from graduate student to professor? Or those moving from a discipline-based teaching and learning environment to a case-oriented professional school? In our seminar on teaching we normally hand out and discuss both the (A) and (B) cases together. The (A) case provides a ready vehicle for discussing potential problems in establishing rapport and maintaining an effective instructor-student learning contract, including the question of how much, if at all, to fraternize with students.

The (B) case describes the instructor's philosophy of case education, and how it has been shaped by his experiences. We usually ask participants to contrast it with "Ernie Budding (D)," another reflective piece read earlier in the seminar. This discussion can be particularly useful in helping seminar members review, integrate, and elaborate upon their own evolving thoughts about case teaching.

Case Summary

"Class on World Hunger" is a richly detailed case which provides a rare opportunity to enter into the experience of a tal-ented newcomer to the case method and to share his insights. We find it helpful to warn participants to allow plenty of preparation time, as the case text is relatively long and "Ernie Budding (D)" must also be reviewed before the seminar session.

The Institutional Context

The case incident takes place in a required course in the first year of the MBA program at Bay Area Graduate School of Business Administration (called "Bay" by most students). Bay has a case-based curriculum with a first-year program of required courses covering most aspects of business practice. Each first-year student is assigned to one of ten sections of 80 students each; sections take all their courses together. Students attend three classes per day, remaining in one classroom (the instructors come to them). The classes last 80 minutes and are scheduled at 8:30 a.m., 10:10 a.m., and 1:00 p.m. Classes meet Monday through Friday.

The Course

Comparative Political Economy (CPE) is a full-year required course dealing with business-government relations. Instructors continue with their sections throughout the entire course. Interim grades are issued at the end of the first half of the course.

The Instructor

Bob Clarkson is in his second year of teaching at Bay. His own graduate training had been in comparative political economy, and he had been a teaching fellow in economics while a graduate student. His Ph.D. was granted during his first year at Bay, winning him an automatic promotion from instructor to assistant professor. He is a young-looking 30-year-old with a wife and two children.

This teaching note was written by Dr. James F. Moore in collaboration with Professor C. Roland Christensen as an aid to instructors in the classroom use of the case series "Class on World Hunger" (A) 9–381–042 and (B) 9–381–043.

The Section

Though Clarkson taught two sections, the case text emphasizes his relationship with Section I, which is described as talented and highly motivated. Several students are identified by name, but only a few of them play major roles in the case and its central incident.

Ian Kahn is a foreign student who has worked in Japan as a businessman. Amanda Brown is a bright and energetic woman, heavily involved in the social activities of the school. Jack Law is the section's social coordinator -- a gregarious person who does not wish to appear to take Bay too seriously. (His CPE grade is adequate, however.) Cynthia Andrews, the section's educational representative, is mature and competent. Before the incident, she asked Clarkson to suggest extra reading related to the day's case. Elliott Farmer is an adequate discussion contributor, but received a low interim grade in the course. He is interested in the problems of world hunger.

The Teacher-Student Relationship

Bob Clarkson uses the metaphor dis-cussion pastures to describe the case method as he practices it in his second year at Bay. As he says in the (B) case, "The instructor polices the fences of a pasture, but lets the cattle graze as they will, without letting the grass become grazed too closely in any one area." Thus Bob tries to manage but not control the discussion -- typically bringing to its attention three questions or areas of consideration during a class period. As he remarks, "If it is managed properly, the students will do all the teacher's work in a lively discussion -- bring up his points, expose each other's reasoning."

On a day-to-day basis, Clarkson seems to judge his effectiveness as a teacher in terms of his sense of rapport with the section and students' seriousness in tackling the case issues. Section I is successful in both respects, and at the end of the year these students give Clarkson a high rating as a teacher.

By the second term, Section I students have begun to create openings for Clarkson to fraternize with them. For example, he is invited to their Friday afternoon beer busts, as well as their first two afternoon baseball games. Clarkson declines these offers, not wishing to become too informal in his relations with the section. He does accept an invitation to join them, with his family, for a scheduled baseball outing where other faculty will be present; and he holds regular, formally scheduled group lunches with the students.

With Section II, on the other hand, Clarkson has trouble both in generating rapport and in the students' classroom performance. At the end of the year Section II rates his teaching considerably lower than does his Section I. Bob attributes his lack of success with Section II in part to his becoming visibly angry and lecturing the class about absenteeism early in the first term. He tries hard not to make the same mistake with Section I. The case descriptions of his in-class experience with Section I suggest that this is not likely. They perform well, he enjoys teaching them and looks forward to his sessions with them, and the text includes examples of light-hearted banter which suggests a good deal of mutual appreciation.

The Incident

The "Class on World Hunger" case is the sixth (out of a total of 23) in the CPE second-term syllabus. As the first of a module of three cases, it sets the tone and conceptual basis for the following discussions. Prior class sessions have gone well, with insightful and energetic discussions.

The class session is on Friday -- the last in the day. The class play -- an important activity for several section members -- has been performed the night before. Amanda Brown warned Clarkson in advance that she might not be as well prepared as usual on Friday.

A second factor affecting the class is that many students have recently found out that their grades, in both Clarkson's course and others, are not good -- and apparently not as good as they had expected. Many of the low grades were received in a marketing course that has now ended, so that students have no way to raise their grades in that course.

Three surprise visitors appear at Friday's class: a prospective student, the wife of a current student, and a friend of his who is considering applying to the program.

Before beginning the session Clarkson receives several signals that the day may be a little unusual. Ian provides a veiled warning that the section is rambunctious and something may be up; Amanda comments that the play was a great success and participants went drinking afterward (implying that they may not be prepared for class);

Jack Law is in a jocular mood, and quite friendly and open to Clarkson; and an unusually large number of students are absent.

After a few moments of informal banter with the students, Clarkson turns to his usual type of case introduction. At this moment Jack Law jumps up and yells "Food fight!" Bread and rolls start flying from all sides.

Clarkson, shaken, retreats behind the desk to avoid being hit. He feels embarrassed in front of the guests -- both as an instructor and for the school. Moreover, he is offended by the symbolism of a food fight among well-fed Americans studying world hunger. And Clarkson feels chagrined not to have read Ian's signal more clearly.

After considering a number of options for action (while still huddled behind the desk), Clarkson decides to suppress his anger. Instead he emerges from behind the desk with an exaggerated look of shock and puzzlement, and asks, "Is it safe to come out now?" His actions evoke laughter. Looking around, he continues, "Frankly, I really don't know how to respond to this." Looking more closely at the individual students, he sees that not all of them seem to be involved, and some appear to be quite concerned.

Finally he asks, "Can someone suggest where we should go from here?" Hands shoot up, people look prepared for discussion. Clarkson calls on Elliott Farmer, who had received a low grade on his exam, who had looked concerned about the food fight, and who, Clarkson imagines, wants particularly to do a good job on this case.

Elliott does an excellent job of laying out and analyzing the case. Clarkson lets him continue for fifteen minutes -- an exceptionally long time in this class. When Elliott concludes, Clarkson calls on other students who seem well prepared and serious. The discussion turns out to be one of the best the section had experienced, with even the ill-prepared students becoming interested and joining in. Clarkson ends the session by thanking Elliott for his careful preparation, and thanking several other students for their contributions. He then summarizes the issues from the discussion, honestly complimenting the class.

Later Cynthia asks, "Did you really think we were going to hit you?" Several students stop by to say that the discussion had been one of the best, and to thank Clarkson. But most of the students seem interested in heading out to the ball field. Clarkson hears nothing from the guests.

In the days and weeks following, Section I continues to do very well in the course, and Clarkson continues to enjoy working with the students.

The (B) Case

The (B) case contains Clarkson's reflections on his first two years of teaching at Bay. He comments on the discussion leader's problem of balancing discipline and order with the need for student freedom. He describes an incident in which he made an angry, disciplinary speech to Section II. In retrospect, he believes this was the wrong approach -- too unilateral and too infantilizing for the section members. It seems to have damaged morale and the ability of section and instructor to work well together.

Clarkson then describes how his philosophy of education has changed during his two years. His early approach involved trying to enhance his power and authority by being unpredictable, and somewhat authoritarian. By the second year he began to realize that, with guidance, the students could do much more work than he had realized -- not only supplying answers, but critiquing each other, generating more questions, and generally managing their own learning. Out of this experience has come his current teaching style of "policing the fences" of discussion pastures.

Clarkson is still growing and questioning, and his current thoughts about leading discussion courses center on the question, "How do you uphold the standards of your own school and the intellectual enterprise without becoming obnoxiously authoritarian so that you destroy or interrupt a delicate rapport?"

A Note on Study and Discussion Questions

Typically we prepare at least two sets of questions for use with each case. The first set (see Exhibit 1) consists of study questions for participants to use when preparing the case before class. The discussion questions (see Exhibit 2) are used by the instructor in preparing for the session and for guiding the case discussion when appropriate. For all discussion questions, but not for study questions, we have provided detailed usage and analytical notes.

A Suggested Process Plan for the Case

"World Hunger" is usually the next-to last case discussed in our seminar. Our overall aim is to provide a great deal of opportunity for general, philosophical discussion of case teaching -- and especially of the role of the instructor. We anticipate that this will help participants integrate the reflections they have made throughout the semester, and strengthen the influence of this learning on their teaching practice.

At the same time, we also want the seminar to consider closely how Clarkson responded to the prank. We especially want participants to realize that Clarkson made an active, considered response; he did not simply avoid acting. In addition, we want them to appreciate that pranks seldom "just happen." Though the food fight could probably not have been predicted, several identifiable factors might have alerted the instructor that the section was ripe for a prank.

We ordinarily hand out and discuss both the (A) and (B) cases at the same time. In a 90-minute session, we typically begin by asking the seminar members to examine the case, gradually focusing more and more closely on Clarkson's series of actions. We generally spend about 30 minutes on this tack. Question 1 asks participants to give a comprehensive interpretation of the case, centering their remarks on an evaluation of Clarkson's response to the prank. Question 2 directs the seminar to a closer analysis of Clarkson's actions. Together, these two questions require participants to integrate analysis, action planning, and generalization in their comments. Earlier seminar discussions, in contrast, have used separate questions to help the participants focus on each of these issues independently. In this session we wish to move rather quickly from the particulars of the case to a more general philosophical discussion. Thus our opening question invites compression of the typical three-part case discussion into a single response.

We then use Questions 3 through 6 to guide the seminar to spend about 30 minutes generalizing from the case. We encourage participants to raise and address their own questions, as well as to consider in more depth the meaning and management of pranks and similar phenomena.

During the final 30 minutes of the session we switch to the (B) case and raise the level of generality even higher. Our questions direct participants to consider the role of the instructor in case teaching. They are asked to compare and contrast their own approaches with those of Bob Clarkson. In some instances, we also ask seminar members to compare the philosophy of Ernie Budding -- whose approach is highlighted in "Ernie Budding (D)" (an earlier case in our syllabus). The resulting dialogue usually provides participants with a valued opportunity to consider their own educational philosophies in light of both "Class on World Hunger" and their overall experience in the teaching seminar.

Notes for Discussion Questions

These notes parallel the suggested discussion questions presented in Exhibit 2. We briefly indicate the pedagogical intent and use of each question and provide our best attempt at a reasoned response. These analytical responses are intended primarily to sensitize the instructor to key issues when preparing for the discussion. They represent our current thinking on the questions raised by the case, not definitive solutions.

The following questions refer primarily to the (A) case:

1. **How well, in your opinion, did Bob Clarkson handle the problem? What is the worst thing he could have done?**

Usage Note

By asking seminar members to evaluate Clarkson's action, this question accomplishes several things. First, it focuses attention on the fact that he was not simply passive but made an intentional response to the prank. Moreover, by asking participants to speculate as to the worst thing he could have done, it helps them appreciate the range of possible actions and/or unplanned reactions. In addition, this question asks seminar members to examine the impact of Clarkson's responses -- that is, to interpret section dynamics during and after the incident. Third, it requires them to take an evaluative stand, thus necessarily making a comparison between their own approaches and Clarkson's. Thus this one question involves action planning, analysis, and generalization.

Analysis

Seminar members vary in their evaluations of Clarkson's intervention, although most see his actions in a favorable light. (After all, it is clear from the case that the situation turned out well.) Clarkson has rolled with the prank itself, maintaining rapport with the section and playing along with the comedy by exaggerating his own perplexity. Then he invited section members who were not involved in (or particularly supportive of) the prank to join him in reestablishing the class as a serious discussion session. Once these members began to speak, Clarkson supported case-related contributions by calling on only those students likely to make good contributions, and by using his end-of-class summary to reward those who were most helpful.

It seems likely that the prank was primarily an expression of the section's need, at that point in the semester, to let off steam. If so, Clarkson's action was probably effective in allowing the release of tension. Had he tried to suppress their actions, he could easily have created more tension, and thus further trouble later in the session and term.

The prank was perhaps also an initiation rite for Clarkson -- simultaneously an expression of students' affection for him and an attempt to get him to loosen up and become socially more "one of them." In this case, Clarkson appears to have succeeded in demonstrating that he can take a joke and even contribute to the fun. Although he may feel that his role as instructor makes it inappropriate for him to socialize with students, he has shown that he is not simply standoffish. In contrast, it might have been disastrous to become angry and lecture them about the prank. This would have been a rejection of the implicit offer of friendship in the prank, and would have established Clarkson as manifestly not "one of them" -- possibly creating a seriously alienated student-teacher relationship.

On the other hand, Clarkson did not let the prank usurp his overall agenda for the day, for he clearly did not want to send the message that class could be sacrificed whenever the section felt more like playing. Moreover, to cancel the session would not have been fair to the students who had prepared for class and wanted to have a discussion, both as an opportunity to raise their grades and as the substantive basis for the rest of the course. Even the pranksters probably did not want the class canceled. Cancellation would make many of them feel guilty about the impact on their sectionmates (who might very well be angry with the disrupters), awkward about having created more of a stir than was intended, and upset -- in retrospect -- at missing out on a case discussion that played a crucial role in the course.

Clarkson chose an effective means of bringing the section back to its academic priorities. In essence he allowed the students to do most of the work of reestablishing order. He called on those who seemed to want to make a serious contribution, and worked with them to create a case discussion in which the others joined.

In our experience this sort of maneuver is very often the best way for an instructor to recover from challenges to his or her authority -- whether the challenges are basically friendly, as in Clarkson's situation, or more hostile. When some members of a group attack or undermine the leader, there are almost always others who, if given an opportunity, will come to his or her aid. Because this support is normally freely given, the best way to mobilize it is often simply to make an opportunity for students to express it. Clarkson did this by simply asking, "Can anyone suggest where we can go from here?" and then calling on students who he thought would support a reestablishment of the conventional norms of the classroom, including his own authority.

2.   **What precisely did he do? What particular aspects of his response do you believe were most helpful? Why?**

Usage Note

This question moves the seminar to a more detailed consideration of Bob Clarkson's response, and helps illuminate the specific series of actions Bob took -- each of which contributed to his effectiveness.

Analysis

Clarkson retreats behind his desk to assess the situation. This was his first effective move, for it gave him time to determine whether the prank was orchestrated (he concluded it was), to experience his initial reactions (shock and surprise, fear about how the incident would look to outsiders, and repugnance at the moral symbolism), and to consider his options and decide how to respond (suppress his anger and magnify his shock, while maintaining rapport with the students).

When he came out from behind the desk, Clarkson appeared stunned -- taking his honest response, exaggerating it, and thus making it comic. This got a laugh, and created rapport with the section. The friendly laughter also reassured Clarkson that the section was not hostile. Appearing stunned and perplexed also bought more time, for this role did not require him to direct the events.

Clarkson then played into the joke even more by asking, "Is it safe to come out now?" and getting another laugh. At this point he noted that it felt like a fraternity setting -- and indeed this sense may have reflected accurately that he had passed his initiation and moved into a new level of emotional acceptance by the section.

The initiation accomplished, Clarkson still had to decide where to go next. He chose to share his uncertainty -- an approach that might seem risky to instructors who equate leadership with a constant facade of assurance. However, Clarkson appears to have made the admission with a certain humorous quality, even conveying a sense that he shared the section's enjoyment of his own discomfiture. Instead of seeming defensive, he was able to retain his authority while deepening his rapport with the section by being honest with them.

Clarkson then looked around carefully, observing individuals. This had the effect of creating even more rapport and contact between instructor and students. Moreover, he noticed that the section was not monolithic in support of the prank, and that several students looked quite concerned. Reaching out to these individuals, he asked, "Can someone suggest where we should go from here?" This appeal mobilized their support, and hands shot up.

Finally, Clarkson was very careful in choosing students to call on. Had he recognized one of the jokers -- for example, Jack Law or Amanda Brown -- the disruption might have continued. But Clarkson picked Elliott Farmer, a student who appeared prepared and motivated to do well.

Elliott performed beautifully, which helped immensely. By laying out the case in detail, and giving a very clear first analysis, Elliott made it possible for students who were not prepared at least to understand the core of the case. Later in the class they even contributed. Moreover, by taking fifteen minutes, Elliott gave both the class and Clarkson time to settle down. Even if Elliott had not done so well, however, Clarkson could probably have made the discussion work. All he needed was a few serious contributions -- not necessarily brilliant -- to set the tone for effective discussion.

After Elliott finished, Clarkson continued to lead the discussion. He was careful not to call on Jack Law -- and presumably others who were involved in the prank -- until they seemed ready to make serious contributions. At the close of the class Clarkson suppressed an urge to comment on the incident. Instead he complimented Elliott and two others on their contributions, thus reinforcing the classroom norms.

Overall, Clarkson managed to go along with the prank and be seen as a "good guy" who can take a joke -- while remaining steadfast in communicating the importance of the central task of the section: case analysis and discussion.

3. What questions does this incident pose for you?

Usage Note

This question encourages seminar members to consider the wider issues raised by the case, leaving them free to decide which of these issues to emphasize.

Analysis

"Class on World Hunger" is apt to suggest a variety of issues to seminar members. As instructors, we work to support the initiative of the section members, while using such tools as bridging and brief summaries to help clarify and crystallize the questions that emerge. Our notes to the discussion questions below include comments on some of the questions that are often raised. For example, what is the role of pranks, and how can they be managed? How can an instructor maintain rapport and good feelings with a section, while at the same time encouraging high performance and maintaining discipline? Given that one wishes to promote student initiative and voluntary involvement, how can one maintain authority in the face of challenges without becoming authoritarian and stifling the enthusiasm and self-direction one hopes to stimulate?

4. Could Bob Clarkson have anticipated this incident? If so, how and when? Could he have prepared for it? How?

Usage Note

This query shifts attention from Clarkson to the section, asking participants to consider the factors that made the section ripe for a prank, and to identify observations that Clarkson might have interpreted as signs of this condition. Further, it encourages participants to consider what can be done with such information before a prank actually occurs.

Analysis

It seems highly unlikely that Bob Clarkson could have predicted the specific incident that occurred. A more experienced instructor, however, might have sensed a risk that the section would come up with something along these lines. Pressure had been high on the section, and no end was in sight. Students had recently learned to enjoy playing together in organized ways -- for example, in baseball and the class play -- and a prank is another expression of this capability. The highly successful (and highly humorous) class play had just been presented; now, on a pleasant Friday afternoon, many students are in a spirited and frivolous mood. Finally, Clarkson -- who is about the same age as many of the students -- has spurned several of their invitations for more informal contact. The students may be looking for a way to break through his formal manner and test his ability to "come down to their level." These factors, which are likely to be raised at this point in the discussion, are examined in more detail under Question 5.

Clarkson might have paid attention to two sorts of signals. First, the section had been trying to involve him in its social life. These overtures may be seen as friendly attempts to rewrite the instructor-student learning contract. While Clarkson may feel he is most effective when he maintains a relatively formal relationship with the section, he should probably respond to these student initiatives for change by attending carefully to the contract issues at this time. It might have been helpful to discuss the situation informally with the educational representative or other students, to get a better sense of students' perceptions of the contract, and the nature and strength of their interest in changing it. Clarkson might thus have become better able to decide what contract he wanted to work toward, and how to go about getting it.

Second, in the days before the prank, Clarkson might have noticed the frivolous mood of some students and their increasing capacity for enjoyment of organized play. Had he attended to the signals offered by Amanda (and probably others), he might have modified his teaching plan; to capitalize on students' desire to work together, for example, he might have asked small groups to prepare for joint in-class presentations. Or he might have put their desire for group games to work in the classroom by asking two groups of students to argue against each other on some point, and then asking the remaining students to vote on which group was more convincing.

Before class began, Ian tried to warn Clarkson of the impending prank. Had he probed Ian's oblique statement a bit farther, he might have learned of the prank. Even so, Clarkson would have had only moments to prepare, and there are limits to what he could do. His best bet might have been simply to go along with the plan, feigning ignorance -- but with the advantage of having a few moments to consider possible responses and to brace for the shock.

5. **Why did the prank happen when it did, at this point in the term? What was going on with the students that may have contributed to its occurrence?**

Usage Note

This question is essentially a specification of Question 4, designed to draw attention to the section dynamics leading up to the prank. This question may not be necessary if these points have been made in response to the previous question.

Analysis

Pressure on the students was building. Even for a competent, hard-working section, case analysis can become tedious. In Clarkson's class alone, they had analyzed 36 cases, with many more to go. Moreover, the fact that many students had received disappointing marketing grades probably contributed to a disenchantment with the system that had kept them in tight harness for so many months.

In addition, the section had learned the joys of organized play. They had moved from beer busts to softball games, and many of the members had been active in the class play -- which is usually a spoof on the school. An organized prank was just another expression of this new-found group capability.

Clarkson's class fell on a beautiful Friday afternoon, and occurred on the day after the play. What better time to orchestrate a prank? Many students were already in a frivolous mood, several were not prepared for discussion, and the class was the last before the weekend.

Many of the members of the class probably saw Clarkson as essentially their own age. He is personable, the section was going well, and the students liked him. As an expression of this liking, the section members had invited him to join in their beer busts and the first baseball game. He had refused, holding himself -- for probably valid professional reasons -- somewhat aloof from socializing with the section. Some members of the section, hoping to change the existing teacher-student contract, may have seen the prank as a way to loosen Clarkson up and bring him down to their level.

Finally, the section probably felt its exceptional competence, the members were learning to enjoy playing as a group, and esprit de corps was very likely high. What better way to symbolize this new-found positive identity than with an organized prank?

6. Why are pranks such a recurring phenomenon in professional schools?

Usage Note

This question leads the seminar to begin actively generalizing from the case, if it is not already doing so.

Analysis

Pranks are characteristic of large groups and seem to happen in educational and organizational settings where regimentation and shared residence bring students together. Regimentation provides a "system" to resist. Regimentation and shared residence foster group cohesion and provide the time and place for plotting together. Pranks seldom happen in classes at "commuter schools" where students have a great deal of autonomy and are dispersed except during class time.

Prank-prone schools and organizations often put members under a great deal of pressure to work hard and perform on demand, and the students look for release. Pranks are exciting, diverting, and great releasers of tension. In addition, the infantilizing effect of highly structured educational programs can be quite irritating to people who are used to more autonomy. Pranks may reflect both students' hostility to their condition of formal powerlessness and their desire to demonstrate their own informal sources of power and autonomy.

Finally, students often chafe at the rigidity with which they are cast in a student role, while others, who may be their own age or younger, are cast as instructors. Student pranks serve to remind instructors that they are human and not gods -- and give everyone a few precious

moments to experience each other out of role. An instructor who responds to the prank favorably demonstrates that he or she is a "regular person." The experience then can lead to a much deeper bond between instructor and students. In many cases the experience is tantamount to initiating the instructor as an honorary member of the section tribe.

* * *

The following questions refer to the (B) case:

7. What do you think of Bob Clarkson's philosophy of education? What do you see as the instructor's primary role in a case discussion?

8. In the earlier case, Ernie Budding argues for an interventionistic style of discussion leadership which seems to contrast with Bob Clarkson's "discussion pastures" approach. How would you characterize your own position, vis-à-vis theirs?

Usage Note

These questions require participants to articulate the educational philosophies of Bob Clarkson and Ernie Budding, to evaluate them, and to compare them with their own ways of thinking about teaching.

Budding and Clarkson can be seen as polar cases on a continuum that runs from interventionistic, content-oriented teaching to a process-oriented approach. Highlighting this continuum focuses attention on the very general question of how an instructor can manage both content and process in case discussions. The range defined by Budding's and Clarkson's approaches is quite wide, and usually stimulates a broad discussion of styles and philosophies of teaching.

All participants are encouraged to read "Ernie Budding (D)" in preparation for class. However, it is too optimistic to assume that all or even most participants will do so. Therefore, we often specially ask two or three participants to prepare for the day by rereading "Ernie Budding (D)." Seeding the section's memory in this way helps ensure a good discussion.

We have combined our analytical notes for Questions 7 and 8.

Analysis

The contrast between Ernie Budding's and Bob Clarkson's educational philosophies may be best summed up in their respective metaphors of teaching. Ernie speaks of "conceptual blocks" of material to be covered in each discussion. He specifies for himself not only the overall content to be taught in his course, but the subordinate topics to be covered in each class period. He organizes these in a logical sequence, creating building blocks of content. He prepares for class very much as one might for a lecture.

In his first year of teaching, Ernie uses sequences of rather closed-ended questions to get the section to consider the major points in his blocks. He asks students to supply key case facts and insights at a relatively low level of generality. After the experiences described in the "Ernie Budding (A), (B), and (C)" cases, Ernie opens up his questioning, and allows more student-initiated discussion. Rather than leading the students through the blocks in a predetermined sequence, Ernie now allows them to raise issues in any order that makes sense within the context of the day's discussion. Even in the (D) case, however, Ernie still sees his course as a series of topics that students must master. The cases are vehicles for bringing these topics to the attention of the students, and for giving them practice in applying key concepts to real situations. Under his ground rules, student excitement comes primarily from the progressive mastery of powerful concepts.

Clarkson, by contrast, uses the metaphor of "discussion pastures" and sees the instructor as a shepherd "policing the fences" -- moving his grazing students to a new area whenever a particular pasture becomes overworked. The cases provide the "fodder" which students digest to produce insights. These insights may be very much like Ernie Budding's "conceptual blocks." In Bob Clarkson's class, however, generalizations are more likely to be introduced by the students, and may well differ from the concepts Clarkson would have drawn out of the same cases. Clarkson does exercise some leadership in guiding students toward particular ideas. But he appears to put more emphasis on the richness and complexity of the cases, and on student generation of insights, than does Ernie Budding.

We believe a course should be supported by an overall conceptual scheme. Moreover, the instructor should consider the most effective order in which to present key concepts. Cases, readings, and other materials should be carefully chosen to introduce and allow the students to explore these concepts. In this sense Ernie Budding is on the right track.

However, we also think it is important that students learn to appreciate the complexity of situations, and to recognize that any situation is richer and more mysterious than the concepts that may be used to explain it. Moreover, history makes it clear that, in any field of knowledge, today's useful concepts will eventually be superseded by others. Thus we must help the students to use our concepts as starting points, rather than as conclusions. To this end, we believe, it is essential that students learn to produce, value, and use their own insights.

Thus we see the discussion class as a workshop in which students can get involved in the raw materials of cases and, under our increasingly light-handed guidance, learn to create usable, action-relevant insights. In this sense, we lean toward Clarkson's approach of grazing in "discussion pastures." We have found, however, that it is also important to incorporate elements of Ernie Budding's teaching style. An instructor must understand the conceptual structure of his or her subject and at times may need to focus student attention on key concepts -- teaching, in the conventional sense, a point.

However, too much teaching of this kind can encourage students to put too much confidence in the particular models presented -- to their future detriment. More important, it can prevent them from testing out and developing their own capacities for understanding and insight. Thus we believe that the most appropriate role for the instructor is often to manage the discussion process -- to "police the fences," as Clarkson puts it.

Clarkson's and Budding's views differ in other interesting ways. Ernie stresses the importance of "rigor" -- and what he seems to mean by the term is that students should learn to pay attention to and account for the facts in the case. That is, as their education progresses, their views should become increasingly grounded in the particulars of situations. This seems to us an important goal. Clarkson's primary concern in contrast, seems to be creating enthusiasm about the course questions. He describes the ideal instructor as being "tinder for discovery." He tries to create rapport with the students, presumably so that they can experience together the excitement of solving the conundrums presented in the cases -- and, by extension, in the professional world.

Both rigor and enthusiasm are needed for a successful case learning experience. Without enthusiasm, the student's rigor will be hollow and pointless. Without rigor, enthusiasm may simply generate a lot of half-baked ideas. However, we would define rigor somewhat more broadly than Ernie does. Rigorous work by students involves developing a logical and plausible understanding of business situations that is based on the facts of the situations and is chosen after an examination of alternative interpretations. Moreover, the understanding they adopt must be considered in light of their implications for action. Commitment to a perspective involves not only accepting a particular view of a situation, but also deciding on a course of action. And finally, the students should attempt to "feel into" these actions, to get a sense of whether they could really live with the decision.

Good teaching, then, combines rigor and enthusiasm. Perhaps significantly, the "Class on World Hunger (B)" case concludes with Clarkson wondering, "How do you uphold the standards of your school and the intellectual enterprise without becoming obnoxiously authoritarian so that you destroy or interrupt a delicate rapport?" It may be that Clarkson sensed a conflict between standards and rapport because he took too narrow a view of rigor, without reference to what the students need and value. In our view rigor is not something an instructor insists upon because it upholds some abstract standards, but rather a means of helping students generate better, more usable ideas. This goal is one that students understand and appreciate, and can become enthusiastic about.

At the outset of their teaching careers, Ernie Budding and Bob Clarkson have radically different views of the instructor-student learning contract, but they move closer together after two years' experience. Ernie originally tries hard to maintain a consistent and relatively explicit contract with the students. Sticking with his contract -- particularly the formal aspects -- seems to be a matter of pride. For example, he promises students that his grades will be based on the quality of class comments rather than the quantity, and takes some satisfaction in the students' shock when he carries through consistently. Ernie also gets into difficulty because he does not notice when his contract no longer fits the students' evolving situation. At the end of the "Ernie Budding" case sequence, he recognizes the need to modify contracts to match the students' needs.

Bob Clarkson, in contrast, starts his teaching career feeling insecure about his ability to maintain authority. He deliberately introduces uncertainty in his behavior, and thus in his contract, with the students as a means of strengthening his control. After some experience with the effects of this strategy, he comes to feel students are better served by more consistency in their instructor.

Interestingly, both instructors seem to be developing a more situationally based understanding of their teaching. Clarkson describes the importance of rapport. Though for him this seems to be largely a matter of enthusiasm and emotional closeness, good rapport inevitably gives him a more detailed understanding of his sections' learning process at any given moment. It is likely to enable him to adjust his contract with them more sensitively. Budding explicitly recognizes the need to become more attuned to his section, so as to be able to shift his contract as the students grow and change.

Suggestions for Building the Seminar Group

This case is often our next-to-last case of the semester, and thus the last for which full preparation and participation can be expected. (The very last class is usually less successful as a discussion than as a ritual of closing and completion -- which is perhaps as it should be.) "Class on World Hunger" provides the participants with an occasion for reflecting on what has come before, thinking philosophically about education, and exploring the connections between the seminar material and their own teaching.

As instructors we help create these moments for reflection. We use bridging, selective attention, and summarizing to highlight the seminar's efforts at generalization. Our questions also contribute to the shift of focus. We may ask more often, "What issues does this case raise for you?" or "What questions does this discussion leave you with?"

We find these last classes are a good time to reemphasize the complexity and mystery of teaching, the importance of becoming better and better at it, and the great value of diversity in approaches. Our overriding purpose in the teaching seminar is to create a setting in which instructors can talk about teaching. This aim is far more important than the particular questions we ask, the concepts we introduce, or the cases we examine. As the seminar concludes, it seems appropriate to underline this goal by showing our appreciation for the variety and richness of perspectives that participants have brought to our discussions.

Exhibit 1

Class on World Hunger

Study Questions

For student use when reading the (A) case:

1. How did Bob Clarkson handle the food fight? What is the worst thing he might have done? Why did his response work out well from both his point of view and from the point of view of many of the members of the class?

*   *   *

For student use when reading the (B) case:

1. Why are pranks a recurring phenomenon in most educational and organizational settings? Can their occurrence be predicted by an instructor? What dangers and opportunities do they present to you, as a section instructor?

2. What do you see as the critical elements in Bob Clarkson's teaching philosophy? In what key dimensions, if any, did it differ from Ernie Budding's? Your own?

Exhibit 2

Class on World Hunger

Discussion Questions

The following questions refer primarily to the (A) case:

1. How well, in your opinion, did Bob Clarkson handle the problem? What is the worst thing he could have done?

2. What precisely did he do? What particular aspects of his response do you believe were most helpful? Why?

3. What questions does this incident pose for you?

4. Could Bob Clarkson have anticipated this incident? If so, how and when? Could he have prepared for it? How?

5. Why did the prank happen when it did, at this point in the term? What was going on with the students that may have contributed to its occurrence?

6. Why are pranks such a recurring phenomenon in professional schools?

*   *   *

The following questions refer to the (B) case:

7. What do you think of Bob Clarkson's philosophy of education? What do you see as the instructor's primary role in a case discussion?

8. In the earlier case, Ernie Budding argues for an interventionistic style of discussion leadership which seems to contrast with Bob Clarkson's "discussion pastures" approach. How would you characterize your own position, vis-à-vis theirs?

Alternative Seminar Outline

James F. Moore

Our course outline has never settled into a fixed, definitive form, but continues to evolve each year. An alternative time-tested approach, however, is contained in the outline shown in Exhibit 1. We have organized a twelve-session seminar into five major units. The first three units explore several basic dimensions of teaching: managing the implicit and explicit contracts between instructor and student, using questions and responses strategically and sensitively, and listening effectively. The fourth unit shifts gears to focus on recurring difficulties faced by most teachers. Insights first developed in the earlier three units can now be used to address a wide range of problems. The fifth unit summarizes and reinforces the guiding outlines used in the professional school teaching seminar.

The first, introductory unit includes readings on the overall philosophy of the case method. Two classic statements -- E.P. Learned's "Reflections of a Case Method Teacher" and Charles I. Gragg's "Teachers Also Must Learn" -- provide excellent insight. We suggest one of two cases to begin the seminar. "Kurt Jacobs" is an intriguing and stimulating case that will give experienced instructors a great deal to chew on. If, however, the seminar consists primarily of younger instructors (especially doctoral candidates and teaching fellows), it may be more effective to begin with "Bill Curtis," which deals with the predicament of a graduate student making the difficult transition to the teacher's role and at the same time wrestling with stage fright. Most of these cases are incorporated into Teaching and the Case Method; the others may be ordered from Harvard Business School Publishing Division.

Our plan for the first day is perhaps worth sketching here. We generally begin with some introductory remarks about the nature of the seminar as a whole, acknowledging its history and aims. We point out that each seminar is different from all others; although there is a syllabus, the group will evolve its own style and priorities. This is as it should be, for we come together not as instructor and students but as colleagues in an exploratory venture. Following this opening, we ask participants to introduce themselves.

We then briefly preview the syllabus outline, noting the five units of the seminar, and say a few words about the process we will follow in our meetings. We point out that the role of the instructor involves posing questions and moderating the discussion, and that for each case the group will tackle three central questions:

1. What is going on?
2. What should the protagonist do?
3. What questions and/or generalizations are suggested by the case?

With this introduction, we then turn to the first case.

The second unit of the seminar, usually consisting of two or three cases, focuses on the issue of instructor-student learning contracts. The readings emphasize the difference between methods of teaching that center on the instructor as dispenser of authoritative knowledge and those that confront students with actual or simulated challenges from their chosen field of practice. A key reading suggestion is the classic piece "Louis Agassiz as a Teacher."

The first case in this unit addresses problems in the establishment and management of the instructor-student learning contract -- problems that we believe arise in all sorts of teaching situations. The second case focuses on issues more specifically relevant to case method teaching. "Henry Jasper" concerns an instructor who is unaware of a critical implicit contract until an accidental violation of it sends a student into paroxysms. "Ernie Budding" describes a case method instructor who must learn to renegotiate the contract when students outgrow the original agreement.

The third unit emphasizes the related arts of listening, questioning, and responding to students. The readings include "Active Listening" by Carl Rogers and Richard Farson, and "Note on Process Observation" by Anne Harlan and John Gabarro, which offers pertinent suggestions for understanding group dynamics. There are only two cases in this unit. "Assistant Professor Graham and Ms. Macomber" -- one of our most popular cases -- concerns a professor whose punishing cross-examination of a student highlights the power of questions and responses -- for good or ill. "Bill Jones" emphasizes the crucial and complementary skill of listening to students.

The fourth and longest unit of the

seminar focuses on a wide range of knotty problems faced by most teachers, experienced or new. "Suzie Simons" deals with grading and plagiarism as well as ways to respond to students who implicitly ask for counseling and/or extra emotional support. In "The Section Just Took Over: A Student's Reflections," a highly controlling instructor's class erupts into chaos over the issue of whether a company described in a case was acting morally, and whether moral issues should be discussed in class at all. Discussion of the case generally focuses on issues of freedom and control in case teaching.

In "We're Just Wasting Our Time," it is the instructor who provides the drama -- storming out after chastising a section on its lack of preparation. The case raises the question of how to deal with student apathy and lack of preparation. In "Trevor Jones," the instructor also causes the drama -- this time by abruptly "firing" a student during an impromptu, unannounced role-playing exercise, deeply angering the rest of the class. The case highlights the risks as well as the benefits of role playing, and leads to a consideration of prudent precautions to take when using involvement-enhancing pedagogical techniques.

The "Class on World Hunger" describes a potentially offensive prank played on a well-liked young instructor. In addition to the question of how to deal with pranks in class, this case highlights the issue of how an instructor can establish (or recover) authority without alienating the students and/or slipping over into authoritarianism. Moreover, because the case text includes the instructor's well-considered reflections on his first two years of teaching, it can stimulate a valuable discussion of educational philosophy, as well as a review and summary of concerns expressed over the course of the seminar.

"What Do We Do Now, Professor?" details a complex situation involving alleged cheating by students in writing up a required report. It poses the difficult question "Where is the line between desired student cooperation and excessive collaboration in the preparation of a written assignment?" The reading for this unit, "Training for Uncertainty," provides a rich backdrop for these cases; it points out

the limits of propositional knowledge in professional practice, and draws implications for teaching.

Part V features the last case on our syllabus -- "Bob Thompson" -- which concerns a student who, backed by a senior faculty member, pressures a young instructor to change his grade. The case gives participants an opportunity to explore the always troublesome issue of grading and to consider the more general question of how to respond to external pressures. The fifth unit also concludes the seminar with Charles Gragg's "Because Wisdom Can't Be Told," a reading which summarizes the benefits of the case method of teaching and, implicitly, other simulation-oriented approaches to professional education:

Teachers, since it is their avowed objective to extend the knowledge boundaries of others, are particularly beset by the temptation to tell what they know -- to point out right paths of thought and action. . . .

Yet, no amount of information, whether of theory or fact, in itself improves insight and judgment or increases ability to act wisely under conditions of responsibility. . . . The body of generally accepted business theory may be equally familiar to all executives, yet the decisions reached by the various individuals are unlikely to be the same or to have equal merit.

We cannot effectively use the insight and knowledge of others; it must be our knowledge and insight that we use. . . . The outstanding virtue of the case system is that it is suited to inspiring activity, under realistic conditions, on the part of the students; it takes them out of the role of passive absorbers and makes them partners in the joint processes of learning and of furthering learning.

To those who decide to experiment with this seminar format, we offer our best wishes. Our own experience has been that seminar discussions provide extraordinary opportunities for meeting and learning from one's colleagues, and for examining and developing one's own discussion leadership skills.

Exhibit 1

Alternative Seminar Outline
for Professional School Instructors

I. INTRODUCTION

Readings: Teachers Also Must Learn
               The Use of Cases in Management Education (9-376-240)
               Reflections of a Case Method Teacher (9-381-006)

Case: Kurt Jacobs (9-376-094)

For groups and participants with limited or no experience with the
case method, we also suggest:

Case: Bill Curtis (9-376-096)

II. ESTABLISHING THE INSTRUCTOR-STUDENT LEARNING CONTRACT

Readings: Louis Agassiz as a Teacher
               The Development of a Professional Self-Image[1]
               Bike Riding and the Art of Learning

Case: Henry Jasper (A) (9-378-036)
               Henry Jasper (B)* (9-378-037)

Case: Ernie Budding (A) (9-381-038)
               Ernie Budding (B) (9-381-039)
               Ernie Budding (C)* (9-381-040)

III. THE RELATED ARTS OF QUESTIONING, RESPONDING, AND
      LISTENING

Readings: Active Listening
               Note on Process Observation (9-477-029)

Case: Assistant Professor Graham and Ms. Macomber (A)
               (9-379-020)
               Assistant Professor Graham and Ms. Macomber (B)*
               (9-379-021)
               Assistant Professor Graham and Ms. Macomber (C)*
               (9-379-022)

Case: Bill Jones (A) (9-378-038)
               Bill Jones (B)* (9-378-039)

IV. LEADING THE DISCUSSION PROCESS: THE CRITICAL OPERATING
     ISSUES

Reading: Training for Uncertainty[2]

Cases: Suzie Simons (A) (9-378-033)
               Suzie Simons (B)* (9-378-034)

---

1. Mary Jean Huntington, "The Development of a Professional Self-Image" in *The Student-Physician*
by R. K. Marton, G. G. Reader, and P. L. Kendall, eds. (Cambridge: Harvard University
Press, 1957).
2. Renee C. Fox, "Training for Uncertainty" in *The Student-Physician.*

Case: The Section Just Took Over: A Student's Reflections
                (9-379-007)

Case: We're Just Wasting Our Time (9-378-035)

Case: Trevor Jones (9-380-016)

Case: Class on World Hunger (A) (9-381-042)
                Class on World Hunger (B) (9-381-043)

Case: What Do We Do Now, Professor? (A) (9-376-161)
                What Do We Do Now, Professor? (B)* (9-376-162)
                What Do We Do Now, Professor? (C)* (9-376-163)
                What Do We Do Now, Professor? (D)* (9-376-164)

V.   SUMMARY

Reading: Because Wisdom Can't Be Told (9-451-005)

Case: Bob Thompson (A) (9-379-004)
                Bob Thompson (B)* (9-379-005)
                Bob Thompson (C)* (9-379-006)

* To be distributed by the discussion leader

Note: Most of the above entries can be found in Teaching and the Case
Method. Identifying numbers may be used to order individual entries from
HBS Publishing Division, Soldiers Field, Boston, Mass. 02163. (Use order
form at back of this book.)

Part III Stand-Alone Mini-Seminar

*"Bill Curtis" Teaching Note (HBS No. 5–384–096) and "Suzie Simons" Teaching Note (HBS No. 5–384–047) may be ordered from HBS Publishing Division, Harvard Business School, Boston, MA 02163. (Use Order Form at end of book.)

Stand-Alone Mini-Seminar

Introduction

Part III includes a sample mini-seminar for those who want to continue the primary seminar program. This mini-seminar focuses on problems encountered on the first day in the classroom and also the challenges encountered in a new instructor's first year.

If you wish to include this Part III mini-seminar in your program, you may order additional copies of the individual cases from the Harvard Business School Publishing Division, Soldiers Field, Boston, Mass. 02163. Order numbers appear in the copyright line on the first page of each case, and an order form appears at the end of this book. Reproduction of these cases is prohibited.

Bill Curtis

Bill Curtis, 26, MBA from the University of Southern California with four years of industrial experience, was in his second year of Metropolitan's doctoral program. Bill was currently working half time writing cases for Professor Wayne Anderson. In addition, as part of the Policy area's doctoral teaching requirement, Bill was sitting in on Policy classes to observe senior instructors at work. The teaching program also required Bill to teach several Policy classes with a "coach" -- professor -- in attendance.

As part of this second assignment, Bill was given the chance to teach a Policy class in the seventh week of the spring semester. In preparation Bill observed five of Professor Anderson's Section A Policy classes. On the first of these visits, Professor Anderson introduced Bill as his research assistant and author of a case studied by the section.

All Policy sections participated in a report program. Three times during the semester each student prepared, and handed in before class, a 1,000- to 1,500-word report on the case to be discussed in class that day. All Policy professors agreed that a report assignment stimulated more than usual student case preparation.

Bill's first Section A teaching assignment occurred on the day Section A's second report was due. The opening question Bill planned to ask was related to, but different from, the specific question assigned to students as their written assignment.

On the day in question, a smiling Professor Anderson opened the class with "I am lucky to get a day off. Bill, as you know, is in the doctoral program and is possibly interested in teaching so we are giving him the opportunity to teach this case." He then sat down in an open seat in the back row near the rear exit of the classroom.

This case was written by Professor C. Roland Christensen for the Developing Discussion Leadership Skills Seminar. While the case is based on data supplied by participants involved, all names and some peripheral facts have been disguised.

The following is Bill's third-person summary of his first teaching experience.

The Filibuster

The big day had arrived! Bill Curtis, a second-year DBA candidate was making his Metropolitan Business School teaching debut before a class of MBA wolves. Bill had only limited teaching experience and was just finishing his second semester of teaching an evening course at a local undergraduate business school. But that school was different from Metropolitan -- it was considered "the minor leagues." The problems there involved getting students to prepare for class and to participate. In "the pit" at Met before a class of second-year MBAs, these would be the least of his problems, especially since the class had the assignment of preparing a written report on the case he was to teach.

Bill had met the day before with Professor Anderson. They discussed general teaching strategies for the case for several hours and, as well, reviewed some of the specific problems associated with class discussion of a case also used for student written report purposes. They also prepared a list of six or eight "strong" students to whom Bill might turn for class contributions. Bill came up with his own teaching plan and questions. He decided to begin the class by asking, "If you were in Ed Roberts's [the general manager of the involved company] position, what factors would you consider in deciding whether to recommend expanding your plant's capacity?"

Bill felt a flutter of butterflies in his stomach as Professor Anderson finished his opening remarks and introduced him to the class. He walked to the center of the room, stood in front of the chalkboard, and spread his 10 pages of yellow notes across the instructor's table. There were good-natured chuckles from the class. What could be a more typical beginning! Bill looked out to the class and wondered if his voice would work; it had the night before when he had asked the empty classroom his opening question at least a dozen times. When you are scared you don't take chances -- you cover all the bases!

His voice was strong and clear, and the student he called on, an articulate Miller Scholar,[1] began to talk. Bill breathed a sigh of relief. "He's talking now and at least I'll get a chance to calm my nerves." Initially Bill began to write the student's key points on the board, but after awhile he stopped and stood behind the instructor's table, listening to the student. About three minutes passed, and Bill began to feel uneasy. The Miller Scholar was talking and not saying much of value. As Bill looked across the class he saw several students beginning to smile. Four minutes passed, then five. By now there were several students talking to their seatmates, and others were sporting broad grins.

"It's a filibuster!" he realized. The Miller Scholar had taken over, and the class was with him . . . six minutes . . . seven. . . .

---

1. The James C. Miller Scholars were selected by the faculty on the basis of academic achievement. Membership was restricted to the top five percent of the class.

The Introduction (A)

> Well . . . Mike is from Westin, Connecticut. He attended Westin Central High School. So far, he likes his roommate. Mike has a red Firebird which he drives too fast. Mike likes to drink, uses cocaine often, has a 21-year-old girlfriend who is . . . [pause], oh yes, and he can't wait for this boring class to get over.

With only a few minutes of class remaining, freshman Dianne Quinn glanced around the room, appearing to look for approval as she completed her introduction of the twenty-sixth and final student in the first meeting of the English Literature and Composition (ELC) class at Pax Vobiscum College (PVC).

Professor Leslie O'Connor felt her face burn with anger. Using a tried and true exercise to help students get to know one another, she had asked the freshmen to pair up and interview one another. Each student would then introduce the other to the rest of the class. Leslie sensed an uneasiness in the room:

> After a few gasps, no one moved. No one even shuffled a paper. The students appeared to be avoiding any eye contact. Many were looking down at their hands. Dianne had gone from the innocuous, to the inappropriate, to playing dirty pool. I was <u>really</u> annoyed. This was the first day of this class's college career.

Pax Vobiscum College

Pax Vobiscum College (PVC) first opened its doors to provide an education to the sons of the swelling Irish and Italian Catholic immigrant population of Metropolis. In time, PVC relocated from its urban beginnings to an idyllic suburban setting resplendent with Gothic spires and green

Additional copies of this case for seminar participants may be ordered from the Harvard Business School Publishing Division. Use HBS Order No. 9-386-146 and the order form at the back of this book.

This case was written by Research Assistant Marina McCarthy in collaboration with University Professor C. Roland Christensen for the Developing Discussion Leadership Skills and Teaching by the Case Method seminars. While the case is based on data furnished by participants involved, all names and some peripheral facts have been disguised.

quads. PVC alums are fiercely loyal; many of its students are the second and even third generation of their families to attend.

Students today still come from predominantly Catholic homes, with both parents and student seeking a strong liberal arts program grounded in Christian values. Despite a more geographically diverse and affluent student body, the character and ethos of the school have remained intact. Having marked its first decade of full coeducation in all of its five colleges and academic departments, PVC was also enjoying one of its healthiest applicant pools in years.

Leslie O'Connor

Leslie O'Connor had a fondness for PVC. Although she was not a graduate, she had cross-registered into the English department during her senior year from a nearby secular university. She remained in touch with her PVC professors over the decade that followed, and was eventually invited to join the faculty to teach freshman English. In fact, she had not applied for a position at PVC; rather, a senior professor had telephoned early one summer to ask her if she would like to teach there. Leslie was pleased with the way her ELC classes were going, and was encouraged by her consistently high reviews.

Leslie had always found student introduction a technique useful in breaking down the strained atmosphere of the first day. Since students were often uncomfortable when asked to speak about themselves, Leslie asked each to socialize briefly with a neighbor before introducing him or her to the class. The result was a lighter treatment instead of the previously stilted and awkward recitations.

Leslie's Version of the Incident

The beginning of that first class was uneventful. My general administrative noise included a welcome to PVC. I jokingly assured the students that they were not "admissions mistakes" and commended the class for making a great choice -- coming to PVC. Introducing myself, I explained that I had been a student in the English department in the early 1970s, had been teaching for the past several years, and was now finishing my doctoral work at another institution, where I also had an additional teaching commitment. I then asked the class to break out of rows and form a circle. While the students were moving their chairs I walked over to the instructor's desk on the raised platform at the front of the room where I had left my briefcase and various papers. As I rummaged through my briefcase looking for the folder containing my syllabus, course description, and 3x5 cards, I thought, "Who on earth would ever actually sit up here? I'd feel pompous!"

Before distributing the syllabus and course description, I asked the class to fill in their names, local phone numbers, and addresses on the 3x5 cards I was passing out. I also asked them to write down if they had a nickname they preferred to be called. Finally, I asked them to indicate where they had gone to high school.

I waited until the other handouts had made their way around the circle before briefly going over course content and expectations. Although I had pushed a student chair for myself into the circle, I continued to stand as I introduced the course.

Explaining that I was adopting a model that I had used in an upper level course the previous term, I announced that we were going to drop one class meeting per week and lengthen the second by fifteen minutes to make time for individual writing conferences. I thought I heard an "Oh goody!" when I mentioned the canceled class, but I just treated the comment as innocuous and proceeded. . . . It just didn't sound funny or humorous enough to pick up on. . . .

I hoped that the class would share my interest and enthusiasm for the experiment, and related how the students last term had specifically found the one-to-one conferences to be very helpful. If anyone did not feel comfortable with the design of the course, I suggested that he or she see me after class so I could suggest another section in the same time slot.

Since there were no questions about the course design, I proceeded to hold up the texts we would be using for the semester. I joked that Strunk and White's Elements of Style would be our bible for the term. A few smiles broke through the intense notetaking. I continued to discuss the syllabus and the course description handout.

To make the transition from texts and syllabi to student introductions, I mentioned the final feature of last term's seminar: two students each week were responsible for bringing refreshments. I asked for a show of hands if they wanted to carry on the tradition. I smiled at the enthusiasm and then reached into my folder to pull out two "sign-up sheets." Chuckling, I said, "I thought you would! There should be enough slots for everyone to sign once; if there are any extra spaces, I'll fill in! Now, to kick off, I'll supply for today. These are store-bought. I don't want anyone to feel the pressure to be fancy." I then retrieved a bag from the desk at the front of the room. Several students began to laugh. One joked, "I thought I smelled baked goods!"

As soon as I asked the students to pair up and interview one another, the noise level in the class rose. I was pleased. For all but one student (I had taken a poll), this was their last class of the day (3:00-4:15). It had been a long day for most of them -- their first day of college. Since all of the first-year classes are large lectures, the group was in its first and only "small" class of the day. The English department feels strongly about keeping the sections small -- "almost like a homeroom," one of my senior colleagues said. Hence, we had 80 sections of freshman English -- give or take a few -- each year.

The atmosphere was light and the introductions began. I was now seated in the semicircle, diligently taking notes as each student spoke. All the while I nodded and maintained eye contact to encourage the speaker. I guess I gave them carte blanche to say what they wanted. I urged the students to find out a bit about their neighbor's background -- where he or she was from, what high school they attended, any talents -- musical, theatrical, athletic.

The group was learning who had played what instrument or what sport in high school, who was from the same section of the same state. A camaraderie was building. I noticed two female students from Florida, who hadn't appeared to know each other, signaling each other to meet after class. Two male students found out that they had both been high school lacrosse players and were going to "walk on" at PVC's varsity tryouts that afternoon.

When Dianne made her inappropriate introduction of Mike, I fumed. Like a high-speed slide carousel, options of what to do flashed through my mind.

Part of me wanted to slam my hand on my desk. A little shock value often goes a long way if you reserve it for emergencies. But I wasn't at a real desk. I had taken a student desk and was facing the class.

I couldn't believe someone would make a wise remark like that on the first day of college. I was angry at myself for having nodded at Dianne as she began her seemingly innocent introduction. I had smiled and encouraged her to continue. . . . Some of the previous students had been a bit nervous speaking up in class. . . .

Though I was furious at Dianne, what about Mike? His chair was turned to the side so I couldn't see his facial expression or reaction. Maybe Mike and Dianne knew each other before coming to PVC. It might have been an attempt at humor on her or both their parts. Regardless -- the tone was inappropriate. Maybe Mike was being naive -- or perhaps a wise guy -- by telling Dianne as much as he did. Perhaps he did not realize that she was naively going to repeat everything. I felt my face getting redder and hotter.

After Class

Back in her third-floor office, Leslie removed her jacket and carefully hung it on the back of her chair. She gave her skirt a customary check for chalk smudges and muttered how she must remember not to wear navy on "teaching days." Seated behind her desk, Leslie put her feet up and leaned back. Her colleague and friend from across the corridor, Jo Smith, noted Leslie's knit brow and, sensing that she was upset, pulled up a chair and closed the door. Jo and Leslie saw eye to eye on many professional and personal issues. Leslie rose and stood with her back to the window, deliberately tapping a pencil in her left palm. The afternoon sun was streaming into the office; Leslie paused for a moment to adjust the curtains. She leaned forward against the window sill, supporting herself with both elbows. Gazing out onto the quad, she began twisting a stray paperclip as she prepared to recount Dianne's introduction of Mike O'Neil. Irritation filled her voice as she began.

Leslie Confides in Her Colleague

This first class today has really hit a raw nerve. One thing I especially enjoy about teaching on the college level is that you don't have to fuss with discipline. The students are here to learn and you don't have to stand on your head to entertain, cajole, and deal with those who don't want to be here. You know, many of the PVC instructors in our department hate to teach freshmen. We often hear them say, "Ugh, a required course. . . . Freshmen are so young and immature. Their skills are getting worse and worse every year." My vantage point is obviously much different. The course may be compulsory, but college is not. I enjoy teaching freshmen. I enjoy teaching. I enjoy talking about teaching. In fact, there are several senior faculty members with whom I regularly get together to talk about pedagogy and ideas about teaching.

Why, just last week, a senior faculty member referred several students to me who were interested in teaching. He thought I might have some advice for them.

Dianne's inappropriate introduction really took me by surprise; but in retrospect, maybe it shouldn't have. Maybe I should have paid more attention to the reaction to my canceling a class per week. That "Oh goody!" is a bit haunting now. But all had been going along so smoothly at that point. I looked at the clock and had only a few minutes to go. The sudden quiet in the class led me to conclude that the students were concerned as well. What would you have done?

The Introduction (B)

Dianne's introduction of Mike O'Neil had clearly jolted Leslie. As Dianne concluded, Leslie slowly sat back in her seat and crossed her arms.

Leslie Recalls the Last Two Minutes

It was over before I realized it. I was too stunned to interrupt Dianne. My first impulse was to use humor to diffuse the situation. I tried to make light of things by exaggerated sarcasm. "Well," I moaned, "now <u>there's</u> a different introduction." I was a bit uncomfortable, however, since the humor seemed to have little effect on the tension in the class. I felt I needed to convey more disapproval. After conspicuously glancing at the clock to convey my concern with time, I then tried to establish eye contact with members of the group. After a short pause, in which I straightened out my papers, I lowered my voice and announced, "See you on Wednesday. You probably all need time to get to the bookstore before the dinner hour." I tried to be deliberate without sounding strained. I hoped that my tone was signaling disapproval of Dianne and Mike to all assembled. Symbolically closing the folders in front of me to emphasize closure, I stood up and went over to the instructor's desk on the raised platform in front of the classroom. I proceeded to file extra syllabi and handouts into my briefcase while nodding and acknowledging students as they somewhat awkwardly left the room.

Students milled about, and connections made in class introductions were slowly pursued. Dianne darted toward me. She began to tell me excitedly that English had been her favorite subject in high school and that she had written a major paper on James Joyce that she wanted to show me during our first

Additional copies of this case for seminar participants may be ordered from the Harvard Business School Publishing Division. Use HBS Order No. 9-386-147 and the order form at the back of this book.

This case was written by Research Assistant Marina McCarthy in collaboration with University Professor C. Roland Christensen for the Developing Discussion Leadership Skills and Teaching by the Case Method seminars. While the case is based on data furnished by participants involved, all names and some peripheral facts have been disguised.

conference. Her attempt to ingratiate herself further annoyed me. Her eagerness did not seem at all sincere. Even if all that she had said in her introduction about Mike were true, her lack of discretion irritated me. I was running through several scenarios of what to say to her; instead, I smiled perfunctorily and kept nodding as the other students and Dianne left the room.

After the Students Left

After the class had left, Leslie turned off the lights and took the elevator to her office. Her ensuing discussion with Jo had not resolved much. Leslie stewed for a couple of days before deciding that she was going to ask both Mike and Dianne to meet with her after the next class meeting. Although much was left up in the air that week, she was glad she had initially let the episode drop. To Leslie's surprise, however, Dianne did not come to the next class.

Since I had not anticipated this turn in events, I dismissed speaking with Mike at all. In a way, I felt a sense of relief -- as if the problem was over. In my mind, the case had solved itself: Dianne had behaved inappropriately and must have decided to change to another section.

The Introduction (C)

Two Months Later

Two months had passed since that first class. Leslie was pleased with the way her freshman section was progressing. The students seemed happy, and there had been a steady stream of roommates and friends of class members asking to be admitted to Leslie's section second semester. Bringing food had not been an issue at all. Each week two members brought provisions. In hindsight, however, Leslie vowed never to be "first" again. The weekly conferences were very successful and the class meetings had taken on the ambience of a seminar as hoped. As Leslie had thought, Mike O'Neil proved not to be a difficulty. Interestingly, they developed a quick rapport.

Returning from lunch one late October afternoon, Leslie and Jo grabbed their mail and a cup of coffee before returning to their offices. As Leslie was unlocking her door, she noticed a scrawled note on the floor. Setting her coffee and mail on the filing cabinet inside the door, she read the note. Shaking her head, she murmured, "He's _only_ 18 years old!" Then she turned to Jo: "Want an update on my 3 o'clock class? Read this."

Dear Professor O'Connor,

I appreciate the extension you granted me on this paper. I apologize for not being able to make the 3:00 Wednesday appointment. I was home from Tuesday morning through Wednesday afternoon to participate in the birth of my child by my girlfriend. _She_ was born Tuesday afternoon and was named Kathryn Hope O'Neil. Once again, I appreciate your understanding. Thank you.

-- Michael O'Neil

This case was written by Research Assistant Marina McCarthy in collaboration with University Professor C. Roland Christensen for the Developing Discussion Leadership Skills and Teaching by the Case Method seminars. While the case is based on data furnished by participants involved, all names and some peripheral facts have been disguised.

Leslie was not surprised by the note. Mike had told her during one of their initial conferences that his girlfriend was pregnant and that they both had decided against marrying. He also admitted to enjoying English class -- his most hated subject in high school, where he apparently did not get along with his English teacher.

Upon rereading Mike's note, Leslie noted that "she" had been underlined. She wondered whether Mike meant her to notice with approval that his new child was a girl. "I guess I should congratulate him the next time I see him," Leslie thought. "It's an awkward situation." She looked back on that first class meeting:

I sensed from Michael that even if he was a culprit that first day of class, he has since decided to straighten out. There's a puzzle here that I'll probably never solve. Further, I have no interest in finding out his role that day -- it's water under the bridge. He seems to have matured tremendously -- in the last several weeks in particular. Perhaps the impending responsibility of a son or daughter began to dawn on him. You know, he seems to have a real need to let a significant adult be aware of his new circumstances. He has an excuse to talk with me since we have scheduled weekly writing conferences of students.

I briefly thought of referring Mike to the counseling or dean of students' offices, but because of previous experiences in which I found them to be of little or no help, I decided to be "Mike's ear."

Leslie Confers with Another Student

Two weeks after receiving the note from Michael O'Neil, Leslie found herself in an intriguing conference with Jack Casey, one of the more active contributors in the class. Jack was a thoughtful and sensitive student who had impressed several of his classmates with his observations and comments. One student, Susan Mangan, specifically referring to Jack one afternoon in a conference, said, "You know, I've never heard guys talk up in class before -- especially about literature!"

Leslie recounts her conversation with Jack:

Out of the blue, Jack asked me if I knew about Mike's new daughter. I nodded affirmatively. Jack appeared distressed. He told me that everyone else in the class knew as well -- apparently it was quite a shock to them. Jack looked up from the essay we had been working on and remarked, "You know, Professor O'Connor, there are several of us who are still angry about the way he treated you that first day of class." I sat back in my chair and realized that although the incident was more or less passe in my mind, it had never been resolved for some or perhaps all of the rest of the class. Did they notice something about Mike's behavior that day that I hadn't? How could I have avoided noticing any subsequent tension in the class? I had often arbitrarily paired and grouped students during class. Were there problems that I had not noticed? What had (or should have) the students expected of me as a result of that first class? Finally, was Jack off base and not representative of the group? This, too, was a possibility. That first class was much more complex than I had realized.

The Introduction

Teaching Note

This teaching note has been prepared as an aid to instructors in the classroom use of the case series "The Introduction" (A) 9-386-146, (B) 9-386-147, and (C) 9-386-148.

Usage

1) "The Introduction" can be used as a springboard for a discussion on <u>what to do on the first day</u> of class. Seminar participants can examine the manner in which Leslie O'Connor chose to begin her class. They may analyze the choices she made, provide alternatives, or offer versions of how they have begun their own first classes.

2) "The Introduction" can also be viewed as a study in <u>dealing with a problem student</u>. Seminar participants may regard one or all three students in the case (Dianne Quinn, Michael O'Neil, and Jack Casey) as "problems" and can probably suggest a variety of options for dealing with them.

A related discussion could evolve here, addressing the issue of <u>control in higher education</u>. Some of the seminar participants may feel that control or discipline "is not what it used to be." Participants may see Dianne or Mike as symptomatic of a larger issue. The discussion leader should not initiate this topic, however, but monitor it should it emerge.

3) Perhaps less obvious for discussion is the issue of <u>consulting with colleagues about a professional concern or problem</u>. We learn in the (A) case that Leslie is open and frank with Jo Smith, a colleague who notices she is upset. Participants may venture into the pros and cons -- risks and benefits -- of sharing one's problems or concerns.

4) Depending on the sequence of the cases, the participants may want to <u>compare "Henry Jasper" with "The Introduction."</u> In both cases, it appears the instructor is "embodying an issue" for a student. Just as Henry Jasper compares his teaching fellow, Carol Cutler, to his castrating elementary school teachers, Mike's later conversation with Leslie [in the (C) case] suggests that he had trouble with his high school English teacher.

Case Summary

The (A) Case

"The Introduction" is about a young but experienced instructor's first class of the academic year -- a required freshman English class at Pax Vobiscum College (PVC). Leslie O'Connor, the instructor, has taught at PVC, a large Catholic university, for several years. In addition to teaching at PVC, she is a doctoral student at a nearby university.

Leslie has taught freshman English before. The model that she used with a mixed-class elective/seminar the previous term had proved to be very effective. She decides to adopt it for use with her freshmen in the fall.

After announcing course requirements, handing out syllabi, and so forth, Leslie has the students form a circle, pair up in twos, and interview one another. They are asked to find out about their neighbors so that each student can then introduce the other to the rest of the class. Introductions are proceeding smoothly until the last (twenty-sixth student) introduction. A female student introduces a male student as follows:

> Well . . . Mike is from Westin, Connecticut. He attended Westin Central High School. So far, he likes his roommate. Mike has a red Firebird which he drives too fast. Mike likes to drink, uses cocaine often, has a 21-year-old girlfriend who is . . . [pause], oh yes, and he can't wait for this boring class to get over.

Leslie is angry. She returns to her office

and recounts "the introduction" to Jo Smith, her colleague from across the hall.

The (B) Case

In (B) we learn what Leslie did with the few remaining minutes of class. She decides to dismiss the group early, hoping that her tone of voice conveys to the group her disapproval of both students involved in the introduction (Dianne Quinn and Mike O'Neil). Leslie then nods and acknowledges students as they leave the room. Dianne attempts to engage Leslie in a conversation about James Joyce after class, but Leslie is perfunctory in her responses and continues to nod and acknowledge the other students as they leave the room. Leslie never notices Mike leave the room; moreover, she never notices his expression or reactions during "the introduction."

After consulting with Jo, Leslie decides that the best resolution would be to ask both Dianne and Mike to see her after the next class meeting. Dianne, however, does not show up in class. Leslie assumes Dianne has transferred to another section and never bothers to pursue talking with Mike. She recalls:

> Since I had not anticipated this turn in events, I dismissed speaking with Mike at all. In a way I felt a sense of relief -- as if the problem was over. In my mind the case had solved itself: Dianne had behaved inappropriately, and must have decided to change to another section.

The (C) Case

Two months pass. Leslie feels the class is going very well. She and Mike O'Neil have developed a good rapport. Mike has told Leslie how much he enjoys English class. He is a faithful contributor to class discussions and generally has a very good attitude. Mike also tells Leslie that he and his girlfriend are anticipating the birth of a child. Leslie notes Mike's increasing maturity as the weeks progress. Upon returning from lunch one afternoon, Leslie finds a note under her door from Mike, informing her that a daughter was born several days before. Leslie confers with Jo about the note. She also reflects back to that first day of class and briefly conjectures about the degree of Mike's involvement in the introduction. She then decides "it's water under the bridge."

Within two weeks of receiving Mike's note, Leslie is in the middle of a student conference with one of the more vocal students in the class, Jack Casey. He unexpectedly changes the topic and asks Leslie if she knows about Mike's daughter. He volunteers that several in the class -- himself included -- are quite shocked. He continues, telling Leslie that he (and others in the class) are still disturbed "over the way Mike treated you that first day in class." Leslie is perplexed. She realizes that although the case is passé in her mind, it was never resolved for Jack and perhaps for others in the class as well. She concludes, "That first class was much more complex than I had realized."

Questions for Discussion

After the (A) case has been read:

1. **What is the teaching situation? Specifically, a) What type of school is PVC? b) What is the physical makeup of the room? c) What is the design of the course?**

    a) PVC is a traditional Catholic university that became completely coeducational only within the last decade. Originally an urban university for the city's immigrant Catholic population, it later moved to its present suburban Gothic campus. It is currently enjoying an exceptionally healthy admission pool for the fifth straight year, and is expanding its facilities and programs while other institutions of higher learning are experiencing retrenchment.

    b) Leslie O'Connor's classroom is a large room, presumably designed for lecturing. It has a raised platform at the front of the room, on which sits a faculty desk. When she initially enters the room, chairs are arranged in rows.

    c) Freshman English at PVC is the only small class that entering students experience during their first term. Classes are intentionally small -- but the case does not indicate whether this choice is made by the university or the English Department. Leslie O'Connor has taught freshman English before but decides to depart from her customary practices because of her favorable recent experience teaching a mixed-level elective.

She drops one class meeting per week, lengthens the second, and adds one-to-one writing conferrences. When members of the group agree to take turns bringing refreshments, Leslie announces she will initiate the tradition and produces a bag of cookies.

2. What do we know about Leslie O'Connor?

Leslie O'Connor is an instructor in a predominantly male department of the university. She is a doctoral student at another institution, though she once had been an undergraduate in the PVC English Department. Her previous success in teaching English is what prompted her old English professor to ask if she would be interested in teaching freshmen at PVC. Leslie is quite friendly with a colleague across the hall from her office.

3. What sequence does Leslie take in opening her class?

a) Distributes her syllabus and discusses course requirements.

b) Informs the group that she is modeling the freshman English class after a mixed-class seminar that she taught the previous term.

c) Substitutes individual student conferences for one class per week. Lengthens the remaining class meetings.

d) Determines first that the class wants to keep the "refreshment tradition," then passes out refreshments (in the spirit of the previous semester's seminar).

e) Asks students to form a circle, pair up and each interview his or her neighbor, then introduce him or her to the rest of the class.

4. How does the class react to Dianne and Mike and "the introduction?"

According to Leslie, the students appear uncomfortable. A few gasp, and silence falls. They appear to be avoiding eye contact.

Evaluation

5. What is your evaluation of Leslie's

opening? What else might she have done?

6. How well did she carry out her plan?

7. What risks, if any, were involved?

(The following is not an answer per se to Questions 5, 6, and 7, but touches on some points to be made and further questions to be raised.)

Leslie could have begun by asking for introductions and then discussing the syllabus. Instead, she wanted to deal with administrative issues first. She felt she needed to inform the class that she was canceling one class meeting per week and lengthening a second. Some students might have commitments -- other classes, jobs, and so forth -- after class. They needed to know about the altered schedule and make arrangements or change sections. Meeting from 3:00 to 4:30 instead of from 3:00 to 4:15 might make a difference to students who worked in the dining hall, for example. Given that the students were "just freshmen," should Leslie have held the announcement for a week?

Each class likes to think of itself as unique. Perhaps Leslie was undiplomatic in giving the impression she was trying to clone a successful class from the previous semester. Conversely, could the freshmen be flattered that Leslie was using an "upperclass" model with them? What were Leslie's assumptions about a _required_ course vis-à-vis an elective?

What is appropriate for one group may not be for another; perhaps passing out refreshments to a group of students fresh out of high school was a mistake. On the other hand, the students seemed eager to talk with their neighbors and introduce each other. The baked goods may have loosened up the tense atmosphere of the first day.

Leslie could have asked students to introduce themselves, but she found that pairing students loosened up introductions. Did the students find the exercise too alien from their experiences -- or their expectation of college? Did they welcome the experimentation?

Finally, how much does one prepare a blueprint for the first day? How much does one allow for flexibility -- "adhocracy"? Should Leslie have asked students to write an in-class essay about their backgrounds and saved the introductions until the next meeting? Then she could have handed back their writing samples (an initial connection-building assignment) before the individual conferences began.

8. **Why was Leslie angry over "the intro-duction?"**

Leslie may have felt betrayed, embarrassed, offended, or stuck. Participants may add their own descriptions.

9. **What risks, if any, did Leslie take in talking with Jo Smith?**

In general, it is difficult to discuss job dilemmas with coworkers. In academia, departmental and academic politics are legitimate concerns of faculty members. What resources do faculty members have to hash out problems and concerns?

Raising this topic, which may seem peripheral to the case, may prompt a fruitful discussion. Some participants may articulate the loneliness of teaching. To stimulate discussion in this area, the discussion leader might read (or have the participants read in preparation for the class) "Sandboxes and Honeybees" by Roland Barth, which addresses the issues of collegiality.

Miscellaneous

10. **Leslie seems haunted by the "Oh goody!" comment in response to her canceling a class per week. With the benefit of hindsight, was this a signal? What else could she have done?**

*   *   *

After the (B) case has been read:

1. **What did Leslie do with the remaining few minutes of class?**

Leslie was angry and unsure of what to do. "Like a high-speed carousel, options of what to do flashed through my mind," she recalls. With only a few minutes of class remaining, she tried to establish eye contact with members of the class, most of whom, however, were "looking down at their hands." Trying to sound deliberate but not strained, Leslie hoped her tone denoted disapproval of Dianne and Mike. She lowered her voice and announced, "See you on Wednesday.

You probably all need time to get to the bookstore before the dinner hour." To further signal closure, Leslie closed the folder in front of her, stood up, and went over to the instructor's desk on the raised platform in front of the classroom. She proceeded to nod to students as they left the room, and was somewhat cool to Dianne, who came up to talk after class.

2. **What was Leslie's plan with regard to Dianne and Mike?**

Leslie decided the best course of action would be to talk with both students after class the following week.

3. **What altered Leslie's plan?**

Since Dianne did not show up, Leslie assumed the problem had solved itself: "Dianne had behaved inappropriately and must have decided to change to another section." Leslie then decided to dismiss talking with Mike at all. "The problem was over."

Evaluation

4. **What is your evaluation of the assumptions Leslie made about Mike and Dianne's involvement in "The Introduction" at the beginning of (B)? At the end of (B)?**

It appears that Leslie's prejudice favored Mike over Dianne -- less so in the beginning of (B) than at the end. She planned to speak with both students, although she had initially been more angry at Dianne (as bearer of the news) than at Mike (who was silent during the first class).

5. **Leslie had an entire week to plan. What alternatives did she have in dealing with Mike and Dianne?**

Since she had collected 3x5 index cards with names and phone numbers, Leslie could have telephoned Dianne or Mike. She could have arranged an appointment with either one or both of them before the next class meeting. Instead, she decided to wait.

*   *   *

After the (C) case has been read:

1. **Two months have now passed. What has happened with regard to the class? With regard to Mike O'Neil?**

The class seems to be moving along smoothly, according to Leslie. Roommates and friends of the students are asking for transfers to the class's second term.

According to Leslie, Mike has been no trouble. On the contrary, he contributes in class and has faithfully attended writing conferences. He apparently has been confiding in Leslie since the beginning of the semester concerning his pregnant girlfriend. He also admits liking Leslie's English class -- in contrast to high school, where English was his most disliked subject.

2. **What is Leslie's reaction to Mike's note?**

Although Leslie knew about Mike and his girlfriend, she still appears to be amazed. She mutters about his "being only 18 years old" and shows the note to her colleague Jo Smith.

3. **What is Leslie's assessment of Mike's involvement in "the introduction"?**

Leslie's assessment in (A) and (B) is that he is a questionable culprit. At the end of (B), however, and throughout (C), it appears that she feels Mike's involvement is unimportant and "water under the bridge."

4. **What do we know about Jack Casey? What are his concerns?**

Jack Casey is described as one of the more vocal members of the class. He is a "thoughtful and sensitive student who had impressed several of his classmates with his observations and comments." Jack apparently is distressed in a one-to-one writing conference with Leslie. He implies that he and some of his classmates were upset about Mike's new "parental" status. He also remarks that "some of us in the class are still angry about the way he [Mike] treated you that first day of class."

Evaluation

5. **Should Leslie ignore the note, congratulate Mike, ask how the mother and daughter are doing, refer Mike to the counseling department or dean of students' office? What should Leslie do?**

Leslie did not contact the counseling department or the dean of students' office about Mike because her previous experiences led her to conclude that they were of little help. Leslie took on Mike all by herself.

6. **Should Leslie have brought up adoption as a possibility? Should she have suggested that Mike get married? That Mike take a term off to support his new family? That he consult his parish priest at home in Connecticut? (Legally, Mike is an adult.) Was Leslie doing all she could just by being an "available ear"? She never mentions the chaplain's office. Could this have been a resource for either her or Mike? (Opinions will vary here.)**

7. **What are the ethics of talking with one student (Jack) about another student (Mike)? How helpful to Jack would discussing Mike be? Is it appropriate?**

Leslie chose to remain silent and did not share her theory that Dianne was the more "guilty one." (Jack probably wouldn't have remembered who Dianne was at this point, since she came only to the first class.) Although Leslie avoided talking about Mike with Jack, the seminar participants may find this a controversial issue and opinions may vary.

8. **Do you think Jack is representative of the group? Is he a "majority of one"? Could Jack have missed Leslie's look after the introduction?**

Jack could have missed Leslie's look since she mentioned that many students were looking down and avoiding eye contact. Perhaps the tone of her voice was not sufficient to convey to Jack her disapproval of Mike and Dianne. On the other hand, Jack may very well not be alone in his assessment.

*   *   *

Wrap-up

Seminar participants may want to consider the "now" versus "later" dilemma in dealing with control issues in a classroom.

1) By waiting until after class or the following week, one may "lose the moment."

2) "Capturing the moment," however, may be dangerous. What one thinks one sees may not be what happened at all.

The tension between (1) and (2) is worthy of discussion. Which is best, considering the case of Leslie O'Connor? Keep in mind that the case says that Leslie was very angry.

Are the issues surrounding "The Introduction" or any other classroom incident really resolved because the instructor feels they are? Is there such a thing as a total resolution for everyone? Or does one have to learn to live with uncertainty for oneself and for others?

Seminar participants may want to venture at this point into a discussion of when (or if) values fit into the curriculum or a faculty-student relationship. The discussion may be specific to PVC, which is religiously affiliated, or may apply to any university. College students are legally adults. Where does an instructor's responsibility lie in the area of personal life, morals, and values?

Suzie Simons (A)

"I'd like to talk with you about my grade," Suzie Simons explained as she walked into Nancy Chamberlain's office, a small room shared with two other graduate students. Clutched in her left hand was her latest written case analysis, a critique sheet with a full page of criticisms indicating that the analysis had received a grade of D minus, and a note from Ms. Chamberlain:

Suzie:

The analysis of this case has some weaknesses which are not characteristic of your regular level of work. Could you please come by my office to discuss it? The paper merits a lower grade than you have previously earned. I will be glad to help you improve your next write-up.

-- Nancy

"Good to see you, Suzie. I thought you would be by. I realize the grade you received was low, but don't you think the quality of this case analysis was below that of your last write-up?"

Suzie, her head lowered, looked up, hesitated for a moment and said, "Yes. The first case write-up was not my own work. Jack wrote it!"

Startled, Nancy Chamberlain asked, "Who is Jack, Suzie?"

"Jack? He's -- he's -- he's -- he was my fiancé. Oh, Ms. Chamberlain, he's gone! He's been helping me with this course. I've used his ideas. But now he has gone and -- and -- I don't want to fail." Suzie burst into tears.

"I was stunned," Nancy Chamberlain recalled. "I felt a responsibility toward Suzie. She had been one of my class's star pupils. In her classroom contributions, she

Additional copies of this case for seminar participants may be ordered from the Harvard Business School Publishing Division. Use HBS Order No. 9-378-033 and the order form at the back of this book.

This case was written by Kathryn Harrigan under the supervision of Professor C. Roland Christensen for the Developing Discussion Leadership Skills Seminar. While the case is based on data supplied by Nancy Chamberlain, all names and some peripheral facts have been disguised.

seemed to me to exhibit wisdom beyond her age and demonstrated knowledge about industrial procurement methods, managerial styles, and strategic alternatives, which might have been expected from a person with business experience rather than from an undergraduate student. I assumed her performance was the result of hours of research and reading. How do I deal with this? I wondered. What's fair? What's fair for Suzie -- and the class?"

Mesa University

Mesa University, a large public institution, was the major university in the state. It had a relatively lax policy regarding admission of state residents, and marginal students could gain admission to the school. The faculty of Mesa was expected to fail those students whose work did not fulfill standard expectations. A bell-shaped grading curve was utilized by the faculty, and there were strong peer pressures on all faculty members to sift out students who could not handle college-level work.

Nancy Describes the Class and Grading Program

The following is a description of the class and the grading system used, as related by Nancy Chamberlain:

Business Policy (BP) was the capstone integrative course in the Mesa University BBA program. With the exception of Policy, the school did not use the case method of instruction for its undergraduate program. Most students found BP to be challenging and rigorous, with preparations for the biweekly meetings requiring much more study time than many other business courses. The course also required a team-consulting report and three individual written case analyses. The latter were used to give the students the feedback frequently badly needed.

For evaluations, I wrote up a page-long analysis of each student's case write-up, which I returned with reports. In my critiques, I pointed out inadequately supported assertions, faulty causation arguments, or other fallacies wherein the student had missed the implications of evidence in the case. I used a checklist of basic issues to be discussed in the papers. However, the checklist was used primarily to ascertain where the weaknesses of the class as a

whole lay. I harbored no absolute convictions of what constituted a "right" answer and tried to communicate this philosophy to my class.

Insightful analysis was valued most highly in my evaluations of the papers. The students, early in the semester, were given a statement of my basic expectations. My report criticisms quickly revealed that I expected my standards of thoroughness and clarity to be pursued as avidly as my expectations of a rigorous classroom analysis.

The students were graded relative to each other on the A through F scale. In the interim, each student received an evaluation of his or her paper, (sometimes containing questions such as "Have you truly thought out this alternative?" or "How close is the content of this paper to the 'brown-nose and bull' lines we agreed not to cross?") These comments were usually of a teasing nature with a sharp edge buried in the joke. The students were evaluated on the basis of improvement over the semester. The comments were my way of gently reminding the students that next time their laxness would not be acceptable. The students' papers also received a numerical grade. (A curve was used to obtain course grades.) Although I always found something to praise in a student's paper, I did not permit sloppiness in reasoning or illogicalities to pass unheeded. I continually urged the class to be ready to support any argument they presented, in print or in class.

The Academic Organization and the Instructor

Nancy Chamberlain was one of the youngest (age 25) graduate students at Mesa University, working as a teaching assistant and the only member of that group not currently enrolled in a Ph.D. program. Nancy, with aspirations to enter a Ph.D. program, was in her second year as an MBA student at Mesa. During her first MBA year she had worked as the course assistant grader for several faculty members, including Dr. John Hawkins.

Dr. Hawkins, a senior tenured associate professor with research as his primary academic interest, had originally been scheduled to teach Business Policy to Section I. With the approval of the department chairpersons, he had given this responsibility to Ms. Chamberlain when he had received a research grant enabling him to work on his book. Nancy's first teaching assignment was only a part of her overall program; she continued her regular grading work for other faculty members and her MBA work.

Dr. Hawkins, Nancy believed, did not really enjoy teaching and seemed only partially at ease in a case discussion. He did make infrequent appearances as a guest lecturer with the section, and met with Nancy several times a fortnight, typically asking, "Are there any problems which you've encountered that might require my assistance?"

In response to an early-in-the-semester query of this nature, Nancy replied, "Well . . . Barry Jenks says his paper will be late. He says he will have trouble typing it in time."

"Oh?" queried Dr. Hawkins, "How will you handle that request, Nancy?"

"I've asked Barry for a photocopy of his handwritten version before class on the day the paper is due. He has a week to turn in the typed copy with no revisions in text," Nancy had responded. "It seems like a fair solution to me."

"Fair? . . . yes, it is fair, I think . . . to Barry and to the other members of the class," Dr. Hawkins said. "It is important to be fair where the class is concerned. . . . How are the students adapting to the case method?"

"It's a trauma for some of them still," Nancy replied. "Some of the students are rather savage to their less aggressive classmates. But I expect the others to catch on soon. In the meantime, I try to keep the attacks civilized."

In commenting about her academic career, Nancy Chamberlain said, "I think Dr. Hawkins gave me this assignment so I might serve as a role model for some of the other young women in the class. I earned my college education alone. I've worked hard to build a career and have high expectations for the capacities of my students. I believe I am somewhat more demanding in my student expectations than other instructors, but I also believe I have a reputation for being 'tough but fair.' For example, I request that all written papers be turned in with identifying numbers only. I do not want my impressions of a student's classroom performance to color my judgments of his or her written analysis."

Nancy Chamberlain Describes Suzie Simons

The following is a description of Suzie Simons as related by the teaching assistant herself:

Suzie Simons had been a good student in my Business Policy class. She was vivacious and very attractive. Suzie's major was marketing. She was especially interested in fashion merchandising, as was illustrated by her flashy wardrobe and tousled, blond-streaked coiffure. At age 21 she was the darling of her father -- a very successful cattle rancher. Despite the fact that Suzie sported a one-carat diamond, she had been an outrageous flirt with the male members of the class, alternating between insightful comments in case discussions and teasing remarks directed toward the introverted men in the class. But Suzie kept the overall level of her remarks in class directed toward the case being discussed; hence she was not a disruptive element in the classroom.

Suzie appeared to be very good in the case-oriented discussions. She seemed to have analyzed her cases carefully and offered innovative solutions to the problems in the cases. Her contributions concerning the case analysis had been thoughtful and frequent. Until recently! I recall a class incident several weeks ago. I had asked another student, Joe Hogan, "What is your assessment of this company, Joe? Is it in good shape? Bad shape? Would you give us your evaluation of its performance, and indicate the factors which have led you to your conclusions?"

Joe Hogan flushed bright red, and stammered, "Well, they . . . ah . . . they seem to be losing money on the rapid transit system."

"Why do you say that, Joe?" I inquired.

"Well, ma'am, they're not earning any," Joe replied.

"Why not, Joe?" I pressed.

"Because nobody is buying their product!" Joe exclaimed.

"And what would you recommend that the company do?"

There had been a painful pause. Joe, like several other students in my class, frequently had problems with case analysis. While some of the students simply did not read the case carefully and made cursory preparations, Joe seemed to prepare for class. However, Joe had difficulty in demonstrating the logical train of thought that was necessary for case analysis. Most of the students had never held jobs.

"They should get some customers, I guess," Joe replied at last.

"Very well; customers are needed," I repeated, trying to weave his comments into the chain of ideas I was trying to present. "How might the firm attempt to do this, Suzie?"

Suzie lifted her head despondently. Her flaxen curls were flat and her roots showed a natural brown color. Her face seemed drained of color and emotion. "I don't know what they should do," she said.

"Won't you give us a plan to explore, Suzie?" I prodded. "What alternatives might it consider?"

Suzie shrugged her shoulders and looked up with a lifeless stare. "I don't know," she repeated.

Finally I said, "Let me tell you about next week's class."

[Nancy continued:]

Besides Suzie's sudden lack of interest in classroom discussion, Suzie's second written case analysis differed greatly from her first. The first paper had been a meticulous analysis of industry structure, comparing the challenge of changing production technologies with a "do-nothing" policy. The paper contained a sophisticated cost-benefit analysis which supported her chosen plan of action. Because Suzie's remarks in class discussion matched the quality of the paper, I had not questioned its authorship. By contrast, Suzie's second written case was a shallow analysis filled with banalities. It contained few ideas concerning how to remedy the problem. The analysis was general. No specific examples were included. It lacked a plan of action.

Suzie had been an average student at Mesa University. Under the A through F grading system, she had managed to maintain a B average in her business courses. Her overall grade-point average was slightly lower. Suzie had failed two distribution requirements when she was younger. Hence, she would not graduate with her class and she would attend summer school to finish her course work.

The Office Visit

After receiving the invitation to consult her teacher about the poor performance on her paper, Suzie Simons went to Nancy Chamberlain and explained that she'd been getting extra help from her fiance, who was no longer around. She then added, "I'm afraid to fail, Ms. Chamberlain. Oh, no . . . I just can't fail." She began crying.

"Suzie, you could take the course again to replace the failing grade if you get an F," Nancy noted, aware that Suzie was not even considering that she could be expelled for plagiarism.

"No! You don't understand! I'll fail college! I've already failed two other required courses," Suzie sobbed. "And if I am flunking out again Daddy won't help me the way he did last time." (Nancy said nothing, fearing that she would be swept into a compromising dilemma.) Suzie murmured in a low tone. "I've tried so hard and I'm still a failure. . . . I just can't go home now." Her tears increased, and Nancy found herself wondering about the level of Suzie's efforts. How hard was Suzie really trying?

Suzie finally regained her composure and looked up at Nancy Chamberlain seated across the room. The image Suzie created in Nancy's mind was that of a little girl -- weak and irresponsible. Nancy looked down. As Suzie spoke, Nancy could feel Suzie's self-confidence dwindling.

"Jack was an engineer, you know. He'd had some management experience. He told me I just couldn't compete with the other students. And he helped me. . . . He told me what to say in class. . . . He even wrote my papers!" Suzie said. Nancy continued to look down. "But he finally decided I wasn't worth his time. He called me a baby. . . . Said I couldn't make decisions. . . . Well, maybe he was right. I'm not good for anything now." Suzie's voice was growing tight and small.

Nancy Chamberlain said firmly, "Couldn't you take this course again someplace and still earn your degree? You could find a job, and start your career."

"No, Ms. Chamberlain, I don't think so. I'd be afraid to do that," Suzie whispered.

Nancy looked at Suzie. She looked trapped and made small, timid motions as tears again ran down her cheeks. Through her tears she looked up at her teacher in an earnest and searching manner. "Please, Ms. Chamberlain," she blurted out, "I don't want to fail. . . ."

Suzie Simons (B)

Suzie Simons stared at the floor in front of her in Nancy Chamberlain's office. It was now three days since her tearful outburst in which she told her teacher that her former fiancé had written her papers and advised her on comments to make in Business Policy class. Nancy had sent her away from the last session, charging Suzie to "consider your situation." Now Nancy said nothing.

At last Suzie broke the silence: "I realize I have violated university rules concerning plagiarism. I am also in danger of failing Business Policy. I would rather not be expelled nor fail the course, but I will, if I cannot convince you that I will improve my performance. I think I can do a better job . . . on my own," she said. "I want you to call on me each day in class. I will be prepared. I want to argue my ideas with the other members of the class. And I will write up each case from now on. It will help my thinking process."

Suzie Simons looked at Ms. Chamberlain. The instructor was silent.

"If I fail this course, I will not protest. I will not ask my father for help," Suzie added. "I deserve to fail. . . . Will I?" she queried.

"I do not know, Suzie," Ms. Chamberlain said quietly. "If you fail, it will be on the basis of your actions. I do not want extra papers from you. That would not be fair to the rest of the class. Your final case write-up will go through blind review with the others. However, your score will be lowered one letter grade when it is recorded. I will not change the grades recorded for you in the past. But, I will not count them either. You may expect to defend your ideas in class with particular energy, Suzie," Nancy added. "Your classmates may be expected to be especially rough in their criticisms." She said no more. Suzie nodded and departed.

This case was written by Kathryn Harrigan under the supervision of Professor C. Roland Christensen for the Developing Discussion Leadership Skills Seminar. While the case is based on data supplied by Nancy Chamberlain, all names and some peripheral facts have been disguised.

One week later Nancy asked Suzie to present her recommendations to the class for a financial program needed by a firm in the case assigned for the day. Suzie explained what she would do. Immediately, Suzie's plan was attacked.

"Now that's plain stupid!" Tom argued. "You haven't left any provision for working capital. How will this company pay their bills?"

"Do you mean that?" challenged Barry. "The company has no remaining debt capacity. How will you persuade any bank to loan them more money?"

"Well, maybe a personal mortgage . . ." offered Suzie, in an uneasy tone.

"On what assets?" demanded Mark. "He has already pledged his house twice."

Suzie, visibly shaken, looked for help from Ms. Chamberlain. Nancy ignored her appeal and waited coolly to see what would happen. Suzie swallowed, accepting the criticism stoically, and said, "I'm sorry. I guess I haven't thought through this problem very well."

————————

"Are there any problems you've encountered that might require my assistance?" Dr. Hawkins asked that afternoon, as he always did at the beginning of their conferences.

"No," said Nancy. "No problems this week."

PART IV   Case Supplements for Distribution to Participants

Note: The Harvard Business School authorizes the seminar instructor to reproduce one copy of each case supplement in this section for each participant who has received a copy of the Teaching and the Case Method book.

Assistant Professor Graham and Ms. Macomber (B)

"Well, well." Professor Graham's words rang in Janet Macomber's ears.

She slumped back in her chair, feeling like a defendant released from hostile cross-examination. The ordeal was over but the verdict was still out. Janet had been disturbed that the class discussion had followed such a different track than her own analysis. It had taken all the courage she could muster to suggest the class was wrong and assert her own point of view.

Janet listened carefully to Professor Graham's closing remarks. To her dismay, he said nothing to indicate her approach had been right -- or wrong. Was it possible that she had been completely off base? Had she made a fool of herself in front of the whole section?

Class was dismissed, and in the minutes before the next class began, Janet was surrounded by her sectionmates. Their comments ranged from good-natured teasing to open incredulity:

"You didn't really. . . . How long did it. . . . Hundreds of numbers. . . . Let me see. . . ." The capstone comment came from Peter Anderson, an already popular figure who usually sat with a group of cohorts in the middle of the right-hand bank of seats. "Janet, you really did it this time," he said, laughing. "We [indicating his colleagues] are going to call your achievement THE MACOMBER MEMORIAL MATRIX!"

Janet made a humorous reply, but inwardly she despaired. Just what I don't need, she thought. In the second week of school, to be typecast as a number-cruncher! I should be more careful in the future about sticking my neck out when I talk in class. She made a silent resolution: this won't happen again.

This case was written by a member of the Developing Discussion Leadership Skills Seminar under the supervision of C. Roland Christensen. While the case is based on data supplied by participants involved, all names and some peripheral facts have been disguised.

Assistant Professor Graham and Ms. Macomber (C)

In the fifth week of the term, Professor Graham was going over his student class cards for first-year QAOM, tabulating notes on individual class participation. On the whole, the section's case discussions were shaping up pretty well. Individually and collectively, the class had come a long way in five weeks. Charles grinned: he supposed that, if surveyed, the class would say the same of him.

Halfway through the pile, Charles stopped at Janet Macomber's card. What, he wondered, is going on there?

In the first weeks of the term, Charles had marked Janet down as very promising. She had come to each class prepared and had participated eagerly in the discussions. Her comments had been intelligent, succinct, and to the point. And on that one occasion (Charles remembered with pleasure), Janet had performed an analytic tour de force, smashing the case wide open in the last minutes of the class.

Charles now counted the case as a watershed in the section's development. He remembered the first hour and ten minutes of that class as everything a case discussion should not be: floundering, disjointed, indecisive, and entirely irrelevant to the company's problems. Since that day, slowly but with increasing confidence, the section was pulling itself together and becoming (on good days) a working forum.

Janet Macomber's behavior was in abrupt contrast to that of the rest of the class. Charles could not fix exactly when the change had taken place, but Janet had become silent, ceasing to voluntarily take part in case discussions. She had begun arriving late to class (QAOM had been meeting after lunch); she no longer took her characteristic back row seat, but changed her position almost every day -- to the point that Charles could not be sure of how many classes she was attending. When Charles had seen her, she had generally seemed sleepy (or bored) and quite evi-

This case was written by a member of the Developing Discussion Leadership Skills Seminar under the supervision of C. Roland Christensen. While the case is based on data supplied by participants involved, all names and some peripheral facts have been disguised.

dently had been barely following the discussion. Charles had refrained from calling on Janet unexpectedly on these occasions; he had a strong presupposition she would be unprepared and felt disinclined to embarrass her. Such tacit benevolence ought not continue, however.

After such an auspicious start, thought Professor Graham, what can be causing Janet to act this way? And what -- if anything -- do I do about it?

Bill Jones (B)

Bill Jones looked at Paige Palmer, who was trying to speak, and then at Fred Wilkens. He realized that Paige Palmer had not meant to say what she had. He walked directly to Fred Wilkens and put his hand on his arm and looked straight at him:

Fred, I know you're hurt and you're probably angry, but she didn't mean to hurt you and she didn't mean to say that. You can't even know how badly she feels right now that she said that. She's probably never felt worse in her life.

Bill turned and looked at Paige, who was flushed and clearly on the verge of tears. Fred turned and looked at her also and simply nodded his head slowly at Bill Jones.

Bill then immediately called on another student to continue class discussion.

This case was written by a member of the Teaching by the Case Method Seminar under the supervision of C. Roland Christensen. While the case is based on data supplied by Bill Jones, all names and some peripheral facts have been disguised.

The Case of the Dethroned Section Leader (B)

Bea Benedict remembered how she dealt with the "revolution" that Jack Kesselman had instigated, and describes it in her own words.

Bea's Description of the "Revolution"

I stood at the board and said: "Hands up, those who want to have no leader."

Jack and Skip raised their hands. Then four other hands went up. Finally, Elke's and Cliff's did, too. I surveyed the democratic assembly that had just ousted me, put the chalk back on the ledge under the board, and sat down.

"Okay, Section," I said, looking at no one in particular. "Discuss."

Jack began to talk about the passage, mainly in terms of personal likes and dislikes. He used phrases like "I think it's phoney of Richard to say so and so," and "If he were somebody I knew, I wouldn't like him."

The other students didn't seem terribly interested in Jack's personal reactions, nor did he offer any analytical statements for them either to agree with or dispute. Discussion was, therefore, desultory and unfocused. Jack dominated, but a few other people did speak. I said nothing.

After the hour was over, Cliff and Elke remained to talk with me. They were both very embarrassed, and Elke expressed chagrin that Jack would now be running things. They saw him as their new de facto section leader, and they were annoyed to be paying for a college education only to be listening to a fellow undergraduate. I was unprofessional enough to admit my anger at Jack, but I did say that I felt I had been fairly and squarely voted out of authority. Only a new vote could restore our former organization. Elke said she would call for a new vote at the next

This case was written by Dr. Abby J. Hansen, research associate, for the Developing Discussion Leadership Skills and the Teaching by the Case Method seminars. Data were furnished by the involved participants. All names and some peripheral facts have been disguised.

meeting. I suggested that she leave things alone for a while and see how the discussion took shape when all the students had had a week to prepare.

The next week's discussion was as formless as the first had been. I sat in the seat farthest from the chalkboard -- no one sat in the "teacher's seat" I had previously occupied, I noted -- and I recall feeling a bit smug at the disarray I witnessed. There was a good deal of vagueness, and some uncomfortable dead silences when no one seemed to know what to say. I thought: maybe I did talk too much as a discussion leader, but at least I gave them substance, and I didn't leave any holes in the discussion.

At the next meeting -- the second after the "revolution" -- Elke called for a new vote. I left the room while the group voted. They didn't tell me by what margin, but I was asked to return and lead the group. I confess I had been expecting this, so I had prepared a series of passages for discussion. I really think the students were relieved to have me back. Before getting the

new discussion under way, I gave a little informal speech in which I apologized for having monopolized the discussion and asked them to let me know when I talked too much. (Skip took that seriously and actually interrupted me later when I began to lecture instead of discuss -- a habit I've always had, and one that my hours of private research had aggravated. Shakespeare was my favorite subject at the time, and I felt like a tightly corked bottle of Elizabethan lore and theories about the plays -- always ready to explode and overflow.)

The rest of the semester went on quite satisfactorily. I had feared that Jack might turn sullen and be a problem in the section, but he behaved quite amiably and settled down to participate. I went out of my way to deal with him fairly -- his final grade was a B+, and frankly, I treated him more charitably than he deserved in order to avoid any suspicion that I might be retaliating against him. It's probably petty of me, but to this day, I still remember him with dislike.

The Day the Heat Went On (B)

Ellen Collins Recalls the Incident

I knew these characters sitting in the top row, and I didn't consider any of them basically hostile, although my instantaneous reaction to the whistle was pure fury. I felt like lashing out, but I immediately rejected the possibility of responding with angry words because it seemed important, somehow, to show that I hadn't been rattled. The idea of calling on a woman student in the hope that she would complain on my behalf occurred to me. That might bolster the women as a group and offer more effective correction than I, as the insulted party, could make.

But I knew that the women in LG VI were demoralized. They were a fairly young group -- their average age was 25 (about two years below the average male age) -- and they had far less than the typical four years of business or government experience the males had. I had noticed that they acted self-effacing. There was a lot riding on me as their only female teacher. If I called on one of them to defend me, not only would I put her on the spot but she might simply swallow the insult and thereby help create an even worse impression of passivity.

I realized that both I and the women students in that room had much to lose by a wrong response. I don't mean that I deliberated for hours before responding to the whistle. But some form of all these thoughts did rocket through my mind as I stood there. What I did was instinctive. I did not look in the direction of the whistle. Instead I waited for a pause from the speaker, wheeled around to face the part of the room farthest away from where the whistle had originated, and called on a male student. I chose a reliable fellow who I knew would have something pertinent to say, and asked him a direct, simple question relating to something I had just put on the board. While he

This case was written by Dr. Abby J. Hansen, research associate, for the Developing Discussion Leadership Skills and the Teaching by the Case Method seminars. Data were furnished by the involved participants. All names and some peripheral facts have been disguised.

answered, I collected my thoughts. The class went on with no further jarring incidents.

Ellen Reflects on Long-Term Consequences

Oddly enough, I think there might be some level on which this incident -- and my not getting rattled by it -- did me some good. I ended up the year with far better teaching evaluations than LG VI gave Charlie Brennan, and he's considered one of the real "old pros" around here. By the way, I think I know who whistled, and I don't think he really meant any harm by it. It was an attempt at humor, quite spontaneous, and flat-footed rather than malicious. The student I'm thinking of happens to be an average guy -- average intelligence, average looks -- but he has a frankness and naivete that are refreshing at Fleming. He's the sort who would offer daring comments in discussion without calculating every syllable for effect in the interests of his precious course grade. In retrospect, I'm still not certain of what that whistle meant. Perhaps it was a sort of compliment -- a recognition that I'd finally joined the club by doing what the men did and teaching without a jacket. I also think this incident could have landed me in real hot water if I'd acted flustered or showed the instantaneous fury that I really did feel. As LG VI's only woman teacher, I was a symbol for all women at Fleming at that moment, and one false step could have crippled my relationship with this group and my credibility as a leader. To me, though, this relatively minor incident is just one of many signs that women live under microscopes at places like Fleming. And -- for the record -- I still wear a jacket when I teach.

Ernie Budding (C)

After delivering his speech of reprimand, Ernie expected to see a distinct improvement in Section I's preparation and participation. The initial results, however, were quite different.

"The Salinas Walnut Company" Case

The next case that was discussed in MM dealt with the Salinas Walnut Company. On that day, several women newly admitted to the next year's MBA program came to visit. Here is Ernie's recollection:

> I listened as Cindy Eakens introduced the visitors, and the section applauded as usual. Then a student introduced his fiancée, whom he had previously introduced as his girlfriend. The section made jokes. I went along with the spirit of things and told the newly admitted women, "We always try to waste the first ten minutes of class if humanly possible." Then I gave the usual introductory sort of stuff and went to Mandy Farmer, who'd had some trouble with participation in the second semester, although her first semester work had been excellent. I had included her in a group of students to whom I'd written notes because their second semester participation was off. The notes were merely invitations to come talk to me if there was a particular problem, but I think some students must have seen the notes in people's mailboxes, recognized my handwriting, and figured there must be something gruesome inside. Gossip, I gather, was wild.

> Mandy said, "Ernie, I'd rather pass on this one."

> Frankly, I was shocked. The Salinas Walnut case _is_ a very confusing one -- I hadn't liked it myself when I prepared it, and I'd even suggested to the other MM teachers that we drop it in coming years -- but I hadn't expected a student simply to refuse to open the case. I had told the section from the first that if they couldn't prepare for a

This case was written by Dr. Abby J. Hansen, research associate, in collaboration with Professor C. Roland Christensen for the Developing Discussion Leadership Skills Seminar. While the case is based on data supplied by participants involved, all names and some peripheral facts have been disguised.

case for some personal or medical reason, all they had to do was tell me beforehand and I wouldn't call on them. That policy had worked well first semester, making "passes" virtually nonexistent, but it obviously wasn't working here.

I said, "Okay," and called on Barry Caslan -- a guy who had performed very well. I could tell people were tense.

Barry said, "Ernie, I'm not prepared either. I pass."

The atmosphere in the classroom got even worse. "Okay," I said again, and turned to another student. "Michael?"

I really think Michael would have liked to pass, too, but things were really very uncomfortable by that time. He started the case, but when I said, "Let's have some analysis," he couldn't do it. Clearly, nobody had understood the case. People were getting more and more tense. Finally, I put the company's options on the board and said, "Now how would you compare these things financially?" People had read the charts in the case, but they hadn't realized that you had to subtract one column of figures from another to do the analysis.

You had to grasp the difference between average cost -- the average of all units -- and marginal cost -- the cost of each additional unit. Absolutely nobody got it, although we had discussed this concept in the Pennsylvania General Steel case, and I thought they'd also done it in Finance. Finally -- it was like pulling teeth -- I said, "Well, who remembers the Penn Steel case?" They slapped their heads and yelled, "Marginal cost."

"What kind of calculation was that?" I said, and continued to put figures on the board. But the calculations gave them real trouble. It was a pretty awful experience.

Also, I recall being pretty annoyed -- saying to myself that after all I said in my speech about not being prepared, I should show them how the numbers go?

That day I tightened the reins and kept them tight. I actually remember forcing some calculations. I took it as a calculation case even though there were a number of important qualitative issues. One certainly could have discussed the case without figures, but given my speech, I was unwilling to accept that approach.

Afterward, a student apologized to the newly admitted women who had visited, saying that the section had had a major paper due in Corporate Strategy that day, and two other big cases as well. Added to this, the complexity of the Salinas Walnut case itself had produced a truly miserable showing. I had become very directive, after having tried quite consciously to hold back, and I had dragged the material out of the students. Even worse, I'm afraid, I didn't conceal my irritation.

A Student's View of the Salinas Walnut Case

Arlene Allen, the educational representative of Section I, also discussed the Salinas Walnut case with the researcher. Here is her account:

I think it's just a poorly written case. It's about cogeneration -- energy from crushed walnut shells. I actually know the professor and research associate who wrote it, and they didn't know what they were doing. It's a screwball case. Ernie cold-called a student who passed without excuse, and then another student passed. Ernie was obviously furious. He raced around the classroom as he talked, going at really high speed. The third guy he called on didn't want to start the case either. It was just a bum case. No opening could have been good. But I think the third guy saw how upset Ernie was and realized he'd better go ahead and say something. When Ernie started to write on the board, he was so furious he broke the chalk. The class got really uptight, partly because of his anger, and partly because nobody understood the numbers in the case.

After this episode, I spoke with quite a few members of the section and they were saying, "Ernie's going to kill us." "He's working us too hard."

"We're really sick of the cold-calling." Yes, there was a certain amount of sloppiness in our classwork at this point, but that's just life at Bay. People are people. They have to relax sometimes. Ernie didn't relax, though, and he didn't want us to, either. But I have to mention that people still liked him at this point. The problem with our relationship with him was that at first, at the beginning of the year, we just loved being told how things went. By the middle of the second semester, though, we all felt calmer, more confident about casework. We didn't want to be led anymore, but he was still leading. It seemed as if we were all on a forced march. [As the section's elected representative] I decided I'd better go and have a talk with Ernie on behalf of the section, to present their views.

Ernie Recounts the Ed Rep's Visit

Arlene said to me, "Your speech, coupled with the section's poor job on the Salinas Walnut case, has created an enormous amount of tension in the classroom. The section is tired after months of classes, and they're neither willing nor able to prepare each and every case completely."

"Standards have to be maintained," I replied.

"But not everyone has your standards. And not everyone wants to do this sort of analysis."

"I think my standards are high, but not unreasonable."

"It is unreasonable to expect students to be able to lay out every MM case in detail. MM is just one of many courses, and your demands -- and your speech -- put everyone on edge."

As I listened to her, I realized that removing the section's tensions had to be my first priority. I explained that laying out a case was necessary for every student to do because it meant producing an organized and systematic approach to the whole problem. But I agreed to step back further. I would still ask probing questions, but I would

channel the discussion less and relinquish my habit of going through the blocks of analysis in order. I also agreed, as an experiment, to stop the cold calls and take volunteers.

Ernie Describes the Rest of the Semester

It seemed to me that the semester turned out quite well once the section's anxieties had been allayed.

I began the first class (after my talk with the educational representative) with a speech in which I announced a new, relaxed approach, and called for volunteers. There was silence at first, and I was afraid that no one would open the case, but finally, Arlene raised her hand. After her opening, the case went smoothly.

I think the whole course ended very well. The buzzwords didn't disappear, but they were bolstered by explanations. The level of analysis remained high. My student evaluations were almost uniformly good, and the students thought that my change at the end was distinctly for the better. Giving up cold calls seems to have gone all right. I don't know if I lost rigor. Maybe it's a trade-off; how much do you buy by going through a logical structure -- A, B, C, D -- versus letting it come out A, D, E, C, B? Maybe it's all right as long as all the pieces are there.

But I'm still not certain that stepping back was really justified. Given that I'd begun to get negative feedback for the first time in the second semester, and that I'd noticed a change in the section and observed different successful teaching styles, I was willing to try to be less directive than formerly. But I'm still not sure it's justified educationally, because the subject matter of MM is largely technical though there are important qualitative elements. All this requires careful attention to details, some of which may be overlooked without prodding from the instructor. I also thought -- and several students agreed with this -- that it was a bit self-serving for them to ask for less direction. They could, frankly, get away with a certain degree of sloppiness.

Ernie Budding (D)

In conversations with the researcher, Ernie Budding reflected on teaching in general, and at Bay in particular. His comments focused on a few central issues: the way an instructor establishes an implicit contract with students; the degree to which it is possible to run a class without intimidation by either the students or the teacher; and the very nature of the Bay MBA program with its enforced grading curve and attendant tensions that lead groups of students to play practical jokes on teachers. The following are extracts from Ernie's statements.

Ernie Describes Contract with Students

For me, the way one establishes a contract with the class is an unresolved issue. Many Bay instructors keep the contract implicit, establishing it subtly, without articulation. For example, I think the pranks my section played on me may have been somewhat restrained.

I made it clear that I'd never treat the students with bad taste and that I expected the same treatment. I tried to keep contracts like that implicit. Similarly, I didn't think I had to say, "Look, I'll prepare for class and so will you." But now I'm not so sure. The students sometimes seemed surprised when I kept my word. Early in the term, for example, I said, "I'll sacrifice quantity in comments for quality any day," and that's exactly how I graded. Some of the students in Section I were gifted orators, but others who clearly thought better did better in my class. Some students said, "Everybody said they'll grade that way, but you're the only one who actually does it." That surprised me.

The matter of the contract -- how you establish it, how you observe it -- is still an open question.

Intimidation

The issue of intimidation -- whether a teacher is intimidated by aggressive stu-

This case was written by Dr. Abby J. Hansen, research associate, in collaboration with Professor C. Roland Christensen for the Developing Discussion Leadership Skills seminar. While the case is based on data supplied by participants involved, all names and some peripheral facts have been disguised.

dents or the other way around -- comes up often in discussions of problems that teachers have with their classes. In Ernie Budding's case, his directive teaching style tended to intimidate some students. Here is Ernie's own report:

> One very good student of mine told me, "I'm not quite comfortable in your class because I have to think more there than anywhere else." I was frankly delighted about that, but if I had thought his remark contained overtones of intimidation, I would have been upset. Some students did tell me late in the year that I had intimidated them at first. That bothers me, and it's something I'd like very much to change. I still wonder how you let people down easily when they're egregiously wrong. One on one, in private conference, I don't have any trouble because I can point out strengths along with weaknesses. But in the classroom it's harder. Some teachers think you shouldn't correct students' errors because they get out of a case only what they bring to it. I disagree. I think you should at least give signposts. But I may have been too obvious.

> One thing some people around here don't seem to realize is that teaching is just another form of human relations -- a unique function, with an authority figure interacting with 80 or 90 people at once. I assumed the students would like me because I'm a nice guy, and I also assumed that my very extensive preparation and academic background would preclude any authority problems in the classroom. It simply never occurred to me to be intimidated by my students. For me, a balance of respect is the most desirable situation.

Teaching Style

Much of Ernie's friction with the section in the second semester seemed to stem from his directive teaching style, and his own consideration of that style was far from finished when he discussed this case with the researcher. In Ernie's own words:

> On reflection, I still think my approach was basically sound, at least for first semester, when everyone was on

edge and students didn't know how to analyze cases. I do have reservations, though, about the way I made the speech or reprimand second semester. I'm afraid it came across as a bit harsh. But how should one deliver a classwide criticism? Is it part of a teacher's job sometimes to be a big bad wolf? Maybe unpleasantness isn't totally bad. The Salinas Walnut case, for example, was one of the starkest teaching moments of the year. Nobody forgot how to do that sort of analysis. It was a miserable experience but it made its point, and they all really learned marginal versus average cost.

> Nevertheless, I think I'll do things differently next year. I'll vary my teaching style from class to class, and try to leave students with questions rather than neat summaries. But I don't want to give up cold calls entirely. I think I'll start with them and announce that I'll switch openings sometime in the future. Cold calls do give me the opportunity to match students with cases. Also, I'll not always channel discussions from A to B; I'll let them flow more naturally. I'm going to step back more. After all, the major advantage of the case method is that it can be used as a springboard into the unknown. In the future, I'll exploit the opportunities for more creative discussions when they may arise.

> Basically, though, the matter of teaching style doesn't really worry me very much. First semester, in fact, I proceeded alone. Consciously, I didn't even attend teaching meetings, because in the first few I attended someone would invariably say, "This is the way you teach this case." My personal feeling is that you have to go with your own style. I deliberately removed myself from the meetings in order to develop and become comfortable with my own way of behaving in the classroom. I attended meetings only in the second semester, when I had already developed a style of my own. The meetings were looser, too, and I found that I could use what was said within my own framework. Now I can pick and choose from others' styles.

> I think part of the reason I don't agonize about style is that I'm just not

self-conscious. I may think about a certain technique in advance, but when I go into the classroom, I'm myself. Some teachers whom I know socially become different people when they step in front of a classroom, but I'm always me. I want the students to learn from me, and I don't believe in mystifying them. One teacher told me, "Never tip your hand. Never tell them what's coming next or what's going on. Hide the information." That's ridiculous. I just don't play those games.

In fact, that leads to another problem I have with the case method. Around here you're so firmly told "Hands off" that you don't always recognize when you really should say "Look, this is the way the numbers go. I'll put them up and then we'll discuss them."

I realize that the section was more comfortable when I just let the discussion drift, but I still wonder if that was rigorous. In the first semester I thought logical build-up was paramount. In the second, I partly changed my view. In the future, I'll vary the two approaches. But one of the best students in Section I did tell me that he thought lower pressure meant lower quality in general.

I do think I erred first semester in equating my understanding of a case with the level of insight that students should take from a discussion. Given the differing amounts of time available for preparation, that's simply unreasonable. Also, in terms of style, I think I may have created an impression that I didn't mean to -- of being more calculating than I am. The business of tossing my notes onto the desk and then not looking at them created a stagey impression that I never intended. I don't like the pretense of infallibility. After all, I spent upwards of 20 hours on some of those cases, and I always reviewed right up until the moment I started teaching. That's why I knew the stuff backward and forward. I think that was one source of some of the intimidation some students felt.

Also, I may have overemphasized terseness and made the mistake of trying to squeeze too much information into the class session. I tried to get, say, eight to ten points with no chaff. Maybe I should have allowed four or five points and some chaff. But still, I mentioned to a student once that I'd like to believe that they were in this for the material and because they enjoyed learning. That's what we did when I was in grad school. Here, I'm aware that some percentage of students simply want to have Bay and the initials MBA after their names. That's an unresolved conflict.

Mainly, I'll try to relax without sacrificing rigor, which is still my main concern. But I won't make the mistake of thinking that every tiny detail of a case is crucial. I think I pushed to make some points that probably could have been dispensed with.

Ernie Describes Climate of the School

I think that the forced-screen system -- which mandates that a certain percentage of every section must be graded Low Pass in a course -- is almost entirely dysfunctional. It creates a pressurized climate that makes the MBA process two very unhealthy years for the students. It seems to use only negative reinforcement, while psychological research has shown that positive reinforcement is far more effective. Nor do I think the grading system is fair. I had to scrape out several Low Passes in my course when those students clearly would have done all right in any other system.

Ernie's View of Pranks

By and large my section's pranks were harmless, I thought, although I have heard of other teachers who have had pretty rough stunts pulled on them. Some stunts, however, were in poorer taste than others, and I did my best to discourage them. In one MM class, for example, we had a case in which an executive had committed suicide. On the day of the case I came in to find a dummy hanging there with, "The John J. Jones Memorial Method of Solving Management Problems" written on it. I took it down and said that just wasn't appropriate behavior for this school.

Some other pranks were actually rather charming. On Halloween I heard a rattling behind the chalkboard (which can be raised and lowered electronically). I raised it, and there stood Al Carpenter wearing a Groucho Marx mask. I stared at him for a second and turned back to the class -- who had all put on Groucho Marx masks! One student had brought a camera to snap my reaction. The photographs are pretty funny.

The pranks students play are just one indication of the level of tension here. I think I was pretty reasonably treated by my section, but, as I've said, I've heard of other pranks that were a good deal rougher. Those often showed real insensitivity to other people's feelings.

The French Lesson (B)

After Jack Sothern slipped out of Bert Peters's French class, Bert stewed for a while. Jack's rather dramatic exit and reappearance had been the only snag so far in an enjoyable class. The other students had been visibly, though not deeply, upset by Jack's behavior, and their general edginess had, in turn, unsettled Bert. The whole thing annoyed him; it would take some doing to recapture the good rapport he had created with that group. Some teachers at Bower thought nothing of insulting, reprimanding, and teasing students in class, but Bert consciously eschewed this style of teaching. Such teachers had made him awfully uncomfortable during his student days, and he didn't want to recreate the unpleasantness of their classes.

Bert called Jack at his dorm that evening.

"You really insulted me," Jack said. "I always prepare for class. You shouldn't have embarrassed me in front of my friends just because I'm not good at languages." Bert told the student he had only meant to let him off the hook, but he apologized for having insulted him, even inadvertently, and suggested that they have a conference to diagnose Jack's difficulties and, perhaps, arrange for private tutoring. Jack's performance improved a bit, but he remained the least talented student in his class. Bert ended the semester by giving Jack a C+, more for effort than accomplishment. Their relations continued to be strained -- Bert noticed that Jack always looked for a way to avoid him when their paths crossed on campus -- and Bert felt the class's mood never recovered its initial level of spontaneous buoyancy.

This case was written by Dr. Abby J. Hansen, research associate, for the Developing Discussion Leadership Skills and the Teaching by the Case Method seminars. Data were furnished by the involved participants. All names and some peripheral facts have been disguised.

The Handicapped Heckler (B)

Paula was really worried. "I was frightened to death of putting Frank down in class," she recalled, "partly because I dreaded hurting him, and partly because I thought a confrontation might turn ugly and trigger some really furious outburst that would upset everybody."

Before the beginning of the seventh week of classes -- just about halfway through the course -- Paula phoned a colleague to seek advice. He could suggest no special techniques for controlling Frank's temper in class, but he did steer Paula to the Office for Disabled Students. The university bureaucracy was so large that many people were unaware of the very existence of some of its services. Paula, who had not known of this office, made an appointment immediately. When she entered the room, a very attractive black woman seated at a neat desk looked up and welcomed her with a smile.

Paula recalled their conversation: The woman knew Frank's case and confirmed Paula's guess that he had been quite athletic. The paralysis had occurred two years previously in a car accident. It was quite severe and the prognosis was not good. His speech had been affected, and his mental state in her judgment was a bit unstable.

"You ought to stand up to him if he's behaving badly," the woman advised.

Paula replied, "I'm not sure I can. I'm so terribly sorry for him. You can see how deeply troubled he is, how much he needs attention. Won't I hurt him terribly if I put him down in class?"

"You might help him," the woman said. "Handicapped people have to live in the real world like everybody else. If you get tough with him, maybe he'll begin to learn that."

(Paula was thinking, "It's easy for you to talk. You don't have problems like his to live with!")

This case was written by Dr. Abby J. Hansen, research associate, in collaboration with Professor C. Roland Christensen for the Developing Discussion Leadership Skills seminar. While the case is based on data supplied by participants involved, all names and some peripheral facts have been disguised.

Just then she noticed a peculiar motion under the woman's desk: a furry tail thumping. A seeing-eye dog, so quiet that she hadn't noticed its presence, had awakened, stretching, from a nap. The woman leaned down to pat the dog's back. Although she had turned in Paula's direction when speaking to her, the woman had not made direct eye contact. Now Paula knew why.

After this interview, Paula returned home determined to meet Frank Edgerton's next outburst with firm resistance. Sure enough, at their next class meeting, he delivered one of his typically irrelevant insults.

"Pardon me, Frank," Paula said calmly, "I don't think that's a useful response to Lois's comment. Rather than just knocking her, could you please address her point more directly?" She got up, walked to the board, then turned back to face the students -- anxious to gauge the effect of her brisk (though, she hoped, polite) put-down.

The Handicapped Heckler (C)

No one was looking directly at Frank, but Paula saw that his face was red. He stared at his hands and remained silent. Paula wrote a few literary terms on the board, returned to her seat in the circle of chairs, and asked a general question on the text. A student answered and the discussion continued.

To Paula, it seemed that the group's morale improved from that day on. The two or three times Frank interrupted she promptly asked him to behave more courteously, and soon his interruptions ceased. He actually joined the class discussion a few times, although Paula noted that there was always a cynical cast to his interpretations.

Paula ended the course feeling rather pleased with the students' progress, although the discomfort of Frank's presence never really disappeared. Still, several students in the group had shown talent and enthusiasm. Clearly, they had profited from the seminar. And Frank's behavior had improved. Paula decided that she hadn't realized how much the students depended upon her to set an example. When she shrank from challenge, her timidity communicated itself to them. As soon as she resisted Frank, the group realized they could rely on her to protect them from insult and interruption. They spoke more boldly, and their discussions improved accordingly.

"My greatest lesson in all this," Paula observed, "was learning how responsible I am for creating the climate of open inquiry and trust without which discussion teaching cannot take place."

This case was written by Dr. Abby J. Hansen, research associate, in collaboration with Professor C. Roland Christensen for the Developing Discussion Leadership Skills Seminar. While the case is based on data supplied by participants involved, all names and some peripheral facts have been disguised.

Henry Jasper (B)

Carol Cutler Analyzes Henry Jasper's Situation

In my view, there are a number of issues involved in this case. Besides the peculiar problems of being a female instructor [which will be discussed below], it is clear in retrospect that probably the biggest mistake that I made in this situation was in altering the "rule of the game." Although I had asked for class participation before, when it was not forthcoming I simply proceeded to answer my own question or solve the problem myself.

Clearly I had violated my implicit "psychological contract" with the class, and Jasper felt that this was not fair play. He refused to play by the new rules -- which I, of course, did not realize I had either promulgated or changed. The lesson of this, in retrospect, is that one must clearly understand the explicit rules which one establishes as well as the implicit rules that become accepted by the very nature of one's behavior in the classroom. I was obviously not aware of either and therefore was not sensitive to the fact that I violated those rules by calling on someone who had not volunteered.

Second, I was completely insensitive to the signals that Jasper was sending to me concerning his general insecurity and his apprehension regarding the statistics course in particular. His visits every week were primarily asking for reassurance rather than indicating interest. His selection of a seat very close to the instructor's desk made it easy for him to ask questions regarding the solution of problems without having to get up and walk to the front -- in other words, he could obtain all the help he needed (substantively and emotionally) without having to signal to the rest of the class that he needed help. His lack of interaction with the rest of the class and his formal orientation in his relation to me should have indicated that he had some problems in his social relationships.

This case was written by Tamara Gilman under the supervision of Professor C. Roland Christensen from data supplied by Carol Cutler for the Developing Discussion Leadership Skills Seminar. All names and some peripheral facts have been disguised.

However, I chose to consistently misread these signs and therefore blundered into the horrendous situation that I did.

That situation was compounded by the fact that I was the only female instructor. In retrospect I recognize that there are two clear and distinct roles that were presented in addition to the ostensible one of "neutral" instructor. This recognition is why I included some background on my disastrous first day of teaching.

The first was that of the helpless "girl" who encountered all those intimidating athletes and who, I'm sure, could not engender respect (and even if I could have, I'm pretty sure they wouldn't have given it). I'm not sure how much of this reaction can be attributed to my own behavior and how much to theirs, but after reflection I am convinced that this is an ever-present problem which a woman instructor faces and a man never does.

The sheer lack of "presence" -- in terms of size, voice, and power -- is one aspect. The fact that men students hesitate to attribute competence to a woman is another. And the socialization process for women, which emphasizes lack of aggression or assertiveness for women, is a very large part. For instance, you will recall that when I realized I was in the middle of a conspiracy that first day, my instinctive reaction was to smile, cajole, and entreat the men to do the work and quit harassing me. That is a typical female-role reaction, and one that I would say is totally inappropriate to developing respect and control in a classroom.

Perhaps the image of the woman professional is changing now, but I would guess that if a woman were to walk into an overwhelmingly male classroom even now, she would still have to do much more than her male counterpart to establish the same atmosphere. I know that personally I am going to have to be much more aware of my most elementary behavior patterns (i.e., smiling) in order to be certain that I don't say something unconsciously that I don't mean to, or that a male student body would interpret differently coming from a female instructor.

Second, in the encounter with Jasper a diametrically different role emerges -- that of the maternal comfort-and-security figure. While this role probably emerges in a minority of cases, it indicates the diversity of interpretations and perceptions that can occur and that are significantly different for women. This role is probably less damaging to the classroom situation, but it has the potential for open hostility when the student perceives himself as betrayed -- (witness Jasper's violent and disruptive behavior). I think that there must be a fine line between being perceived as genuinely supportive and being perceived as a security figure, and I do not as yet have any idea how to establish that line. I hope that I will by the time I find myself "in the pit."

I Felt as if My World Had Just Collapsed! (B)

Sue Roper Recalls the Incident

I turned back to Sarah and said the only thing I could think of: "Please take out your minidrama so you can see which one you and Carrie will perform." I was thinking, "Damn it, there's no way I'm going to let Carrie get away with this sort of behavior in my class!" The group was still unnaturally quiet, watching me, aware that I was really upset. Then I turned to Carrie and said, "It doesn't matter if you aren't in the same dorm. You can exchange phone numbers, or get together in the student lounge, or meet in the library, or work in the dining room after dinner. There's absolutely no reason you can't work together."

I didn't wait for an answer, but turned to another student, making a conscious decision not to look at either Carrie or Sarah again for the rest of the class. Somehow I managed to continue pairing students for the minidrama exercise, but I acted wooden because I felt so disturbed. I didn't, in the larger sense, know what to do. This had been an unacceptable display of racism and rejection that had upset me deeply. My heart was pounding and my head had already started aching as I went through the motions of finishing the class. I kept wondering: Should I immediately stop the class to confront the issue that I perceived as racial prejudice? Should I ask Carrie to come see me in my office? Should I ask Sarah? Maybe call the two of them in? Should I inform Cynthia Wilson, one of our black deans? Should I lodge some sort of formal complaint?

I had let the initial remark go by without a direct verbal reaction to its clear undertone of racism, but I felt the issue was terribly important and I was haunted by what long-term action I should take as a person and professor in an epoch and a setting of supposed awareness and sensitivity to social equality.

This case was prepared by Dr. Abby J. Hansen and Joy Renjilian-Burgy in collaboration with Professor C. Roland Christensen for the Developing Discussion Leadership Skills seminar. Although based on data supplied by participants involved, all names and some peripheral facts have been disguised.

During the rest of that class I wondered whether I'd done the right thing by not directly confronting Carrie's unacceptable behavior, but I was terrified of not being able to handle the situation and of humiliating both the girls and myself.

When a teacher humiliates a student, it shows the teacher's weakness, not the student's. I also realized that calling further public attention to the incident would only worsen Sarah's hurt. But I knew that something serious had happened, and I felt completely out of control.

I decided to say nothing about the incident to either girl until they had performed their minidrama. It was a matter of integrity to me that they should do this assignment in class. But having had to force the issue so overtly made me feel like a failure because my larger life purpose -- creating an open, accepting, interactive atmosphere -- had been undermined.

When they did their dialogue in class the next week, I was struck by its inocuousness. They had memorized Sarah's script, which contained lines such as "I've got a blind date tonight; I wonder what he'll be like. What shall I wear?" Both students spoke well and acted pleasant and courteous during the presentation. I gave them each B+ for their work, but I couldn't let the matter rest there. That would have been irresponsible. The underlying issue was too important. I had to take some long-term action to straighten this out. But what?

I Felt as if My World Had Just Collapsed! (C)

Sue Roper Recalls Long-Term Outcome of Troubling Events

I always hold individual midterm conferences with each student. I took these interviews with Carrie and Sarah as an opportunity to discuss the incident. The conferences were about one week after they had done the minidrama in class. Carrie acted embarrassed and defensive when I asked her what she had meant by initially refusing to work with Sarah. She completely denied that her remark had been racist. When I suggested that she and Sarah might have become friends through working together, Carrie said that black girls were cliquish at Greenwood. They all ate together, lived near each other in one particular dorm, and played the same loud music. This was exactly the sort of stereotypical comment I remembered hearing over a dozen years before. I later found out that Carrie had initially been assigned a black roommate, but had asked to have her room changed.

With Sarah, the midterm conference went quite differently. She said, rather fatalistically, "I know Carrie didn't want to work with me because I'm black. There's plenty of racism at Greenwood, and this was just another example of it. One teacher here assigns a textbook that describes blacks as inferior. If the teachers are racist, what can you expect of the students?" She said that only her parents' feelings had kept her from leaving the school. They were a working class family, very anxious for her to graduate from a good college and have a career. They were proud of her, and her success meant a lot to them. I told her, "I have an assignment for you: Sit with Carrie again. Make conversation. You've got to make an effort; you can't always expect other people to assume the burden of friendship."

I continued, I admit, to feel distant from Carrie because she had deceived me. I had been honest with the class

This case was prepared by Dr. Abby J. Hansen and Joy Renjilian-Burgy in collaboration with Professor C. Roland Christensen for the Developing Discussion Leadership Skills seminar. Although based on data supplied by participants involved, all names and some peripheral facts have been disguised.

and told them my feelings about prejudice. But she had given me absolutely no clue to her feelings until -- wham! -- she openly rejected Sarah. To me that was a betrayal of trust. I still feel that Carrie duped me. And I still feel that I somehow failed the whole group and failed myself. I was self-conscious with them for the whole rest of the semester.

In a very unpleasant way, this incident revealed to me my own ignorance. I had thought I knew the rules and had developed a comprehensive system: how to create a cohesive atmosphere in the classroom, how to communicate with students and get them to communicate with each other. I had also thought my intuition was sharp enough

to prevent me from pairing the wrong people, or maybe I mean that my classroom was open enough to allow me the pairing of any two people. But there it was. I had been wrong.

I still ponder the incident. I did mention it to Cynthia Wilson informally, and she shrugged it off as a common experience for blacks. But Sarah thought it was patently racist, and I did, too. Still, Carrie absolutely denied it. Yet I still feel that, after years of lofty idealism, I acted like a coward in front of all fifteen girls and myself. What, I wonder, was I really facing in that classroom? And what will I do the next time I experience racism in my classroom?

A Night School Episode (B)

Sylvia Nevins tried first to minimize the personal aspect of the confrontation by asking the class at large if anyone else had been offended.

Half a dozen women shook their heads, but half a dozen men nodded. Sylvia groaned inwardly: polarization -- women against men -- was the last thing she wanted in the classroom! She decided, therefore, to change tack by directing attention back to the material. "Frankly," she said, "I find the entire Victorian ideology offensive." This seemed to mollify the man who had objected, and the class resumed its discussion. Afterward, the man disappeared quickly; Sylvia was relieved at not having any opportunity to speak with him privately.

The next class meeting went normally, with Sylvia lecturing for the first hour. but she noticed that the man who had objected the previous week was scowling, and this began to make her feel uncomfortable. During the class break, seeing him sitting alone, Sylvia gathered her courage and walked over to him. Smiling hypocritically, she said: "I'm sorry I missed you after class last time, because I wanted to thank you for your honest, forthright class comments." He looked surprised. "I thought you'd be mad at me for criticizing you in class," he said. "Oh, no," she went on -- letting her instinct to placate dominate her instinct to tell him how annoyed she really had been -- (in fact, at the time, she had wanted to tell him to shut up or leave) -- "I was pleased that you spoke up."

Upon reflection, Sylvia was glad she had trusted the urge to make peace. The man became a more cheerful, friendly, and active member of the class. When he handed in his term paper, she discovered that his views on family life were extremely conservative -- ideologically quite far from her own. But she saw no personal animosity in his attitudes.

This case was written by Dr. Abby J. Hansen, research associate, from material submitted by Dr. Elaine Tyler May for the Developing Discussion Leadership Skills and the Teaching by the Case Method seminars. Data were furnished by the involved participants. All names and some peripheral facts have been disguised.

To Sylvia, the incident held several lessons. Her initial feeling of having been personally attacked had been an overreaction. Her attitude -- expressed hypocritically -- of welcoming honest comments even when they criticized her in public had been the correct one, the one she should have had. Her lack of awareness of the intrinsic sensitivity of some of the material had been unfortunate. And, finally, the success of her "private" class break with the man showed her that classroom dynamics can be greatly improved by informal, out-of-class contacts.

The Offended Colonel (B)

As Ben Cheever scanned the classroom at the Commanding Officers' Senior Executive Institute, he read outrage in only the colonel's expression. But, on the other hand, none of the other participants had leaped to his rescue. It occurred to him to ask the woman her opinion. Her face certainly conveyed no anger to Ben, and he was skeptical of the colonel's accuracy in speaking on her behalf. But Ben realized that she might not want to embarrass her colleague; his predicament might worsen.

Ben considered his colloquial style merely casual and the profanity it often included well within "normal bounds." Never, since he had first begun teaching as a graduate student, had anyone called his language offensive. Part of him was tempted to retort, "Hey, fellow, are you really serious? I learned this language from a Marine!" But he didn't want to insult a workshop participant. Nonetheless, he thought that apologizing might imply intimidation or shame on his part -- neither of which he felt. Besides, apologizing might damage his dignity and lessen the group's respect.

The colonel's expression and stance clearly showed that he was expecting the apology he had demanded.

"Look, it would be hypocritical of me to say I'm sorry," Ben told him. "So I won't. This is the way I talk. I'm just being myself, and that's it."

The colonel stiffened. "If that's the case, well, I don't feel I care to stay." He began to make his way out of the row of seats. Another officer, also in uniform, arose and accompanied him from the room. No one else left, nor did anyone say anything.

This case was written by Dr. Abby J. Hansen, research associate, for the Developing Discussion Leadership Skills and Teaching by the Case Method seminars. Data were furnished by the involved participants. All names and some peripheral facts have been disguised.

After their exit, Ben continued the discussion, making no further reference to the exchange. Among those who came to speak with him directly after the session, the woman in question appeared to say that she certainly had not been offended by his language and had, furthermore, enjoyed the case discussion enormously. After the lunch break, several others apologized to Ben for the colonel's hostile remarks and mentioned that he happened to be a "born-again Christian." Ben left the institute feeling that on the whole he'd handled this situation appropriately.

One Teacher's Nightmare (B)

Slowly, Jeff Freeman's resolve crumbled. He boiled inwardly as he recalled Matt Crane's insulting tone, but as he revolved the issue in his mind, he began to see more and more merit in the fellow's argument. Football, Jeff knew, was a passion to many students at Southwestern. It happened to be a passion Jeff didn't share, but then most of the students didn't get excited about the Napoleonic Code. To each his own. Jeff began to think that, since football obviously meant the earth to this boneheaded Bob Crane, and nobody had elected Jeff Freeman Supreme Arbiter of Student Fate in Charge of Ruining Bob Crane's Life, he might as well go ahead and change the damned grade.

Feeling queasy, Jeff took out a Grade Change form and made the necessary pen strokes to keep Bob Crane on the football team. But part of him winced as he wrote "No Credit." He continued to feel uncomfortable with this decision.

This case was written by Dr. Abby J. Hansen, research associate, for the Developing Discussion Leadership Skills and the Teaching by the Case Method seminars. Data were furnished by the involved participants. All names and some peripheral facts have been disguised.

The Section Was Mine to Lose (D)

Ed Sherman Describes the Next Class

I simply went in there at our next meeting and "worked the crowd" like a professional entertainer. I wore my bright red plaid "Christmas" vest as a signal of general good spirits, made no mention of our past problems, and made sure I had picked on a good, strong student to start the case.

We had a good discussion, and, in fact, the section turned out very well. They say around here if you have an easy fall, you'll have a tough spring and vice versa. Well, this section and I had a tough fall. Spring was good. We started tight, so when we loosened up, things were fine.

This case was written by Dr. Abby J. Hansen, research associate, for the Developing Discussion Leadership Skills and the Teaching by the Case Method seminars. Data were furnished by the involved participants. All names and some peripheral facts have been disguised.

The Section Was Mine to Lose (E)

Hayes Latham Describes the Next Class

When we next met with Edward, this is the way he handled things: he reveled in floating around talking to people before class, and that's what he did this time. He wore his red plaid vest, too -- it later became known as a sort of trademark -- and he called on a very strong student to open. The class went very well that day, and Edward worked hard to make sure that things were very positive. I wrote him a note saying, "Good, fine, just continue doing what you're doing and stop thinking too much about process. That was a good class."[1]

Our annoyance with Edward became a closed issue. There was no confrontation. I think it's important to avoid such things. It's like running downstairs. If you think about how you're taking each step, you're going to fall right over on your face. Examining the teacher's relationship with the section face to face at length is appropriate to Industrial Psychology but to no other class. Besides, Edward is aloof by nature. He likes to make people laugh, to be funny, and to be smart.

I should mention that Edward is very impressive. The class felt he had terrific control of the material and that he had handled this problem in our relationship very well. Not every teacher reacted so cooperatively to complaints from students. Personally, I thought his reaction was fantastic!

---

1. See Exhibit 1 for the text of this note.

This case was written by Dr. Abby J. Hansen, research associate, for the Developing Discussion Leadership Skills and the Teaching by the Case Method seminars. Data were furnished by the involved participants. All names and some peripheral facts have been disguised.

Exhibit 1

The Section Was Mine to Lose (E)

Bay Area Graduate School of Management

MEMORANDUM

TO: Edward

FROM: Hayes

DATE: October 16

Just a quick note to say the class responded really well to today's class. Specifically, in the class meeting, people commented that they felt you had the class on <u>building points</u> by not allowing people to change the subject until the point was complete. Also some good comments on the comparison between the cases. A few commented that they felt it was one of the best classes of the year!

P.S. Writing down names did come up in the meeting so I explained that you had not intended it to have that effect and were going to stop. Also, Charles responded that he felt his whole experience had been positive and that you had been helpful. Subject moved on, point was closed, and I haven't heard a word since.

*   *   *

Researcher's Note: Ed Sherman commented on this note, saying, "It should have made me feel good, but it made me feel bad because it meant they were judging me!"

PART V   Synopses of Additional Teaching Cases

Synopses of Additional Teaching Cases

This section contains abstracts of additional teaching cases, developed by Joyce Wadsworth, which you may want to use at your school. These cases are available from the Harvard Business School Publishing Division, Soldiers Field, Boston, Massachusetts 02163. Identifying case numbers are included at end of each abstract. Use the order form at end of this book.

*　　*　　*

Assistant Professor Brian Duncan

Case Overview

(A) *Case*

In August of 1976 Brian Duncan, 33, resigned as assistant to the vice president of operations of a Pittsburgh, Pennsylvania, firm and accepted an assistant professorship in the Business Department at Mountain State College (MSC). In the first case in the series we learn why Brian Duncan made the move, what he encountered at MSC, and how he attempted to solve what he considered a serious problem: the fact that the majority of his students not only had little grasp of material fundamental to his courses but that they lacked "personal standards."

The case gives background information on MSC, a branch of the state's university system -- located in an eastern U.S. mountain resort area -- with an enrollment of 3,000 full-time students. In brief, it was founded as a teachers' college but expanded in the sixties under the direction of a president who developed undergraduate degree programs in the liberal arts and business administration. The student body is predominantly white, with in-state students coming largely from working-class families, and out-of-state students tending to be affluent and -- according to Brian -- a "breed of fun-loving, academically underachieving recreational jocks." MSC has an open admissions policy for in-state students and while this policy has helped the college to grow, Brian feels that it contributes to the sense of inferiority pervading the institution.

We learn how Brian introduced himself to his students as a professional manager, not a professional teacher; how Managerial Control (MC) would be like a math course with each step built on preceding steps; and that managerial control was "the use of managerial accounting information in decision making." We then read about early student feedback and Brian's reactions to it. His students, although willing, had real trouble with the problems presented, and their efforts indicated weak preparation in accounting. They considered many of the problems unfair because they were distracted by irrelevant data. Brian reminded them that in the working world neat problems were rare, and that choosing relevant data from irrelevant data was essential. Students expressed anxiety about the upcoming exam; Brian told them what sorts of problems to anticipate and scheduled optional review sessions. He then asked a colleague how his section of MC was going -- expecting similar sorts of difficulties -- and was surprised to hear that all was going smoothly. A student told him later that the colleague had "mostly just been lecturing so far."

(B) *Case*

Brian grades his Labor Relations midterms and expresses his exasperation to his wife. He shows her, for example, one exam where the student attempts to answer a question with one sentence. He gives the exam an F. By the time he has finished grading Managerial Control and Labor Relations, he has given over 70 F's.

(C) *Case*

Four years later, we see the results of Brian's steady attempts to improve students' personal standards as well as faculty grading standards at MSC. First we read Brian's critique of a grade monitoring report submitted by the Academic Standards Committee (ASC) in 1977. He comments on the almost total absence of D's and F's and the extremely high percentage of A's for education majors. Making his feelings known to the faculty, he is elected to the ASC and by 1979 has become its chairperson. By 1980 Brian has prepared a new type of grade monitoring report which holds each teacher accountable for his or her grades.

Case Issues

This case series focuses on the efforts made by a professor to improve the motivation, standards, and ultimately the self-image of students at a little-known state college. We read his initial reactions of dismay and exasperation, and then see how, over a period of four years, he is able to make significant and fundamental changes, while remaining a well-respected teacher and colleague. What were the secrets of his success? How was he able to avoid being thought of by students as condescending, punitive, or destructive? How was he able to persuade certain faculty members that they were not meeting their responsibilities to students, and how was he able to do this without alienating them? What sorts of values did he espouse, and how did those values sustain him? How was he able to communicate those values to his students in a way that motivated them to change?

Case Information

This case series is seven pages long and divided into three units. It would be particularly useful for teachers who find themselves in situations where both faculty and students seem to have low self-esteem, or where they try to motivate -- while grading fairly -- students with a low self-image.

HBS Case Nos. (A) 9-381-121;
(B) 9-381-122; (C) 9-381-123.

*   *   *

Assistant Professor Donna Oscura and Ms. Sarah Summers

Case Overview

This case series describes a teacher's handling of what she perceives to be a suicide threat from one of her students. First we read the student's emotional and ambiguous comments, after which we are given background on the academic institution and the teacher.

(A) Case

Assistant Professor Donna Oscura teaches in the Humanities Department at Central State University. She feels out of place at Central, alone in her commitment to excellent teaching. Even though she pub-

lishes, Donna feels that in the eyes of her colleagues the time she spends with her students [instead of devoting to research] reflects negatively on her impending tenure decision. She feels a victim of sexist discrimination at Central, and to make matters worse, her marriage is currently unstable.

Sarah Summers is a student who seems different from the others, but it takes Donna many weeks to realize that Sarah has emotional problems. In the meantime her response to Sarah differs from her response to other students. For example, she reacts with sympathy to Sarah's complaints, and sets no limits on the length of time or number of Sarah's visits. One week after telling Donna that she is going to stop seeing her counselor, Sarah says, "I've been thinking that I really ought to listen to those voices inside me that tell me to give it all up." Stunned, Donna wonders what to do.

(B) Case

After consulting with another teacher, Donna locates Sarah and asks her to come to her office. She asks Sarah directly whether or not she means to hurt herself. Sarah shrugs off the concern and says she was only speaking metaphorically. Later Donna is able to talk to Sarah's counselor who tells her that in his opinion, Sarah will not attempt suicide.

(C) Case

Several years later, Donna reviews the incident. She realizes that Sarah's behavior was a kind of emotional blackmail and that her suicide threat was a bid for attention, yet she is glad that she did not rely on her own judgment and that she sought professional counsel.

Case Issues

This case describes a teacher's response to a student's apparent suicide threat. It also describes the relationship between the teacher and student, and we watch as the teacher unwittingly encourages the student's disturbed behavior. She finally takes steps to remedy the situation. Among the issues for the reader to consider are the sense of alienation teachers can experience at institutions that do not share their values, how such feelings of alienation can influence their behavior, and how an unhappy home situation can also influence their behavior -- often without their knowing. The readers also consider the symptoms of disturbed behavior and what might be done in response to those symptoms.

Case Information

This case is approximately eight pages long and divided into three units.

HBS Case Nos. (A) 9-380-218; (B) 9-380-219; (C) 9-380-220.

*   *   *

Assistant Professor Patrick Grady

Case Overview

(A) Case

Patrick Grady, a hard-working assistant professor of history in his second year at Brown University, is faced with making a decision that might have profound consequences for one of his students. He has just turned in a failing grade for Tom Morrow -- a student who failed to hand in his term paper despite two phone calls from Grady and two clearly defined extensions. Four hours later, Tom calls the weary Professor Grady, saying his paper will be ready by the next morning. He pleads with his instructor to tell the registrar that the failing grade was a clerical error. And he informs Grady that he (Tom) is on probation and will be dropped if he fails the course.

(B) Case

After some discussion, and though he wavers fleetingly, Professor Grady tells his student that he would benefit from taking time off from school -- and sticks with the failing grade.

Case Issues

This case series takes on the subject of when to make exceptions for students. How does one deal with rule infractions? What are conditions for leniency, for clemency, for finality? How much effort should a professor put into these problems, before or after the fact? Should an evaluation or grade be influenced by the professor's knowledge of the student's personal situation? Are there factors regarding a professor's personal life that can influence a student's evaluation? Does a teacher's responsibility end with giving a grade?

Case Information

This case series is two and one-half pages long and divided into two units of unequal length (the second case consists of one paragraph). It could be used most effectively in a liberal arts seminar.

HBS Case Nos. (A) 9-380-221; (B) 9-380-222.

*   *   *

Bob Lunt

Case Overview

(A) Case

Martha Elliot, a new assistant professor at the San Francisco Bay Area Graduate School of Social Policy, fumes over a final exam in Financial Management 220 handed in that day by her student, Bob Lunt. She rereads what she thinks is a hostile paragraph: Lunt states that he refuses to "play with numbers," because "in realities outside the classroom, numbers comprise a game rather than part of a publicly shared form of objective inquiry." She wonders if his failure to answer the exam means that she has failed as an instructor.

We are then given background on the instructor, the student, and the course. In brief, Martha is 29, and had recently received her doctorate in public service management. Bob Lunt was in his late thirties (considerably older than most students in the course). A former professor of English at San Francisco State College, he had decided to change careers. Financial Management 220 was difficult for many first-semester students because it was heavily quantitative. Martha prided herself on being able to "humanize the numbers."

Martha reflected on the class's composition -- the "back-row mafia" who avoided number-crunching but offered management recommendations, and a front-row group that offered numerical solutions to everything. There were a few other scattered categories, but Bob Lunt fit into none of them. He was soft-spoken, polite, articulate, and different. At first he seemed interested in class material. He always arrived early for class, as did Martha; but Martha usually found herself besieged with questions from the "number crunchers" and never quite got around to speaking with Bob Lunt. She observed his aloofness from the class but attributed it to his age difference.

The case reviews the take-home final exam used in the course. It consisted of a balance sheet for a hospital and information describing the plan of the department head to keep an expensive dialysis unit open at the hospital. The department head had to present his argument to the hospital director who thought the unit too costly to run. Each student had to analyze the whole case, complete with figures and recommendations.

(B) Case

The (B) case reports Martha Elliot's note of response to Bob Lunt's bluebook. Her anger clearly carries over into her comments. She tells him he "guessed wrong" and explains why. Then she confronts his "attitudinal" problem. She reminds him why, in her opinion, quantitative analysis is essential for the field he has chosen to enter, and proceeds to guess at the causes of his hostility, basically telling him he should resolve his conflicts or quit the field.

(C) Case

One year later we review Martha Elliot's reflections on the events involving Bob Lunt. The reader is asked to think about the fears and anxieties of a new instructor, the ease of misreading a student's signals, and the power a teacher has to help or hurt a student and to mold a student to fit the instructor's negative or positive expectations.

Case Issues

This case raises questions about a teacher projecting her fears and anxieties onto a student, thus setting him up to fulfill her worst expectations. It also raises questions about a student's "signals" and what gets in the way of an instructor "reading" them correctly. We are reminded of two ways in which a teacher has power over a student -- power to hurt a student professionally and power to mold a student into what the teacher thinks the student should be.

Case Information

This case series is twelve pages long and divided into three sections.

HBS Case Nos. (A) 9-382-054;
(B) 9-382-055; (C) 9-382-056.

*   *   *

Bob Peters

Case Overview

In this case series we watch how a teacher's condescending remark in class toward one of his students backfires dramatically. It is his first teaching experience, and we anticipate trouble as we catch glimpses of his in-class behavior. His remark humiliates a student in front of her classmates, and though he later offers an apology and hopes that the incident will be forgotten, the student threatens retaliation, gangster-style, the night of the final exam.

(A) Case

Bob Peters teaches Introduction to Economics I, a course offered in the Evening Division of Newtown Community College (NCC). We learn that the Extension Division attracts students who work full time, that for many of these students tuition is reimbursed by their employers, and that some of the employers stipulate that their employees earn at least a C in order to be reimbursed.

Bob Peters received his MBA from Wharton and felt, five years later, that his marketing management career had reached a plateau. He responds eagerly to an advertisement for part-time teachers at NCC, hoping to explore teaching as a second career. Bob determines that in his class of fifteen there are a few bright students, but also a sizable minority weak in simple arithmetic. He compromises and puts together a course that he considers the bare minimum level of attainment.

On the night of the review class for the final exam, Donna Gardella, a student who received a D on the midterm, asks a question. Bob proceeds to try to drill the answer out of her. As she finally falters, he provides the answer, only to see Donna walk out of the room.

(B) Case

Bob looks for ways to convince himself that the episode is minor. He telephones Donna to apologize. When she does not sound angry he is relieved, and offers her any special help she may need.

(C) Case

In the two weeks before the final exam Bob has convinced himself that Donna, in fact, has apologized for blowing out of proportion his remark in class. He is shocked, therefore, on the evening of the exam when she tells him she needs a C in the course to get reimbursed by her employer; if she doesn't get the C, Peters will be in trouble, as she "has friends" and she knows where he lives.

Case Issues

In this case a teacher is threatened with "retaliation" for a humiliating remark he made to a student in his class. The teacher does not always seem aware of his "superior" attitude, but it quietly pervades his opinion of Newtown and his approach to teaching. A key teaching question is, How could Bob Peters have handled this situation differently, will he be able to learn from the experience, and what should he learn from the experience?

Case Information

The case series is seven pages long and divided into three units.

HBS Case Nos. (A) 9-381-015; (B) 9-381-016; (C) 9-381-017.

*   *   *

The Case of the Disgruntled Student

Case Overview

In this case we witness a series of encounters at DuBois College between an angry black Vietnam veteran and a highly educated young black instructor. The instructor is teaching for the first time and has introduced the case method to his Business Policy class -- the capstone integrative course in the business administration program. The veteran feels that his teacher and classmates are naive, and that he is wasting his time listening to case method "speculation." He purposely disrupts class. The instructor seems at a loss when faced with the student's provocations. The tension escalates and erupts into an explosion in class.

The instructor, Larry Young, 29, a graduate of the MBA program at Charles River Graduate School of Business, plans to enter the doctoral program at Charles River but hopes to obtain college-level teaching experience first. We learn that many students in Business Policy are perceived to have less than adequate skills in communication and mathematics.

The "disgruntled student," Johnny Davis, 27, is one of the oldest students at DuBois. We learn that he had been suspended from State University during his freshman year and had subsequently spent four years in the Navy. He returned to college at 24 to obtain a B.A. in business administration. In addition to interrupting Larry, Johnny constantly arrives late to class, takes no notes, and stares out the window. Larry tries to speak with him after class, but Johnny's manner is offensive, and he insists on being called "Mr. Davis."

We watch as Larry develops the case method successfully in Business Policy. As the class becomes more sophisticated in working with cases, Johnny's dissatisfaction grows. Larry still does not know how to handle his disruptive comments. We then read about "the explosion," a shouting match that erupts in the classroom. Once again, Johnny arrives late but he is more disruptive than usual. He listens impatiently as the class tries to analyze a case and come up with strategic recommendations. He shouts out his recommendation -- a market research study. At this point another student, Hank Nelson, without waiting to be recognized, lambastes Johnny's suggestion, and ends with barbed personal comments. Johnny jumps to his feet and shouts at the class, saying he spent four years in the Navy defending the likes of them and that he "didn't come back to school to speculate. . . ." Then he leaves the room.

Case Issues

This case touches on an exceedingly complex situation -- the feelings that developed between an angry black Vietnam veteran and his black instructor during a course. The instructor is able to take risks when it comes to teaching (introducing the case method to students who were comfortable only with lectures) but he is unable to take risks over personal confrontations. The student seems to enjoy confrontations. When the instructor consistently ignores the student's provocative remarks in class, everyone's tension escalates (class, instructor, student) until the student responds with an enraged outburst.

The case ends with the outburst and the instructor knows he must take the situation in hand -- but how?

Case Information

This case is one unit, nine pages long, and would be useful to any seminar wishing to discuss the topic of how to handle an angry, disruptive student. The topic is enriched by its setting -- that of complicated relationships within a minority group.

HBS Case No. 9-380-017

*   *   *

The Case of the Frustrated Feminist

Case Overview

(A) Case

Penny Steers is a 39-year-old mid-level administrator in personnel at Midwestern University. In the course of interviewing faculty women about their benefits, she has heard from many of them disquieting news about male/female faculty relations: to wit, that in some departments the atmosphere is still unpleasantly chilly toward women, who are still a tiny percentage of all faculty at Midwestern. She has written up a report of her interview findings, and at the suggestion of her male boss (the director of personnel), has presented it to <u>his</u> boss (the provost), Gloria Barnes. Gloria, one of the highest-placed women in the university, has been cordial to Penny, and is known to be an advocate for women.

We meet Penny coming out of Gloria's office in a shocked and agitated state. In the hall outside she fortunately meets her friend, Shirley Napier (professor of economics). Through their conversation, we learn that Gloria Barnes has reacted in a hostile way to the report, suggesting that its conclusions are unrepresentative of the atmosphere at Midwestern and going so far as to question the accuracy of Penny's reporting.

In the rest of the case we learn more about Penny (a divorced mother of two), her feminist convictions, and the situation women face at a large co-ed university in the Middle West. Penny and Shirley discuss some of Penny's options: the question is, What should she do now? Shirley

advises her to "bury" the report ("<u>You</u> don't have tenure, kid!"); Penny, while admitting that she is loathe to "fight," feels it would be wrong to suppress the stories that women faculty were so eager to tell her.

Two (B) Cases

"The Frustrated Feminist" is unusual in having two (B) cases. In one, despite Penny's efforts, the report remains suppressed. In the other, it is incorporated into a larger, more general report on the status of women at the university. As a discussion leader, you might choose to use the one that runs counter to the expectations of your group about the outcome: e.g., if most group members would expect the report to be suppressed, use the (B) case in which the institution goes far beyond what Penny expected it to do in reporting on the condition of women at all levels.

The (B) cases begin similarly. In both, after anxious deliberation, Penny sends the report to all the faculty women she interviewed, along with a form asking each to (1) assess how accurately her comments were reported; (2) suggest whether the report should be sent to all female faculty, all faculty, or to no one; (3) comment on whether the report would discourage female faculty from coming to Midwestern. The responses are the same in both (B) cases: favorable to Penny and to dissemination. Gloria Barnes, given the responses, answers in a memo: "Okay to go to women faculty, but not yet." It is at this point that the two (B) cases diverge.

(B1) Case. A few months later, Gloria Barnes announces that she wants to do her own study of female faculty. Penny's boss -- Danny Morris, an amiable and adroit administrator (who happens to be black, sympathetic to feminism, and respectful of Penny's work) -- sees this as an opportunity to get support from both the president and from Gloria for a complete study of the climate for women. The study is carried through under Penny's supervision, and (after much debate) made public.

(B2) Case. Over the course of a year, Penny quietly manages to bring her report to the attention of two committees entrusted with oversight of the status of women at the university -- one composed entirely of women faculty and the other composed jointly of men and women trustees. No action ensues. The efforts of a few female faculty members to persuade Gloria Barnes that the time is ripe for tackling the problems mentioned in Penny's report are also of no avail.

In both cases Penny Steers leaves Midwestern to take a job in a smaller college as dean of students.

Case Issues

"The Case of the Frustrated Feminist" focuses on a crucial moment in the life of an individual woman with a modest amount of power and influence when she feels she has an opportunity to help other women, and is stymied -- and personally wounded -- by the initial institutional reaction to her endeavor. The fact that the institution's reaction is expressed by another woman -- and a woman whom she has known and liked and respected -- is another complicating factor of the case. In trying to bring about change in such circumstances, how does a woman handle her feelings -- particularly when there is some tension between her career ambitions and her idealistic goals? In a complex institutional setting, what are her strategic choices at various points? How does she decide where her responsibilities end?

Case Information

The (A) case is three pages long; each (B) case is about two pages. "The Case of the Frustrated Feminist" is particularly appropriate for a single session of discussion; or it could be used in an early session of a series of discussions.

HBS Case Nos. (A) 9-387-002; (B1) 9-387-003; (B2) 9-387-004.

*   *   *

Cathy Ross

Case Overview

Tim Walsh, one year out of business school, teaches Control, a required course in the first-year of an MBA program. The course deals with issues in accounting and behavioral science that would be relevant to a corporate controller. Tim thinks back over the completed course and wonders what part he played in losing the active involvement of one of his stronger students. Despite two appointments and one telephone conversation with the student, he does not fully grasp the changes in her

performance and attitude, nor what message she may have been trying to convey to him.

The student was Cathy Ross, an engineer from Texas with solid work experience, enthusiastic and popular, adept at the case method, and an active participant in class. She had worked for Hightech Limited for three years immediately prior to coming to business school. In mid-October the section was assigned a case on Hightech Limited. Tim entered the classroom fifteen minutes early and listened to Cathy as she talked to a large cluster of students about her former company, commenting on its management control system and its evolution in the ten years since the case was written. Tim was impressed by her comments and by the signs of respect from the students, and asked her to recap her analysis for the benefit of the entire class. The presentation turned out to be impressive, eliciting questions from usually reticent students, and she received a standing ovation. Tim made closing comments and openly acknowledged Cathy's expertise.

Cathy's presentation on Hightech became a model for other student contributions. The continual comparisons to her earlier presentation, however, finally elicited quiet hissing from disenchanted students. Cathy's class participation began to drop off. Tim saw no reason to intervene formally but looked for an opportunity to broach the topic indirectly; Cathy avoided such opportunities. When Cathy finally scheduled an appointment (after doing well on the midterm), they had a conversation in which her approach was indirect. Whatever points she was trying to make did not get across.

Three weeks after Christmas Cathy made another appointment and said she became engaged over Christmas, that she couldn't "get excited" about cases in his course but that she would get by. Subsequently Cathy remained quiet in class with some increased participation toward the end of the course. Her final exam was in the middle range and her final grade was a Satisfactory. Cathy called Tim to register surprise over her grade. After the conversation he wondered if his handling of the Hightech case had been a factor in losing Cathy's active class participation.

Case Issues

This case concerns the challenge of getting the most out of gifted students without damaging their image in the eyes of the class. It also points up subtle issues in teacher-student dynamics. How does a teacher follow up on a student's exceptional performance without setting the student up for a fall? If there is a significant decrease in an active student's class participation, under what circumstances is it the teacher's responsibility to find out the reason? In teacher-student meetings, what are effective methods of asking questions? Similarly, what are effective listening techniques? In these meetings what sorts of considerations inhibit students from being direct? What are some inherent difficulties when the teacher and students are approximately the same age or when the teacher has only recently been a student?

Case Information

This case is one unit, four pages long, and could be used in either a liberal arts or a professional school.

HBS Case No. 9-381-223

*   *   *

Dick Johnson

Case Overview

Dick Johnson, an idealistic young professor of Marketing Strategy, is facing a perplexing teaching situation. Two weeks into his course with undergraduates at Inner City University he asks for guidance on how to handle a student who works hard to prepare for class but who consistently presents superficial in-class comments and seems unable to "hear" opposing arguments. Professor Johnson describes a similarly frustrating earlier teaching situation with an evening MBA course. He describes that class in detail -- its composition, the mixed mode of teaching with both lectures and case discussion, the marketing case under discussion and how it was approached by students and professor, the particular student involved, and finally the professor's teaching style. Not wanting to experience failure again in front of his students or in his own eyes, he asks for help.

Case Issues

This case hinges on the age-old issue of how to balance the needs of regular and slow learners. In addition, it raises the issue of how to develop one's own effective teaching style. Keeping these two themes

in mind, the following questions would be useful: How does an instructor develop techniques for asking effective questions? How does one build section support and get students to help teach other students? How does one balance support and criticism of students? How does one get a student who talks glibly to give a more reasoned, logical explanation? If a variety of strategies fail to get a particular student to modify his class preparation and contribution, what does the instructor do?

Case Information

This case is one unit, five pages long. Because it presents a marketing strategy case in detail, it would be used to best effect in a seminar or where business administration students are in the majority.

HBS Case No. 9-379-024

*   *   *

The Final Exam

Case Overview

Ted Brown, an assistant professor in the MBA program at Far Western State, needs help in thinking through a problem. One of his good students, Paul Clark, has refused to complete the final exam and instead has articulately written up his reasons for taking this action. Ted asks his grader, a Ph.D. candidate, to help him resolve the problem.

First, we read Paul Clark's written statement entitled, "Business Policy II -- Second Term Final Exam." It is clear that he has read the case carefully but that he has many principled objections to going through with a tedious exercise that he considers an affront to the class's intelligence and irrelevant to what the class has been learning. In brief, he feels that the Business Policy department (and thus the exam case) is preoccupied with the role of a consultant who appears, makes suggestions, and disappears -- whereas the class, many of whom are prospective middle managers, need to wrestle with issues in which they themselves make critical decisions. He ends his remarks saying that if Professor Brown would like him to write on a more relevant problem he would be happy to do so.

The case outlines information on the background of the course, including Ted

Brown's statement of course organization and objectives. We are also given personal data on professor and student. Finally we are given information about the exam case.

Professor Brown acknowledges that the section's reactions to this particular exam are overwhelmingly negative, yet Paul Clark is the only student who refused to take it. He tells his grader that the situation is a "hornet's nest of questions and uncertainties" for him, and that he needs help in assessing Paul Clark's statement in order to come up with his final grade.

Case Issues

This case looks at a thorny issue: how to give a final grade to a student who -- on principle -- refuses to complete an exam but whose argument, articulately stated, resonates with the instructor. How does the teacher sort out his decision? Where lies fairness: is it fair to other students if he makes a principled exception? Is it fair to the student in question to let him sacrifice his grade, yet later improve the course and the exam? How does the teacher (in this case a relatively inexperienced assistant professor) balance his ethical responsibilities to himself and to school bureaucracy?

Case Information

This case is one unit, five pages long. Because of its focus on the Business Policy course, it would be used to best advantage in a seminar where business administration students are in the majority, although it raises issues about grading that would be useful in other seminars as well.

HBS Case No. 9-377-120

*   *   *

HB I

Case Overview

(A) Case

The class of second-quarter MBAs at City University's evening MBA program waits for the new instructor of Human Behavior (HB) to arrive and for the first class of the quarter to begin. They speculate as to what the teacher will be like -- they know only that his name is Calvin

Banks and that he has been hired as a part-time instructor. Most of the students expect the class to follow the pattern of other courses in the MBA program in which they receive a syllabus and hear introductory remarks about the subjects to be covered. This pattern generally fits well with their busy schedules, as most of them hold full-time jobs.

Five minutes after class is to have begun, not one, but two instructors enter the room -- Calvin Banks who is black, and Ed Jones, who is white. Contrary to the class's expectations, they ask all class members to say something about themselves. The instructors discuss their own backgrounds, and how they have taught career development seminars together (rather than Human Behavior). Then Calvin Banks asks the class to suggest "course objectives" in order to establish "a contract." It becomes apparent that the instructors know little about the material previously covered in the first quarter of HB.

Gradually the students offer various course objectives but the discussion lags. One student, a white woman who is vice president of an advertising firm, states her lack of respect for this teaching method and leaves the room. Another student, a black man who is an architect, angrily tells the class that they are prejudiced because their instructor is black.

Neither the class nor the two instructors know how to proceed. Calvin Banks looks mystified, trying to comprehend what has gone wrong.

(B) Case

Calvin Banks attempts to salvage the class, and continues in the manner in which he feels comfortable, asking the class their thoughts rather than stating his. We follow the rest of the semester in which discussions go poorly and the instructor comes to interpret the students' poor performance as personal hostility. In his last class he tries a new technique and the class explodes in anger. One week later the dean of the College of Business schedules a meeting with Calvin Banks and presents him with students' negative interpretations of each of his teaching techniques. Calvin is astonished at their interpretations but is given no chance to defend his approach.

Case Issues

This case series concerns several interesting issues, such as the critical decisions an instructor makes on his first day of class, the resistance of students to new or different methods of teaching, the hidden agenda of racial prejudice, and how to regroup when a class gets out of control. What are the basic responsibilities of instructors to their classes on the first day (knowledge of previous semester course, arriving on time, and so on)? What opportunities do they grasp if they meet these responsibilities, and conversely, what traps do they fall into if they do not? Do these decisions vary if a teacher is experienced (as opposed to being a doctoral student)? When students are comfortable with one method of teaching, in what ways can a teacher effectively present a different method of teaching? And finally, what can instructors do when their first class goes badly? What changes can one make if resistance continues throughout the semester?

Case Information

This case series is five pages long, divided into two units. It is of special interest to instructors who teach in the evening or in work/study programs.

HBS Case Nos. (A) 9-380-018; (B) 9-380-019.

*   *   *

Janice Posner

Case Overview

Three weeks into the semester, Janice Posner, a marketing professor at Far Western State University Business School, wonders who or what is responsible for the negative and provocative dynamics in one of her marketing sections. Could it just be a "bad section"? Is something about her teaching style at fault? Is it a bit of both, or something else altogether? She reviews the background of the course, her impressions of Section Q, and the progression of the first five classes.

Janice reviews her introduction to Section Q and tells us how, after the first class, she feels distinctly uncomfortable with the section. The students seem caustic and cliquish, as if they don't like each other. She concludes she would not really like most of them as individuals either. After the second class, she continues to feel uncomfortable. During the third class,

as she writes on the chalkboard, she hears a student leave the class. She feels there is a "message" in this exit, but makes no comment. Later in the day, she happens to meet a member of Section Q and asks him the name of the student who left class. She is told that the student is Brian Thomas (an Afrikaner, 28 years old, with impressive work experience in the field of mining), and that he has challenged authority in various ways in other classes as well. During this conversation Janice is also told that she may be "too nice" to this particular section. Janice defends herself to us, however, saying that she likes to run a "free and open" style of discussion and that she doesn't "saw students' heads off."

The fourth class brings no problems; Brian Thomas is present, though silent. Soon after, Janice reviews the section with Tom Harris, a junior faculty member who was Section Q's first-quarter production instructor. Tom tells Janice that he had to "sit on" the section several times and that he once called Brian Thomas into his office. Janice decides to invite a senior course professor to sit in on her fifth class. We learn that the discussion gets off to a slow start, that after forty-five minutes Brian Thomas makes another exit, and that the entire section seems to be waiting for her reaction.

Case Issues

This case focuses on the elusive phenomenon of negative "class vibes," of provocative group behavior. How does a section develop a personality? What difference do a few student personalities make? What contributes to the evolution of a section that does not seem to like each other? What are effective ways for a teacher to analyze negative class dynamics -- for example, what response is class behavior trying to elicit? When the behavior seems purposeful, what are effective responses and when should they be made? How are the issues further complicated when the professor is female (or, as in this case, a woman who is not assertive)? How can one help a section become more likable?

Case Information

This case is short -- one unit, three pages long. It would be useful in a seminar where teachers wish to analyze and respond to provocative class behavior. (If the focus is to include the development of a "section personality," this case might be discussed in conjunction with another short case, "The Mechanical Hand.")

HBS Case No. 9-379-205

*   *   *

Kho Tanaka

Case Overview

Kho Tanaka, a native Japanese, first-year MBA student at Metropolitan Graduate School of Business, is devastated after reading his instructor's negative comments on his Business Writing paper -- effectively an evaluation of his first six weeks' performance. At the start of a holiday weekend he has no one with whom to talk over his reactions; his few Japanese classmates are out of town. He wonders if he can live down his disgrace and whether or not, with his level of English, he can ever graduate from Metropolitan.

We are then given Kho's background and a description of his adjustment to an American business school. Almost immediately we sense cultural differences in American and Japanese attitudes toward teamwork, colleagues, competition, obligations, success, failure, and dishonor. And even though Kho's company, footing the bill for his graduate education, expects him simply to develop a broad, international business sense, as a Japanese Kho feels intense personal pressure to complete the program successfully.

Kho's main stumbling block is his English language ability. His company had sponsored his attendance at an eight-week language course in Tokyo and he had also spent a summer studying English on a midwestern university campus. Nevertheless, at Metropolitan he has enormous difficulty with reading assignments and class discussions, and he has felt threatened by the school's performance evaluation policy. We learn that when classes end for the day Kho spends the next twelve hours preparing for the following day. We learn of his sense of shame when he cannot follow large segments of class discussions, and of his frustration when his instructors, during office meetings, suggest that he speak more in class. An American sectionmate who values Kho's presence in class tries to help Kho but observes how class vocabulary cannot be simplified in order to accommodate him. And even an English course given for foreign students on Saturday mornings is of little help. In short, Kho has made every attempt to improve his English and master his courses, but the comments on his paper indicate his attempts have failed.

Two of Kho's instructors comment on the issues provoked by foreign students. One acknowledges that many business cases are "culture bound." He also mentions his worries about Kho's silence in class, underscoring the necessity for class participation. The other instructor speaks of the impasse that he gets into in class with foreign students -- how he doesn't want to embarrass the student and how the student doesn't want to be embarrassed; the easy solution is to "back away." He wonders how to change the pattern.

Case Issues

This case concerns problems inherent in language difficulty and cultural diffences (highlighted specifically by a Japanese student attending an American business school). What are the benefits gained when the instructor understands customs and traditions of other cultures? Conversely, what are the losses when such viewpoints are not understood? Armed with some knowledge, what changes might be made (the wording of written comments on a paper, a mutual understanding about office meetings, and so on)? In what circumstances might exceptions be made for a foreign student? How could one enlist student support for fellow students with language difficulty? What institutional support systems are available to foreign students and how could they be made more helpful?

Case Information

This case is one unit, four pages long, and could be used in any seminar wishing to discuss the special instructional challenges of working with non-English-speaking students in a case method academic situation.

HBS Case No. 9-381-127

*   *   *

The Mechanical Hand

Case Overview

With the help of the section's education representative, Professor Simons reviews an incident that happened in his class. The section educational representative feels that Professor Simons was justified in reprimanding the class "clown" for his antics; the professor, however, feels that he would not have been so angry had he not been embarrassed over two gaffes he had just made in class.

The case details the cause of his embarrassment. That week Professor Simons has been particularly overextended and he is tired. He listens to a student in Section J lead off the class with a mediocre presentation. The class discussion in turn is slow. After thirty minutes it becomes more animated, and Professor Simons feels some relief. He refers to his "call list" and calls on one of the quiet foreign students; he addresses him by the wrong name, however, and calls him "Christian" -- the name of another quiet foreign student. The class laughs good-naturedly, Professor Simons apologizes, and the discussion continues. Shortly thereafter Professor Simons calls on a third foreign student but makes the same mistake -- he addresses him as "Christian" also, and the class roars with laughter. The professor apologizes but feels "like sinking through the floor." Mitch Menron the class "clown" decides to perform one of his pranks. He has constructed a "mechanical hand" from erector set pieces and he cranks it up, making a loud mechanical whirring sound. Professor Simons is furious and interrupts the class laughter by shouting at Mitch. The class is startled into silence, and a chagrined Mitch Menron slouches into his seat. All eyes are on the professor.

Case Issues

This case concerns the issue of how to deal with problem behavior in class. What are appropriate responses from the teacher to a student prankster? In what ways can section dynamics be expected to solve the problem of student misbehavior? How can the teacher steer section dynamics toward solving the problem? In what ways can a teacher's personal reactions interfere with appropriate responses to provocative behavior?

Case Information

This case is very short -- one unit, approximately two and one-half pages long. It would be useful to a seminar group wishing to discuss the development of section "personality" or appropriate responses from a teacher to student antics. (It might well be discussed along with another short case, "Janice Posner.")

HBS Case No. 9-381-021

*   *   *

Michelle Grinald

Case Overview

Michelle (Mickey) Grinald is faced with a vaguely troubling political issue. What is the right thing to do and how should she go about it? Before we learn the issue, we learn about Mickey and her environment. She is a part-time faculty member at a small private college, the University of Cranston, in Cranston, New York. It is her first year of teaching and she is into her second semester. She is a 24-year-old CPA with a B.A. degree in accounting. In addition to teaching two sections of Cost Accounting at U.C., she works full time as controller of a local, nonprofit organization. After three years of work experience, Mickey has become concerned about ethical issues in accounting. She thinks that by entering the academic world she will have the best leverage to affect problems in the field. Before committing herself to graduate school, however, she is trying out teaching to see if she likes it -- hence her double load of teaching while working full time.

We go back to the beginning of Mickey's first semester and learn that her department is headed by a dynamic young man, that two sections of Cost Accounting are taught by another young woman (Linda) with whom Mickey feels an instant rapport, and that one section is taught by an older man (Mr. Wilson), a senior financial administrator of the school. It is Linda who helps Mickey at the start of the first semester, giving her the course outline, course requirements, and the textbook that has been used for years. Mickey describes the tension in her early classes where she faces thirty students (most of whom are older than she) with more work experience, and how she gradually relaxes as the semester progresses -- receiving positive feedback.

As a second-semester teacher and beginning to feel like an "old hand," she takes over Mr. Wilson's evening section. Although she has not formed an opinion of Mr. Wilson, she has heard many negative rumors about his teaching. During the second meeting of Mickey's new evening section, a bright student makes comments to her during class break -- not only about his wasted semester with Mr. Wilson but about the poor textbook that Mr. Wilson used and the one Mickey continues using. He asks if Mickey has considered changing the textbook. Not wanting to comment negatively about a colleague or her department, Mickey uncomfortably mumbles a reply about it being too late to change the textbook but that she hoped to improve the course. Later Mickey wonders what her position should be and how she should deal with it: should she report student criticism or should she pass it by because she will be at Cranston for only a year? How can she present negative feedback from students without appearing critical of her department?

Case Issues

This case deals with being caught between student criticism and department politics. How does a new, inexperienced teacher deal with student criticism of departmental decisions? How does one decide which issues are important enough to report? How does one balance an allegiance to students with sensitivity to departmental politics (what if the teacher needs a recommendation for graduate school)?

Case Information

This case is one unit, three pages long. It may be of special interest to instructors who are teaching for the first time.

HBS Case No. 9-379-015

*   *   *

ORG-10

Case Overview

"ORG-10" presents a class situation seen first from the perspective of two graduate students, and second from the perspective of two professors. In the first account we share the students' frustrations and incredulity; in the second we try to understand a theoretical perspective that hardly seems to describe the same experience.

(A) Case

Organizational Theory and Practice (ORG-10) at the Bay Area Graduate School of Public Health was a required course for first-year doctoral students, though other students could elect to take it as well. All students in ORG-10 were required to participate in a small group project on the application of organizational theory to analyze and improve group process within ORG-10 itself.

Doctoral student Louise Bray described events from the first day of class which she perceived as contrived and confusing. For example, Professors Barton and Ford pointed out how students might get a "yes" from one and a "no" from the other, and, after saying that they didn't want master's degree students to feel like "second-class citizens," dismissed them early in order to serve wine to the doctoral students. Louise recounted that despite criticism from the class, the course did not improve.

The case history also notes the point of view of doctoral student Hank Grivers who described his Project Intervention Group. In brief, he was enthusiastic about his group and about the relevance of their task -- a class survey designed ultimately to improve group process within ORG-10. Hank then described an event that greatly angered him. At the end of a class, his survey results were distributed and discussed by the professors. When he and another group member tried to raise objections, their comments were cut short by the professors.

(B) Case

Barton and Ford presented their viewpoints to the school's curriculum committee in a report entitled, "Some Explanations for Why ORG-10 Unfolded as It Did." They acknowledged that student dissatisfaction was higher this year than last. They stated that, due to their interest in organizations, they were interested in learning the explanation for the dissatisfaction.

Case Issues

ORG-10 depicts a situation in which two graduate students on the one hand, and two professors on the other, present dramatically different perspectives on a shared experience. What inferences can be drawn from the different types of reports (direct and emotional reporting from the students, vague and theoretical reporting from the professors)? How is it that two professors with good credentials and good reputations taught a course that was inferior to the one they taught the previous year, alienated a sizable portion of the students, and seemed impervious to criticism? ORG-10 raises questions about professor credibility, student credibility, trust, teacher-student communication, teacher-student contracts, and the ability to use feedback constructively.

Case Information

ORG-10 is a long case series -- 10 pages -- and is divided into two units. It would be especially stimulating in a seminar where students have some background in Organizational Behavior, though such background is not a necessity.

HBS Case Nos. (A) 9-381-008;
(B) 9-381-084.

*   *   *

Sheila Lund

Case Overview

Sara Andrews has just had an unpleasant and unsettling confrontation with Sheila Lund, one of her graduate students. The conversation left her perplexed. Even though she instinctively feels that the department chairperson will support her position, she wonders if Sheila, with nothing left to lose, will sabotage the remaining weeks of class. Sara looks back on the semester and tries to figure out how she let the situation slip out of her control.

Sara is 31, and a first-year assistant professor of English at Eastern, a small, illustrious private university. She recently completed her Ph.D. at Metropolitan -- another excellent university. One of her first teaching assignments at Eastern was a graduate seminar entitled Methods of Literary Analysis. The purpose of the course was to introduce doctoral students to research techniques and skills of analysis and critical argument. The grade depended heavily on one long paper and its defense in class.

We meet Sara as she enters her classroom on the day that the long papers are due. After the students hand in their papers, Sheila Lund informs Sara that she was ill over the weekend, could not complete her paper, and will "have to take an incomplete." Sara says she will see Sheila during office hours, and class continues (as students begin the process of presenting and defending their papers). During their appointment Sheila once again asks for an incomplete. Sara denies the request. Condescendingly Sheila says she will speak to "Fred," the department chairperson, about Sara's decision, and calmly walks out of the room.

At a subsequent appointment Sara denies Sheila's request to do the long report along the lines of a feminist analysis. During that conversation Sara thinks fleetingly that some of Sheila's comments have truth to them, but she insists that Sheila's paper be less "polemical." Sheila leaves the office without a word.

After this episode Sheila changes her behavior in class. She vehemently and angrily argues against "male perspectives," "objective standards," or books written by males that were "degrading to women" (such as Daisy Miller by Henry James). She accuses a female student of having "male eyes." She is sometimes quiet and sullen, but whenever she participates the class seems to get out of control.

Case Issues

This case describes how a teacher's handling of a potentially valuable discussion topic -- a feminist analysis of literature -- turns the topic into a political battleground. The focus of the case is not the political content; instead it is how and for what reasons a teacher misses important cues and opportunities, lets her anxieties and politics interfere with her judgment, and alienates the student in question. What are some behavior patterns we fall into when we feel threatened? In this case, how might the teacher have handled the situation differently (such as further conversations with the student in order to know her better or understand her point of view, attempts to understand her term paper proposal, attempts to help her make it more "professional" and less "polemical")? How might she have enlisted the support of the class? What kept her from trying to help the student? What kept her from realizing she might need advice on how to handle the situation? Once the student had her first outburst in class, what sorts of interventions would have been effective? And as the teacher predicts disaster for the last two weeks of class, what should she do now?

Case Information

This case is one unit, eight pages long. It raises extremely important issues about personal reactions to students who seem threatening, as well as the handling of topics which seem threatening to the teacher or to the class.

HBS Case No. (A) 9-381-216

*   *   *

Student Boycott/Teacher Strike for Divestiture of South African Holdings

Case Overview

(A) Case

This case series focuses on the circumstances confronting Assistant Professor Neil Larson in deciding whether or not to participate in a strike/boycott organized by the Coalition for Awareness and Action at Harvard University in the spring of 1979. The purpose of the strike was twofold: divestiture of Harvard's South African holdings and support for its Afro-American Studies Department.

Neil Larson is one of three junior faculty members teaching Biology 124 -- a "slightly revolutionary new introductory biology course" -- which received glowing student evaluations. Neil is 31, described by a former student as an excellent teacher -- disciplined, demanding, and accessible. We learn from Neil that he was politically active in high school but at college turned his energies toward educational reform. By 1979 he had been teaching biology and doing research for about five years. He expects to be appointed to an associate professorship in July.

The (A) case describes how Neil came to his decision about the boycott. He felt that he had to choose between holding class and not holding class but that neither choice was a politically neutral action. Holding class was a political statement. Canceling class would impose his views on students. Postponing class would deprive certain students of their right to make a political statement. Letting students vote on the matter would mean an abdication of his responsibility for the decision.

(B) Case

This section of the case series details Neil Larson's account of his handling of the lecture period immediately preceding the proposed boycott/strike. At the start of class he handed out a statement concerning his views on the upcoming boycott. He announced that he would leave time at the end of class for discussion. We read his policy statement which made three general points (including one which stated his belief that in all but the most extreme cases it was wrong to champion political beliefs in the classroom). He presented the options of holding class as usual, canceling class, and postponing class, and followed with his reasons for rejecting those options. Instead he suggested that he hold two classes -- one during the day of the boycott at the regularly scheduled time, and one the following morning. He would not lose valuable teaching time and would provide a class for those who had opposing views on the boycott. At the end of his prepared lecture, Neil discussed the reasons for his decision with the class.

(C) Case

The final case in the series details the outcome of Neil's decision. On Monday, April 23, approximately 75% of his class attended the regularly scheduled lecture, and the other 25% came to the alternate lecture the following day. Neil reported that there was no further discussion of the boycott, either in class or in confidential course evaluations. A teaching fellow for Biology 124, interviewed about the class's reaction to Neil's statement preceding the boycott, said that Neil had "stopped apathy dead in its tracks. He forced everyone's actions to be seen as political."

Case Issues

This case focuses on the relationship between politics and academia, and raises questions of the following sort: Is it possible to separate politics and academia? Is there a place for politics in the classroom? Is it possible to teach anything completely objectively without personal opinions and politics influencing the presentation of facts? Is there such a thing as a politically neutral action? Would teachers' responses to these questions vary according to the academic institutions in which they teach or their particular status in those institutions? Why?

Case Information

This case series is fifteen pages long and divided into three units.

<u>HBS Case Nos.</u> (A) 9-381-018; (B) 9-381-019; (C) 9-381-020.

*   *   *

That Discussion Just Fell Apart

Case Overview

Frank Taylor, on tenure track at Metropolitan, a well-known graduate business school, has recently concluded a class in which the discussion simply disintegrated. He reveals his mixture of feelings as he recalls the discussion -- his incredulity, frustration, anger, and uncertainty. Although Frank has an excellent reputation as an effective case teacher and is teaching Corporate Strategic Planning -- a required first-year MBA class -- for the third time, he is uncertain as to what went wrong, what he might have done to rescue the situation, and how he might handle a similar situation if it were to recur.

We meet Frank as he talks over the disastrous discussion with a researcher and tries to analyze the class from beginning to end. The section of students is described: Frank thinks of them as a competent group who display a quality he values highly -- that of listening to each other. He goes on to describe the subgroups in the section, showing that with attention to this sort of detail he has been able to lead effective discussions without one group monopolizing the floor.

He discusses at length his own preparation for the discussion of "Addison Meats," a long and complicated case with much industry-specific terminology and cost data. He then describes the procedure he used for selecting the lead-off speaker, and the various reasons why this decision was important. Because he grades 50% on classroom contribution, opening a case gives a student a special chance to demonstrate competence. Frank recalls how the night before class he narrowed a list of ten potential lead-off speakers down to four and he discusses these four in some detail. He gives his reasons for not choosing three out of the four as he finally settled on Neil Haffner, an intelligent young man with experience in the meat-packing business.

Frank then turns to a review of the class itself. He describes his dismay as Neil Haffner bounds into class -- not the slightest bit tentative or diffident -- and gushes enthusiasm for the case's technical topic, which turns out to have been the subject on which he had written his senior honors thesis. For a moment Frank debates whether or not Neil's technical overpreparation will kill class discussion, but sticks with his decision. As soon as Neil begins, however, Frank immediately senses the class's resistance to his overenthusiastic approach. We listen as Neil launches into the meat-packing business in great detail -- occasionally making a sensible point which gives Frank hope, but then lapsing into an irrelevant and tedious presentation. Neil rarely touches on the management issues which are critical to a case discussion at Metropolitan. Finally the actual discussion begins. In short, students are contentious or bored -- and for once not listening to each other. Frank tries to refocus the discussion with increasingly pointed or directive questions, but he cannot engage the class. The section mood becomes increasingly hostile, with long silences between comments which in turn are unrelated mini-speeches. When the class finally ends, he goes to a trusted colleague to review the events of the class.

Case Issues

This case focuses on the phenomenon of the disintegrating class discussion. Here we have a professor who is reasonably experienced, with an excellent reputation, and who enjoys teaching this particular section. For a teacher (or student), what are the differences between preparing a case thoroughly and being able to start up an effective class discussion? Where do the teacher's responsibilities lie? Is it as important to risk giving a diffident student a chance to open the class as ensuring a stimulating discussion by choosing an excellent student? How can one rescue a discussion when it starts to fall apart? At what points should one follow one's instincts (such as choosing a different lead-off speaker when sensing the student's overpreparation)? How can one retrench and salvage a discussion as it continues to fall apart? And if no methods seem to work during the class, is there a way to conclude the class with humor and optimism? What should one look for when retrospectively analyzing a class, so as to prevent a discussion from disintegrating again?

Case Information

This case is one unit, eight pages long, and divided into eight sections in order to organize an analysis of the class. Although it would be useful in any seminar discussing the phenomenon of a discussion falling flat, it would be used to best advantage in a professional school seminar, preferably when business school students are in the majority.

HBS Case No. 9-383-039

*   *   *

Timothy D'Olivier, Jr.

Case Overview

(A) Case

Professor Hamid Morabak of the Bengali Institute of Management (BIM) has assigned a discussion topic concerning bribery and corruption to his class in Environmental and Social Analysis. He is slightly uneasy, as only a few students volunteer to participate, and those who do participate speak only in lofty generalizations. For reasons we learn later, he hesitates before choosing Tim D'Olivier, an American and the only non-Bengali student eager to participate. When finally called on, Tim launches into a condescending critique of corruption in the host country. As classmates become angry and Professor Morabak contemplates how best to intervene, Tim is interrupted by a Bengali student who challenges him about a well-known American scandal.

The case gives detailed information about the Bengali Institute of Management and the composition of faculty and student body. We learn that BIM is an excellent institution with high standards, modeled on Western business schools. Scholarships are provided for highly qualified international applicants, most of whom are from Asia and the Middle East. We learn about the current class (in particular how the high-pres-

sure atmosphere inevitably increases the competition among students, especially in classes where the case method is used), how students from Asian countries learn to coexist in school, how the Westerners find the adjustment process difficult, and what contributes to the students' sense of polarization. We are then given a detailed description of Tim D'Olivier, the contentious American student, and Professor Hamid Morabak's background.

(B) Case

In this section of the series we come back to the incident of Tim's original condescending outburst. Professor Morabak walks to the center of class amidst cries of "Yankee, go home" and the class hushes. As he assembles his thoughts and is about to comment, Malik -- a thoughtful, well-respected student from Indonesia -- raises his hand. Professor Morabak calls on him. Malik gives a sensitive quasi-lecture, first on corruption's place in social-cultural history, and second on business situations in which the students may one day find themselves -- faced with having to make difficult moral decisions. There is a round of applause, the class seems calmed, and Professor Morabak gives a closing statement.

(C) Case

This third section follows up on the eventful class. We learn that Tim is effectively isolated from most of the students who expect him to make a gesture of reconciliation. Tim, however, sees no need for any such gesture and associates only with international students. He was described sympathetically by his dorm-room neighbor. We learn that contributing to Tim's low spirits is his worry as to whether or not he had passed his bar exam back home.

Case Issues

What is an effective way to organize a discussion around a threatening topic (graft, corruption) or one that bears on personal morals and values? Where do the professor's responsibilities lie when a student has adjustment or personal problems, when students are polarized in and out of class? Where do those responsibilities end? How do racial or cultural differences affect a competitive situation? How does one build a supportive atmosphere in a highly competitive environment?

Case Information

This case series is seven pages long and is divided into three sections. It would be particularly useful for an international seminar or a graduate seminar dealing with cultural differences in a discussion class.

HBS Case Nos. (A) 9-379-008; (B) 9-379-009; (C) 9-379-010.

Suggested Readings for Seminar Leaders

TITLE	AUTHOR	HBS NUMBER
On the Balance Between Skill and Knowledge	Joseph Bailey	From *Organizational Behavior and Administration: Cases, Concepts, and Research Findings* (Homewood, Illinois: Richard D. Irwin, Inc., 1961)
Use of Cases in Management Education	E. Raymond Corey	376-240
Because Wisdom Can't Be Told	Charles I. Gragg	451-005
The Development of a Professional Self-Image	Mary Jean Huntington	From *The Student Physician* (Cambridge: Harvard University Press, 1957)
Barn Raising: Collaborative Group Process in Seminars	Don McCormick and Michael Kahn	From *Exchange: The Organizational Behavior Teaching Journal*, Vol. VII, no. 4 (1982), pp. 16-20.
Teaching Mathematics as Though Students Mattered	Joseph Katz, ed.	Jossey-Bass, Inc., San Francisco, 1985 (pp. 39-48)

ORDER FORM

HARVARD BUSINESS SCHOOL
Publishing Division
Operations Department
Boston, MA 02163

Ref. No. _____

Batch No. _____
Code No. 220

Fill in completely and simply mail to address above or call (617) 495-6117, Monday through Friday, 9-5 EST.

Instructor _____

Ordered by _____

Phone No. (___ ___ ___) - ___ ___ ___ - ___ ___ ___ ___

Billing Address _____

_____

_____

_____

Shipping Address _____

_____

_____

_____

Customer Code _____

Purchase Order No. _____

Minimum order fee
$10.00 for all orders

Shipping and handling
5% shipping and handling, continental U.S.; 15% elsewhere. For special shipping requirements, charges will be billed at cost.

_____
Preferred carrier and method

Payment Method
☐ Check enclosed, payable to HBS Publishing Division.

☐ Charge my ☐ VISA ☐ MasterCard. Expires ___ / ___ / ___
mo   day   year

Acct. No. [ ][ ][ ][ ][ ][ ][ ][ ][ ][ ][ ][ ][ ][ ][ ][ ][ ][ ]

Signature _____

Verification of Teaching Status (required for purchase of teaching notes and researcher's perspectives)

(___ ___ ___) - ___ ___ ___ - ___ ___ ___ ___
Phone number of Dean's Office or Personnel

Order Number	Title (one line per title)	No. of Copies	x Price (see reverse)	= Total
CASES and TEACHING NOTES (Part III)				
9 - 3 7 6 - 0 9 6	Bill Curtis			
9 - 3 8 6 - 1 4 6	The Introduction (A)			
9 - 3 8 6 - 1 4 7	The Introduction (B)			
9 - 3 8 6 - 1 4 8	The Introduction (C)			
9 - 3 7 8 - 0 3 3	Suzie Simons (A)			
9 - 3 7 8 - 0 3 4	Suzie Simons (B)			
5 - 3 8 4 - 0 9 6	Bill Curtis, Teaching Note			
5 - 3 8 4 - 0 4 7	Suzie Simons, Teaching Note			
CASES (Part V)				
9 - 3 8 1 - 1 2 1	Assistant Professor Brian Duncan (A)			
9 - 3 8 1 - 1 2 2	Assistant Professor Brian Duncan (B)			
9 - 3 8 1 - 1 2 3	Assistant Professor Brian Duncan (C)			
9 - 3 8 0 - 2 1 8	Assistant Professor Donna Oscura and Sarah Summers (A)			
9 - 3 8 0 - 2 1 9	Assistant Professor Donna Oscura and Sarah Summers (B)			
9 - 3 8 0 - 2 2 0	Assistant Professor Donna Oscura and Sarah Summers (C)			
9 - 3 8 0 - 2 2 1	Assistant Professor Patrick Grady (A)			
9 - 3 8 0 - 2 2 2	Assistant Professor Patrick Grady (B)			
9 - 3 8 2 - 0 5 4	Bob Lunt (A)			
9 - 3 8 2 - 0 5 5	Bob Lunt (B)			
9 - 3 8 2 - 0 5 6	Bob Lunt (C)			
9 - 3 8 1 - 0 1 5	Bob Peters (A)			
9 - 3 8 1 - 0 1 6	Bob Peters (B)			
9 - 3 8 1 - 0 1 7	Bob Peters (C)			

(Order Form continued on reverse side)

Subtotal _____
(carry to reverse side)

Order Number	Title (one line per title)	No. of Copies	x Price (see below)	= Total
	CASES (Part V, continued)			
9 - 3 8 0 - 0 1 7	The Case of the Disgruntled Student			
9 - 3 8 7 - 0 0 2	The Case of the Frustrated Feminist (A)			
9 - 3 8 7 - 0 0 3	The Case of the Frustrated Feminist (B1)			
9 - 3 8 7 - 0 0 4	The Case of the Frustrated Feminist (B2)			
9 - 3 8 1 - 2 2 3	Cathy Ross			
9 - 3 7 9 - 0 2 4	Dick Johnson			
9 - 3 7 7 - 1 2 0	The Final Exam			
9 - 3 8 0 - 0 1 8	HB I (A)			
9 - 3 8 0 - 0 1 9	HB I (B)			
9 - 3 7 9 - 2 0 5	Janice Posner			
9 - 3 8 1 - 1 2 7	Kho Tanaka			
9 - 3 8 1 - 0 2 1	The Mechanical Hand			
9 - 3 7 9 - 0 1 5	Michelle Grinald			
9 - 3 8 1 - 0 0 8	Org-10 (A)			
9 - 3 8 1 - 0 8 4	Org-10 (B)			
9 - 3 8 1 - 2 1 6	Sheila Lund			
9 - 3 8 1 - 0 1 8	Student Boycott/Teacher Strike for Divestiture (A)			
9 - 3 8 1 - 0 1 9	Student Boycott/Teacher Strike for Divestiture (B)			
9 - 3 8 1 - 0 2 0	Student Boycott/Teacher Strike for Divestiture (C)			
9 - 3 8 3 - 0 3 9	That Discussion Just Fell Apart			
9 - 3 7 9 - 0 0 8	Timothy D'Olivier, Jr. (A)			
9 - 3 7 9 - 0 0 9	Timothy D'Olivier, Jr. (B)			
9 - 3 7 9 - 0 1 0	Timothy D'Olivier, Jr. (C)			
	READINGS			
9 - 3 7 6 - 2 4 0	The Use of Cases in Management Education			
9 - 4 5 1 - 0 0 5	Because Wisdom Can't Be Told			
	Additional materials may be ordered in the space below.			
- -				
- -				
- -				
- -				
- -				
- -				
- -				
- -				
- -				
- -				
- -				
- -				
- -				
- -				
- -				
- -				
- -				

Subtotal _____

Subtotal (carried forward from other side) _____

Shipping and handling 5% in U.S.A.; 15% elsewhere. _____

TOTAL $ _____

(Please include customer code on check)

Terms

(1) Orders shipped within four working days.
(2) Examination copies not available free of charge.
(3) No returns accepted.
(4) Prices are subject to change.
(5) Prices not valid for orders from Europe, Mid-East, or North Africa.

	CURRENT PRICES ($10.00 minimum order fee)	
	PRICE PER ITEM*	
TYPE OF ITEM	List Price	*Educational and Bookstore Price
Cases	$3.50	$1.75
Teaching Notes	$3.50	$1.75
Readings	$3.50	$1.75

* Buyers ordering material for use at institutions whose primary purpose is education are eligible for a 50% discount on cases and notes.
Buyers ordering material for use in educational programs of companies and consulting firms are not entitled to the discount.

ORDER FORM

HARVARD BUSINESS SCHOOL
Publishing Division
Operations Department
Boston, MA 02163

Ref. No. _____

Batch No. _____
Code No. 220

Fill in completely and simply mail to address above or call (617) 495-6117, Monday through Friday, 9-5 EST.

Instructor _____

Ordered by _____

Phone No. (___ ___ ___) - ___ ___ ___ - ___ ___ ___ ___

Billing Address _____

_____

_____

_____

Shipping Address _____

_____

_____

_____

Customer Code _____

Purchase Order No. _____

Minimum order fee
$10.00 for all orders

Shipping and handling
5% shipping and handling, continental U.S.; 15% elsewhere.
For special shipping requirements, charges will be billed at
cost.

_____
Preferred carrier and method

Payment Method
☐ Check enclosed, payable to HBS Publishing Division.

☐ Charge my   ☐ VISA ☐ MasterCard. Expires ___/___/___
                                        mo day year

Acct.
No. | | | | | | | | | | | | | | | | | | |

Signature _____

Verification of Teaching Status (required for purchase of teaching notes and researcher's perspectives)

(___ ___ ___) - ___ ___ ___ - ___ ___ ___ ___
Phone number of Dean's Office or Personnel

Order Number	Title (one line per title)	No. of Copies	x Price (see reverse)	= Total
	CASES and TEACHING NOTES (Part III)			
9 - 3 7 6 - 0 9 6	**Bill Curtis**			
9 - 3 8 6 - 1 4 6	**The Introduction (A)**			
9 - 3 8 6 - 1 4 7	**The Introduction (B)**			
9 - 3 8 6 - 1 4 8	**The Introduction (C)**			
9 - 3 7 8 - 0 3 3	**Suzie Simons (A)**			
9 - 3 7 8 - 0 3 4	**Suzie Simons (B)**			
5 - 3 8 4 - 0 9 6	**Bill Curtis, Teaching Note**			
5 - 3 8 4 - 0 4 7	**Suzie Simons, Teaching Note**			
	CASES (Part V)			
9 - 3 8 1 - 1 2 1	**Assistant Professor Brian Duncan (A)**			
9 - 3 8 1 - 1 2 2	**Assistant Professor Brian Duncan (B)**			
9 - 3 8 1 - 1 2 3	**Assistant Professor Brian Duncan (C)**			
9 - 3 8 0 - 2 1 8	**Assistant Professor Donna Oscura and Sarah Summers (A)**			
9 - 3 8 0 - 2 1 9	**Assistant Professor Donna Oscura and Sarah Summers (B)**			
9 - 3 8 0 - 2 2 0	**Assistant Professor Donna Oscura and Sarah Summers (C)**			
9 - 3 8 0 - 2 2 1	**Assistant Professor Patrick Grady (A)**			
9 - 3 8 0 - 2 2 2	**Assistant Professor Patrick Grady (B)**			
9 - 3 8 2 - 0 5 4	**Bob Lunt (A)**			
9 - 3 8 2 - 0 5 5	**Bob Lunt (B)**			
9 - 3 8 2 - 0 5 6	**Bob Lunt (C)**			
9 - 3 8 1 - 0 1 5	**Bob Peters (A)**			
9 - 3 8 1 - 0 1 6	**Bob Peters (B)**			
9 - 3 8 1 - 0 1 7	**Bob Peters (C)**			

(Order Form continued on reverse side)

Subtotal _____
(carry to reverse side)

Order Number	Title (one line per title)	No. of Copies	x Price (see below)	= Total
	CASES (Part V, continued)			
9 - 3 8 0 - 0 1 7	The Case of the Disgruntled Student			
9 - 3 8 7 - 0 0 2	The Case of the Frustrated Feminist (A)			
9 - 3 8 7 - 0 0 3	The Case of the Frustrated Feminist (B1)			
9 - 3 8 7 - 0 0 4	The Case of the Frustrated Feminist (B2)			
9 - 3 8 1 - 2 2 3	Cathy Ross			
9 - 3 7 9 - 0 2 4	Dick Johnson			
9 - 3 7 7 - 1 2 0	The Final Exam			
9 - 3 8 0 - 0 1 8	HB I (A)			
9 - 3 8 0 - 0 1 9	HB I (B)			
9 - 3 7 9 - 2 0 5	Janice Posner			
9 - 3 8 1 - 1 2 7	Kho Tanaka			
9 - 3 8 1 - 0 2 1	The Mechanical Hand			
9 - 3 7 9 - 0 1 5	Michelle Grinald			
9 - 3 8 1 - 0 0 8	Org-10 (A)			
9 - 3 8 1 - 0 8 4	Org-10 (B)			
9 - 3 8 1 - 2 1 6	Sheila Lund			
9 - 3 8 1 - 0 1 8	Student Boycott/Teacher Strike for Divestiture (A)			
9 - 3 8 1 - 0 1 9	Student Boycott/Teacher Strike for Divestiture (B)			
9 - 3 8 1 - 0 2 0	Student Boycott/Teacher Strike for Divestiture (C)			
9 - 3 8 3 - 0 3 9	That Discussion Just Fell Apart			
9 - 3 7 9 - 0 0 8	Timothy D'Olivier, Jr. (A)			
9 - 3 7 9 - 0 0 9	Timothy D'Olivier, Jr. (B)			
9 - 3 7 9 - 0 1 0	Timothy D'Olivier, Jr. (C)			
	READINGS			
9 - 3 7 6 - 2 4 0	The Use of Cases in Management Education			
9 - 4 5 1 - 0 0 5	Because Wisdom Can't Be Told			
	Additional materials may be ordered in the space below.			
- -				
- -				
- -				
- -				
- -				
- -				
- -				
- -				
- -				
- -				
- -				
- -				
- -				
- -				
- -				
- -				

Subtotal _____

Subtotal (carried forward from other side) _____

Shipping and handling 5% in U.S.A.; 15% elsewhere. _____

TOTAL $ _____

(Please include customer code on check)

Terms

(1) Orders shipped within four working days.
(2) Examination copies not available free of charge.
(3) No returns accepted.
(4) Prices are subject to change.
(5) Prices not valid for orders from Europe, Mid-East, or North Africa.

CURRENT PRICES ($10.00 minimum order fee)		
	PRICE PER ITEM*	
TYPE OF ITEM	List Price	*Educational and Bookstore Price
Cases	$3.50	$1.75
Teaching Notes	$3.50	$1.75
Readings	$3.50	$1.75

* Buyers ordering material for use at institutions whose primary purpose is education are eligible for a 50% discount on cases and notes.
Buyers ordering material for use in educational programs of companies and consulting firms are not entitled to the discount.

ORDER FORM

HARVARD BUSINESS SCHOOL
Publishing Division
Operations Department
Boston, MA 02163

Ref. No. _____

Batch No. _____
Code No. 220

Fill in completely and simply mail to address above or call (617) 495-6117, Monday through Friday, 9-5 EST.

Instructor _____

Ordered by _____

Phone No. (___ ___ ___) - ___ ___ ___ - ___ ___ ___ ___

Billing Address _____

_____

_____

_____

_____

Shipping Address _____

_____

_____

_____

Customer Code _____

Purchase Order No. _____

Minimum order fee
$10.00 for all orders

Shipping and handling
5% shipping and handling, continental U.S.; 15% elsewhere. For special shipping requirements, charges will be billed at cost.

Preferred carrier and method

Payment Method
☐ Check enclosed, payable to HBS Publishing Division.

☐ Charge my ☐ VISA ☐ MasterCard. Expires ___ / ___ / ___
mo   day   year

Acct. No. | | | | | | | | | | | | | | | | | | |

Signature _____

Verification of Teaching Status (required for purchase of teaching notes and researcher's perspectives)

(___ ___ ___) - ___ ___ ___ - ___ ___ ___ ___
Phone number of Dean's Office or Personnel

Order Number	Title (one line per title)	No. of Copies	x Price (see reverse)	= Total
CASES and TEACHING NOTES (Part III)				
9 - 3 7 6 - 0 9 6	**Bill Curtis**			
9 - 3 8 6 - 1 4 6	**The Introduction (A)**			
9 - 3 8 6 - 1 4 7	**The Introduction (B)**			
9 - 3 8 6 - 1 4 8	**The Introduction (C)**			
9 - 3 7 8 - 0 3 3	**Suzie Simons (A)**			
9 - 3 7 8 - 0 3 4	**Suzie Simons (B)**			
5 - 3 8 4 - 0 9 6	**Bill Curtis, Teaching Note**			
5 - 3 8 4 - 0 4 7	**Suzie Simons, Teaching Note**			
CASES (Part V)				
9 - 3 8 1 - 1 2 1	**Assistant Professor Brian Duncan (A)**			
9 - 3 8 1 - 1 2 2	**Assistant Professor Brian Duncan (B)**			
9 - 3 8 1 - 1 2 3	**Assistant Professor Brian Duncan (C)**			
9 - 3 8 0 - 2 1 8	**Assistant Professor Donna Oscura and Sarah Summers (A)**			
9 - 3 8 0 - 2 1 9	**Assistant Professor Donna Oscura and Sarah Summers (B)**			
9 - 3 8 0 - 2 2 0	**Assistant Professor Donna Oscura and Sarah Summers (C)**			
9 - 3 8 0 - 2 2 1	**Assistant Professor Patrick Grady (A)**			
9 - 3 8 0 - 2 2 2	**Assistant Professor Patrick Grady (B)**			
9 - 3 8 2 - 0 5 4	**Bob Lunt (A)**			
9 - 3 8 2 - 0 5 5	**Bob Lunt (B)**			
9 - 3 8 2 - 0 5 6	**Bob Lunt (C)**			
9 - 3 8 1 - 0 1 5	**Bob Peters (A)**			
9 - 3 8 1 - 0 1 6	**Bob Peters (B)**			
9 - 3 8 1 - 0 1 7	**Bob Peters (C)**			

(Order Form continued on reverse side)

Subtotal _____
(carry to reverse side)

Order Number	Title (one line per title)	No. of Copies	x Price (see below)	= Total
	CASES (Part V, continued)			
9 - 3 8 0 - 0 1 7	The Case of the Disgruntled Student			
9 - 3 8 7 - 0 0 2	The Case of the Frustrated Feminist (A)			
9 - 3 8 7 - 0 0 3	The Case of the Frustrated Feminist (B1)			
9 - 3 8 7 - 0 0 4	The Case of the Frustrated Feminist (B2)			
9 - 3 8 1 - 2 2 3	Cathy Ross			
9 - 3 7 9 - 0 2 4	Dick Johnson			
9 - 3 7 7 - 1 2 0	The Final Exam			
9 - 3 8 0 - 0 1 8	HB I (A)			
9 - 3 8 0 - 0 1 9	HB I (B)			
9 - 3 7 9 - 2 0 5	Janice Posner			
9 - 3 8 1 - 1 2 7	Kho Tanaka			
9 - 3 8 1 - 0 2 1	The Mechanical Hand			
9 - 3 7 9 - 0 1 5	Michelle Grinald			
9 - 3 8 1 - 0 0 8	Org-10 (A)			
9 - 3 8 1 - 0 8 4	Org-10 (B)			
9 - 3 8 1 - 2 1 6	Sheila Lund			
9 - 3 8 1 - 0 1 8	Student Boycott/Teacher Strike for Divestiture (A)			
9 - 3 8 1 - 0 1 9	Student Boycott/Teacher Strike for Divestiture (B)			
9 - 3 8 1 - 0 2 0	Student Boycott/Teacher Strike for Divestiture (C)			
9 - 3 8 3 - 0 3 9	That Discussion Just Fell Apart			
9 - 3 7 9 - 0 0 8	Timothy D'Olivier, Jr. (A)			
9 - 3 7 9 - 0 0 9	Timothy D'Olivier, Jr. (B)			
9 - 3 7 9 - 0 1 0	Timothy D'Olivier, Jr. (C)			
	READINGS			
9 - 3 7 6 - 2 4 0	The Use of Cases in Management Education			
9 - 4 5 1 - 0 0 5	Because Wisdom Can't Be Told			
	Additional materials may be ordered in the space below.			
- -				
- -				
- -				
- -				
- -				
- -				
- -				
- -				
- -				
- -				
- -				
- -				
- -				
- -				
- -				

Subtotal _____

Subtotal (carried forward from other side) _____

Shipping and handling 5% in U.S.A.; 15% elsewhere. _____

TOTAL $ _____

(Please include customer code on check)

Terms

(1) Orders shipped within four working days.
(2) Examination copies not available free of charge.
(3) No returns accepted.
(4) Prices are subject to change.
(5) Prices not valid for orders from Europe, Mid-East, or North Africa.

CURRENT PRICES ($10.00 minimum order fee)		
	PRICE PER ITEM*	
TYPE OF ITEM	List Price	*Educational and Bookstore Price
Cases	$3.50	$1.75
Teaching Notes	$3.50	$1.75
Readings	$3.50	$1.75

* Buyers ordering material for use at institutions whose primary purpose is education are eligible for a 50% discount on cases and notes.
Buyers ordering material for use in educational programs of companies and consulting firms are not entitled to the discount.

ORDER FORM

HARVARD BUSINESS SCHOOL
Publishing Division
Operations Department
Boston, MA 02163

Ref. No. _____

Batch No. _____
Code No. 220

Fill in completely and simply mail to address above or call (617) 495-6117, Monday through Friday, 9-5 EST.

Instructor _____

Ordered by _____

Phone No. (___ ___ ___) - ___ ___ ___ - ___ ___ ___ ___

Billing Address _____

_____

_____

_____

Shipping Address _____

_____

_____

_____

Customer Code _____

Purchase Order No. _____

Minimum order fee
$10.00 for all orders

Shipping and handling
5% shipping and handling, continental U.S.; 15% elsewhere.
For special shipping requirements, charges will be billed at cost.

_____
Preferred carrier and method

Payment Method
☐ Check enclosed, payable to HBS Publishing Division.

☐ Charge my ☐ VISA ☐ MasterCard. Expires ___/___/___
mo   day   year

Acct. No. [ ][ ][ ][ ][ ][ ][ ][ ][ ][ ][ ][ ][ ][ ][ ][ ][ ][ ]

Signature _____

Verification of Teaching Status (required for purchase of teaching notes and researcher's perspectives)

(___ ___ ___) - ___ ___ ___ - ___ ___ ___ ___
Phone number of Dean's Office or Personnel

Order Number	Title (one line per title)	No. of Copies	x Price (see reverse)	= Total
	CASES and TEACHING NOTES (Part III)			
9 - 3 7 6 - 0 9 6	Bill Curtis			
9 - 3 8 6 - 1 4 6	The Introduction (A)			
9 - 3 8 6 - 1 4 7	The Introduction (B)			
9 - 3 8 6 - 1 4 8	The Introduction (C)			
9 - 3 7 8 - 0 3 3	Suzie Simons (A)			
9 - 3 7 8 - 0 3 4	Suzie Simons (B)			
5 - 3 8 4 - 0 9 6	Bill Curtis, Teaching Note			
5 - 3 8 4 - 0 4 7	Suzie Simons, Teaching Note			
	CASES (Part V)			
9 - 3 8 1 - 1 2 1	Assistant Professor Brian Duncan (A)			
9 - 3 8 1 - 1 2 2	Assistant Professor Brian Duncan (B)			
9 - 3 8 1 - 1 2 3	Assistant Professor Brian Duncan (C)			
9 - 3 8 0 - 2 1 8	Assistant Professor Donna Oscura and Sarah Summers (A)			
9 - 3 8 0 - 2 1 9	Assistant Professor Donna Oscura and Sarah Summers (B)			
9 - 3 8 0 - 2 2 0	Assistant Professor Donna Oscura and Sarah Summers (C)			
9 - 3 8 0 - 2 2 1	Assistant Professor Patrick Grady (A)			
9 - 3 8 0 - 2 2 2	Assistant Professor Patrick Grady (B)			
9 - 3 8 2 - 0 5 4	Bob Lunt (A)			
9 - 3 8 2 - 0 5 5	Bob Lunt (B)			
9 - 3 8 2 - 0 5 6	Bob Lunt (C)			
9 - 3 8 1 - 0 1 5	Bob Peters (A)			
9 - 3 8 1 - 0 1 6	Bob Peters (B)			
9 - 3 8 1 - 0 1 7	Bob Peters (C)			

(Order Form continued on reverse side)

Subtotal _____
(carry to reverse side)

Order Number	Title (one line per title)	No. of Copies	x Price (see below)	= Total
	CASES (Part V, continued)			
9 - 3 8 0 - 0 1 7	The Case of the Disgruntled Student			
9 - 3 8 7 - 0 0 2	The Case of the Frustrated Feminist (A)			
9 - 3 8 7 - 0 0 3	The Case of the Frustrated Feminist (B1)			
9 - 3 8 7 - 0 0 4	The Case of the Frustrated Feminist (B2)			
9 - 3 8 1 - 2 2 3	Cathy Ross			
9 - 3 7 9 - 0 2 4	Dick Johnson			
9 - 3 7 7 - 1 2 0	The Final Exam			
9 - 3 8 0 - 0 1 8	HB I (A)			
9 - 3 8 0 - 0 1 9	HB I (B)			
9 - 3 7 9 - 2 0 5	Janice Posner			
9 - 3 8 1 - 1 2 7	Kho Tanaka			
9 - 3 8 1 - 0 2 1	The Mechanical Hand			
9 - 3 7 9 - 0 1 5	Michelle Grinald			
9 - 3 8 1 - 0 0 8	Org-10 (A)			
9 - 3 8 1 - 0 8 4	Org-10 (B)			
9 - 3 8 1 - 2 1 6	Sheila Lund			
9 - 3 8 1 - 0 1 8	Student Boycott/Teacher Strike for Divestiture (A)			
9 - 3 8 1 - 0 1 9	Student Boycott/Teacher Strike for Divestiture (B)			
9 - 3 8 1 - 0 2 0	Student Boycott/Teacher Strike for Divestiture (C)			
9 - 3 8 3 - 0 3 9	That Discussion Just Fell Apart			
9 - 3 7 9 - 0 0 8	Timothy D'Olivier, Jr. (A)			
9 - 3 7 9 - 0 0 9	Timothy D'Olivier, Jr. (B)			
9 - 3 7 9 - 0 1 0	Timothy D'Olivier, Jr. (C)			
	READINGS			
9 - 3 7 6 - 2 4 0	The Use of Cases in Management Education			
9 - 4 5 1 - 0 0 5	Because Wisdom Can't Be Told			
	Additional materials may be ordered in the space below.			
- -				
- -				
- -				
- -				
- -				
- -				
- -				
- -				
- -				
- -				
- -				
- -				
- -				
- -				
- -				

Subtotal _____

Subtotal (carried forward from other side) _____

Shipping and handling 5% in U.S.A.; 15% elsewhere. _____

TOTAL $ _____

(Please include customer code on check)

Terms

(1) Orders shipped within four working days.
(2) Examination copies not available free of charge.
(3) No returns accepted.
(4) Prices are subject to change.
(5) Prices not valid for orders from Europe, Mid-East, or North Africa.

CURRENT PRICES ($10.00 minimum order fee)		
	PRICE PER ITEM*	
TYPE OF ITEM	List Price	*Educational and Bookstore Price
Cases	$3.50	$1.75
Teaching Notes	$3.50	$1.75
Readings	$3.50	$1.75

* Buyers ordering material for use at institutions whose primary purpose is education are eligible for a 50% discount on cases and notes.
Buyers ordering material for use in educational programs of companies and consulting firms are not entitled to the discount.